The Cambridge Companion to Bruckner

This *Companion* provides an overview of the composer Anton
Bruckner (1824–96). Sixteen chapters by leading scholars investigate
aspects of his life and works and consider the manner in which
critical appreciation has changed in the twentieth century. The first
section deals with Bruckner's Austrian background, investigating the
historical circumstances in which he worked, his upbringing in Upper
Austria, and his career in Vienna. A number of misunderstandings
are dealt with in the light of recent research. The remainder of the
book covers Bruckner's career as church musician and symphonist,
with a chapter on the neglected secular vocal music. Religious,
aesthetic, formal, harmonic, and instrumental aspects are considered,
while one chapter confronts the problem of the editions of the
symphonies. Two concluding chapters discuss the symphonies in
performance, and the history of Bruckner-reception with particular
reference to German Nationalism, the Third Reich and the
appropriation of Bruckner by the Nazis.

Cambridge Companions to Music

Instruments

The Cambridge Companion to Brass Instruments
Edited by Trevor Herbert and John Wallace
The Cambridge Companion to the Cello
Edited by Robin Stowell
The Cambridge Companion to the Clarinet
Edited by Colin Lawson
The Cambridge Companion to the Guitar
Edited by Victor Anand Coelho
The Cambridge Companion to the Organ
Edited by Nicholas Thistlethwaite
and Geoffrey Webber

The Cambridge Companion to the Piano
Edited by David Rowland
The Cambridge Companion to the Recorder
Edited by John Mansfield Thomson
The Cambridge Companion to the Saxophone
Edited by Richard Ingham
The Cambridge Companion to the Violin
Edited by Robin Stowell

Composers

The Cambridge Companion to Bach
Edited by John Butt
The Cambridge Companion to Bartók
Edited by Amanda Bayley
The Cambridge Companion to Beethoven
Edited by Glenn Stanley
The Cambridge Companion to Berg
Edited by Anthony Pople
The Cambridge Companion to Berlioz
Edited by Peter Bloom
The Cambridge Companion to Brahms
Edited by Michael Musgrave
The Cambridge Companion to Benjamin Britten
Edited by Mervyn Cooke
The Cambridge Companion to Bruckner
Edited by John Williamson
The Cambridge Companion to John Cage
Edited by David Nicholls

The Cambridge Companion to Chopin
Edited by Jim Samson
The Cambridge Companion to Debussy
Edited by Simon Trezise
The Cambridge Companion to Handel
Edited by Donald Burrows
The Cambridge Companion to Mozart
Edited by Simon P. Keefe
The Cambridge Companion to Ravel
Edited by Deborah Mawer
The Cambridge Companion to Schubert
Edited by Christopher Gibbs
The Cambridge Companion to Stravinsky
Edited by Jonathan Cross
The Cambridge Companion to Verdi
Edited by Scott L. Balthazar

Topics

The Cambridge Companion to Blues and
Gospel Music
Edited by Allan Moore
The Cambridge Companion to Grand Opera
Edited by David Charlton
The Cambridge Companion to Jazz
Edited by Mervyn Cooke and David Horn
The Cambridge Companion to the Musical
Edited by William A. Everett and Paul R. Laird

The Cambridge Companion to the Orchestra
Edited by Colin Lawson
The Cambridge Companion to Pop and Rock
Edited by Simon Frith, Will Straw and
John Street
The Cambridge Companion to the String Quartet
Edited by Robin Stowell

The Cambridge Companion to

BRUCKNER

. . . .

EDITED BY
John Williamson

CAMBRIDGE
UNIVERSITY PRESS

CAMBRIDGE UNIVERSITY PRESS
Cambridge, New York, Melbourne, Madrid, Cape Town, Singapore,
São Paulo, Delhi, Dubai, Tokyo

Cambridge University Press
The Edinburgh Building, Cambridge CB2 8RU, UK

Published in the United States of America by Cambridge University Press, New York

www.cambridge.org
Information on this title: www.cambridge.org/9780521008785

© Cambridge University Press 2004

First published 2004

A catalogue record for this publication is available from the British Library

ISBN 978-0-521-80404-2 Hardback
ISBN 978-0-521-00878-5 Paperback

Transferred to digital printing 2009

Contents

Part IV • Reception

Notes on contributors

Christa Brüstle has worked as a researcher and teacher at the Free University of Berlin since 1992, becoming Wissenschaftliche Mitarbeiterin in the special research centre Kulturen des Performativen in 1999. In 2002 she became chairwoman of the Berliner Gesellschaft für Neue Musik. Her Ph.D. thesis, completed in 1996, was concerned with the reception history of Anton Bruckner, particularly during the period of National Socialism in Germany, and formed the basis of a book, *Anton Bruckner und die Nachwelt* (1998). Current research projects include performance issues in modern and experimental music as well as relationships between music and theatre. Recent publications include articles on performance art and music, concert platform as stage, sound art, Tippett, and Kagel.

Andrea Harrandt has worked on the staff of the Commission of Music Research at the Austrian Academy of Sciences since 1984 and for the Anton Bruckner Institut Linz since 1980. She has contributed to the *Bruckner Gesamtausgabe* for which she has edited *Studien & Berichte* as well as the first volume of the letters (with Otto Schneider†); she is currently working on the second. Since 2002, she has been secretary general of the Mozartgemeinde Wien. Recent publications include *Vergessene Komponisten des Biedermeier* (Hans Schneider, 2000) and *Künstler und Gesellschaft im Biedermeier* (Hans Schneider, 2002), both with Erich Wolfgang Partsch.

Paul Hawkshaw's principal scholarly activity has been as editor of the Collected Works Edition of Anton Bruckner. His new score of the Mass in F minor and extensive critical report are now in press, and his critical report on the Psalms and Magnificat, of which he edited five volumes, appeared in 2002. His articles on Bruckner have been published in *The Musical Quarterly, 19th Century Music*, and the *Bruckner Jahrbuch*. He co-edited *Perspectives on Anton Bruckner* (Ashgate, 2001) with Crawford Howie and Timothy L. Jackson as well as *Bruckner Studies* (Cambridge University Press, 1997) with Timothy L. Jackson, and is currently working on a biography of the composer. He has been a member of the Faculty at the Yale School of Music for eighteen years including eleven as Associate Dean.

Julian Horton is a College Lecturer in Music at University College Dublin. He has been a Research Fellow of Trinity College, Cambridge, and has also taught analysis at King's College, London. His doctoral research concerned the theory and analysis of nineteenth-century tonality, and took Bruckner's Eighth Symphony as an extended analytical example. He has recently published in *The Musical Quarterly* on the relationship between postmodern philosophies and the critique of musical analysis, and is currently working on a study of Bruckner's symphonies for Cambridge University Press.

A. Crawford Howie lectures in music at the University of Manchester. His teaching and research interests are in the nineteenth century in general, with particular emphasis on the sacred music of Schubert and Bruckner. He has contributed several articles and signed reviews to learned journals, is associate editor of the *Bruckner Journal*, co-edited *Perspectives on Anton Bruckner* (Ashgate, 2001) and is the author of the recently published two-volume *Documentary Biography* of the composer (Edwin Mellen, 2002).

Benjamin M. Korstvedt is Assistant Professor of Music at Clark University in Worcester, Massachusetts and author of *Bruckner: Symphony No. 8* (Cambridge University Press, 2000), as well as a number of articles on Bruckner and related topics. He recently completed preparation of the first modern edition of the 1888 version of the Fourth Symphony, which will be published in 2002 as part of the Bruckner *Gesamtausgabe*.

Margaret Notley, who teaches at the University of North Texas, has published widely on topics such as musical life in turn-of-the-century Vienna and compositional reception of Beethoven in the nineteenth and twentieth centuries and is currently focused on finishing a book on late Brahms. For the article 'Late-Nineteenth-Century Chamber Music and the Cult of the Classical Adagio' which appeared in *19th Century Music*, she received the American Musicological Society's Alfred Einstein Award in 2000. Her other research interests include the music of Stravinsky and the phenomenon of twentieth-century neoclassicism.

Derek B. Scott is Chair of Music at the University of Salford and researches into music, culture, and ideology. He is author of *The Singing Bourgeois* (Open University Press 1989, rev. edn, Ashgate, 2001) and editor of *Music, Culture, and Society* (Oxford University Press 2000). His latest book is *From the Erotic to the Demonic: on Critical Musicology* (forthcoming 2003). He is also a composer.

Kevin J. Swinden is Assistant Professor of Music Theory at Wilfrid Laurier University in Waterloo, Ontario, Canada. He is a music analyst, interested primarily in the music of the late nineteenth century and of Anton Bruckner in particular. His work is published in the journal *Music Analysis*.

John Williamson is Professor of Music at the University of Liverpool. He is the author of *The Music of Hans Pfitzner* (Oxford University Press, 1992) and *Strauss: 'Also sprach Zarathustra'* (Cambridge University Press, 1993). He has published extensively on Liszt, Mahler, Strauss, Wolf, and their contemporaries in *Music & Letters*, *Music Analysis*, *The Music Review*, and other journals, and contributed articles to the most recent edition of *Grove*. He is currently writing a monograph on Eugen d'Albert.

Acknowledgements

I should like to thank Penny Souster and her team at Cambridge University Press for their help and persistence in encouraging me to produce this book. The early stages of planning were facilitated by a period of study leave granted by the Arts and Humanities Research Board in 1999–2000. My daughter acted as a sounding-board for matters relating to readability and translation. George Bremner helped me with one particularly awkward passage of translation. The Department of Music at the University of Liverpool was virtually rebuilt around me while I was writing the book, but still managed to provide some important resources. My biggest thanks are to my contributors, who set me the usual problems and have patiently put up with my attempts to solve them.

A version of Chapter 8 first appeared in the *Bruckner Journal*.

Chronology

1824	4 September, Bruckner born in Ansfelden in Upper Austria.	Birth of Smetana.
1827		Death of Beethoven.
1828	Begins to study music with his father.	Death of Schubert.
1833		Birth of Brahms.
1835	Studies with his cousin Weiss at Hörsching; period of earliest compositions.	Birth of Saint-Saëns. Death of Bellini.
1836	Returns to Ansfelden.	
1837	7 June, death of his father. Boy singer in St. Florian. Begins studies with Michael Arneth, prior of St. Florian.	
1839		Birth of Musorgsky. Birth of Hermann Levi.
1840	Studies with Dürrnberger in Linz.	Birth of Tchaikovsky.
1841	Assistant schoolmaster in Windhaag bei Freistadt.	Birth of Dvořák.
1842		Founding of the orchestra that became the Vienna Philharmonic.
1843	Assistant schoolmaster in Kronstorf bei Steyr. Beginning of study with Zenetti.	Founding of the Wiener Männergesangverein. First performance of *Der fliegende Holländer*. Birth of Hans Richter. Birth of Grieg. Birth of Peter Rosegger.
1844		Birth of Nietzsche.
1845	First assistant teacher at St. Florian.	First performance of *Tannhäuser*.
1847		Death of Mendelssohn.
1848	Begins composing the Requiem in D minor on the death of his friend Franz Sailer.	Revolution in Vienna; accession of Franz Joseph. Liszt starts to compose his Weimar cycle of symphonic poems. Death of Donizetti.
1849	15 September, first performance of the Requiem.	Death of Chopin.
1850	Provisional organist at St. Florian.	First performance of *Lohengrin*.
1851	Confirmed as organist at St. Florian.	Wagner completes *Oper und Drama*.

1852	First visit to Vienna.	
1854	Death of Arneth.	Hanslick's *Vom Musikalisch-*
	Bruckner writes the *Missa solemnis* in	*Schönen*.
	B♭ for the induction of his successor	Birth of Janáček.
	(14 September).	
	Organ examination in Vienna's	
	Piaristenkirche (9 October).	
1855	Visits Simon Sechter in Vienna and	Concordat with the Papacy restores
	becomes his pupil.	ecclesiastical authority in educa-
	Failed attempt to become cathedral	tion and other matters.
	organist at Olmütz (Olomouc).	Birth of Arthur Nikisch.
1856	Becomes cathedral organist at Linz.	First performance of Liszt's 'Gran'
	Member of the Linz Liedertafel	Mass.
	Frohsinn.	First Steinway grand piano is
		produced.
		Birth of Felix Mottl.
		Birth of Freud.
		Death of Schumann.
1857		First edition of Baudelaire's *Fleurs*
		du mal.
		Birth of Josef Schalk.
		Birth of Elgar.
1858		Birth of Hans Rott.
1859		Darwin's *Origin of Species*.
		Birth of August Göllerich junior.
1860	Bruckner appointed director of the	Birth of Mahler.
	Linz Liedertafel *Frohsinn*.	Birth of Hugo Wolf.
	11 November, death of Bruckner's	
	mother.	
	Completion of Psalm 146.	
1861	Completes course with Sechter.	
	Examination as organist in Piaris-	
	tenkirche.	
	Obtains diploma from the Vienna	
	Conservatory.	
	Begins to study modern orchestral	
	forms with Otto Kitzler.	
	Conducts *Frohsinn* in Nuremberg.	
1862	Completion of String Quartet.	Birth of Debussy.
		Birth of Klimt.
		Birth of Arthur Schnitzler.

1863	*Tannhäuser* under Kitzler in Linz. Studies with Dorn. Completion of the Overture in G minor. Composition of the Symphony in F minor and *Germanenzug*.	Birth of Franz Schalk. Birth of Ferdinand Löwe. Birth of Weingartner.
1864	Publication of *Germanenzug*. Mass in D minor; 20 November, first performance.	Birth of Richard Strauss.
1865	Bruckner visits Munich, hears *Tristan*, and meets Wagner. Attends the first performance of *Die Legende von der heiligen Elisabeth* in Budapest. Begins the First Symphony. 5 June, first performance of *Germanenzug*, Linz.	Opening of the Ringstrasse. First performance of *Tristan und Isolde*. Birth of Sibelius. Birth of Nielsen.
1866	Present when Berlioz conducted *La Damnation de Faust* in Vienna. Completes the First Symphony and composes the Mass in E minor.	Prussia defeats Austria and excludes it from German affairs.
1867	Nervous breakdown leads to four months in a sanatorium in Bad Kreuzen. Bruckner applies unsuccessfully for posts in Vienna. Begins the Mass in F minor. 10 February, Herbeck conducts the Mass in D minor in Vienna.	Execution of Emperor Maximilian of Mexico. The *Ausgleich* establishes the Dual Monarchy of Austria-Hungary. Death of Simon Sechter.
1868	Conducts the closing section of *Die Meistersinger von Nürnberg* in Linz. Appointed to a professorship at the Vienna Conservatory. Completion of the Mass in F minor. 9 May, first performance of Symphony No. 1 in Linz.	The 'May laws' lead to a crisis between church and state in Austria. First performance of *Die Meistersinger von Nürnberg*. Death of Rossini. Suicide of Adalbert Stifter in Linz. F. X. Witt founds the Allgemeiner Cäcilien-Verein.
1869	Performs in an organ-playing contest at Nancy, then in Paris. Composition of the Symphony in D minor. 29 September, first performance of the Mass in E minor, Linz.	First performance of *Das Rheingold*. Birth of Pfitzner. Birth of August Halm. Death of Berlioz.

1870	Appointed teacher at the college of St. Anna.	Dedication of the Musikverein. First performance of *Die Walküre*. Wagner's *Beethoven*.
1871	First Symphony rejected by the Vienna Philharmonic Orchestra. Performs in the Royal Albert Hall and the Crystal Palace. Begins to compose the Second Symphony.	Conclusion of Franco-German War leads to founding of German Empire. Birth of Zemlinsky.
1872	Second Symphony completed but rejected by the Vienna Philharmonic Orchestra. Possibly begins work on the Third Symphony. 16 June, first performance of the Mass in F minor.	Foundation of the Wiener Akademischer Wagner-Verein. Birth of Skryabin. Birth of Vaughan Williams. Birth of Siegfried von Hausegger. Death of Grillparzer.
1873	Bruckner joins the Wagner-Verein. Composition of the first version of the Third Symphony. Bruckner shows the Second and (draft) Third Symphonies to Wagner, who accepts the dedication of the latter. 26 October, revised Second Symphony performed in Vienna by the Philharmonic under Herbeck.	Beginning of world-wide financial crisis. Birth of Rakhmaninov. Birth of Reger.
1874	Leaves the college of St. Anna. Composes the first version of the Fourth Symphony. Revision of the Third Symphony. Sends a copy to Wagner.	Wagner at Wahnfried First performance of *Die Fledermaus*. Birth of Schoenberg. Birth of Franz Schmidt. Birth of Ives. Birth of Karl Kraus. Birth of Hofmannsthal.
1875	Appointed to the post of lecturer at the University of Vienna. Vice-archivist at the Hofkapelle. Third Symphony rejected by the Vienna Philharmonic Orchestra. Begins work on the Fifth Symphony. Starts on the revision of the Second Symphony.	Wagner visits Vienna for the last time. Hans Richter comes to Vienna. First performance of Bizet's *Carmen*. Birth of Ravel.

1876	Bruckner visits Bayreuth. Revision of the three masses. Fifth Symphony completed. Starts the second version of the Third Symphony and writes an 'intermediate' version of the slow movement. Further revision of the Second Symphony. 20 February, first performance.	First Bayreuth Festival and first complete performance of *Der Ring des Nibelungen*. Brahms's First Symphony receives its première in Karlsruhe. Birth of Bruno Walter.
1877	Bruckner teaches theory to Josef Schalk. Mahler attends Bruckner's University classes in harmony. Revises the First Symphony, producing a version usually described as the 'Linz' version. Revision of the Fifth Symphony. New version of Second Symphony. Revises the Third Symphony. 16 December, fiasco of Third Symphony at first performance in Vienna.	Edison's phonograph. Death of Johann Herbeck.
1878	Bruckner teaches theory to Franz Schalk. Additional coda for the Scherzo of the Third Symphony. Completion of the Fifth Symphony. Begins to revise the Fourth Symphony, including the composition of a new Scherzo and the 'Volksfest' Finale.	Fontane's *Vor dem Sturm*. Death of Pius IX.
1879	Theodor Rättig publishes the Third, the first of Bruckner's symphonies to appear in print. Completion of the String Quintet. Begins work on the Sixth Symphony.	Appointment of Taaffe as prime minister marks the beginning of Austrian Liberalism's decline. Completion of the Votivkirche.
1880	Revised version of the Fourth completed with the composition of a third Finale.	Birth of Max Auer. Death of Anselm Feuerbach.

1881	Sixth Symphony completed.	Birth of Bartók.
	Begins to compose the Seventh Symphony.	Death of Musorgsky.
	Starts work on the Te Deum.	
	Further revision of the three masses and of the Fourth Symphony.	
	20 February, first performance of the Fourth Symphony under Hans Richter in Vienna.	
	10 December, Mottl conducts the Fourth Symphony in Karlsruhe.	
1882	Bruckner visits Bayreuth.	Georg von Schönerer founds the Deutschnationaler Verein in Vienna.
	Revision of the Mass in E minor.	First performance of *Parsifal*.
		First edition of Riemann's *Musiklexikon*.
		Birth of Stravinsky.
		Death of Raff.
1883	Seventh Symphony completed.	The first sections of Nietzsche's *Also sprach Zarathustra* are published.
	Completion of the Te Deum (first version).	
	11 February, performance of the middle movements of the Sixth Symphony in Vienna under Wilhelm Jahn.	Birth of Webern.
		Death of Wagner.
1884	Completion of the Te Deum (second version).	Meeting of the *Dreikaiserbund*.
	Starts to compose the Eighth Symphony.	Death of Smetana.
	Revision of the String Quintet.	Death of Bishop Rudigier.
	Revision of First Symphony.	Death of Emanuel von Geibel.
	30 December, success of Seventh Symphony at its first performance under Nikisch in Leipzig.	Death of Hans Makart.
1885	First meeting with Hugo Wolf.	Brahms's Fourth Symphony receives its première in Meiningen.
	Honorary member of the Wiener Akademischer Wagner Verein.	Friedrich von Hausegger's *Musik als Ausdruck*.
	Publication of the Seventh Symphony in the version by Löwe and Franz Schalk.	Birth of Berg.
	Publication of Te Deum.	Birth of Otto Klemperer.
	4 October, first performance of the revised Mass in E minor in Linz.	

1886	Receives the Order of Franz Joseph. Further revision of the Fourth Symphony; first performed in New York. 10 January, first performance of the Te Deum under Richter in Vienna.	Krafft-Ebing's *Psychopathia sexualis*. Birth of Wilhelm Furtwängler. Birth of Ernst Kurth. Birth of Kokoschka. Birth of Robert Haas. Death of Liszt.
1887	The first version of the Eighth Symphony is completed but is rejected by Hermann Levi. First sketches for the Ninth Symphony. Begins the revision of the Eighth. Begins a further revision of the Third Symphony.	First performance of Verdi's *Otello*. Death of Borodin.
1888	Third version of Fourth Symphony first performed on 22 January under Richter in Vienna.	Accession of Wilhelm II as German Emperor. Birth of Hans Knappertsbusch.
1889	Honorary member of the Wiener Akademischer Gesangverein. Completes the revision of the Third. Revision of First Symphony. Continues to revise the Eighth. Publication of the Fourth Symphony in the version edited by Löwe and Franz Schalk.	Founding of Christian Social Party. Publication of Wolf's Mörike and Eichendorff song-books. Mahler's First Symphony receives its première in Budapest. Strauss's *Don Juan* receives its première in Weimar. Birth of Ludwig Wittgenstein. Birth of Alfred Orel. Death of Ludwig Anzengruber.
1890	The Eighth is completed in the revised version. Starts to revise the First Symphony. Franz Schalk's edition of the score of the Third Symphony published. 21 December, first performance of the revised Third Symphony under Richter in Vienna.	Fall of Bismarck. Rise of operatic Verismo. Foundation of Neuer Richard Wagner-Verein. Birth of Egon Schiele. Death of Franck.

1891	Retires from the Conservatory. Honorary Doctor of the University of Vienna. Starts to compose the Ninth Symphony. Completes the revision of the First (the 'Vienna' version). 13 December, first performance of the revised First Symphony under Richter in Vienna.	Birth of Prokofiev.
1892	Composition of Psalm 150, first performed on 13 November. Revision and publication of Second Symphony (ed. C. Hynais). Publication of Mass in D minor. Publication of the Eighth Symphony in the edition by Josef Schalk and Max von Oberleithner. 18 December, first performance of the revised Eighth under Richter in Vienna.	
1893	Composition of *Helgoland*. Publication of the First Symphony in the 'Vienna' version. 8 October, first performance of *Helgoland* in Vienna.	Death of Tchaikovsky. Death of Gounod.
1894	Completes the first three movements of the Ninth Symphony. Publication of Mass in F minor. 9 April, first performance of the Fifth Symphony in a version by Franz Schalk. 25 November, first performance of the second version of the Second Symphony under Richter in Vienna.	Birth of Karl Böhm.
1895	Bruckner is granted apartments in the Belvedere. Begins work on the Finale of the Ninth Symphony.	Beginning of the political crisis over Karl Lueger's election as Mayor of Vienna. Birth of Hindemith.
1896	11 October, Bruckner dies. Publication of the Fifth Symphony in the version by the brothers Schalk, and of the Mass in E minor in Franz Schalk's edition.	Otto Wagner's *Moderne Architektur*.

1899	Unveiling of bust of Bruckner in Vienna's Stadtpark.
	Publication of *Helgoland*.
	26 February, first performance of Symphony No. 6 in the version by C. Hynais (published in the same year) under Mahler.
1903	Publication of Löwe's edition of the Ninth Symphony, which is performed on 11 February in Vienna under Löwe.
1909	12 December, original Scherzo of Fourth Symphony performed in Linz.
1913	31 October, second movement of the Symphony in F minor performed in Vienna under Löwe.
1923	18 March, first and fourth movements of the Symphony in F minor performed in Klosterneuburg under Moissl.
1924	17 May, first performance of third and fourth movements of the Symphony in D minor.
	12 October, first complete performance of the Symphonies in F and D minor in Klosterneuburg under Moissl.
1932	2 April, first performance of the original version of the Ninth Symphony in Munich under Hausegger.
1935	23 October, first performance of the original version of the Fifth Symphony in Munich under Hausegger.
1939	5 July, first performance of Robert Haas's version of the Eighth Symphony.
1946	1 December, first performance of first version of the Third Symphony in Dresden under Keilberth.
1954	2 May, the first movement of the first version of the Eighth Symphony is performed in Munich.

1973   2 September, the BBC broadcasts a performance of the first version of the Eighth Symphony under Schönzeler.

1975   20 September, first version of the Fourth Symphony performed in Linz under Wöss.

Abbreviations

In the notes the following abbreviations are used:

ABSW Anton Bruckner, *Sämtliche Werke: kritische Gesamtausgabe*, ed. Leopold Nowak (Vienna, 1951–)

B-J *Bruckner-Jahrbuch*

B-P *Bruckner-Probleme: internationales Kolloquium 7.–9. October 1996 in Berlin*, ed. Albrecht Riethmüller (Stuttgart, 1999)

BS *Bruckner Studies*, ed. Timothy L. Jackson and Paul Hawkshaw (Cambridge, 1997)

EKB Ernst Kurth, *Bruckner*, 2 vols. (Berlin, 1925; repr. Hildesheim and New York, 1971)

Göll-A August Göllerich, *Anton Bruckner: ein Lebens- und Schaffens-Bild*, ed. and completed by Max Auer, 4 vols. (Regensburg, 1922–37) (volumes cited as I, II/1, II/2, III/1, III/2, IV/1, IV/2, IV/3, IV/4)

H-S1 Andrea Harrandt and Otto Schneider (eds.), *Briefe 1852–1886*, Anton Bruckner Sämtliche Werke, vol. XXIV/1 (Vienna, 1998)

H2 Andrea Harrandt (ed.), *Briefe 1887–1896*, Anton Bruckner Sämtliche Werke, vol. XXIV/2 (Vienna, forthcoming)

MQ *The Musical Quarterly*

NCM *19th Century Music*

PAB *Perspectives on Anton Bruckner*, ed. Crawford Howie, Paul Hawkshaw, and Timothy [L.] Jackson (Aldershot, 2001)

PART ONE

Background

1 Introduction: a Catholic composer in the age of Bismarck

JOHN WILLIAMSON

Psychology and environment

Within the last two decades, the study of Bruckner and his music has begun to change radically. For long a generalized picture was current that depicted a simple religious man, ill at ease in society, an anachronism in his age who suffered neglect, misunderstanding, and the malice of critics.[1] The martyrdom of the life bred the mysticism of the artist; the social anachronism became the timeless prophet. Much of this rested on flimsy evidence and critical misunderstanding. When the Bruckner number of *Musik-Konzepte* appeared in 1982, Norbert Nagler could still bemoan the tendency of anecdotes to swamp analysis.[2] The evidence of recent Bruckner scholarship suggests that criticism and analysis of his music is now flourishing as never before, and with the full arsenal of modern techniques. Anecdotes have also to some extent given way to more complex questions in the area of biographical study. As a result interpretation has acquired new directions that are not simply to be traced in specialized Bruckner scholarship.

That Bruckner's life and times impinged upon his music is now a given of scholarship, and is reflected in the attention devoted specifically to his personality in recent conferences. At least one distinguished scholar has noted that this was not always the case.[3] It is arguable that what has changed is the need to subscribe to one or other of the myths about Bruckner that enrolled him either as a mystic or as a simpleton. Such constructs lead to value judgements about the work; embarrassment at their inadequacy was just as likely to lead to an exclusion of the life from critical accounts.

A decisive moment came when modern psychological and sociological criticism began to suggest that beneath the standard picture there lay a deeply fractured personality, torn by neuroses that were different from, but hardly less striking than, those of Mahler, with whom for long Bruckner seemed to stand in a musico-biographical comparison. Constantin Floros documents a moment at a symposium in 1977, when a speaker raised the possibility of mental illness in Bruckner, as indicative of a change in the way that he was regarded.[4] Within five years more sophisticated analysis began to appear that related Bruckner's mental life to the world of his music.

Norbert Nagler's essay of 1982 sparked off a reinterpretation that extended to the writings of Peter Gülke and Martin Geck. While it would be inaccurate to say that they share a consistent point of view, they do form a kind of unity, in which biographical, ideological, and critical factors have come together to consider what kind of Bruckner picture should be dominant, at least in the German-speaking world. Factors of historical and sociological provenance shaped Bruckner's personality towards a decisive moment marked by his nervous breakdown of 1867. The transition to psychological analysis does not entirely throw off the world of the Bruckner anecdote, since the new interpretative tradition could hardly exist without the stories that emphasise his 'tendency to necrophilia, counting mania and compulsion to control, and fanatical observation of religion'.[5] Even within this tradition there are misgivings, a fear of 'greedy demands from the psychological or sociological viewpoints'.[6] There is little doubt, however, that Bruckner interpretation has to account for such phenomena, which have passed into general knowledge through the increasing emphasis on late nineteenth-century Vienna as city of 'nervous splendour'.[7] Equally it has to consider how far the old picture served an agenda that had much to do with 'German-ness' in the decades after Bismarck excluded Austria from the new Reich.

Later chapters will address the circumstances of Bruckner's upbringing, Catholic education, and attitude to Vienna. My intention in raising them here is to underline the necessity of seeing that his upbringing in the period of the *Vormärz* (before the Revolution of 1848), his exposure to patriarchal 'despotic-feudal' interaction, the resulting 'subservient mentality', and the 'codified asceticism' of his Catholic education have their place in the new picture of the neurotically driven Bruckner.[8] If these generated a compulsion to overachieve coupled with fantasies of power, then the effect on his artistic personality must have been considerable. In its most remarkable expression, there is the idea that Bruckner 'strangled' his personality in order to realize his inner life in music.[9]

Born into the world of Metternich and Biedermeier, Bruckner passed through the years of revolution, and arrived in Vienna at the point when Liberalism approached its climax. By his death, however, Liberalism had collapsed in Vienna before the forces of what is often regarded as 'irrationalism' in the all too real forms of anti-Semitic Christian Socialism and German Nationalism. This journey from a quasi-feudal world to the verge of the twentieth century is illuminated retrospectively by the widely influential interpretation of Carl Schorske, the representative of a view of the Viennese *fin de siècle* as revolt of the sons against the fathers: crudely expressed, the deflection of failed political Liberalism into an artistic avant-garde. In recent years, this picture from the history of ideas has been increasingly adjusted in the light of research by students of sociology and politics.

Such changing perspectives were not really available to Nagler or Gülke when they began their seismic shift in perspectives on Bruckner. For Nagler, there is a clear break between the world of the first compositions, with their emphasis on choral society and church, and the works that followed 1867. In the light of recent research into the phenomenon of 'voluntary association', it may be that Bruckner research has too unthinkingly accepted the Biedermeier image of Bruckner's earliest creative phase. Although social organizations (including choral societies) were notionally apolitical (but nevertheless 'patriotic') before the *Ausgleich* of 1867, it has been suggested that 'voluntary association' in the form of social societies formed the basis for discussions that contained implicitly 'moral and political goals'.[10] Since it was a dogma of Nagler's interpretation that the composer's complete lack of political involvement was a relic of his upbringing in the *Vormärz* and determined his later subservience and social repression, a more sophisticated picture of the social circumstances in Austria after 1849 would have considerable impact on our estimate of Bruckner's personality. Here is one area where the fluidity of current research into Austrian circumstances may inflect our picture of Bruckner.

The moment of Nagler's break, around 1867, is more likely to require interpretation. Andrea Harrandt's chapters show clearly the hesitations and personal ambitions which warred within Bruckner at this fateful point in his career. The Nagler–Gülke interpretation, however, has seen this as also an inner artistic crisis that may reflect the assimilation of Wagner (and of Berlioz and Liszt). When Martin Geck refers in disparagement to a 'Wagner irritation', he may be attempting to create a purely artistic crisis out of what in reality was a combination of personal and artistic factors. More interesting is the idea of a crisis after the First Symphony's composition that arose from an 'unresolved conflict between creativity and the compulsion to conform'.[11]

At this junction, the student of Bruckner is confronted with three strands to interpret the change that came over Bruckner's compositions. The psychological strand, that the later symphonies arose from a brilliant compromise between creative genius and the ritualizing of formal and technical procedures, goes alongside the socio-historical strand of Bruckner's 'gründerzeitliche Monumentale Symphonie': Bruckner's type of symphony after the 'Nullte' was formed in the heady days of the Liberal upswing, shared characteristics with Vienna's rebuilding, and represented a kind of compromise of the 'new' Vienna with older monarchical impulses that still continued and were fundamental to Bruckner's world-view.[12] Slightly apart from this is the brilliantly provocative view of Gülke: if we are to accept any truth in the interpretation of Bruckner as mystic (and each of the three interpreters has misgivings here), then we must recognize the plebeian insurrectionary element in all mysticism and acknowledge its essentially heretical character: '[Bruckner's] heresy lay in his composing symphonies.'[13]

Conflation of these ideas is really an attempt to answer why Bruckner emerged from his crisis with a radically new style of symphony. The psychological and sociological nexus that scholars sought to explain in the 1980s and 1990s revolved round the perception that such personality traits as Bruckner's counting mania corresponded to features of his music. The compromise between creativity and ritualizing was a matter of replacing 'endless melody' with 'metrical predetermination' (the equation of counting mania with quadratic phrasing is a theme that constantly recurs in more recent Bruckner studies). Bruckner thus was disturbed at a deeply personal level by the experience of Wagner but did not emerge from his crisis as a Wagnerian symphonist. In place of the seamless rhetoric of music drama came the juxtaposition of contrasts, for which literary and architectural comparisons quickly suggested themselves, and an element of violence that stood opposed to the religious elements in Bruckner's symphonies; for the creators of the new Bruckner picture did not reject the religious interpretation of Bruckner (represented here by Derek Scott's reinterpretation in Chapter 8) but placed it in neurotic tension with socio-psychological factors. In the face of such an interpretation, the old certainties of the Bruckner anecdotes crumbled. Even Bruckner's notorious gaucheness amidst the liberal bourgeoisie of Vienna began to look like a strategy; moral cowardice and servility became peasant cunning.[14] In short, Bruckner ceased to seem like an anachronism in pre-Freudian Vienna.

Political implications of a non-political life

If Bruckner became a man of his time, however, there is now considerable debate as to what kind of time he represented. Scholars have revalued the picture of late nineteenth-century Vienna from two angles that impinge on Bruckner studies. The school that sees a strong interpenetration of artistic factors with social and political history, the descendants of Schorske, has begun a process of self-criticism that may yet trickle into ideas of Bruckner. At the same time, the study of the circumstances of Viennese musical life has advanced to the point that Bruckner studies must start to take account of it. This point of view, more directly related to Bruckner the musician, has remained in the background by comparison with the historico-political complexities of the first.

The picture painted by Nagler of a 'monarchist' Bruckner in a liberal age had the advantage of fitting the little that was known about Bruckner's political views. It also rendered Bruckner relatively easy to locate in Vienna's intellectual map, defined as a gradual substitution of 'an aristocratically based *Gefühlskultur* for the liberal culture of reason and law' which 'was a decisive symptom of Austrian society's sickness unto death'.[15] The Bruckner whose upbringing took place in the *Vormärz* instinctively and without need of revolution anticipated Schorske's elevation of art and culture over rationality; it was hardly surprising that in the half-century after his death Bruckner interpretation should have been overgrown by the irrationality documented in Chapter 16 by Christa Brüstle.

Some of the most striking research into aspects of Bruckner in recent years has concerned this irrationalism in the form of the use made of his music in the Third Reich. Various scholars have considered a number of ways in which Bruckner's life and works were coordinated with the cultural policy of the Nazis. Inevitably this has led to some consideration of the extent to which Bruckner's career had prepared this nemesis. The degree to which he was infected with anti-Semitism is central to this and follows naturally from the Nagler–Gülke interpretation. Already in their writings, it was noted that he was no stranger to religious anti-Semitism, though it is surprising how grudgingly this has trickled into general accounts.[16] In practice it would have been surprising, given Bruckner's connections, if he had not been anti-Semitic. This is less a matter of his Wagnerian associations and visits to Bayreuth than of specifically Austrian circumstances.

The question of the origins and nature of Viennese anti-Semitism is peculiarly complex. Although it found a characteristic home in Karl Lueger's Christian Socialism, it was also present within the liberal movement. The traditional view of Austria's socio-political development has been to stress the manner in which the question of the Habsburg Empire's various nationalities destroyed the liberal dominance. More recent research has tended to show that Liberalism was compatible with Nationalism, which could and intermittently did advocate a liberal agenda. Since Nationalism in this form stressed inclusiveness, both anti-Semites and Jews could find places within movements that promoted liberal ideas and programmes. The unfortunate effect was to legitimize anti-Semitism even within Liberalism.[17]

To place Bruckner within a kind of aristocratic-monarchical *Gefühlskultur* or to emphasize his connections to German Nationalism does not really differentiate him sufficiently from his liberal contemporaries in such a shifting political landscape. An additional problem is that, under close examination, Schorske's thesis of a revolt by Vienna's artists at the turn of the century began to appear implausible. The constitutional monarchy mostly contained the strains, largely because of the extent to which it was involved in artistic life and decision-making.[18] Bruckner may be said to have anticipated this without any particular effort on his part. His recognition in Vienna extended to rewards from official circles.

Yet the sense of Bruckner's marginality within Vienna has always been strong, whatever the point of view of the writer. Marginality in the wider sense has been defined in terms of 'different social backgrounds and positions, different religions and political affiliations'; at its most extreme this could become ' "multiple marginality", a growing alienation from the threatening reality of Vienna'.[19] Bruckner's admirers laid particular weight on the degree to which he, the authentic German, had been rejected by the liberal (with more than undertones of Jewish) opinion makers. Even without this extreme formulation, there is a sense in which Bruckner represented something marginal to the more intellectual classes of the capital city. This lay in his Catholicism.

The most authoritative look at the rise of Liberalism's nemesis, the Christian Socialist movement, has revealed the degree to which anti-Semitism grew out of the mixture of 'racial hatred' and 'economic protest' of the artisan class, but has also noted the manner in which a radicalized clergy gave it a helping hand.[20] In Bruckner studies, there is little need to place excessive weight on the 'subculture of crackpot journalists and district political leaders' that underlay movements such as Schönerer's Pan-Germanism.[21] The church provided him with a model closer to hand.

That liberalism of an anti-clerical kind and anti-Semitism were at loggerheads within Vienna was part of the peculiarly poisonous circumstances of Bruckner's society. Among liberal voices, the charge that the church was anti-Semitic was virtually a topos and inspired much animus within the world of Vienna's press. This was a particularly critical issue in the light of the restored position of Catholicism and its hierarchy within society and education as a result of the Concordat of 1855; Catholicism and the role of the clergy were of critical importance in Austria (in contrast to the situation in Germany, where the 'Catholic bourgeoisie was slowly driven to a sort of internal exile out of disappointment with the conservative attitude of the clergy').[22] The suggestion that this became a canker within the liberal outlook and contributed substantially to its eventual downfall is a central part of the argument put forward by John Boyer. In one of the most striking, yet 'ineffective and degrading', episodes of the conflict between state and bishops, Bruckner's patron Bishop Franz Rudigier of Linz was sentenced to fourteen days imprisonment (subsequently commuted by Franz Joseph) for his contribution to a 'wave of Episcopal anarchism'.[23]

This dramatic confrontation between church and state on the question of (*inter alia*) the supervision of schools took place in the year that Bruckner moved to Vienna. It is hard to imagine that Bruckner, however unpolitical, had no opinion on this matter. Unfortunately, even in the most recent treatment of the Rudigier episode it is difficult to find substantial evidence that bears directly on Bruckner's life; a strong element of supposition therefore marks the conclusion that to speak of his religious anti-Semitism is to overlook that it carried a distinct political charge.[24] In the German Reich anti-Semitism became a means for Catholics to prove their national credentials in the face of a Protestant ascendancy.[25] The Austrian way was less 'political' in a modern sense but no less destructive. From Rudigier at the mercy of the liberals to the radicalized clergy of a generation later was a short step once the church entered the political arena. It was also to shape the political mainstream far more than the Pan-Germans whose anti-Semitism was combined with, rather than opposed to, anti-clericalism.

Bruckner's Catholic background was augmented by the German-National activities of his various admirers referred to by Andrea Harrandt in Chapter 3 and dealt with by her more fully elsewhere.[26] How this made the leap from specifically Viennese circumstances through such channels as the 'mystic' and the 'German' Bruckner to the era of the Third Reich is explained by Brüstle in Chapter 16. The full extent of the taking over of Bruckner in a full party- and state-promoted ritual in 1937 was made clear to an English readership by Bryan Gilliam in a twice-published essay.[27] In an unexpected way this also made an impact on Bruckner's music.

Ethics, editions, and performing styles

Since the 1960s, the issue of which versions of Bruckner's symphonies to sanction had tended to run in favour of the first *Gesamtausgabe* of Robert Haas, for reasons that are reviewed by Benjamin Korstvedt in Chapter 10. Although few Bruckner specialists were unaware of individual oddities in that *Gesamtausgabe* from the purely musicological point of view, Gilliam stressed to a greater extent than before its entanglement with the cultural politics of Germany, Austria, and the approaching *Anschluss*. Whereas an earlier Bruckner biographer like Erwin Doernberg had noted regretfully that Haas' achievements had been threatened by 'the political events of the last twenty-five years', it quickly became apparent that Haas' reputation had more than musicological sins to expiate.[28] The unity of Bruckner's life and works was once more revealed in an all too startling manner.

The first publication of Gilliam's essay prompted a controversy in the pages of *The Musical Quarterly* that was side-tracked to some degree by allegations of lack of communication between German- and English-speaking Bruckner specialists, which may have been true of earlier generations but could hardly apply to the highly impressive work done by American scholars in the last ten years. Manfred Wagner raised an objection that the speech by Goebbels marking the state ceremony of 1937 was of minor significance because it had merely reassembled a ragbag of clichés already present in Bruckner's own time and stated particularly forcefully in obituaries.[29] That the continuity or revival of this 'intellectual tradition' in the 1930s was of some interest to Bruckner scholars seemed to be by-passed by Wagner.

In his introduction to the controversy, Leon Botstein acknowledged this by accusing Wagner of pushing to the margin the question of the continuity of an Austro-German tradition in the origins and development of National Socialism, and it is precisely in this area that one important 'Bruckner problem' lies: why Bruckner's career attracted a German-National mentality that in the larger historical framework proved ruinous for Austria.[30] Austrian treatment of the problem seems as yet not to have made up its mind about this. In a recent essay by Monika Glettler, we meet again Bruckner as friend of Rudigier, as composer of choral works oriented towards a German-National standpoint, and as perhaps more deeply implicated in cultural politics through his relationship to the Wiener Akademischer Gesangverein. She draws to a close, however, by noting that 'open politicization' did not make significant advances before 1914, and by repeating Wagner's objection against the 'American' thesis that seemed to claim that Goebbels had some priority in assimilating Bruckner to a 'German' image: again the 'clichés' of the obituaries stood against consideration of issues that Gilliam had only implicitly raised (as his reply to Wagner noted, continuity had not been his primary concern; nor was he in any sense describing Goebbels as a pioneer in the politicization of Bruckner).[31]

Gilliam's article, as he pointed out, had as underlying issues the myths of martyrdom and religion that underlay the old Bruckner picture; by religion, he was thinking specifically of the Nazi concept of *Gottgläubigkeit*, but there is a more general sense of this issue, in that religion in Bruckner studies is an extensible concept.[32] Far from leading to Biblical hermeneutics and sophisticated deconstruction such as colour Scott's chapter below, earlier concepts had a flavour compounded of German romantic mysticism and nationalism of which the banalities of *Gottgläubigkeit* are only one dimension. Perhaps the non-comprehension which Wagner and Glettler displayed towards Gilliam came from the belated manner in which German musicology had addressed these. Underlying the controversy, however, was not the degree to which Bruckner could be considered a 'Nationalist' or a 'forerunner'. There was also the problem of how to perform Bruckner.

In this context it is hardly surprising that there is both an ethical and an aesthetic dimension. In the course of the *Musical Quarterly* controversy, Botstein referred to his fears that to perform Bruckner in the 'original versions' (to use the language of the liner notes and CD covers) was to risk 'perpetuating a set of aural signifiers closely linked with radical evil'.[33] In itself this is worrying both as a possibility and for what it implies about musical texts. It would be easy to dismiss it for purely 'common sense' reasons (one instinctively, perhaps mistakenly, recoils from the idea that musical texts can be implicated of themselves in the kind of evil to which Botstein refers), but, if it is to be refuted, it really has to be done on solid theoretical grounds. I suspect that musicology, sooner rather than later, will make such an attempt. For the moment, however, Botstein has presented a problem that would be rich in comic potential were it not so serious. Calling for 'a new scholarly methodology', he advocated the resurrection of the versions in which 'the contemporaries of Mahler, and later Schoenberg and Hartmann, got to know Bruckner in the first place' with the object of 'reinventing' a 'new but oddly traditional pre-Nazi Bruckner'.[34]

Most major orchestras nowadays hold copies of both Haas and Nowak editions. Whichever is performed, audiences or buyers are assured that they are hearing 'original' Bruckner. For musicology to step in and say that, on reflection, it should have thought a little longer and harder about endorsing these 'originals' risks the wrath of too many interested parties. But a reconsideration of the supposedly discredited and now seldom performed versions associated with Bruckner's friends and disciples is precisely what musicology is currently doing, both in Austria, through Thomas Leibnitz's careful re-evaluation of the relationship of Bruckner and his disciples, and in America.[35] A by-product has been to muddy the pool even further by revealing that some of the disciples, notably Josef Schalk, had made their own contribution to 'evil' by spreading the image of the 'German Bruckner' in the composer's lifetime.[36] That Bruckner's image can be reinvented in quite the way that Botstein advocates seems doubtful; nonetheless, true to his word, Botstein subsequently recorded the now rarely heard Schalk score of the Fifth Symphony, a performance to which I shall return in Chapter 15.

If the ethical issue is as yet unresolved, the aesthetic argument (which is by no means independent) is also open and goes beyond the question of which versions should be played. Here it is a matter of how the versions are to be played. An argument against the disciples' scores had always been that they represented 'Wagnerized' versions that distorted the block sonorities and contrasts of the originals. American scholarship in particular has pointed out that this is a simplification, perhaps even a misconception. Their implication is that a 'Wagnerized' way of performing Bruckner now exists, even among conductors who have used the 'original' scores.[37] Has the legacy of the Nazi reading of Bruckner been the recordings and performances of the post-war era? Oddly enough, some of those German conductors who lived through the Nazi period have left recorded evidence of a more 'mercurial' style. In such a subjective area it is only to be expected that inconsistencies in argument occasionally arise. Furtwängler appears among the 'Wagnerized' in Botstein's list (though he does not use the term), but represents the 'mercurial' tradition for Korstvedt (which may reflect how complex an interpreter he was).[38] The demand for a new, lighter style of Bruckner performance is already being met, though whether this should be attributed to specific features of Bruckner reception or to trends in twentieth-century performance practice is as yet an open question.[39]

The problems of Bruckner's relationship to his own time and of its dangerous legacy will not go away. In the case of performance, however, their status is more than usually metaphorical. All of the contributors to the controversy raise it in some way, though it would be possible to relate it to aspects that are already present in the literature and which return to the *Gründerzeit* to which Nagler referred. Manfred Wagner compared the relationship of Wagner reception in Vienna to the architectural 'megalomania' of the Ringstrasse.[40] The environment and musical culture in which Bruckner was first performed are moving towards the centre of music historiography of the late nineteenth century. It would be easy to forget in considering the religious in Bruckner that at least a few of his major works were designed for church performance in liturgical context (which is examined below in Chapters 4 and 5). The manner in which Bruckner's musical language sought to make the leap from church to concert hall was another likely factor in the crisis of the 1860s. It bears on how contemporaries viewed the symphony and what audiences expected of Bruckner's music.

Historicism

At the heart of the question of Bruckner and his relationship to his own time is the degree to which he can be said to have departed from the mainstream of musical modernism, usually defined in largely harmonic-contrapuntal terms from Wagner to Schoenberg. That he did depart is a theme common to interpreters of quite different approaches. Thus what is considered anachronistic in one theory is defined as 'ossification' in another; where one writer tended to see an irreconcilable gulf between 'composing with symbols' and modern 'absolute' theories of art, another felt that it was more of a tangential relationship; essentially they are talking about similar things, the elevation of aesthetic categories to thematic material (the 'sublime'), the ritualized use of choral, song, and march, simplified metre and rhythm, stereotyped successions, pre-classical cadences.[41] These seem to be the characteristics of a style with a strong historicizing tendency analogous to the dominant style in the architecture of the time.

That this is not a random comparison is suggested by the widespread prevalence of the idea of the Gothic cathedral as metaphor for Bruckner's symphonic music. A recent essay has drawn attention to the degree to which the nineteenth century accepted equations (raised by no less a figure than Goethe) between Gothic and German and between Gothic and the organic reflection of nature (an idea to which I shall return in Chapter 9 and to which Brüstle refers in Chapter 16). The impetus for the Gothic revival in Germany and (to a lesser extent) in Austria in part came from that identification. The romanticized picture of the mediaeval cathedral became a baffling aesthetic touchstone for the appearance of buildings in 'a century of mechanization, industrialization, and technical progress'.[42] Yet without the appearance of an industrialized society in the aftermath of Bismarck's wars, the great religious buildings of the second half of the century would hardly have come into being with such impressive speed. The anachronistic, 'prefabricated' aspects of Bruckner's music were essentially an aspect of this historicizing tendency transformed by the increasingly large-scale symphony orchestra in the concert hall as temple of art. Even in his religious music a strain developed between its external material splendour and claims to mystic insight; of Psalm 150 it has been noted that the 'reality of the music changes to irrational statements'.[43]

It has been claimed that the modernist direction taken by Viennese religious art after 1900 was towards the cultic.[44] The religious note detected in Bruckner's music, the priestly devotion of his 'disciples', stand together in this field of tension between historicism and cult. The cult, however, saw the universal in Bruckner's symphonies, as Margaret Notley has demonstrated: a heady compound of popular oration, monumentality, and the religious sublime.[45] This aspect was intensified by the manner in which certain institutions in Vienna seemed to his admirers to be closed to his music. There appeared to be a strong contrast between the praise bestowed upon him in Germany from the mid-eighties onwards and the 'carping and narrow-minded' reviews that sometimes appeared in the Viennese press. As Andrea Harrandt shows in Chapter 3, this was a one-sided picture of Bruckner's Viennese reception, but such is the nature of artistic cults. The tendencies in Bruckner interpretation towards the monumental, solemn, 'Wagnerized', and priestly grew out of this desire for his music to embrace a universality that was in reality a passing aspect of a fashion of his time towards historicism and neo-Romanticism. That it did not die finally after 1945 may be a reflection of a rather different and no less questionable cult, that of the great conductor. But no cult should inhibit us from playing Bruckner's well-defined repertory in styles which seem appropriate to our age. The following essays can only be a snapshot of how Bruckner was received at a specific point in the history of his reception. If they do not completely answer 'Bruckner problems', it is because the solutions involve a deeper understanding of the man and his time, and the evolution of performance style in an age that has rediscovered historicism without overcoming the need for 'authenticity' of experience. Bruckner problems are persistently alive.

2 Musical life in Upper Austria in the mid-nineteenth century

ANDREA HARRANDT

From assistant teacher in the 'Land ob der Enns' via professor of music to university lecturer in the capital city of Vienna: that is the astonishing career of Anton Bruckner, who finally in 1891 was also created an honorary doctor of the University of Vienna.

Bruckner was born into the Metternich era. Upper Austria, the land above the Enns, was an agrarian crown land of the Danubian monarchy that was stamped by a patriarchal social structure. The church and its representatives acquired great importance in that the spiritual was regarded as absolute authority. In cultural matters, the visual arts outranked music. From 1854 to 1861 the novelist Adalbert Stifter (1805–68) ran the Oberösterreichischer Kunstverein (founded in 1851) as vice-president, in which capacity he took steps to support numerous artists. On his instigation the Oberösterreichische Landesgalerie was founded. In poetry Stifter (who was also a painter) and the dialect poet Franz Stelzhamer (1802–74) achieved great influence. The dilettantism of the Biedermeier period initially played a great role in music. In the countryside folk music was intensively cultivated while in the towns and cities the nobility and art-loving bourgeoisie emerged as the driving force. The monastic foundations also played an important role in nurturing art and music.

Bruckner was the son of a schoolteacher in Ansfelden, a little village south of Linz that is still of interest nowadays for its parish church (incorporated since 1682 into the foundation of St. Florian) and the vicarage built in Italian renaissance style by Carlo Antonio Carlone. He grew up as the eldest of twelve siblings in a teacher's household with a meagre income that required him even at an early age to help in his father's various activities. Anton Bruckner senior was not only a teacher but also choirmaster, organist, and sexton as well as being in demand as a dance musician on the violin. Regular Sunday performances in the church and visits to the nearby monastery of St. Florian provided the child with his first artistic impressions.

Bruckner's first thirty years were spent mainly in country conditions in the small villages and towns of the land above the Enns. In his eleventh year, Bruckner took up lodgings in Hörsching, south-west of Linz, with his cousin Johann Baptist Weiss (1813–50), a teacher, composer, and in his time one of the best musicians in Upper Austria. He gave the boy (in addition to a primary school education) his first knowledge of theory and organ playing. In the autumn of 1836, Bruckner returned to Ansfelden where he received tuition in music from the teaching assistant Franz Perfahl. After her husband's death in 1837, Theresia Bruckner took her eldest son to St. Florian, where he was admitted to the monastery of the Augustinian canons as a boy singer. As a result the richly equipped Upper Austrian monastery made an indelible impression on his youthful imagination. In the church choir with the second largest organ in Austria Bruckner learned not only the splendour of the monastic ceremonies as well as the power and the standing of the church, but also got to know the works of the church composers of his time.

Mentioned for the first time in 888, the monastery had its heyday in the thirteenth and fourteenth centuries. Monastery and church were rebuilt in the Baroque period according to the design of the architect Carlone (with the construction being completed by Jakob Prandtauer). The great organ, which was to exert such a decisive influence on Bruckner as an artist, was the creation of Franz Xaver Chrismann (1770–74). In the nineteenth century the monastery was again a place of learning. Apart from theology, the study of history stood at the centre of the work of Franz Kurz, Jodok Stülz, and Franz Pritz. In 1847 a department of philosophy and theology was founded. The canons made their mark on higher education in Linz through the professors whom they educated.

Music-making was one of the main subjects in a monastic education. In the nineteenth century church music as well as 'secular' music-making experienced an upturn (as lists of performances prove) and this coincided precisely with Bruckner's own era where the mediaeval institutes for boy singers were concerned. Michael Arneth (1771–1854, Provost of the Monastery from 1823 to 1854) introduced a new regulation transferring the education and training of the boy singers for church and chamber music to the schoolteacher and his assistants. In Bruckner's time Eduard Kurz was the monastery's *regens chori* from 1810 to 1841 with responsibility for choice of music.[1] Bruckner also received technical tuition in organ-playing and encouragement to the independent study of harmony and thorough-bass from Anton Kattinger (1798–1852), organist of the foundation.

In St. Florian Bruckner answered 'schoolteacher' when questioned by the prelate about his future career. Later he reproached himself with not having requested a course of study. His progress was so great, however, that he could enter the teacher training course in Linz. Bruckner now spent almost a year (1840–1) in the provincial capital and gathered new experiences. Linz was then a city 'with 20,000 inhabitants, 12,000 houses, nine churches, a bishopric, five monasteries, and twelve institutes of education'.[2] Two personalities shaped Linz's musical life in the first half of the nineteenth century. One was the multi-talented Franz Xaver Glöggl (1764–1839), who practised various musical activities: *Thurnermeister*, theatre director, orchestra and opera director, concert conductor, cathedral and parish *Kapellmeister*, music teacher, seller, and publicist. In this last capacity he produced Austria's first music journal. The second was Johann Baptist Schiedermayr (1779–1840), a musician from Bavaria who was an outstanding organist and esteemed composer, as well as a music teacher and theatre conductor.[3]

In 1821 a Gesellschaft der Musikfreunde was founded in Linz which was renamed in 1864 Musikverein für Linz and was to play a significant role in the musical life of the city. Its first orchestral conductor was Anton Mayer, a teacher and choir leader. He was followed by – among others – Anton M. Storch (1815–87) and Engelbert Lanz (1820–1904).

The Normal-Hauptschule in Linz – known for short as *Präparandie* – at that time was under the direction of Johann Nepomuk Pauspertl von Drachenthal (1796–1864), an outstanding pioneer in the improvement of teacher training in Upper Austria. Great attention was also paid to musical training, because 'church singers, organists, and sextons' were trained in this school.[4] The music teacher was Johann August Dürrnberger (1810–80), from whom Bruckner received his first regular and sound musical instruction and who was later to play a decisive role in Bruckner's life as friend and adviser. Later, as teacher at the Conservatory in Vienna, Bruckner based his own study plan on Dürrnberger's *Elementar-Lehrbuch der Harmonie- und Generalbasslehre* (Linz, 1841).

Having successfully completed his basic training at the *Präparandie*, Bruckner became a teaching assistant in Windhaag an der Maltsch (in the extreme north of Upper Austria) which at that time was particularly remote, numbered about 200 inhabitants, and comprised twenty houses. The parish belonged (and still does today) to the foundation of St. Florian. Living in the most humble circumstances and suffering under his superiors, Bruckner had to augment his salary by various activities. Among the tasks of the teaching assistant, who had to be at the same time teacher, organist, music copyist, sexton, and farm-hand, were the 'ringing of the morning bell and mowing, then dressing the priest, playing the organ, fetching the wine, serving at the altar, taking the children's practice', 'writing out a lot of music', 'getting the lunch', 'after-school hay-making, threshing, potato-digging, and ploughing', 'prayer-reading', 'ringing lights out', and more.[5] Bruckner was a teacher, servant, and farm-labourer in one. He obtained some scanty additional earnings when he played for weddings and church festivals (which were really forbidden to a teacher). The 'dance floor', however, also became a musical stimulus. Bruckner got to know the richness of Upper Austrian folk dances: alongside those like the Ländler, the quintessential Upper Austrian folk dance around 1860, and the *G'strampften*, there was also the farmworker's *Rockn'geigen*.[6] Here is Friedrich Eckstein on this period: 'He frequently told me how in his early years as village schoolteacher in Windhaag in Upper Austria, he was frequently forced to sustain the bare necessities of life by playing all night at the peasants' dances for a silver twenty-kreuzer piece…'[7]

For his further musical education Bruckner was thrown back upon his own resources. He appeared as a violinist with like-minded people at light-music concerts and dances, he had Joseph Jobst as a violin teacher, he made music in duos and trios with the family of Süka the weaver, and he got the opportunity to practise on a clavichord.

His new place of activity from January 1843, Kronstorf, in one of the richest and most fertile parts of Upper Austria, brought no higher payment, but did result in friendlier surroundings, a more favourable climate, people more receptive to the arts, and a more understanding superior. Although smaller than Windhaag, Kronstorf (with approximately 100 inhabitants) had the advantage of lying between the cultural centres of Enns, Steyr, and St. Florian. His passion for learning led Bruckner to Enns and to Leopold von Zenetti (1805–92), the organist and choir leader of the municipal parish church, with whom he deepened and expanded his knowledge of harmony as well as studying the works of the Viennese classics.[8] In Steyr he was permitted to practise on the Chrismann organ of the parish church, and he still visited St. Florian. Florian Födermayr, a wealthy peasant, not only gave Bruckner financial help but placed a spinet at his service.

In September 1845 Bruckner was employed as assistant teacher in the primary school of St. Florian and so returned to a place of his youth, where he dedicated himself assiduously to study of the organ, natural sciences, and Latin. He earned additional income from private lessons for the Count of nearby Tillysburg, where he was also invited to festivals. After the departure of the monastery organist Anton Kattinger, with whom he had studied organ, Bruckner was appointed as his provisional successor in 1850 – he was never to achieve a permanent appointment. His ten-year spell as monastery organist certainly turned him into one of the best artists on the organ of his time. For a time there also existed in St. Florian a male-voice quartet with which Bruckner himself collaborated and for which he wrote a few compositions.

Because of his impoverished origins, Bruckner always strove to obtain a secure income and place in society. Accordingly in 1853 he applied for 'a position appropriate to a person of his abilities and knowledge' in the court at St. Florian. His ambition and his eagerness to learn led Bruckner repeatedly to seek testimonials; he voluntarily sat rigorous examinations, took the secondary school teacher's examination in Linz, studied from 1855 with the most celebrated theorist of his time, Simon Sechter (1788–1867), in Vienna, and submitted to an examination in 1861 by a commission of the Gesellschaft der Musikfreunde. The first photograph of Bruckner to be preserved (from the period around 1854) shows a self-confident young man with a roll of music paper in his hand.

His fanatical search for knowledge drove him to ceaseless study with the object of making himself completely independent as a craftsman; he already contemplated moving to Vienna and travelled there in 1852 for the first time to dedicate his Psalm 114 to the court conductor Ignaz Assmayr. In a letter to Assmayr Bruckner described his personal situation in St. Florian: 'There is no-one here at all to whom I might open my heart and I remain unappreciated in many respects, which is often a source of secret difficulty for me. Our foundation treats music and therefore musicians with complete indifference…'[9]

Encouraged by someone else, Bruckner participated in the auditions for the position of Cathedral and Municipal Parish Organist in Linz, which had become vacant on the death of Wenzel Pranghofer (1805–55). Ferdinand Ruckensteiner, who worked in the court at Linz, offered some advice that proves how completely naïve Bruckner was in social dealings: 'To my astonishment I hear every day that you who want the job of organist in Linz after all have not even sorted out your finances for the same… Furthermore I feel that it is my duty to tell you that it has been noticed that you have appeared during the taking of vows in an overcoat that even lacked a button, with a scarf around your neck, and with galoshes. Such behaviour is thoroughly improper, I have excused you, but you shouldn't let it happen a second time…'[10] After his financial solvency had been successfully demonstrated, Bruckner was appointed in 1856 Cathedral and Municipal Parish Organist in Linz. With that he took a further step up the ladder of social advancement.

By 1855, Linz, capital of the Imperial and Royal crown land of Upper Austria, contained approximately 27,000 inhabitants. The new age of communications also highlighted the favourable state of the provincial capital: in 1832 the first horse-drawn railway on the continent was constructed between Linz and Budweis, to be followed in 1858 by the Empress Elisabeth West Railway from Vienna to Linz and finally from 1860 to Salzburg. Bruckner's journeys to Vienna were thus made easier, for he had at first to make them by boat.

Bruckner was now one of the leading men of Linz's musical life alongside the opera director Karl Zappe and the current director of the Liedertafel *Frohsinn*. After holding appointments in Prague, Graz, and Vienna, Karl Zappe senior (1812–71) came to Linz in 1834 and fulfilled numerous musical functions. From 1834 to 1866 he was orchestral director in the theatre, from

1839 until 1855 and from 1867 to 1871 violin teacher in the school of the Linz Musikverein, as well as Glöggl's successor as Cathedral and municipal parish conductor. Zappe was also the expert on the examining board at Bruckner's audition on 13 November 1855.

For Bruckner, brought up in the countryside and afraid of the city, Linz meant 'noise and hazard'. Now he found completely different conditions there: a provincial city with a bourgeois milieu and fixed rules of social conduct. Here too we meet the gregarious Bruckner as he ever was in spite of shyness and reserve, the Bruckner who visited carnival evenings and dances as an eager participant. Soon he became a member (and later archivist and on two occasions – 1861 and 1868 – chorus master) of the Liedertafel *Frohsinn* (founded in 1845) and in this capacity came to know the male-voice choir repertory of his time. Singing in such choirs was an essential part of the social structure of the time. The emancipated bourgeoisie's cult of song represented a certain force not only socially but musically, which united the duty of sociability with the cult of patriotic feelings and ideas. Bruckner contributed a few characteristic pieces to this genre. In performances he also often helped out as a critically acclaimed pianist. It was with *Frohsinn* too that he first travelled abroad to the Pan-German Song Festival at Nuremberg.

Bruckner's work-place, the Alter Dom, built to sketches by Pietro Francesco Carlone, was first the Jesuit Church, and from 1785 until 1909 Cathedral of the newly established diocese of Linz. The organ, which came from Engelszell, was brought to Linz in 1789 and adapted for the Cathedral by Franz Xaver Chrismann. Bruckner valued it highly. Its redesigning from 1856 to 1867 claimed the entire period of Bruckner's activity and was carried out by the Ottensheim organ builder Josef Breinbauer (1807–82). On its completion the *Linzer Zeitung* reported: 'So now Linz has an organ again that in fullness and strength of tone numbers among the best in all Austria and sings the praises of the Lord under the masterly hand of our cathedral organist Bruckner.'[11] On this instrument he played private improvisations for Bishop Franz Joseph Rudigier, and here too his Mass in D minor was given its première. At his second place of work, the Municipal Parish Church, the organ built by Ludwig Mooser (1807–81) was in a poor condition. For the third important church in Linz, the Neuer Dom (the Cathedral of the Immaculate Conception) built from 1862 to 1924 in the historicizing style of French High Gothic, Bruckner wrote on commission from Rudigier the Festival Cantata to celebrate the laying of the foundation stone as well as the Mass in E minor for the dedication of the votive chapel.

Even then Bruckner's organ playing was exciting admiration. On the occasion of a recital in Vienna in 1858 there was also a report in Linz:

> In this age of musical aridity you will understand if now and again we visit private musical treats that we can then review without reluctance in public, if they should be of some importance. Recently we had an unaccustomed pleasure when we heard the cathedral organist of Linz, Herr Anton Bruckner, who was spending some time in Vienna for his training, play the organ in Josefstadt's Piaristenkirche. Herr Bruckner possesses a successfully completed teaching course in harmony, as well as the most splendid testimonials to his skill in the art of preludizing, from Professor Sechter. But when he sat at the splendid instrument in the Piaristenkirche and began to improvise freely, we also noticed that he had in practice flown far beyond his theoretical school... His great skill, his inspired efforts, and the all too apparent lack of solid organ players should ensure that he does not lack a splendid future...[12]

Beside his activities as organist, Bruckner earned extra income from piano teaching, gathered a circle of pupils around him, travelled to the houses of the burghers of Linz, and thus had access to the city's public life. In Bishop Rudigier he found a patron ready to help. His friends included the government official Moritz von Mayfeld, whose wife Betty, a pianist, helped him in artistic and social matters. Because he now had reached a professional level corresponding to his education, he was able to think about marriage. However, his courtships, which stretched into advanced old age, remained unsuccessful.

In 1861, a great future was already prophesied for Bruckner: 'Herr Bruckner is also recommended as an excellent teacher of music at the Conservatory and instructor of residential pupils. May a musician as efficient as he is modest be so lucky as to find a position in Vienna appropriate to his talent and ability.'[13] Bruckner still wanted further education, however, and on completing his studies with Sechter he turned to Otto Kitzler (1835–1905) to complete his training in composition by the study of form and instrumentation. Kitzler was conductor at the Linz Theatre from 1858 to 1860 and from 1861 to 1863. In the latter year he conducted Wagner's *Tannhäuser* in Linz with the express permission of the composer, an event of decisive importance for Bruckner's ideas in sound. The first of the larger works for orchestra came into being while Bruckner studied with Kitzler, and they remained in contact in the future.

The Linz Theatre, founded in 1803, had a chequered history. Changing administrations had repeatedly altered the focus of repertory-building: at one point plays had dominated, then opera performances increased again, though of variable artistic quality. Its heyday was under the direction of Franz Stöckl (1852–55), husband of the singer Klara Heinefetter, and of Emanuel Kreibig (1857–63). In Bruckner's time there also took place performances of Wagner's *Der fliegende Holländer* and *Lohengrin,* which the composer probably attended.

Kitzler's successor as conductor of the Linz Theatre was Ignaz Dorn (1829/30–72), who worked less as a teacher in the strict sense than as a guide to the modern musical world of that time: Wagner, Liszt, and Berlioz. He supervised the origins of the First Symphony and the Mass in D minor.

In 1863, Bruckner applied on invitation to succeed Engelbert Lanz as artistic director of the Linzer Musikverein. Because of his excessive demands as much in artistic as material terms, Bruckner did not get the post. His higher musical and artistic demands were already clear at that time:

> to make artistic improvements I am quite willing to apply the full powers of my knowledge and abilities as well as hard work in the task of artistic leadership, if the path is smoothed for me by specific development and organization. That I must still place my heartfelt wish for a yearly salary of the given amount for the great effort and responsibility of the artistic direction of the society cannot possibly be regarded as presumptuous on my part by those gentlemen who have an idea of the cost and terrible labour of a thorough musical education; who understand what it means in musical terms to have a society; and who moreover know my circumstances.[14]

In the same year Bruckner also travelled to the great music festival in Munich where he introduced himself to a few personalities and presented his own compositions to Franz Lachner. Even from Linz he was in regular contact with Vienna. Rudolf Weinwurm, the brother of Alois (1824–79), founding chorusmaster of the Male Voice Choral Society *Sängerbund* in Linz, played the role of contact with Sechter and 'billeting officer' for Bruckner's periods of study in Vienna. 'What always filled me with the greatest pleasure was the complete conviction that the man I acknowledged as my only true friend also thought the same of me, of which every letter from you and others from Vienna have become my guarantee...'[15] His dissatisfaction with Linz conditions is clear in numerous letters to Rudolf: 'I am heartily glad to have put Linz behind me. I shall tell you much in which you will suspect, and even clearly recognize, real provincial characters.'[16]

Further journeys also took Bruckner to Munich, in 1865 to the first performance of *Tristan und Isolde,* and in 1868 to *Die Meistersinger von Nürnberg.*

On 20 November 1864 the performance of the Mass in D minor created 'excitement and emotion' in the Alter Dom in Linz.[17] It was 'the most outstanding work of recent times in church music... With this, Herr Bruckner has taken a decisive step into the future.'[18]

The first Upper Austrian Singing Contest took place in 1865 and the second prize went to Bruckner's chorus *Germanenzug* behind Weinwurm's

Germania, which led to a short-lived annoyance between the two friends.[19] 'From what we have heard, the visiting aesthetician Herr Eduard Hanslick asked Herr Bruckner for the score of the prize-winning chorus *Germanenzug* in order to undertake a detailed critique of this beautiful work.'[20]

'Dissatisfaction with himself and his surroundings, his growing artistic resolve, and his striving for a more respected livelihood' soon brought plans to fruition for finally quitting Linz. Bruckner had already applied in vain in 1861 to the Cathedral Music Society and Mozarteum in Salzburg, in 1867 to the Vienna Hofkapelle, and for the post of court organist in Munich, and finally toyed with the idea of going together with Rudolf Weinwurm as organist to the court of the Emperor Maximilian in Mexico. He wrote to Weinwurm: 'Recently I was told that you had thought of emigrating to the court chapel in Mexico. Is there any truth in that? I too ought to make such an application...Let's go to Russia or wherever if they won't recognize us in our fatherland. You see what my level of satisfaction is and how I love the citizens of Linz for such recognition.'[21] In his numerous applications he didn't exactly hide his light under a bushel: 'incidentally the applicant has no reason to avoid inquiries about his personality in Vienna, Linz, or [St.] Florian; on the contrary, the stronger the efforts to recognize his character, the more it meets his approval'.[22]

Not only his professional and artistic situation but also his private unhappiness are clear in Bruckner's letters: 'At odds with world and man again, I seek there some alleviation of the villainous state of affairs in Linz...'[23] Hence his repeated rejoicing at contacts with the outside world: 'Withdrawn on principle from all society here and also deserted, I am amazed and delighted in the highest degree that some one from far off still thinks of me.'[24]

In spite of this, the application for a Conservatory position in Vienna developed into a long personal struggle: the security of his place in Linz against an uncertain future in a great city. Already in 1866 he confided in Johann Herbeck: 'I lay my destiny and future in your hands! My innermost prayer is "Rescue me"! Or else I am lost. Now is the moment for your intervention and your power. I know your favour for me. Never withdraw this from me, highest one!'[25] Worry about the future finally led in 1867 to a crisis in his health.

Certainly even Herbeck could offer no security:

> You yourself know best how much I did then and am doing now to bring you to Vienna, and precisely for this reason I have the duty as a man of honourable intentions again to say: I absolutely cannot advise you to take an honourable position in Vienna that is still not screwed down in the material sense and give up your present certainly also honourable position that is profitable and additionally still offers personal insurance against a possible accident...[26]

Even in June 1868 Bruckner turned to Hans von Bülow in Munich 'lest I should be passed over in my fatherland, because I cannot stay forever in Linz…'[27]

In the end, however, the decision went in favour of Vienna, even if he cherished long doubts about its correctness. Herbeck had to offer repeated encouragement: 'Don't disengage "from the world" but go "into the world"; no despair unworthy of a man and artist of your type, you have no reason for it.'[28]

He still made certain of a way back to Linz:

> While the undersigned sends his most hearty thanks to the most reverend Episcopal Ordinariate for the trust placed until now in his previous effectiveness as cathedral organist, he most humbly acknowledges hereby that he has taken the place offered him at the Vienna Conservatory as a consequence of renewed requests, and begs the most reverend Episcopal Ordinariate to accept his most humble plea that his previous position as cathedral organist be most graciously reserved for a few years. The gracious granting of this request, as greatest proof of such high good will, would be of the greatest consolation and extraordinary reassurance to the undersigned.[29]

What mattered now was the chance to take advantage of improved social status and better himself professionally. To a musical institute Bruckner brought skills in playing the organ, hard-learned knowledge, and practice in music theory.

In the late Linz period, Bruckner could already register a strong presence in the local press. Shortly before his departure from Linz, the following appeared: 'Herr Bruckner is on the best path to fame and already his name is mentioned with the highest respect in wider musical circles.'[30]

The last months in Linz were still marked by artistic successes. Richard Wagner let the Liedertafel *Frohsinn* and its chorus master Bruckner have the final song of his still unperformed opera *Die Meistersinger von Nürnberg*: 'we congratulate also the Liedertafel on its chorus master, whose outstanding organ-playing and talent for composition we have already had earlier opportunity to appreciate, and who has now also won well-deserved laurels as chorus master for himself, as was only to be expected'.[31]

On 9 May 1868 the première of the First Symphony finally occurred in the presence of Bishop Rudigier in the Redoutensaal, the largest concert hall in the city. The orchestra was made up of music groups from the two regiments stationed in Linz and members of the Theatre orchestra, as well as a few dilettantes: 'Bruckner's outstanding talent resolutely confronts us even here and we wish that he soon may find a place in the capital city of Vienna corresponding to his abilities and musical knowledge, in order to be able to discharge his creative responsibilities at leisure. Meanwhile may he march further down the path he has entered; rewards beckon him on.'[32]

He received good wishes from Linz too on the way:

> Everything in our backwater is as usual. The great pleasures of art are already starting up. Musikverein, *Frohsinn, Sängerbund*, the choral society, various other artists' societies, etc. in short the poor old public should have a good choice. I might ask you to take something to heart. Use your patrons as long as the iron is hot. Those who provided you with the court title have quite certainly the power to provide you with a salary. There are enough funds for so worthy an artist as you to be provided for in the most acceptable manner. So don't let these gentlemen rest, it must work, I am convinced it can and will work.[33]

In spite of this Bruckner continued to be a loyal ally of his homeland in Upper Austria, spent his holidays in St. Florian, Steyr, or Vöcklabruck, and took part in the great festivities of the Linz diocese: Bishop Rudigier's twenty-fifth jubilee (1878), the centenary of the diocese (1885), and the twenty-fifth anniversary of the laying of the foundation-stone of the new cathedral (1887), for each of which he wrote compositions. According to his wish, he was also buried under the organ of the monastic church of St. Florian.

(*Trans. John Williamson*)

3 Bruckner in Vienna

ANDREA HARRANDT

Historical and social environment

The imperial capital and residence of Vienna, the central melting pot of the Habsburg monarchy's empire of four million people, contained roughly 600,000 inhabitants at the end of the 1860s and had spread far beyond its old city walls. New architecture quickly determined the city's image. The entire city was a building site: in 1857 the Emperor Franz Joseph I had ordered the razing of the fortifications and in their place the new Ringstrasse emerged with its official buildings and various palaces of the grand bourgeoisie.

Even if Austria's power had declined in 1866 because of its defeat by Prussia, the liberal constitution of 1867 still led to the equality of all citizens. The loosening of the phase of political Restoration as well as Liberalism brought a general commercial upswing followed by a long stagnation after the stock market crash of 1873. The subsequent downfall of Liberalism led in the final decades of the century to the rise of anti-capitalism and anti-Semitism. The Taaffe government's swing away from Liberalism in 1879 led to increased political activity and socio-religious ferment. The strong growth of population and the doubling of the inhabitants up to 1890 revealed new problems in a great city, as also intermittently did problems of nationality through the immigration of essential labour.

The influence of the metropolitan bourgeoisie made itself felt as public concert life demanded a wide diversity of activities from virtuosity to mass organizations. The new Court Opera House (built in 1869 by August Sicard von Sicardsburg and Eduard van der Null) and Musikverein (built in 1870 by Theophil Hansen) provided an important foundation for public concert life and an essential vehicle for presenting the Viennese bourgeoisie in society. In 1888, the Burgtheater moved into its new building on the Ring (built by Gottfried Semper and Carl von Hasenauer).

Bruckner's professional activity in Vienna

From 1858 Bruckner had travelled regularly to Vienna to study with Sechter and to visit Rudolf Weinwurm. The following report had already appeared in Vienna in 1867 on the occasion of the performance there of the Mass in

D minor: 'And now in conclusion we shall talk about an old favourite idea when we wish Herr Bruckner success in permanently establishing himself musically in Vienna. We could grab hold of this artist, who cultivates an almost criminal modesty, in Vienna on two grounds: his great theoretical knowledge and his truly important organ playing. Has no church been built for him? No chair of learning vacated for him? His abilities as teacher we don't really know at first hand but his mastery of the organ we have experienced again and again.'[1] A year later Bruckner moved to Vienna, where he first took up residence in the Währinger Strasse. As a follower of Sechter he now flaunted the title of professor of harmony and counterpoint and later of the organ at the Conservatory of the Gesellschaft der Musikfreunde (founded in 1816 for the education of professional musicians) after Johann Herbeck had exerted persistent pressure for his appointment. Bruckner gathered a circle of pupils around himself who were later to develop into disciples and champions of his works: among them Franz and Josef Schalk, Felix Mottl, and Ferdinand Löwe. His teaching was universally esteemed, so that he could already report in 1869: 'My examinations are over. My examination in counterpoint aroused extraordinary enthusiasm. There was general astonishment and congratulations on all sides.'[2] By the time that he reached retirement in 1891, he had earned the praise and thanks of his superiors: 'It is not only superfluous, therefore, to recall the outstanding work that you have achieved during twenty-two years as teacher of theory and organ in the institution, always with equal dedication and loyalty to duty. Your numerous pupils join us in gratefully honouring the memory of the man who guided them thoroughly on the path that leads to the broad realm of composition.'[3]

For four years (1870–4) Bruckner also worked as teaching assistant in piano, organ, and theory at the Teacher Training Institute of St. Anna. The so-called 'St. Anna affair' (in which he was investigated over his relationship with his female pupils) represented a deep humiliation for him, even if he was rehabilitated.

For a long time Bruckner had toyed with the idea of becoming Court Organist, first showing interest in the post in 1851. At first he became the Court Organist 'apparent' (i.e. unpaid), then vice-archivist and second singing teacher of the boy choristers in the Hofmusikkapelle in 1875. In 1878 he was finally promoted to a real position and made a member of the Kapelle before in 1880 being appointed Court Organist. After Herbeck's death in 1877 Joseph Hellmesberger, the new Court Conductor (who was simultaneously Director of the Conservatory), kept a marked distance from Bruckner. As a result he had climbed a further rung in social prestige and public standing though he was certainly denied a great wish in spite of many efforts: to become chief or assistant Court Conductor.

Bruckner had already made his first attempt to be appointed teacher of musical composition at the University of Vienna in 1867; in 1875 he finally became unpaid lecturer in harmony and counterpoint in spite of the opposition of Eduard Hanslick and evidently with the support of Karl von Stremayer, Minister for Culture and Education. On 24 April 1876, he gave his inaugural lecture, and for the first time in 1880 he was able to obtain an award of the normal semester's remuneration. His students provide numerous reports of his unconventional style of teaching. Bruckner's ideas and his methods attracted many of the curious who nevertheless approached him with respect. Among his students were Alois Höfler, later professor of pedagogy at the University of Vienna, and Rudolf Steiner, the founder of anthroposophy.

Bruckner's numerous professional activities did not remain unrewarded. In 1886 he received the Knight's Cross of the Franz Joseph Order, and in 1891 he was finally promoted to honorary doctor of the University of Vienna, a long-sought ambition, thanks to a report by Hellmesberger and Hermann Levi. He set particular value on the formula in the document, 'Life-long profession as symphonist'. At the time, he was the first musician in Austria to receive this honour. The subsequent celebration of the Akademischer Gesangverein was intended as a mass demonstration of a nationalist kind. How far Bruckner was aware of this is unknown. The explosive nature of the event could have been considerably defused had the earlier chairman of the Verein, Franz Schaumann, read the ceremonial address instead of the well-known German Nationalist militant August Göllerich.

All of Bruckner's attempts to further his career were linked to his lifelong search for security. During his life, therefore, he made a number of petitions for different positions, a few of which were crowned with success: 'The most respectful undersigned has taken the liberty of begging the high-ranking imperial and royal Ministry for Culture and Education most humbly for the gracious award of an artist's stipend for this year! Hitherto the same has always carried out his protracted studies without any support.'[4] His applications and letters for the most part were also connected to his complaints about his financial situation.[5]

Others, however, report his thoroughly well-established income:

> On the whole he had a very good financial set-up in Vienna; from the court orchestra 1,500 florins that he increased by 300 florins; 1,500 from the Conservatory; 800 and college money from the University; private tuition and 1,000 florins a year from the Emperor for the publishing of his works. And there he was complaining eternally that he had no money, that he was doing very badly. If I had had 1,500 florins for the whole family, we would have been in paradise. You could guess how much the Viennese paid for him from the fact that he could devote his time entirely to composition.[6]

Performances of Bruckner's works and the struggle for recognition

Bruckner's struggle for recognition and for his place in the musical life of Vienna may be simply described with the help of a few reviews of performances of his works. Bruckner's move to Vienna had gradually increased his field of action. After occasional accounts in the Viennese press came regular reviews of his activities and of performances of his works. In 1869 and 1871 he had his first successes abroad in France and London, admittedly as organist, which moved Eduard Hanslick to write:

> In the professor of the local Conservatory, Anton Bruckner, we possess one of the most outstanding organ virtuosos, who at the last music festival in Nancy, then in Paris … performed on the famous organs of St Epvre, St Sulpice, and Notre-Dame with such success that he defeated the most renowned Belgian and French organists in formal competition. Only in Vienna is it impossible to hear Bruckner, for until now he, the Imperial Court Organist, has not been allowed to use the organ for a recital or even only for private practice.[7]

Hanslick was by no means a champion of the conservative point of view, but defended the alliance of new music with classical forms and opposed everything 'unnatural', Richard Wagner, and as a consequence also Bruckner. While he esteemed the organist and theoretician, he could find no sympathy for Bruckner as a composer.

The music criticism of Bruckner's age was a result of the freedom of the press won in 1848, which threw the critic's consciousness back on individual point of view, particular education, and personal estimate of what was heard. A high musical knowledge was taken for granted.

At first Bruckner appeared before the Viennese as a composer of church music. After the great success of the Mass in D minor on 10 February 1867 in the chapel of the Hofburg, Bruckner was commissioned to compose another mass. The Mass in F minor was finally performed on 16 June 1872 in the court chapel of St Augustine by the imperial orchestra under the composer's direction. In his review, Eduard Kremser spoke of Bruckner's talent that had been displayed 'in such a completely significant way'.[8]

The first important performances of the symphonic works took place in the Viennese Academic Wagner Society. Founded in 1873, the Viennese Society, like its model in Germany, aimed to promote and disseminate the works of Richard Wagner. Numerous pupils and students of Bruckner belonged to it. Apart from Wagner's works, it also advocated those of Liszt, Hugo Wolf, and Bruckner. In the so-called 'Internal Evenings' and weekly meetings of the Society Bruckner's symphonies were performed in arrangements for piano (two or four hands) mostly in the Bösendorfer-Saal or in the small hall of the Musikverein. The pianists in charge at these were Hans Paumgartner, Felix Mottl, Josef Schalk, Franz Zottmann, and Ferdinand Foll. Later the Society also organized full performances of the symphonies in the Musikvereinssaal under the direction of Hans Richter.[9] Richter (1843–1916) ought to be reckoned one of the most outstanding interpreters of Bruckner's music. He was one of the regular conductors at the Bayreuth Festival and conducted all of Bruckner's symphonies up to the Fifth and Sixth in the composer's lifetime not only in Vienna but also abroad. Bruckner himself joined the Society after his return from Bayreuth in October 1873 and remained a member to the end of his life.[10] In 1885 he was made an honorary member. At the end of the 1880s a few members left for political reasons and in 1890 founded a 'New Richard Wagner Society' with an outlook that was fundamentally German nationalist. In this society, too, piano performances of Bruckner's works took place.

The first orchestral work by Bruckner to be performed in Vienna on 26 October 1873 at a concert of the Gesellschaft der Musikfreunde (the closing concert of the Vienna World Exhibition) was the Second Symphony in the version of 1872 (with revisions from 1873) under the composer's direction.[11] Hanslick described the symphony in the *Neue Freie Presse* as:

> a composition laid out on the largest scale, which is no less to be denied a very serious, pathetic character as countless beautiful and important details. Although the total impression is diminished by an insatiable rhetoric and a mosaic-like form that was far too broad and sometimes weakly fell apart, it still made a favourable impression on the public and its reception was really enthusiastic. For today we will make do with reporting this splendid outward success that should not be begrudged the modest energetic composer.[12]

Ludwig Speidel spoke of applause 'that bordered on enthusiasm', while Franz Gehring was of the opinion that 'Herr Bruckner should not be denied inspirations of a beautiful and original kind and yet his musical language gives the impression that speaker and listener after a time know neither in nor out.'[13] Bruckner himself sent the Vienna Philharmonic an exuberant thank-you letter. His offer to dedicate it to the orchestra, to be sure, remained unanswered.

On 16 December 1877, the Third Symphony followed in the version of that year, similarly under Bruckner's direction in a concert of the Gesellschaft in the Musikverein. This time the omens were less favourable. Herbeck had scheduled the work for December in the Gesellschaft's concerts, but died on 28 October, and so Bruckner himself took over a concert that turned into a scandal. The composer's interpretation and the work's length contributed fundamentally to its rejection. If Hanslick's review of the

Second had still been relatively favourable, this time things sounded very different:

> It is not our wish to harm the composer whom we rightly respect as man and artist, for his artistic intentions are honest, however oddly he employs them. Instead of a critique, therefore, we would rather simply confess that we have not understood his gigantic symphony. Neither were his poetic intentions clear to us – perhaps a vision of how Beethoven's Ninth made friends with Wagner's *Walküre* and ended up under her horse's hooves – nor could we grasp the purely musical coherence. The composer...was greeted with cheering and was consoled with lively applause at the close by a fraction of the audience that stayed to the end for the flight of the rest.[14]

The length of Bruckner's work was a particular difficulty for a public used to mixed programmes:

> Even before Herr Bruckner raised the baton, part of the audience began to stream out of the hall and this exodus assumed ever greater proportions after each movement, so that the Finale, which exceeded all its predecessors in oddities, was only experienced to the last extreme by a little host of hardy adventurers.[15]

Shortly after that, on 30 December 1877, Brahms' Second Symphony on its first performance by the Philharmonic under Richter won a satisfactory success. At this time Brahms, who had also taken up residence in Vienna in 1868, was in contrast to Bruckner already a composer who had 'arrived'. He lived as an independent professional composer with the financial security of royalties from his publisher Simrock and soon played a leading role in Vienna's musical life. His partisans were above all the conservative press with Hanslick and Max Kalbeck as well as the 'conservative' concert-going public. In origin, education, religious feeling, and life-style the two bachelors were completely different.

By 1880 Bruckner was already known throughout the city, as could be gathered from a feuilleton entitled 'Anton Bruckner (Porträt eines Wiener Musikers)':

> Since then Vienna has possessed not only one of the most splendid organ virtuosos who, despatched to the World Exhibition in London as the most competent of Vienna's artistic community, triumphed there and won first prize on the gigantic organ of the Albert Hall, not only the most professionally qualified successor to Simon Sechter in the chair of counterpoint at the Conservatory and the University, at which he has given much-visited specialized lectures for some years, not only a brilliant master of organ improvisation, but also moreover an original artist and human being.[16]

The organist was still valued more than the composer.

The Fourth Symphony followed on 20 February 1881 in the version of 1878–80 in a Philharmonic concert under Richter. Although the performance was a success, a 'heated war of opinions' broke out.

> Under such circumstances it is proof of great impartiality that they used the first opportunity that presented itself to acquaint the Viennese musical public with the symphony, on account of which its author would have been proclaimed almost a martyr to his art by a certain party.[17]

Gehring did not evaluate the work positively ('nothing but decorative music to which the form of the classical symphony was applied in a rough and ready way'). Eduard Kremser by contrast called Bruckner the 'Schubert of our time'.[18] The symphony quickly achieved great popularity, however, and was quite frequently played in Austria and Germany even in Bruckner's lifetime.

Only the two middle movements of the Sixth Symphony were performed on 11 February 1883 under Richter's successor Wilhelm Jahn (1835–1900). Thus a work by Bruckner was heard for the first time in the Philharmonic's subscription concerts, an event noisily celebrated by his supporters. The press proved rather uncomprehending, as in Hanslick's case:

> It has become ever harder for me personally to achieve a proper relationship with these peculiar compositions in which clever, original, and even inspired moments alternate frequently without recognizable connection with barely understandable platitudes, empty and dull patches, stretched out over such unsparing length as to threaten to run players as well as listeners out of breath . . . Bruckner enjoys general good will because of his honourable, sympathetic personality, the love of his pupils for his educational activity, in the last resort, thanks to his rapturous admiration for Wagner, the strongest support from the 'party'. The latter, however, would act in Bruckner's own interest if they would express their sympathies in less brusque forms.[19]

In contrast Brahms' Third Symphony on 2 December 1883 proved to be the greatest success yet for the composer in Vienna.

In December 1884, Bruckner's pupil Friedrich Eckstein lamented the condition of music in Vienna and complained of the numerous piano performances, 'that magnificent orchestral works by a native master must be performed on the piano if the public is to get to know them at all!'[20] Hugo Wolf, at that time critic of the *Wiener Salonblatt*, agreed:

> Thus it is well worth the trouble to pay rather more attention to this brilliant radical than has been the case hitherto, and it is a truly distressing sight to see banned from the concert hall this extraordinary man who has the first and greatest claim among living composers (Liszt naturally excepted) to be performed and admired.[21]

In January 1885 the following appeared: 'Nevertheless we look in vain for Bruckner on our concert programmes and can calmly swear that ninety-five per cent of our musical world knows not much more about him than his name.'[22]

On 21 March 1886 the Seventh Symphony, after its resounding successes in Leipzig (1884) and Munich (1885), was finally performed in Vienna too – after a few piano performances – and experienced 'a splendid success' under Richter. Bruckner was presented with a laurel wreath with the inscription, 'To the German symphonist, Master Anton Bruckner, in faith and veneration from the Vienna Academic Wagner Society'.[23] There was sharp criticism again from Kalbeck and from Hanslick, who wrote:

> The audience admittedly did not show much 'resistance'; it fled in part even after the second movement of this monstrous symphonic serpent, in droves after the third, so that only a small remainder stayed to enjoy the Finale. But this courageous Bruckner Legion applauded and rejoiced with the force of thousands . . . Bruckner is the new idol of the Wagnerians. One cannot say that he has become the fashion, for nowhere does the public want to follow it; but Bruckner has become an army command and 'the second Beethoven' in the articles of faith of the Richard Wagner community.[24]

Kalbeck was of the opinion that 'We have as little faith in the future of the Brucknerian symphony as in the triumph of chaos over the cosmos.'[25] In contrast Theodor Helm could not restrain his joy at the success of 'the great Seventh Symphony of our patriotic composer Anton Bruckner' in entering 'even the concert hall of the Vienna Philharmonic, and with a success commensurate to the importance of the work'.[26] Even Johann Strauss communicated his enthusiasm to the composer by telegram: 'Am entirely shaken, it was one of the greatest experiences of my life.'

On 20 April 1887 Josef Schalk and Franz Zottmann played the Fifth Symphony in a version for two pianos. The work had its first orchestral performance in Graz on 8 April 1894 under Franz Schalk – Bruckner himself was never to hear it in this form. Although Bruckner had at first expressed himself against a piano performance, the concert in the Bösendorfersaal was still a success for the composer.

When Hans Richter conducted the Fourth Symphony in the version of 1887–8 on 22 January 1888 with 'the most splendid success conceivable', Helm wrote:

> Let us leave the subscribers to the Philharmonic Concerts their charming Robert Fuchs, their agreeable Hugo Reinhold, and all their other good and capable 'professional composers'; the serious and profound Bruckner remains for his friends and admirers as well as for all those who are in any

other way genuinely interested in his affairs – as the attendance at the last concert showed, in total at least a truly impressive congregation completely sufficient to fill Vienna's Grosser Musikvereinsaal in all its areas.[27]

Even if his works were now able to score successes in Vienna, Bruckner always found renewed cause to complain that 'In Vienna everything is as of old', that 'Old friends have again become opponents', and that 'Without Hanslick – nothing happens in Vienna.'[28] His critique of Richter ('in the foremost rank' of 'the Brahms cult') and the programme-planning of the Philharmonic Concerts was thoroughly justified, as can be gathered from this preview of the Philharmonic season of 1889–90:[29]

> It is exceptionally annoying to find yet again this year the total neglect in the repertory of the most brilliant of living symphonists, Anton Bruckner, and in our opinion one of the two Brahms and Schumann symphonies could certainly have made room for his absolutely imperative representation in these concerts. Perhaps the grave sin of omitting a national(!) composer can still be made good.[30]

On the occasion of the performance of the 1889 version of the Third Symphony on 21 December 1890 Hanslick remarked:

> In Bruckner's compositions we miss the logical thinking, the purified sense of beauty, the sifting and surveying understanding of art. That the D minor Symphony received the liveliest applause would be to say much too little. There was stamping, raging, and screaming... I am delighted for the talented and honourable man who has been my friend for thirty years at this rejoicing with which it is impossible for me to concur.[31]

Helm thought on the other hand:

> Hitherto the gentlemen had only dared twice to present their own regular audience with a Bruckner symphony; probably they were also afraid of the well-known anti-Bruckner clique in the press. Under the influence of yesterday's storms of applause they might worry a little less in the future, I imagine, about the latter.[32]

He also maintained in comparison with the first performance under Bruckner:

> Yesterday in the performance conducted by Hans Richter the enthusiasm knew no end and it was by no means merely the product of the intimate connoisseurs of the affair, but was contributed to by the overwhelming majority of the audience.

Josef Stolzing, critic of the *Ostdeutsche Rundschau*, took as his theme the controversy about Bruckner:

> Might it well ... be a riddle to many that Anton Bruckner, who is certainly
> not suspected by the press and the public of German-National beliefs, is
> attacked in the style of so-called public opinion? ... but the critic has
> broken his staff over Bruckner. His love and reverence for Wagner
> delivered into the hands of the enemies of that truly German man the
> weapon with which to fight him in exactly the same way as Wagner.[33]

The new arrangement of the First Symphony was able to achieve a 'completely decisive success' on 13 December 1891 even though 'the astonishingly
polyphonic work [that] assuredly belongs among its creator's most interesting, daring, and magnificent' contained music among 'the most complicated, difficult to understand, and peculiar in detail' that Bruckner had
presented to Vienna.[34]

After the performance of the Eighth Symphony (in the version of
1887–90) on 18 December 1892, Theodor Helm wrote enthusiastically to
Bruckner:

> The artistic triumph that you celebrated on 18 December belongs to the
> most splendid of your glorious life, for the storm of applause derived not
> merely from your admirers and friends but from the whole audience. Near
> where I was sitting everyone applauded with delighted expressions
> particularly after the incomparable Adagio – and yet there was hardly a
> face among them that was known to me.[35]

Hanslick spoke about a 'fundamentally German and New German symphony' but nevertheless was frank about his problems with Bruckner's
works:

> This most recent, like everything I know of the Brucknerian symphony,
> has interested me in details but alienated, indeed repelled me as a whole ...
> Of the extraordinary 'depth' of Bruckner's C minor Symphony there have
> already spread so many irritating advance rumours that I didn't fail to
> prepare myself properly by studying the score and attending the
> *Generalprobe*. But I must nevertheless confess that the mystery of this
> world-embracing composition was first revealed to me when
> understanding was pressed into my hand in the shape of an explanatory
> programme.[36]

Performances of Bruckner's works were demanded repeatedly. So
thought the *Deutsche Zeitung* in 1893, believing that one could win 'new
friends and admirers of the national master precisely among the exclusively
conservative ranks of the core subscribers to these concerts' by performing
the Fourth Symphony.[37]

The performance of the Second in the published version on 25 November
1894 became 'a bone of contention among public and critics', as Helm wrote:

Admittedly in Sunday's concert one noticed personally nothing of a 'battle of the parties'; there was only more or less general, sometimes passionate, applause, and the hisses that one of the most enthusiastic satellites of the Viennese 'critical pasha' thought he noticed after the first movement were probably heard by no-one but him. But after the concert, in the most glaring contrast to the honest enthusiasm of the majority of the gathering, there was certainly such unbelievable superficiality, pettiness, and spitefulness displayed by that circle of the Philharmonic subscribers who only attend these performances to be fashionable that one could only regret that the Philharmonic has to set its precious gifts before such musical semi-barbarians. Who there did not think of the parable of the pearls and the swine? [38]

On 5 January 1896, Bruckner yet again heard his Fourth Symphony in a Philharmonic Concert. Another item on the programme (amongst even more) was Richard Strauss' *Till Eulenspiegel*. Helm reported:

Yet again Bruckner's 'Romantic' Symphony shook us with its mighty imprint! While we are still quite sated with this resounding wonder of the world . . . now the subsequent grumbles of the various incorrigible, doubly small Viennese Beckmessers come out among us. But what should one reply when the famous Beckmesser-in-chief, who 'respectfully excused' himself from the 'Romantic' Symphony . . . detected in the great applause for the delightful Mozart symphony, which was played at the beginning, an 'advance demonstration' against the later items by Richard Strauss and Bruckner?[39]

Contrary to widespread opinion Bruckner possessed a thoroughly public reputation. The period in Vienna that he himself called his 'time of sorrows' contained numerous perfectly successful performances of his works. Close reading of the numerous reviews reveals a balance of pro and contra. In his lifetime, Bruckner was in no way unknown, but a fiercely controversial artist caught up in the debates around Richard Wagner by his supporters. In the course of his life he received public recognition as is evident from the numerous honours bestowed on him (inter alia, honorary membership of the Gesellschaft der Musikfreunde in 1891).

To be sure Bruckner did not frequent the middle-class salons, somewhat like his opposite Brahms, but preferred to surround himself with his pupils in simple inns and taverns and cultivated his deliberately Upper Austrian manner. Because he was not invited to elegant drawing rooms, opportunity was denied him to present his works to an interested public, as Brahms, for instance, managed with his chamber music. Accordingly he achieved no social prominence and felt himself a teacher all his life. On the other hand he was perfectly in position to use the behavioural patterns of bourgeois society to his advantage.

Thus his importance can be read from the interest of musical Vienna and from (to take an example) one of his numerous obituaries, published under the headline, 'One of the most original and strange phenomena in the musical life of Vienna':

> In Vienna Anton Bruckner had many friends and also such men as did not completely approve of his compositions, but applauded his selfless artistic endeavour and knew the high value of the brilliant organist, the outstanding teacher of composition, the venerable human being full of friendly kindness . . . The fanatical reverence for his compositions displayed by his admirers is not in the least to be ascribed to the influence of Bruckner's personality. His death leaves behind a sad gap that will not easily be filled in the world of Viennese music, which counted him among its most characteristic representatives.[40]

Theodor Helm expressed it thus:

> In my decided opinion, however, there are hardly any good arguments against the view that in Bruckner one of the greatest musical inventors and contrapuntists in particular, as well as a noble spiritual heir of Wagner as of Beethoven, especially one of the most brilliant composers of symphonies and church music, has gone from here.[41]

(Trans. John Williamson)

PART TWO

Choral music

4 Bruckner's large sacred compositions

PAUL HAWKSHAW

> I climbed to the organ gallery, the cheapest section of the Grosser
> Musikvereinsaal, and stood with Bruckner … through a badly cut and
> poorly prepared performance of the Berlioz Te Deum … The master was
> completely captivated, though he had a threatening expression on his face.
> After the concert, although the work had clearly made an impression, not a
> word escaped his lips for a long time. He quickly and firmly grabbed my
> arm and stormed off to the restaurant Stadt Frankfurt where he invited me
> to his favourite meal in those days, capon and apple puree. Suddenly he
> gave me a hefty poke in the side with his elbow and burst out with a
> summary of his conflicting deliberations: 'and ecclesiastical it isn't!'[1]

August Göllerich relates this anecdote in his chapter about Viennese concert
life and Bruckner's work on his own Te Deum in 1884. In the context of
a discussion of Bruckner's large sacred compositions, while admitting the
futility of trying to read the composer's mind through Göllerich's filter,
it is tempting to speculate as to the nature of the deliberations inspired
by Berlioz's monumental work. At the very least it is safe to say that 'and
ecclesiastical it isn't!' states the obvious: the Berlioz performance had not
taken place in church. Göllerich's narrative suggests a more critical stance on
Bruckner's part. Perhaps the composer was pondering issues of musical style:
had Berlioz, whom he admired, provided an appropriate setting for a sacred
Latin text – a text that had been very much on Bruckner's mind in recent
months? Or by 'kirchlich' did he mean 'liturgical', thus questioning the
appropriateness of the Berlioz work for use as service music? Perhaps venue
and content intersected in Bruckner's mind, and the Berlioz performance
caused him to deliberate on broader, one might say Wagnerian, issues of
where and how sacred and secular overlap. He had already been accused
himself of turning the Credo of the F minor Mass into a religious 'Wolf's Glen
Scene'.[2] Given that he would finish his career with a symphony dedicated to
God, and propose his Te Deum as a suitable Finale, it may not be far fetched
to speculate that weighty aesthetic questions of meaning and function in
sacred as opposed to secular music were on his mind as he climbed to and
from the organ gallery that evening in 1884.[3]

Anton Bruckner was the most important composer since Johann Sebas-
tian Bach to spend almost his entire professional life in the employ of the
church. Since his days as a choirboy in St. Florian (1837–40) he had wrestled

Table 4.1 *Masses*

Title and volume in the Bruckner Collected Works edition	WAB	Setting	Date
Mass in C major 'Windhaag'(XXI)	25	A solo, 2 hns, org.	1842?
Mass in D minor 'Kronstorf' (XXI)	146	SATB chorus	1844?
Mass in F major for Maundy Thursday (*Christus Factus Est*, XXI)	9	SATB chorus	1844
Requiem (XIV)	39	SATB solos, SATB chorus, 3 trbns, str., org.	1849 rev. 1892
Missa solemnis (XV)	29	SATB solos, SATB chorus, orch., org.	1854
Mass no. 1 in D minor (XVI)	26	SATB solos, SATB chorus, orch., org.	1864 rev. 1876, 1881, 1882
Mass no. 2 in E minor (XVII, 1–2)	27	SSAATTBB chorus, ww., brass	1866 rev. 1876, 1882
Mass no. 3 in F minor (XVIII)	28	SATB solos, SATB chorus, orch., org.	1867–8 rev. 1876, 1877, 1881, 1893?

Table 4.2 *Psalms, Cantatas, Magnificat, and Te Deum*

Title and volume in the Bruckner Collected Works edition	WAB	Setting	Date
Entsagen (XXII/1)	14	S or T solo, SATB chorus, org. or pf.	1851?
Psalm 22 (XX/2)	34	SATB solos, SATB chorus, pf.	1852?
Psalm 114 (XX/1)	36	SAATB chorus, 3 trbns	1852
Magnificat (XX/3)	24	SATB solos, SATB chorus, orch., org.	1852
Psalm 146 (XX/4)	37	SATB solos, 2 SATB choruses, orch.	c. 1855?
Festgesang (*Festlied*, Jodok Cantata, XXII/1)	15	STB solos, SATB chorus, pf.	1855
Festkantate (XXII/2)	16	TTBarBB solos, TTBB chorus, ww., brass, timp.	1862
Psalm 112 (XX/5)	35	SATB solos, 2 SATB choruses, orch.	1863
Te Deum (XIX)	45	SATB solos, SATB chorus, orch., org.	1881–4
Psalm 150 (XX/6)	38	S solo, SATB chorus, orch.	1892

with problems of style, content, function, performance quality, and appropriate venues for religious music. In the process he must have developed an acute musical and social sense of 'ecclesiastical' – one that was shaped spiritually, in his case, by intense piety and devout Roman Catholicism.[4] No doubt Göllerich included the anecdote in his biography by way of reminding his readers of his view that Bruckner's deep-rooted sense of 'ecclesiastical' informed not only his assessment of Berlioz, but also the composition of his own Te Deum and, by extension, all his sacred music. Göllerich knew as well as anyone that, translated into specifics of musical content and function, the composer's perception of 'ecclesiastical' had, in fact, changed considerably over the years. By the time of the Berlioz concert, Bruckner had explored an entire spectrum of styles from old-fashioned through consciously retrospective to avant-garde in his sacred music, and he had supplied religious pieces for sacred and secular venues in almost equal measure.[5]

His large sacred compositions fall roughly into two categories: Masses (including the Requiem) and a less homogenous group of psalms, cantatas, the Magnificat, and Te Deum (see Tables 4.1 and 4.2).[6] The Masses form a unified group in that they set, with minor additions and omissions to be discussed below, the Common Latin texts of the Roman Catholic liturgy and were conceived as service music. Of the pieces in the second group, only the Magnificat was composed for a specific liturgical purpose – the Vesper service at St. Florian.[7] The early German psalm settings (22 and 114) were concert pieces for the entertainment of the priests at St. Florian; Psalm 112 was a composition exercise for Otto Kitzler; and the others were occasional pieces.[8] As biographer, Göllerich was well aware of something else about Bruckner's career as a composer of sacred music: a glance at the dates in Tables 4.1 and 4.2 will confirm that, other than the Te Deum and Psalm 150, the large sacred compositions date from the early and middle periods of his life (see Tables 4.1 and 4.2). Although Bruckner is best remembered as a composer of symphonies, it is in these sacred compositions that one must track his growth into a mature composer. As Elisabeth Maier observed: 'Between the "Windhaager" Mass (1842) and the Mass in F minor (1867–8) lies the complete span of artistic development from run-of-the-mill utilitarian church style to individual mastery.' The following remarks will trace that span and, in the process, offer some observations on what Bruckner might have perceived as ecclesiastical in his own compositions.

Windhaag (1841–1843), Kronstorf (1843–1845), and St. Florian (1845–1855)

Bruckner's early life was inextricably bound to the Upper Austrian school house. He was born into a schoolteacher's family; his first music instructor, Johann Baptist Weiss, was the teacher in Hörsching; his early education in St. Florian and Linz was designed to prepare him to follow in his father's profession; and his first three positions were as assistants in the school houses of Windhaag, Kronstorf, and St. Florian. As assistant schoolteacher, it was Bruckner's responsibility to play the organ and muster the meagre resources available for liturgical music in the village church. His first three Masses were products of this local amateur environment. The Mass in C major (WAB 25) for alto solo, two horns and organ, was composed for one Anna Jobst in Windhaag, and the two early *a cappella* Masses in F major and D minor (WAB 9 and 146) survive from his sojourn in Kronstorf. The F major Mass was composed in 1844 for Maundy Thursday without a Kyrie and Gloria, but including the Gradual and Offertory propers for that feast – 'Christus factus est' and 'Dextera Domini'.[9] The D minor Mass (WAB 146) composed for the Lenten season, *sine Gloria*, survives only in a fragmentary state: the manuscript has two blank pages with an autograph indication that they were to contain a Credo in F major.[10] The Sanctus is a modified version of the one in the F major Mass.

All three of these early works are in the *Landmesse* tradition with ab-breviated Gloria and Credo texts that Bruckner encountered as a child in Ansfelden and Hörsching. Their texture is predominantly homophonic with occasional contrapuntal interruptions (hence the designation *Choral-Messe* even though there is no borrowed chorale material). The harmonic language stems from the eighteenth century in keeping with principles Bruckner would have learned in his studies in harmony and thorough bass with Dürrnberger.[11] Remnants of Baroque practices are common. The alto solo part of the Windhaag Mass, for example, bears the designation *concerto*, and the organ part consists of the alto solo line and an unfigured (largely unrealized) bass from which Bruckner must have performed himself.[12] The Credo of this Mass is notable for its reference to the chant intonation that serves as the basis for the opening phrase of the Alto solo and returns in the final seven bars of the movement.[13] Bruckner continued to borrow from chant in his Latin church music as late as the F minor Mass.

In 1845 the composer achieved something of a career objective, re-turning to his beloved St. Florian where his musical investigations could proceed to levels far beyond those of a village schoolteacher. He resumed his organ lessons with Kattinger and began to study Friedrich Wilhelm Marpurg's *Abhandlung von der Fuge*, continuing periodic visits to Zenetti with whom he had studied on a regular basis while he lived in Kronstorf.[14] The church music repertoire at the monastery was extensive and featured Mass and Vesper music by Austrian pre-classical and classical composers including Michael Haydn (1737–1806), Franz Xavier Aumann (1728–97, former chorus master at St. Florian), Johann Albrechtsberger (1736–1809), Joseph Eybler (1765–1846), Joseph Haydn, and Wolfgang Amadeus Mozart. A few Baroque composers such as Antonio Caldara (1671?–1736) were also represented.[15] A testimony to the diligence with which Bruckner pursued his investigations is that copies of music by all these composers are extant in his hand from the St. Florian years.[16]

Bruckner's Latin church music from this period is a stylistic hybrid of the music he heard every Sunday. Viennese Classicism became the model with older rhetorical references and technical devices interspersed. His first major work for chorus and orchestra was the Requiem in D minor (WAB 39) composed for the anniversary of his friend Franz Sailer's death, 13 September 1849. Elisabeth Maier has observed that, with its tonality and literal citations from Mozart's Requiem, it could almost be subtitled 'Hommage à Mozart'.[17] His provincial background is still evident as much of the choral writing remains homophonic, with the orchestra weaving figu-rations reminiscent of organ chorale preludes around it (e.g. the Agnus Dei).

Imitative interruptions are more numerous and extensive than in the earlier chorale Masses, and the Requiem has the distinction of containing Bruckner's first extended fugue at 'Quam olim Abrahae promisisti' ('which you once promised Abraham'), also a fugue in Mozart's Requiem. The Latin text-setting, while awkward at times, can be effective, such as the breathtaking appearance of 'lux' (light) at the end of the Agnus Dei (bar 23), and there are premonitions of later orchestral writing in the lovely French horn solos in the Benedictus.[18] Late in his life as he surveyed his early pieces, Bruckner described the Requiem as 'not bad' and considered it good enough to dedicate to another friend, Franz Bayer of Steyr.[19] Modern audiences have accepted the composer's assessment, and the Requiem along with the *Missa solemnis* of 1854 are two St. Florian pieces that continue to obtain performances in both liturgical and concert settings.

Mozart's influence is also obvious in the Magnificat of 1852, scored for the same forces as the Vespers K. 321 and 339, and again in the *Missa solemnis* where the reference to the 'Recordare' of the Requiem at the beginning of the Credo has been identified.[20] Composed for the investiture of Bruckner's patron Friedrich Mayr as Abbot, 14 September 1854, the *Missa solemnis* is the culmination of Bruckner's activity as a composer in St. Florian. In addition to the Mozart reference, the Gloria contains a citation from Haydn's 'St Bernard' Mass (Gloria, bar 219) at 'Quoniam tu solus sanctus' ('For you alone are holy'). In keeping with Classical tradition the Gloria and Credo end with fugues, the second of which ('Et vitam venturi saeculi' – 'and the life of the world to come') is arguably Bruckner's strongest effort to date in the genre. He later showed the Mass to Sechter, who was impressed enough by the fugal writing to accept him as a student.[21] The predominantly Classical writing of the *Missa solemnis* is punctuated by the occasional old-fashioned rhetorical gesture such as the rising chromatic figure in *stile agitato* representing the trembling of the earth at the beginning of 'Et resurrexit' ('And he rises') and the extended passage of choral octaves at 'Et unam sanctam catholicam' ('And one holy catholic...church'), bar 80 of the same movement. Bruckner would use the same gesture again at the same place in the Credo of all three of his Linz Masses. Here the string accompaniment recalls the bass line from the 'Recordare' reference that opened the movement. The chant-like melodic figures at the beginning of the Kyrie and Gloria point out once again Bruckner's cognizance of the Gregorian roots of Roman Catholic church music.

In addition to its ongoing regimen of church music, surviving handwritten programmes demonstrate that the monastery hosted an impressive series of concerts by professionals and amateurs who performed solo compositions, chamber music, reductions of symphonies, operatic excerpts, as well as both sacred and secular choral works. Bruckner's lifelong admiration for the music of Schubert and Mendelssohn, neither of whom were featured as a regular part of the monastery liturgy before 1855, can be traced directly to these concerts.[22] He must have been particularly enamoured of Mendelssohn's music during the early 1850s. In a letter of 20 September 1853, Franz Scharschmidt cautioned the composer:

> You are wrong to model yourself after Mendelssohn alone. At the very least you must also draw from the same source as he has: from Johann Sebastian Bach, whom you must study thoroughly. Like M[endelssohn], you will easily set aside the things in Bach that are no longer contemporary, but you cannot be deep and thoroughly grounded without him.[23]

Scharschmidt was extremely perceptive on two counts: at the time Bruckner's knowledge of Bach was limited to chorales and keyboard music, and there can be little question that he saw himself emulating Mendelssohn in his own German psalms and occasional works up to and including the *Festgesang* of 1855.[24]

More retrospective than their Mendelssohn models, Bruckner's pieces of this type resemble cantatas with combinations of arias, recitatives, choruses, chorales, and often, though not always, a closing fugue. Instrumental accompaniments vary from piano or organ (Psalm 22, *Entsagen*, and *Festgesang*) to full orchestra (Psalm 146), and the vocal forces range from vocal quartet (parts of Psalm 22) to double chorus (Psalm 146). Arias and solo passages often feature *basso continuo* (with and without figures) and a florid obbligato wind part (see for example the fourth and fifth movements of Psalm 146) reminiscent of the Baroque. Choral movements (not the fugues) consist of a series of phrases, by no means always symmetrical in length, which are often imitative in texture. Melodic material is usually not related from one phrase to the next, though passages may return to lend a movement an overall formal cohesion (for example Psalm 114, bars 68 and 101). Bruckner's penchant for writing movements in compound metres (9/8 or 12/8) while he lived in St. Florian is evident throughout his psalms and occasional pieces.

Although these works lack Mendelssohn's thematic organicism and orchestral fluidity, and their rhetorical gestures are somewhat dated, they contain some effective passages. Two examples from Psalm 114 will serve by way of illustration. Trombones were a standard instrument in liturgical practice at the monastery and, in the finest eighteenth-century tradition, were regularly featured in Bruckner's music from St. Florian for texts associated with death (as in the Requiem, for example).[25] In Psalm 114 he relied on the trombones to reinforce contrasts delineated by the silences that would become so poignant in his later music. At bar 41, the text 'Es umgaben mich die Schmerzen des Todes' ('I am cloaked in the pains of death') is set apart by the shift to minor, the contrast in texture between the four-part cadence and subsequent choral octaves, the change in dynamics and return to Tempo I, the entrance of the trombones, and two crotchet rests. Silence and the trombones help create a stronger contrast at bar 96 where Bruckner may have intended the third relation between E and C as a harmonic rhetorical gesture for the text 'Kehre zurück meine Seele' ('Go back my soul'). At this point the piece begins a brief harmonic journey home for the closing fugue in G major.

Gregorian chant as the functional representative of ecclesiastical tradition in Bruckner's Latin church music is replaced in his vernacular pieces by chorales which he composed himself, rather than borrowing from other sources. They contain some of the more interesting technical features of this repertoire. One of the few attempts at thematic integration between movements, for example, is found in Psalm 22 where the principal subject of the fugue serves as the bass line for the first phrase of the closing chorale and is repeated in the soprano two phrases later (compare bars 43–6 with 115–18 and 123–6).[26] In the chorale of Psalm 114 the Phrygian melody of the opening phrase beginning on e^1, recurs transposed to A in the bass in phrase 2, to e in the tenors and basses in phrase 3, and finally to a in the tenor in phrase 4. Perhaps Bruckner was hoping to impress the Viennese Kapellmeister Ignaz Assmayr to whom he dedicated Psalm 114 in the hopes of enlisting his assistance in obtaining a position elsewhere.[27] Otherwise, apart from its ecclesiastical connotations, there is little musical explanation for the presence of the chorale in this piece. Among other things, its Phrygian mode clashes with the G major tonality of the rest of the composition.[28]

From a biographical perspective the most enigmatic composition that can be traced to St. Florian is Psalm 146, an enormous yet little-known work that poses as many unresolved chronological problems as any of his entire oeuvre. When it was written, for whom, and why it was allowed to languish unperformed are all unanswered questions. Its cantata-like structure, obligation to Mendelssohn, and stylistic affinity with the *Missa solemnis* place it in the late St. Florian years, though its enormous dimensions – both length and performance forces – are difficult to reconcile with the resources of the monastery.[29] Its closing Alleluia (bars 512ff.) is Bruckner's most extended fugue prior to the Fifth Symphony. Psalm 146 is also remarkable as the first piece in which Bruckner experimented with organic thematic integration on a large scale; not only are the closing chorus and fugue melodically linked in an obvious way, but all the movements are connected by motivic combinations of a perfect fourth with a major or minor third (see, for example, bars 1, 4, 24–7, 41–3, 111–13, 167–70, 179–85, 200, 349–50, and 431–2).

The chorale, which is an integral part of the fourth movement rather than tacked on at the beginning or end of the psalm, is organically linked by orchestral figurations (bars 274ff.) to the rest of the composition. Psalm 146 also deserves to be heard more often for the lovely string *pianissimo* in its opening bars that foreshadow the beginning of both the D minor and F minor Masses.

Linz (1856–1868)

When Bruckner left St. Florian at the end of 1855, he was a world-class organist and a provincial church composer with talent. He is said to have been told by at least one knowledgeable observer, the organist and composer Robert Führer (1807–61), that he needed to study if his composition career was to amount to anything.[30] To his credit, he began to do so with a vengeance, first with Sechter and then with Otto Kitzler.[31] Under Sechter Bruckner formalized his investigation (largely undirected until now) of counterpoint and fugue, eventually achieving a level of expertise that qualified him to succeed his teacher as Professor of Harmony and Counterpoint at the Vienna Conservatory in 1868. Kitzler brought Bruckner *au courant* with contemporary practice, broadening his horizons in standard non-liturgical repertoire such as the Beethoven sonatas and instructing him in the fundamentals of form and orchestration.[32] Psalm 112 with its periodic phrases and clear repeat structure is a product of his tutelage. Kitzler must also be given credit for introducing his pupil to the music of Wagner.[33]

The eight-year study period was followed by a few small choral works before Bruckner's pent-up compositional energies erupted with the Mass in D minor, composed between June and 29 September 1864.[34] Nothing in his previous work could have prepared even the most astute observer for the wonders of the new Mass. The composer himself described it as 'very serious and original'.[35] It is mature Bruckner – monumental in conception, symphonic in development, economic in material and dramatic in expression. Wagner's influence is evident as the orchestra plays a major role setting the stage, developing material and intensifying the drama. The tritones, fifths, and semitones in the strings of the opening bars set a dark tone and provide motivic cells for much of the rest of the Mass. Instrumental figuration is integrated with the motive fabric and propels the waves of *crescendo* so characteristic of Bruckner's mature style (e.g. Kyrie bars 82–94 or Credo bars 175–84). The orchestration in choirs of like instruments adds Wagnerian contrasts in colour to the dramatic palette. If one were to pick a single passage by way of illustrating Bruckner's new-found theatricality and orchestral mastery it might be the death and resurrection section of the Credo from bar 97 onward. The plaintive *a cappella* setting of 'passus et sepultus est' ('died and was buried') is reflected in *pianissimo* woodwind (or organ) and brass chorales before the strings propel a tremendous *crescendo* to a triumphant re-entry of the chorus at 'Et resurrexit'.[36] The unifying figure of the falling semitone is heard throughout.[37]

The premiere of the Mass in the old Linz Cathedral on 20 November 1864 was successful enough that a second performance was given less than a month later at a *Concert spirituel* in the Redoutensaal. Bruckner's friend, Moritz von Mayfeld, who looked somewhat askance at the obvious Wagnerian presence in a piece of church music, nevertheless wrote a laudatory review that included the following passage:

> The future biographer of Bruckner might express his views as follows: '18 December 1864 can be designated as the day that Bruckner's star in all its lustre rose shining on the horizon. On that day the intelligentsia of the entire city expressed its admiration for his powerful and intense musical spirit (which, as with Beethoven and Schubert, had heretofore concealed itself under a cloak that, for superficial observers, was hardly attractive). Work after work followed (as hopefully the biographer will be able to continue), and each was a step forward on a boldly trodden path.' Is one allowed to write a Mass in the style that Bruckner has chosen? The answer to this question is as follows: not only is it allowed, it is eminently desirable if a work of such significance can be produced ... The astonishment and admiration for Bruckner's genius grows, when one realizes that his acquaintance with masterworks of older and more recent times is relatively limited and consequently, he creates from within himself.[38]

While Mayfeld may not have been entirely accurate in his assessment of Bruckner's knowledge of earlier repertoire, he was able to continue his remarks with the insightful prediction that the composer would soon enter the 'symphonic realm with utmost success!'[39] A second critic, Franz Gamon in the *Linzer Zeitung*, also alluded to Bruckner's potential as a symphonic composer and ranked the D minor Mass along with the music of Liszt in the highest echelon of modern church music.[40]

After a diversion for the first symphony (1865–6), Bruckner composed two more Masses before he moved to Vienna: No. 2 in E minor (August – 25 November 1866) and No. 3 in F minor (14 September 1867 – 9 September 1868). The formal characteristics of the three Linz Masses can be outlined roughly as follows beginning with a chart of the principal tonalities of the movements:

	Ky	Gl	Cr	S	B	A
No. 1	d	D	D	D	G (D)	d
No. 2	e	C	C	G	C	e
No. 3	f	C	C	F	A♭ (F)	f

In all three Masses only the Kyrie and Agnus Dei are in the minor tonic; all the other movements are in a major tonality. The Gloria and Credo of each Mass are in the same key, and the Benedictus movements of Nos. 1 and 3 end in the same tonality as the Sanctus because the 'Hosanna' is repeated verbatim.

Each Kyrie is tripartite ('Kyrie eleison', 'Christe eleison', and 'Kyrie eleison') with the middle section in the relative major. In the first and third Masses the 'Christe eleison' is sung, in classical tradition, by soloists, and its material is related by inversion to the opening. Each second Kyrie is a development of its respective opening section. Each Gloria is in A–B–A[1] form; the slower B section begins at 'Qui tollis peccata mundi' ('Who takes away the sins of the world') or slightly earlier at 'Agnus Dei, Filius Patris' ('Lamb of God, son of the Father') in the Mass in D minor. The A section is subdivided in two as a new idea in a new tonality (in a different relationship to the tonic in each Mass) begins at 'Gratias agimus tibi' ('We give you thanks'); in the F minor Mass the end of the A section (bars 76–115) is extended to the point where Max Auer compares it with the closing group of a Bruckner sonata movement.[41] A varied reprise begins, again in classical tradition, at 'Quoniam tu solus sanctus' ('For You alone are holy'), though in the F minor Mass Bruckner reverses the return, using the theme from 'Gratias agimus tibi' first (bar 179) and reserving the opening theme for an imposing statement in octaves at 'Cum sancto spirito' ('And with the Holy Spirit'; bar 215). The Gloria ends with a fugue in all three Masses, another classical feature. Each Credo also has a slower middle section beginning at 'Et incarnatus est' ('And he was born') and modified reprise at 'Et in Spiritum Sanctum' ('And in the Holy Spirit'). Bruckner reserved his most expressive, if not his most Baroque, rhetorical gestures for the middle sections of these movements.[42] In the Masses in D and F minor the mystery of the virgin birth is captured by solo voices in a remote tonality a major third higher than the outset of the movement; the E minor Mass 'Et incarnatus' begins in F major. The subsequent passion of Christ's suffering, death and burial inevitably ends in a chorale with trombones and is followed invariably by his resurrection in the midst of a musical earthquake.[43] Only the F minor Mass follows the classical practice of ending the Credo with a fugue. The Sanctus and Benedictus are separate movements performed before and after the Consecration respectively. The Mass in E minor is unique in that neither movement has a faster tempo at 'Pleni sunt coeli'; and the second 'Hosanna' is newly composed using material from the Benedictus. In the Agnus Dei movements, the second and third petitions are variations on the first one; in the Masses in D and F minor the closing text 'dona nobis pacem' ('grant us peace') is the occasion for an extended coda. In all three Masses the cyclic impulses of Bruckner's symphonies are evident in the waning bars where melodic references to the preceding movements, particularly the opening Kyrie, are explicit.

If models for Bruckner's earlier sacred music are found in eighteenth-century rural Austria and the Viennese classics, the Masses in D and F minor are in the tradition of larger and later works: the *Missa solemnis* of Beethoven, Schubert's Masses in A♭ and E♭ major and Liszt's 'Gran' Mass. In contrast, the E minor Mass, composed with wind accompaniment for performance outdoors at the dedication of the Votive Chapel of the new Linz Cathedral, 29 September 1869, is a more compact work. The quasi-modal, Palestrina-style counterpoint and chant-like quality of much of its melodic material (e.g. the opening of the Gloria and Credo) give it an especially ec-clesiastical quality that is reinforced by a heavy reliance on plagal cadences (Kyrie, Gloria, Sanctus, and Agnus Dei) and plagal secondary tonalities (after bar 20 of the Gloria and after bar 55 of the Credo).[44] The Mass has often been connected with the Cecilian movement, although Bruckner could never empathize with the anti-modernist sentiment of Franz Xaver Witt (1834–88) and his followers.[45] Its consciously retrospective elements may be better attributed to a desire to provide a musical analogue to the neo-Gothic aesthetic of the new building. A popular contemporary per-ception of Palestrina as official historical representative (at least in the contrapuntal realm) of Roman Catholic church music and Bruckner's in-nate fascination with different types of counterpoint were easily recon-ciled in the E minor Mass. The extent to which he was able to absorb the Palestrina style can be seen in his technical mastery of canon in the Sanctus.

The adjectives monumental, symphonic, and dramatic used to describe the Mass in D minor are even more applicable to the Mass in F minor that Bruckner began in 1867 after a stay in the convalescent home at Bad Kreuzen. So far as is known there is no truth to Leopold Nowak's assertion that it was commissioned by the Viennese Court Chapel, although it received its first performance with forces from the Chapel in the Augustinerkirche, Vienna, on 16 June 1872, with Bruckner conducting.[46] In his review Eduard Hanslick (who was still supportive of Bruckner at the time) recognized Beethoven's *Missa solemnis* as a worthy predecessor and called for a concert performance where the F minor Mass could receive more rehearsal and obtain a wider public.[47] Hanslick's reference to the *Missa solemnis* could have been prompted by any number of passages in the new work. In particular it is easy to surmise that Bruckner had Beethoven's Benedictus in mind as he composed the 'Et incarnatus est' (Credo, bars 117ff.) with its solo violin and viola in delicate counterpoint around one of his most beautiful melodies.[48] Hans Ferdinand Redlich has pointed out that Gregorian chant served as a building block for the entire Mass:

> The thematic material of the Mass in F [minor] is fertilized by plainsong to an even greater extent than that of the two preceding Masses; it is also closely organized by virtue of a common root-motive of unmistakably liturgical flavour: a falling or ascending fourth that determines the thematic subject matter in all parts of the work, thereby assuring its symphonic coherence.[49]

Redlich traced the fourth motive to the priest's intonation of the Gloria (*Cunctipotens Genitor Deus*) that is the basis for the opening phrase of Bruckner's Gloria.[50]

Vienna (1868–1896)

After 1868, Mayfeld's prediction that Bruckner would turn to symphonies proved true to an extent that no-one could have foreseen. While the Viennese Court Chapel, where the composer was employed as organist until October 1892, served as an important performance outlet for his Masses and motets, it was not a major stimulus for composition.[51] The only large sacred works from the Vienna years are the Te Deum, which he began in 1881 and left unfinished until 16 March 1884, and Psalm 150, completed on 11 July 1892. Bruckner is reported to have referred to the Te Deum, which has become one of his most popular pieces, as the pride of his career and his best composition.[52] It has all the hallmarks of his late style beginning with the open fifth and octave of the principal subject and its string figuration. In the contrasting second and fourth sections of the work, the poignant petitions in quasi-recitative ('Te ergo quaesumus', 'We beseech You therefore', bars 175ff., and 'Salvum fac populum tuum', 'Save Your people', bars 257ff.) precede two brief lyrical verses of tenor solo reminiscent of 'Et incarnatus est' in the F minor Mass. The extended chant-like modal passages in choral octaves (bars 99–120 and 227–40) can be seen as the composer's way of reminding his audience, yet again, of the plainsong origins of all Roman Catholic church music. Characteristic of Bruckner's late style are series of parallel first-inversion chords (chorus, bars 129ff., and the lower voices, bars 149–50) that reappear at the climax of the fugue in Psalm 150 (bars 211ff.) in a passage that might call to mind the 'Magic Fire Music' from Wagner's *Die Walküre* for some listeners.

Some of Bruckner's time in Vienna was absorbed revising and publishing his sacred compositions. In the summer of 1876 he did a metrical analysis of the three Linz Masses. He returned to No. 1 again in 1881 and 1882, No. 2 in 1882, and No. 3 in 1877, 1881, 1883, and 1893. His revisions affected primarily phrase structure and performance directions and, to a lesser extent (F minor Mass Credo, bars 117ff.), voice leading and instrumental figurations. Although none of these changes could be described as extensive in comparison with those in some symphony scores, it is possible to distinguish two versions of the Mass in E minor (1866 and 1882) and two of the Mass in F minor (1883 and 1893).[53] The first of Bruckner's major sacred works to be published (by Rättig of Vienna in 1885) was the Te Deum with a dedication 'Omnia ad majorem Dei Gloria' ('All for the greater glory of God'), followed by the D minor Mass (Innsbruck: Gross, 1892), Psalm 150, and the Masses in F and E minor (Vienna: Doblinger, 1893, 1894, and 1896 respectively).

Two musical elements that are evident in the entire repertoire of Bruckner's large sacred compositions are plainchant and the chorale. A third that began to appear in works from his St. Florian years and that he continued to cultivate as late as Psalm 150 was the fugue. Even his earliest efforts in the genre, while sometimes awkward as many commentators have observed, are ambitious such as the double fugues in the Requiem ('Quam olim Abrahae') and Psalm 114 (bars 119ff.).[54] After his studies with Sechter he produced some of the century's most stunning technical *tours de force* – e.g. the closing fugue of the Te Deum (bars 402ff.) or 'Et vitam venturi' at the end of the Credo in the F minor Mass (bars 337ff.). The latter is a double fugue in which the counterpoint of the principal subject (derived from the opening phrase of the movement) and countersubject is punctuated throughout by chorale-like outbursts of 'Credo, Credo'.

   'I believe' is an appropriate phrase with which to draw a discussion of Bruckner's sacred music to a close; the literature is full of commentary on his compositions as expressive outlets for his religious beliefs. Although such observations are difficult to quantify, one would be hard pressed to question his Fear of the Lord at the 'Judicare' ('He will come to judge'; Credo, bars 260ff.) or the sincerity of his faith in the Benedictus of the F minor Mass, for example.[55] Bruckner's perception of what was appropriate technically in sacred music was shaped at first by the remote parishes of Upper Austria and then by the relatively sophisticated, though conservative, musical establishment at St. Florian. After a few years in Linz he had to find a delicate balance between the dictates of his earlier experience and the newly discovered attractions of the modern musical world, particularly those of Wagner. Ernst Kurth has observed that Bruckner's mature church music is an extraordinary amalgam of the modern and the conservative.[56] As he walked from the concert hall with August Göllerich that December evening in 1884, perhaps Bruckner felt that Berlioz had overstepped a fine line towards the modern or neglected something from the past in his Te Deum. By that point in his career, Bruckner's struggle to achieve a balance had produced some of the finest sacred music of the century.

5 Bruckner and the motet

A. CRAWFORD HOWIE

Introduction

The majority of Bruckner's smaller sacred works belong to the period in which he was either partly or wholly devoted to the composition of church music – from 1841 in Windhaag until his move to Vienna in 1868. After this, Bruckner was still involved in church music as an organist at the Hofkapelle until October 1892, at the court parish church of St Augustine where he played at two services each month from 1870 to the late 1880s and, occasionally, at other churches in Vienna and its suburbs; but the composition of orchestral music took precedence and sacred works were composed sporadically. Most of these sacred miniatures fall into the category of 'occasional music', composed specifically or by demand for church choirs in St. Florian, Linz, and Kremsmünster, but it is a measure of Bruckner's greatness that several of them transcend the limitations of their fairly confined medium and can stand favourable comparison with the three great Masses, the Te Deum and Psalm 150.

The early works (c. 1835–1855)

Bruckner's first faltering attempts at composition were made in the mid-1830s while he was staying with his cousin Johann Baptist Weiss in Hörsching. Weiss gave him organ lessons and some basic instruction in harmony and counterpoint, and the *Pange lingua* in C major, WAB 31, a setting of St Thomas Aquinas' hymn for unaccompanied four-part choir in a simple homophonic style, is the obvious fruit of this teaching. Bruckner thought highly enough of this early motet to revise it more than fifty years later.[1]

The only surviving sacred work of the Windhaag period is a Mass in C major written for solo alto, two horns, and organ, no doubt a reflection of the extremely limited resources Bruckner had at his disposal in this rather isolated village. The sacred compositions written during the Kronstorf period (1843–5) are not quite so restricted and provide evidence of a clearer grasp of traditional styles and an improved technical facility for which his teacher, Leopold von Zenetti, should no doubt take much of the credit. Some pieces have been lost, including a setting of *Salve Maria*

(WAB 134) and a *Requiem* for male voices and organ (WAB 133), composed in memory of his friend Johann Nepomuk Deschl, schoolmaster in Kirchberg, and first performed in March 1845 with Bruckner playing the organ. Of the works still extant, which include another Mass setting, the *Maundy Thursday Mass*, not all can be dated precisely and it is possible that one or two of the smaller pieces were written either just before or immediately after his move to St. Florian in September 1845. The *Libera me* in F (WAB 21) – the first of Bruckner's two settings of the text from the Absolution at the end of the Requiem Mass – the three settings of the antiphon *Asperges me* (WAB 3/1 and 2, and WAB 4), and the two settings of the *Tantum ergo* from Aquinas' hymn *Pange lingua* (WAB 32 in D major and WAB 43 in A major) are all for four-part mixed-voice choir and organ accompaniment, with the exception of WAB 4 and WAB 32 which are a cappella. Plainchant phrases are integrated in the *Asperges me* settings. Otherwise, all have an attractive Schubertian melodiousness in spite of dependence on well-tried cadential formulae.[2]

As one would expect from a young composer who became increasingly involved with church music at St. Florian in the years 1845–55, there are several short sacred works from this period. Most of them are no more than competent but Bruckner was happy to return to five of them, all settings of the *Tantum ergo*, viz. *Vier Tantum ergo*, WAB 41 (1846), for mixed-voice choir and organ (ad lib.) and a *Tantum ergo* in D major, WAB 42 (1846), for five-part mixed-voice choir and organ, and revise them in 1888.[3] Yet another setting of the text – a *Tantum ergo* in B♭ major, WAB 44 (c. 1855), scored for mixed-voice choir, two trumpets, violins and organ – has a typically 'busy' string accompaniment but is more adventurous melodically and harmonically.[4]

As well as providing a secular piece, *Die Geburt*, in 1852 for his friend Josef Seiberl in Marienkirchen, Bruckner also sent him two funeral songs, *Totenlieder*, WAB 47 and 48, for unaccompanied mixed-voice choir.[5] In the first of the two songs we are transported momentarily to the world of the last three symphonies with the tremendous soprano surge at 'seek only the kingdom of God', a bold false relation in the penultimate bar serving to heighten the effect. In similar vein, but for the mellow combination of three trombones, are the two *Aequale*, WAB 114 and 149, written in January 1847 possibly in memory of his aunt, Rosalia Mayrhofer.[6]

The death of Michael Arneth, the prelate of St. Florian abbey, in 1854 came as a bitter blow to Bruckner. For the funeral procession he set music to a poem by the St. Florian priest Ernst Marinelli – *Vor Arneths Grab* (WAB 53) for male voices and three trombones – and for the benediction at the end of the Requiem Mass, he wrote a setting of *Libera me* (WAB 22), also in F minor. It is a noble and quite extended composition – by far the longest of the smaller sacred works up to this time – and is imbued with something of the grandeur of the contemporary *Missa solemnis* in B♭ minor. It is certainly derivative in places, Mozart's *Requiem* being the most obvious source of inspiration, but there are several passages in which Bruckner begins to flex his contrapuntal muscles – the five-part double fugue exposition in the contrapuntal middle section and the extensive use of canonic imitation at the words 'dies illa' (bars 42ff.) are the two most obvious examples – and others in which he succeeds in bringing the words to life, for instance the arresting soprano entry at 'et amara valde' (bar 55) and the extremely tender 'Requiem aeternam' before the recapitulation of the 'Libera me'.

The two *Totenlieder* are examples of settings of texts in the German ver-nacular. Bruckner was attracted to the Evangelical chorale and wrote some chorale or hymn-like compositions during the Kronstorf and St. Florian periods: *Dir, Herr, Dir will ich mich ergeben*, WAB 12 (1844 or 1845), for mixed voices *a cappella*, *O du liebes Jesukind*, WAB 145 (1845 or 1846), for solo soprano and organ, *Herz Jesu-Lied*, WAB 144 (c. 1846) for mixed voices and organ, and *In jener letzten der Nächte*, WAB 17 (c. 1848), a hymn for Passion week which exists in two versions, the first for voice with organ accompaniment, the second for mixed voices *a cappella*.

The Linz works (1856–1868)

Bruckner's appointment as organist at both the Cathedral and the Parish Church in Linz meant that he was able to devote himself entirely to church music for the first and only time in his career. That he enjoyed a good work-ing relationship with Bishop Rudigier, who not only admired and sought to encourage his musical gifts but also had a pastoral concern for his wel-fare, was of undoubted value to him as he began to spread his wings as a composer.[7]

From the beginning of the Linz period comes a setting of the *Ave Maria* (WAB 5) for four-part mixed-voice choir, cello, and organ. Written on 24 July 1856 and dedicated to Ignaz Traumihler, director of the St. Florian abbey choir, it provides a good example of Bruckner's contrapuntal facility shortly after the beginning of his marathon course in harmony and coun-terpoint with Sechter. Bruckner is not entirely successful in his attempt to combine the old – it is the last of his sacred works to contain a figured bass – and the new. Significantly, it was with another setting of the same text – the *Ave Maria* (WAB 6) for unaccompanied seven-part mixed-voice choir – that Bruckner ended his self-imposed abstinence from original composition during his studies with Sechter.[8] It was composed specially for the an-niversary celebrations of the *Frohsinn* choir in Linz and first performed on 12 May 1861 in Linz Cathedral as an offertory hymn during a sung Mass by Lotti. Like the contemporary *Afferentur regi*, it was frequently included in later performances of the D minor Mass and the threefold 'Jesus' phrase allotted to different voice combinations (bars 15–20) is a kind of blueprint for the 'Et resurrexit' passage in the Credo of this Mass. In the following 'Sancta Maria' passage the antiphonal answering phrases overlap to produce a gloriously rich sound spiced with seventh and ninth chords, the repeated high A for sopranos in bars 25–6 marking the climax of the whole piece. No less effective are the hushed descending sixth chords over a pedal C at 'ora pro peccatoribus' (bars 31–3) and the expressive sequential octave leaps at 'mortis nostrae' (bars 39–41). *Afferentur regi* (WAB 1) was written a few months later, on 7 November, and first performed at St. Florian on 13 December. It was unaccompanied originally but Bruckner added three optional trombone parts later. The offertory begins imitatively and works up to a joyous shout for full choir with trombone underlay at 'afferentur tibi in laetitia' (bars 13–15). The bass descent to a pedal A at 'exsultatione' looks forward to the mighty phrase for solo bass in the 'Salvum fac' section of the Te Deum, while the sixth chord harmonies over this pedal and the imitative voice entries at the beginning and elsewhere no doubt provided material for the 'Qui cum patre' section in the Credo of the D minor Mass.[9]

Four years elapsed before Bruckner's next small-scale sacred piece. In the meantime he had written the first of his three great settings of the Mass, the Mass in D minor, WAB 26 (1864). *Trauungschor* (WAB 49), set to a German text by Dr Franz Proschko, is really a semi-sacred composition, an occasional work for male-voice choir and organ written in January 1865 to celebrate the wedding of Karl Kerschbaum, the president of *Frohsinn*, and Marie Schimatschek, a concert singer and the daughter of Franz Schimatschek, his Linz copyist.[10]

Just as the *Ave Maria* and *Afferentur regi* motets are closely associated with the D minor Mass, a motet written near the end of the Linz period – *Pange lingua* (WAB 33) – has modal (Phrygian) and thematic connections with the E minor Mass, its Kyrie movement in particular. It was composed on 31 January 1868 and Bruckner's original intention was to have it performed at the same time as the first performance of the Mass in Linz on 29 September 1869; but he had to wait twenty years before hearing it.[11] In the 1880s, Franz X. Witt, founder of the Allgemeiner deutscher Cäcilienverein in 1868 and one of the leaders of the Cecilian reform movement in Catholic church music in the second half of the nineteenth century, included this small motet in a collection of *Eucharistic Songs* and, to Bruckner's great annoyance, 'corrected' the slight dissonance near the end of the piece which presumably did not meet with his approval![12] Although 'archaic' elements such as the unison opening, restricted voice ranges, pure chordal progressions and modal cadences recall sixteenth-century polyphony, Bruckner does not adhere strictly to the 'rules' of strict counterpoint but makes extensive use of dissonance at 'corporis mysterium' (bars 9–13) and 'quem in mundi pretium' (bars 19–23), driving home the climax at 'generosi' (bars 26–7) with a diminished seventh chord.[13] Like the majority of his church music colleagues, with the notable exception of Ignaz Traumihler in St. Florian, Bruckner was unsympathetic to the more 'hard-line' attitude adopted by the German wing of the Cecilian association, which rejected the orchestral Mass and required contemporary church music to be deliberately archaic and modelled on sixteenth-century vocal polyphony, and preferred the much more moderate Austrian stance adopted by Johannes Evangelist Habert, director of church music in Gmunden, who advocated a balanced mixture of the best aspects of the old and the new.[14]

Bruckner wrote two other small church works during his final year in Linz. The offertory *Inveni David* (WAB 19) for male voices and four trombones was composed on 21 April for the anniversary celebrations of *Frohsinn* and first performed on 10 May. In the same key as its great contemporary, the F minor Mass, and sharing such common features as the opening phrase in unison octaves, the motet makes great demands on the voices, particularly in the closing 'alleluja' section, introduced by a tremendous downward sweep in the second basses with trombone support. The four trombones intensify the frequent antiphonal effects and dynamic changes, of which the most striking is undoubtedly the sudden whisper of 'manus enim mea' after three *ff* trombone chords (bars 13–15).[15] In contrast, *Iam lucis orto sidere* (WAB 18) is a hymn for mixed-voice choir *a cappella*, probably written during the summer months for the Gymnasium pupils in Wilhering Abbey. It is a very simple, modally inspired strophic piece and homophonic throughout.[16]

The Vienna works (1869–1892)

Like the 1868 *Pange lingua*, the gradual *Locus iste* (WAB 23, later dedicated to Bruckner's friend Oddo Loidol) for unaccompanied mixed voices was written in August 1869 for the dedication of the new cathedral's Votivkapelle in Linz at the end of September. It begins with Mozartian phrases, but soon introduces characteristic Brucknerian progressions such as the sequential 'inaestimabile sacramentum' (bars 13–20). The short middle section comprises a threefold repetition of the words 'irreprehensibilis est' with chromatic descending movement in the tenor part initially. The final section recapitulates both the words of the first section and the music as far as bar 39. After a strong affirmation of 'Deo' followed by a bar's silence, the work ends peacefully and serenely.

The first smaller sacred work composed for performance in Vienna, specifically the Hofkapelle where he had an unpaid 'reserve organist' position, is the gradual *Christus factus est* (WAB 10), scored for eight-part mixed-voice choir, three trombones and strings and written towards the end of 1873 – at the time that Bruckner was completing the Finale of his Third Symphony.[17] In the context of the normal *a cappella* four-part setting for Bruckner's smaller sacred works, this scoring is unusual. A striking feature is the wide variety of textures, beginning with the sopranos and altos in unison with a contrapuntal accompanying part for unison first and second violins, followed by a fugato for four-part mixed voices *a cappella* ('propter quod est Deus', bars 12–14) and gradually leading to the *tutti* of all eight parts supported by strings and trombones, with an impressive climax at the words 'dedit illi nomen'. But what follows is even more remarkable. As in the later, third setting of the text (1884), Bruckner places particular emphasis on the words 'quod est super omne nomen' ('[the name] which is above all names'). Over a bass A♭ pedal, the ascending scale of E♭ major (beginning on the submediant) is distributed among the voices in a terraced structure, culminating in a C major cadence. The same generative process, albeit in slightly altered form, is repeated for the second statement, and the final climax is reached in the tonic major key (D major). The final section, imitative and full of characteristic suspensions, is remarkably similar to the closing section of the later setting. Furthermore, both share a thematic relationship with the 'in aeternum' passage in the Te Deum.[18]

There is a gap of five years before Bruckner's next motet, *Tota pulchra es* (WAB 46), written in Vienna on 30 March 1878. This Marian antiphon was commissioned for the twenty-fifth anniversary celebrations of Bishop Rudigier's episcopate and first performed at a special benediction service held in the Votivkapelle of the new Linz cathedral on the evening of 4 June. The scoring for tenor soloist, mixed-voice choir, and organ enables Bruckner to alternate plainchant-like phrases for the tenor precentor and harmonizations of the same material for chorus in a responsorial fashion. The work is clearly fertilized by plainchant or plainchant-like material, but Bruckner does not allow himself to be restricted by modality or to be fettered by Cecilian considerations.[19] The passage at 'mater clementissima' (bars 49–52) where the choir diverts the previous tenor phrase into the key of D♭ major and provides a startling dynamic contrast illustrates his desire to be faithful to the text and use elements of melodic and harmonic expressivity to accomplish this. The ending is most original. F major is reached at bar 71, but the basses descend a semitone to E and the antiphon ends in an ethereal E major, clinched by a plagal cadence.[20]

In spite of his lack of sympathy with the ideals of the Cecilian movement, Bruckner responded to an invitation from Ignaz Traumihler to write a motet for the feast of St Augustine on 28 August by composing *Os justi*, WAB 30, for mixed voices *a cappella*. A week after completing the motet in July 1879, Bruckner sent it, with an accompanying letter, to its dedicatee and went out of his way to stress the deliberately archaic style of the piece, underlining the avoidance of sharps, flats, seventh chords and other 'modern' features.[21] Its asceticism is in complete contrast to the luxuriant string writing of the String Quintet in F major which was completed only a few weeks earlier. It is tripartite and strictly modal, beginning and ending in the Lydian mode but with a fugal middle section which moves towards a Mixolydian cadence. There are suitably hushed repetitions of an F major chord at the end before the 'Alleluia'.[22]

Bruckner's third setting of the Marian hymn *Ave Maria* (WAB 7) is in the same key – F major – as the two earlier settings but differs from them in being composed not for choir but for solo voice with organ or harmonium accompaniment. It was written on 5 February 1882 and dedicated to Luise Hochleitner, a young contralto from Wels who had attracted the composer's attention when he visited the town probably during his summer vacation in 1881. Bruckner's interpretation of the text is remarkable for its wide dynamic range (*fff–ppp*) and contrast between passages in which there is much enharmonic change ('Sancta Maria...peccatoribus', bars 39–41) and unison plainchant-like phrases ('nunc et in hora mortis', bars 53–5). In the final 'amen', the soloist makes an impressive two-octave descent to a low f.[23]

During 1884, a year which was largely taken up with negotiations with Arthur Nikisch concerning the first performance of the Seventh Symphony and with the completion of the revised version of his Te Deum, Bruckner had time to compose two short sacred pieces, his third setting of *Christus factus est*, WAB 11, and *Salvum fac populum*, WAB 40. They are at opposite stylistic extremes and illustrate Bruckner's ability to write with equal facility in modern and traditional musical languages. *Christus factus est* was written on 28 May and dedicated to his young friend, Oddo Loidol, in Kremsmünster. Although there are close motivic connections with the Seventh Symphony, Te Deum and later Eighth Symphony, it is the allusion in several places (at the words 'exaltavit illum' in bars 23–4 and 27–8, for instance) to the 'Grail' motive from Wagner's *Parsifal*, a work which he had heard for the first time in Bayreuth in the summer of 1882, which makes an immediate impact. Throughout the motet the skilful voice-leading, the smooth stepwise progression of the outer voices, and the many beautiful dynamic changes and exquisite modulations combine to produce an effect of great nobility. Timothy Jackson has also drawn attention to the religious implication of the gradual enharmonic shift from Db (in bar 19) to C♯, the long-held leading note of D minor (in bar 39).[24]

It is not known for what purpose Bruckner wrote his *Salvum fac populum*, a setting of lines from the Te Deum for four-part mixed-voice choir composed in Vienna on 14 November. It is possible that he intended it for inclusion in a Cecilian publication or for performance at either St. Florian or Kremsmünster. Plainchant-like phrases for bass, short sections in a fauxbourdon-type homophony and equally short polyphonic enclaves alternate.[25]

Bruckner's setting of *Veni Creator Spiritus* (WAB 50), which dates from 1884 at the latest, is nothing more than a simple organ accompaniment to the plainchant melody, typical of the period and no doubt similar to the unobtrusive type of accompaniment he would have provided when accompanying monophonic plainsong in the Hofkapelle or elsewhere.[26]

In 1885 Johann Burgstaller, the music director of Linz Cathedral, asked Bruckner to provide a work for the centenary of the Linz diocese in October, specifically a sacred composition to accompany the procession of the bishop into the cathedral. Bruckner wrote his *Ecce sacerdos magnus* (WAB 13) for double choir, three trombones, and organ at the end of April and sent it to Burgstaller together with an accompanying letter on 18 May, but it had to wait another twenty-seven years for its first performance.[27] It comes from the same spring as the Te Deum, and the bare fifths at the opening, the rapid harmonic transitions, the modal tendency of the harmonies, the mediant relationship of keys, and the majestic ceremonial mood all point to that work. The most enthralling feature of the motet is undoubtedly the antiphonal writing of Gabrielian grandeur at 'Ideo jure jurando' (bars 64–6). The third and final appearance of these rising sequences makes an even greater impact as it follows the plainchant doxology ('Gloria Patri et Filio').[28]

One of Bruckner's finest motets, *Virga Jesse floruit* (WAB 52) for *a cappella* mixed-voice choir, was completed on 3 September 1885 at the end of a short visit to St. Florian. Like *Ecce sacerdos*, it was possibly intended originally for the Linz diocesan centenary celebrations the following month. Bruckner draws on so many different ideas (psalmodic, homophonic, and polyphonic) in this work and yet succeeds in fusing them into a successful whole. A plainchant-inspired motive literally blossoms ('floruit') into the 'Grail' motive in the two opening phrases. The expressive minor sixth leap for sopranos at 'Virgo Deum' (bars 21ff.) recalls the 'Tu Rex Gloriae' phrase in the Te Deum and foreshadows the glorious horn phrase at the opening of the Ninth Symphony (bars 20–1). The preparation of the first great climax in bars 49–51 is effected with an economy of means and deceptive simplicity. The earlier rising minor sixth is complemented by a descending minor sixth at 'in se reconcilians' (bars 52–4) and once again a rising chromatic bass leads to a breathtaking enharmonic change and a cadence in E major. And it is in this key (the key of the contemporary Seventh Symphony) that the final section begins and ends, with memorable expansive 'Alleluia' phrases for tenors and basses.[29]

In the seven years between *Virga Jesse* and *Vexilla regis*, the last of his smaller sacred works, Bruckner concentrated almost entirely on orchestral composition, including the revision of some of his earlier symphonies, the production of the original and revised versions of the Eighth Symphony and ongoing work on the Ninth. In 1886, however, he wrote a short piece, *Ave regina coelorum* (WAB 8) for the novitiate priests at Klosterneuburg to sing on Annunciation Day (25 March). It is similar to *Veni Creator Spiritus* in its scoring for unison voices and organ accompaniment but it is a paraphrase rather than a harmonization of the original plainsong.[30]

Vexilla regis (WAB 51) is a Passiontide motet for *a cappella* mixed voices, written between 4 and 9 February 1892 – possibly in response to a request from Bernhard Deubler, Ignaz Traumihler's successor as choir director at St. Florian, for a hymn for the Good Friday liturgy. Bruckner's reference to his 'inner compulsion' to compose it, however, may indicate that the motet was not commissioned.[31] Indeed the remarkable mixture of the old and the new in this strophic piece could perhaps be interpreted as an attempt to sum up his life's work, albeit on a smaller scale than the coda of the third movement of the Ninth Symphony, by synthesizing a wealth of stylistic elements. The old is represented by the Phrygian modality, the plainsong-inspired melodic phrase at the opening of each verse and some of the cadential formulae. The new can be seen in references to the 'Grail' motive and the enharmonic transformations symbolizing the change from 'death' to 'life' near the end of each verse.[32]

Conclusion

Bruckner's first motet, a setting of *Pange lingua*, dates from 1835, and his last one, *Vexilla regis*, was written in 1892, the year in which he also composed his final large-scale sacred work, Psalm 150. In the motets written during these fifty-seven years we are presented with a fascinating microcosm of Bruckner's development as a musician, from the first tentative steps to the confident strides of a fully mature composer. We see an engagement with both old and new stylistic elements, ranging from monophonic plainchant to late nineteenth-century chromatic harmony, a process also observable in the church music of his great contemporary Franz Liszt. We observe Bruckner's suspicion of the more extreme manifestations of Cecilianism and his deliberate avoidance of 'rules' which would have hindered true originality. Above all, we marvel at his ability to bring the different sacred texts to life. These motets are the most intimate and, arguably, the most profound expressions of his Christian faith.

6 Bruckner and secular vocal music

A. CRAWFORD HOWIE

Background

The social upheavals that followed the French Revolution and its wars brought accelerating change to musical and concert life, including the rise of vocal and choral societies in many countries. Not only did they fulfil a social need, they enabled people to express feelings of patriotism which became more pronounced as the political map of Europe changed. The great choruses in Verdi's *Risorgimento* operas had their counterparts in the inspirational pieces for male-voice choir (*Liedertafel*) which became a vital part of music-making throughout Germany and Austria.

Germany led the way with Zelter's Berlin *Liedertafel* in 1809, followed by others in Leipzig, Breslau, Magdeburg, and Stuttgart. The first German choral festival took place in Plochingen (Württemberg) in 1827. In Austria, Metternich regarded any kind of popular movement with suspicion and initially refused to allow the establishment of choral societies. The founding of the Wiener Männergesang-Verein in 1843, however, provided the necessary impetus, as did the culturally and politically motivated cultivation of Austrian folksong.[1] Frequent contacts between societies resulted in joint tours and choral festivals as symbols of 'choral solidarity'. Beginning in the 1850s, choral festivals grew increasingly common in the 1860s, while enlarged bodies emerged such as the 'Upper Enns Choral Association' proposed by Josef Hafferl (the president of Linz's *Frohsinn*), Alois Weinwurm (the conductor of its *Sängerbund*), and August Göllerich senior in 1863.[2] Its objects were to provide support for new and existing societies, to encourage the writing of new choruses by native composers, and to institute festivals such as the first *Oberösterreich-salzburgische Sängerbundesfest* in Linz from 4 to 6 June 1865.

The choral repertoire in the nineteenth century

A transition took place in the male-voice repertory from the convivial choruses of the late eighteenth and early nineteenth centuries to choruses of a more folk-like, and eventually of a much more patriotic, nature. An inspection of the annual reports of *Frohsinn* and *Sängerbund* during the period 1855–68 reveals, besides works about nature, love, and drinking, the presence of patriotic songs which were to receive new impetus from German unification and the related struggle in Austria between Pan-Germans and conservative monarchists.[3] The often highly charged political significance of these choruses assured their success. Prominent composers included Franz Abt, Karl Santner, Jakob Eduard Schmölzer, Anton M. Storch (choirmaster of *Frohsinn* until 1860), Hans Schläger (choirmaster of the Wiener Männergesang-Verein from 1856 until 1861), and Rudolf Wein-wurm, founder and choirmaster of the Akademischer Gesangverein and conductor of the Wiener Männergesang-Verein. Choral pieces by Johann W. Kalliwoda, Konradin Kreutzer, Friedrich W. Kücken, Franz Lachner, and Heinrich Marschner were sung regularly, and the two choirs also performed works by Beethoven, Haydn, Mendelssohn, Mozart, and Schubert.

Bruckner would have been familiar with much of this repertory through his involvement with *Frohsinn* and *Sängerbund* in Linz, the Wiener Männergesang-Verein (conducted between 1866 and 1880 by his friend Weinwurm), and other societies in Wels, Steyr, and Vöcklabruck. He was held in high esteem by these choirs, many of which elected him an honorary member.[4]

Bruckner's secular vocal compositions

Bruckner's secular vocal compositions are of varying quality, forming a relatively large but well-nigh forgotten part of his output. The majority are for male-voice choir but there are also works for mixed-voice choir, male-voice quartet, and the 'mottoes' (*Sprüche*) or short signature-tunes which Bruckner wrote for several choral societies. These works cover virtually his entire compositional career (1843–92) and were mostly written for specific occasions and dedicated to acquaintances or colleagues.[5] Many details of their first performance are obscure and manuscript sources are sometimes missing (as for WAB 91–2, 95 and 95b). There are also some songs for solo voice with piano accompaniment.

The smaller-scale works

Among the acquaintances Bruckner made in Enns while receiving lessons from Zenetti was the parish priest Joseph von Pessler, for whose birthday he wrote his earliest surviving chorus, *An dem Feste*, to words by the Kronstorf priest Alois Knauer. The unaccompanied male-voice piece (first performed on 19 September 1843) is of particular interest because, fifty years later, Bruckner made some corrections, added dynamic markings, and had new words provided by Karl Ptak. The most striking alterations occur in the cadential bars in which a semitone shift in the harmony gives added spice to an otherwise unpretentious perfect cadence. With its new title *Tafellied* it was performed by the Wiener Akademischer Gesangverein in March 1893 and was reviewed favourably in the *Deutsche Zeitung* and the *Deutsches Volksblatt*. In the former, Theodor Helm drew attention to the 'unpretentious but successful choral writing of the nineteen-year-old Upper Austrian school assistant who at that time had certainly no inkling that he would become one of the greatest masters of the symphony and church music'.[6]

Eight compositions were written during the St. Florian period: six for male-voice chorus – *Das Lied vom deutschen Vaterland*, *Der Lehrerstand*, the first setting of *Das edle Herz*, *Die Geburt*, *Vor Arneths Grab*, and *Des Dankes Wort sei mir gegönnt*; and two for his own male-voice quartet in which he sang second bass – *Ständchen: Wie des Bächleins Silberquelle* and *Sternschnuppen*. The only work to have a specific date (see Table 6.1) is *Die Geburt*, an appealing work with a fondness for Schubertian mediant relationships.[7] We can also be certain of the date of *Vor Arneths Grab*, as it was written specifically for Michael Arneth's funeral on 28 March 1854. The majority of these works are through-composed, and two are fairly substantial: *Der Lehrerstand*, in several sections differing in key, time-signature, and setting (chorus, soloists' ensemble), and *Des Dankes Wort*, which has a cantata-like character, choral homophony alternating with recitative-like solo sections.[8] The first of the two male-voice quartets, *Sternschnuppen*, reveals a strong Mendelssohnian influence; the second, *Ständchen*, is essentially a tenor solo with a three-part 'humming' accompaniment which is wordless at first but later has words added.[9]

It has been assumed that Bruckner composed the chorus *Lasst Jubeltöne laut erklingen* for the reception of the future Empress Elizabeth in Linz on 22 April 1854. According to the *Frohsinn* chronicles, the choir sang a 'festal chorus' when she arrived and a 'serenade' in the evening. There is no mention of Bruckner's composition in contemporary reports and publications, however, and several stylistic features of the music (the two-against-three rhythm which became more prevalent in his works from the 1860s onwards, chains of sixth chords, and enharmonic changes untypical of the St. Florian works) point to a later date.[10]

With the exception of the second setting of *Das edle Herz*, Bruckner wrote no new works during the period of his study with Sechter. It is not known if this work was written for a specific occasion.[11] Marinelli's poem about the compassionate and unselfish treatment of one's fellows prompted no more than an adequate musical response from Bruckner.

Bruckner's first contact with *Frohsinn* was in 1853 when it visited St. Florian as part of a 'choir excursion'. In March 1856, not long after moving

Table 6.1 *Chronology of Bruckner's secular music for vocal ensemble (ABSW, XXIII/2)*

Title	WAB	Setting	Date
An dem Feste	59	TTBB	rev. 1843, 1893
Tafellied	86		22 Feb. 1893
Das Lied vom deutschen Vaterland	78	TTBB	?1845
Ständchen	84	T, TTBB	?1846
Der Lehrerstand	77	T, T, B, B, TTBB	?1847
Sternschnuppen	85	TTBB	1848
Zwei Sängersprüche: Ein jubelnd Hoch;	83/1 and 2	TTBB	1851
Lebt wohl, ihr Sangesbrüder			
Das edle Herz	65	TTBB	?1851
Die Geburt	69	TTBB	19 March 1852
Vor Arneths Grab	53	SATB, 3 trbns	March 1854
Des Dankes Wort sei mir vergönnt	62	T, B, TTBBB	c. 1850
Das edle Herz	66	SATB	December 1857
Am Grabe	2	TTBB	February 1861
Du bist wie eine Blume	64	S, A, T, B	5 Dec. 1861
Der Abendhimmel	55	TTBB	Jan. 1862
Lasst Jubeltöne laut erklingen	76	TTBB, 2 hns, 2 tpts, 4 trbns	after 1861
Zigeuner-Waldlied	135		
Um Mitternacht	89	A solo, TTBB, pf.	12 April 1864
Herbstlied	73	2 S, TTBB, pf.	19 March 1864
Trauungslied	49	SATB	8 Jan. 1865
Vaterländisches Weinlied	91	TTBB	c. Nov. 1866
Vaterlandslied	92	T, B, TTBB	c. Nov. 1866
Der Abendhimmel	56	TTBB	6 Dec. 1866
Das Frauenherz, die Mannesbrust	95	SATB	c. 1868
Des höchsten Preis	95b	TTBB	?1850
Two mottoes: Im Wort und Liede wahr und treu;	148	TTBB	28 Oct. 1869
Wir alle jung und alt			
Mitternacht	80	T, TTBB, pf.	Nov. 1869
Freier Sinn und froher Mut, motto	147	TTBB	21 March 1874
Das hohe Lied	74	(T, T, T, B, TTTTBBBB)/ (T, TTTTBBBB, 2 vlas, cellos, kbd, 4 hns, 3 trbns, tuba)	31 Dec. 1876
Nachruf	81	TTBB, org.	19 Oct. 1877; rev. 1886
Trösterin Musik	88	TTBB, org.	
Abendzauber	57	T, 3 yodellers, TTBB, 4 hns	13 Jan. 1878
Zur Vermählungsfeier	54	TTBB	27 Nov. 1878
Sängerbund	82	TTBB	3 Feb. 1882
Volkslied	94	TTBB	winter 1882
Um Mitternacht	90	T, TTBB	11 Feb. 1886
Träumen und Wachen	87	T, TTBB	15 Dec. 1890; rev. 4 Feb. 1892
Das deutsche Lied (Der deutsche Gesang)	63	TTBB, brass	29 April 1892

to Linz, he joined the choir, becoming assistant librarian on 31 October. He resigned from the choir in September 1858, possibly because of voice problems, but succeeded Storch as principal choirmaster in November 1860 after making a very favourable impression when conducting the choir for the first time at a concert in October. Contemporary reports confirm that he was a conscientious conductor, taking great care over details of articulation, intonation, and breath control; regularly praised in the *Linzer Zeitung* and *Linzer Abendbote*, he was credited with raising the choir's standard to a level at least the equal of other choirs in the region. During 1861 he directed the choir in festival performances in Krems and Nuremberg, but resigned in September as a result of some unspecified contretemps.[12] Nevertheless, he seems to have remained on reasonably good terms with the choir and took up the baton again in 1868, his final year in Linz. The results he achieved, including the first performance of the final chorus from *Die Meistersinger* during the choir's centenary celebrations, were no less impressive.

A sign of Bruckner's greater maturity in word-setting and harmonic treatment comes with *Am Grabe* for male voices, sung at the funeral of the mother of the president of *Frohsinn*. Composing at short notice, he used the same text as in *Vor Arneths Grab*, omitting the final verse and avoiding an identical musical treatment, apart from some motivic connections at the opening; 'not so much a revision designed to update an earlier work as ... a new composition using material from an older one', it was the first of Bruckner's choral works to be performed publicly in Linz on 11 February 1861 and to be reviewed in the following day's *Linzer Zeitung*, which highlighted the 'atmosphere of gentle feeling' that pervaded the work.[13]

Shortly after his resignation from *Frohsinn*, Bruckner wrote two pieces for vocal quartet: *Du bist wie eine Blume*, an undistinguished setting of Heine's famous poem for mixed voices and *Der Abendhimmel*, the first of two settings of Joseph Christian Zedlitz's three-verse poem. In comparison with his earlier choral works, the latter displays a much tauter formal structure, a tripartite song form with varied reprise (a structural model increasingly used in his subsequent choral works). The piece has a serenade-like character and is indebted harmonically and melodically to Schubert. The second setting of the text for unaccompanied male voices was completed nearly five years later. Not surprisingly, it reveals how much richer and more varied Bruckner's harmonic language had become in its mixture of chromaticism, archaic chordal progressions, and harmonic shifts to keys a third apart. The sudden break from four-part harmony to unison octave writing in bars 15–16, for instance, is reminiscent of many passages in the three great Masses and early symphonies.

Between the settings of *Der Abendhimmel* (while working on *Germanenzug*), Bruckner wrote two choral pieces for male voices, female soloists, and piano, a combination not otherwise found in choral works. *Herbstlied* (dedicated to Josef Hafferl), a setting of a poem by Friedrich von Sallet, includes parts for two soprano soloists. The *Linzer Zeitung* deemed it well composed but found the initial soprano entries too prominent above the *pp* choral description of the echoes of nightingale song. As in the contemporary *Um Mitternacht*, *Herbstlied* begins in the minor but ends in the tonic major with an eloquent musical portrayal of the 'thousand kind stars' which are hidden behind the dark clouds. *Um Mitternacht* uses a text by Robert Prutz that Bruckner set again in Vienna more than twenty years later, writing for similar forces but using a solo tenor instead of a solo alto. After the original's first performance by *Sängerbund* under Bruckner (11 December 1864), the *Linzer Zeitung* referred to its 'unusually sombre mood' at the beginning (which is not long maintained) but singled out the solo alto entry in E major and the work's 'truly delightful conclusion' for particular mention.[14] The first section, for male voices and piano, makes extensive use of choral unison and cadences in Eb major. With the entry of the alto soloist comes the sudden move to E major and descending chromatic movement in the bass effects a modulation to F major and thence to A major for the end of the second section. A return to the material of the opening in a brighter F major and with the solo alto echoing the choral phrases gives added interest to the final section which concludes with voices in unison underpinned by a Schubertian piano arpeggio accompaniment.

Three male-voice pieces were written in quick succession at the end of 1866, the second setting of *Der Abendhimmel*, and two choruses – *Vaterländisches Weinlied* and *Vaterlandslied* (*O könnt ich dich beglücken*) – to texts by August Silberstein that reflect the patriotic mood generated by the Austro-Prussian War of that year. Storch, as conductor of the Niederösterreichischer Sängerbund, had asked Bruckner to send him a chorus for male voices and the composer made reference to this request when he wrote to Rudolf Weinwurm on 2 December.[15] On 11 December Bruckner thanked Storch profusely for his request and sent him the three pieces, dedicating *Vaterlandslied* 'to your excellent choir because I considered it to be the most substantial of the three'.[16] Whereas *Vaterländisches Weinlied* is a mere twelve bars, culminating in a rousing treatment of the final words, *O könnt ich dich beglücken*, a setting of a four-verse poem for male-voice choir with tenor and baritone soloists, is the most extended of the unaccompanied works. The tonic Ab is changed enharmonically to G♯ to become the third of E major in the third verse as soloists and chorus give impassioned expression to the words 'I will not leave you, land full of noble truth!' The quiet ending of the final verse over an Ab pedal is in complete contrast to the closing bars of *Vaterländisches Weinlied*.[17]

During the St. Florian, Linz, and early Vienna years Bruckner wrote several very short 'mottoes' for different choral societies. Some of these are of uncertain date, others can be dated accurately. *Ein jubelnd Hoch in Leid und Lust* and *Lebt wohl, ihr Sangesbrüder* were requested by his friend Josef Seiberl for the use of the Eferding *Liedertafel* in a Song Festival at Passau. *Das Frauenherz, die Mannesbrust* was probably given its first performance by the combined men's and women's choirs of *Frohsinn* during an outing to the Kiernberger forest on May 1868. The words are by Karl Kerschbaum, a friend of Bruckner and president of *Frohsinn* at the time. The motto *Des Höchsten Preis*, with words by A. Mittermayer, was probably written for the *Liedertafel* in Sierning, near Steyr. Its simpler harmonic style suggests an earlier date. The two mottoes in C major and D minor for unaccompanied male voices (settings of Johann Kajetan Markus) were written in memory of Sechter. Finally *Freier Sinn und froher Mut*, also for unaccompanied male voices, was written in March 1874 for the Grein Choral Society.

After his move to Vienna, Bruckner continued to write male-voice choruses when the opportunity arose. In August 1869 *Frohsinn* asked for a choral piece for the society's anniversary celebrations in May 1870; in November he wrote to the choir committee to thank them and inform them that Rudolf Weinwurm had helped him to find a suitable text.[18] In *Mitternacht*, Bruckner provided a highly effective piece for male voices and piano accompaniment. He complemented the atmospheric words – flowers and trees bathed in moonlight and a gentle breeze – with a pulsating repeated quaver right-hand part in the accompaniment. As the poet is moved to feelings of great devotion and imagines the sound of the organ and hymn-singing, the piano accompaniment changes to unison octave semiquavers.

During the years 1876–8, dominated by symphonic composition and revision, Bruckner wrote four pieces for male-voice choir which illustrate his highly imaginative use of the medium and reflect, albeit in much condensed form, some of the arresting stylistic features in his symphonic works. These choruses put much greater demands on the singers than the Linz choral works, which are more closely orientated to contemporary performing practice and performance standards. The range of colour in *Das hohe Lied* for male voices, tenor and baritone soloists, and in some other Bruckner choral works of this period, is increased by the use of a small 'humming chorus' which provides an atmospheric background sound. Bruckner composed the chorus at the end of 1876 and dedicated it to the Akademischer Gesangverein, possibly out of gratitude for their performance of *Germanenzug* in Vienna earlier in the year. Because of the technical difficulty and exposed nature of the 'humming chorus', Richard Heuberger, the conductor of the choir, suggested that the parts be doubled by a string quintet (two violas, two cellos and double bass). Bruckner also took the opportunity of adding brass instruments (four horns, three trombones, and bass tuba) to support the voices. The different images and moods of the poem are captured onomatopoeically by Bruckner: oscillating semiquavers for humming voices suggest the obtrusive sound of the millwheel as it 'disturbs the wanderer's song'; descending diminished sevenths depict the darkness of the wood (bars 12–14), rising E major arpeggios graphically portray the ascent of the mountain (tenor soloist alternating with chorus, bars 15ff.); further alternation between soloists and chorus describes 'the echo of the sound resounding more and more strongly' (B major second inversion chords, bars 37–9); full homophony with typical Brucknerian surges conveys the sense of excitement as the summit is reached (bars 44ff.). There is a hushed ending as the song rises up into the stratosphere.[19]

Nachruf for male voices and organ was written in October 1877 in memory of Seiberl, and was premiered at St. Florian during the unveiling of a memorial plaque on 28 October. Bruckner played the organ part. To make the work more accessible he later had the original text changed by August Seuffert to one with less specific sentiments. Under its new title *Trösterin Musik*, it was given its first performance in Vienna in April 1886 by the Akademischer Gesangverein conducted by Weinwurm. The most effective part of the piece is at the end where, in the original version, the contrasting images of the 'stormy chords of the organ' and the organist (that is, Seiberl) 'resting in peace' are portrayed musically.[20]

Abendzauber (dedicated to Karl Almeroth, one of Bruckner's Steyr friends) was written in 1878 for male voices (who hum until the final section where there is a proper text underlay), tenor/baritone soloist, three distant yodelling voices and four horns. According to Franz Bayer, another of Bruckner's Steyr friends, the yodelling parts were intended for female voices and were modelled on the Rhinemaidens' music. Bruckner appears to have chosen the key of Gb major and frequent tranquil pedal points deliberately to suggest a Romantic moonlit seascape with the 'magical sound of songs' drifting upwards.[21]

The marriage of Bruckner's landlord, Dr Anton Oelzelt-Newin, in November 1878 was the occasion for the unaccompanied male-voice chorus *Zwei Herzen haben sich gefunden* (*Zur Vermählungsfeier*). It contains the normal Brucknerian fingerprints of sudden semitone shifts in the harmony and unison octave phrases.[22] Nearly four years elapsed before *Sängerbund*, composed in February 1882. First performed in a choral festival held in Wels in June 1883, its theme is the strength of German choral singing and its ability to foster patriotic feelings, underlined by some bars quoted from Kalliwoda's famous *Deutsches Lied* in the second verse. Bruckner sets the four verses of the poem similarly, with the exception of the slightly longer second verse and the end of the fourth where he makes an appropriate harmonic change at the words 'the song sounds forth right to death's door' before the final fanfare-like exaltations of 'freedom' and 'fatherland'.[23] When *Sängerbund* was performed again at the forty-first anniversary concert of the Steyr *Liedertafel* in 1891, the *Alpenbote* commented on Bruckner's treatment of the patriotic words in the chorus which 'in its powerful chords sealed the vow of everlasting faithfulness to German song in every phase of the destiny of the German people'.[24] Contemporary with it is the work erroneously called *Volkslied*, also with patriotic overtones. Bruckner intended it for a competition for 'a hymn for the German people in Austria' to be written as a 'beautiful, simple folk-like melody'. The jury came to the decision that none of the 1,320 entries (which presumably included Bruckner's) fulfilled these conditions.[25]

During 1886, while he was working on the Eighth Symphony, Bruckner composed the second version of *Um Mitternacht* (WAB 90). It was written specifically for a special Bruckner concert in Linz in April planned by *Frohsinn*. Bruckner's response to Prutz's textual imagery is just as keen as it is in the first setting, and there are some similarities between the two; both are in F minor and both begin with an organ-point effect, in the piano in the earlier version, in the bass voices in the later. The second and third verses are now set for tenor solo with an evocative humming accompaniment for the choir, which provides a rich, frequently shifting harmonic background. *Frohsinn* found this extremely awkward to sing, however, and a supporting harp accompaniment was provided at the first performance.[26]

Bruckner's last two works of this kind were both connected with the Akademischer Gesangverein. Although preoccupied during 1890 with revisions of earlier works, Bruckner found time to write a short male-voice chorus, *Träumen und Wachen*, a setting of words by Grillparzer in concise A–B–A form with a central section for solo tenor and 'humming voices' which he conducted during the University of Vienna's celebrations to mark the centenary of Grillparzer's birth on 15 January 1891. The cordial relations between composer and choir, strengthened by a successful Bruckner evening in December 1891, led to Bruckner being invited to write a choral piece specially for the Deutschakademisches Sängerfest in Salzburg at the beginning of June 1892. Bruckner obliged with *Das deutsche Lied* for male voices and brass ensemble. The words were provided by Aurelius Polzer ('Erich Fels') from Graz. The work was given its first performance by three massed choirs, including the Vienna Akademischer Gesangverein, in the *Aula academica*, Salzburg on Pentecost Sunday, 5 June. As in *Sängerbund*, Bruckner quotes deliberately from Kalliwoda's *Das deutsche Lied*. Antiphony between the brass and the voices reinforces the patriotic words and the combined forces apostrophize the power of German song as it resounds through the 'endangered land'. Bruckner the symphonist is very much in evidence throughout and it was climactic moments such as the chromatically rising first inversion chords at the words 'so sound forth, terrify the enemy and awaken our sleeping comrades' which no doubt prompted one of the reviewers of the first performance to describe the work as being 'shot through with the titanic power of his symphonic creations'.[27]

The larger-scale works

The only large-scale secular piece to survive from the Kronstorf period is the first of the 'name-day cantatas', *Vergissmeinnicht* (WAB 93). It has a cantata-like format and is scored for eight-part mixed voice choir, four soloists and piano accompaniment. Its three versions (all dating from 1845) vary only in slight changes to the accompaniment figuration. There are seven short movements, all in a simple melodious style, though the final unaccompanied eight-part chorus shows a keen awareness of vocal colour and achieves a pleasing textural variety.[28] *Entsagen* (WAB 14) was composed c. 1851 for soprano or tenor soloist, mixed-voice choir and organ or piano. It is a 'spiritual song' in three sections, the outer sections in the form of a Protestant chorale and the middle section, for soloist, rather repetitious and unappealing in its arid three-part semi-contrapuntal style.[29]

More substantial are three occasional cantatas: *Heil, Vater! Dir zum hohen Feste* (WAB 61), a setting for six-part mixed-voice choir, three horns, two trumpets, and trombone of a text by Marinelli for Arneth's name-day in 1852 and first performed at the abbey at the end of September; *Auf, Brüder! auf, und die Saiten zur Hand* (WAB 60), for male-voice quartet, male-voice choir, mixed-voice choir and wind band, written in July 1855 for Friedrich Mayr's name-day; and the *Festgesang 'Sankt Jodok spross aus edlem Stamm'* (WAB 15), for soloists, mixed-voice choir, and piano, completed in December 1855 for the name-day of Jodok Stülz, the St. Florian parish priest, and perhaps intended as a parting musical gift. In the coda of the second we have our first real glimpse of later Bruckner as the basses span almost two octaves and the pre-cadential harmonic movement colourfully avoids the obvious.[30]

By 1862 Bruckner was well established in the musical life of Linz. After his course with Sechter, he was beginning to spread his wings again under Kitzler's tuition and had a renewed confidence in composing after a long self-imposed period of musical silence. Bishop Rudigier's request for a cantata for the laying of the foundation stone of the Neuer Dom on 1 May 1862 fired Bruckner's enthusiasm and he responded with the *Festkantate 'Preiset den Herrn'* (WAB 16), to words by the theology professor Maximilian Prammesberger. It was written in about a month, scored for four-part male-voice choir, solo quartet, bass soloist, wind band, and timpani, and performed by *Frohsinn*, invited guest singers, and members of a local regimental band conducted by Lanz. There are eight short movements; material from the opening chorus is repeated twice – in the third and eighth movements – to bind the work together. In the fourth movement, the expansive phrase for bass soloist, 'the building reaching like a giant into the blue heaven', and repeated quaver accompaniment were clearly blueprints for similar gestures in the later sacred and secular vocal music.[31]

Thirty years separate Bruckner's two arguably most 'patriotic' choruses, *Germanenzug* (WAB 70; 1863–4) and *Helgoland* (WAB 71; 1893), both settings of texts by the Viennese poet and journalist Dr August Silberstein.[32] Bruckner entered *Germanenzug* for a competition at the first Oberösterreichisches Sängerbundesfest, scheduled for August 1864 in Linz but postponed until June 1865 when its name was changed to the Oberösterreichisch-Salzburgisches Sängerbundesfest. His original intention was to use his *Zigeuner-Waldlied* (WAB 135) as the basis for his entry, but correspondence with Silberstein and Weinwurm during the summer of 1863 makes it clear that he discarded this and requested a more patriotic text.[33] Bruckner's and Weinwurm's entries were two of the eight compositions chosen to proceed to the final stages.[34] On the day of the competition (5 June 1865) first, second and third prizes were awarded according to the volume of popular applause, and *Germanenzug* had to take second place to Weinwurm's *Germania*.

Clearly conceived primarily for outdoor performance, *Germanenzug* is scored for male voices accompanied by a brass ensemble consisting of four horns, two cornets, four trumpets, three trombones, a tenor horn, and tuba. Structurally it is in three main sections, each with internal repetition. The first (comprising verses 1 and 2) is in D minor and the sharply dotted leaping octave motive at the beginning is a slightly altered variant of the beginning of *Preiset den Herrn*. There are also obvious links with other D minor works written before and after, the Requiem, Mass, and Symphonies '0' and 3. The slower middle section (verses 3 and 4) is the most adventurous harmonically. The third section (verses 5 and 6) begins with an exact repetition of the first section but then proceeds to D major and new material for the stirring conclusion of the piece. The outer sections portray German warriors going into battle, and the middle section (for male-voice quartet and four horns) is a song of the Valkyries who describe the delights of Valhalla, the destination of heroes who are killed in battle.[35]

Helgoland was commissioned by Eduard Kremser and the Wiener Männergesangverein for their fiftieth anniversary in 1893. Dates on the autograph and references in his letters give us some indication of Bruckner's slow but steady progress on the composition of the work between April and August, subsequent corrections, and concern that sufficient rehearsal time be spent in preparing it for performance.[36] The chorus, scored for male voices and symphony orchestra, was given its first performance at the Männergesangverein's anniversary concert in the Winter-Reitschule of the Hofburg palace on 8 October. Silberstein's poem narrates the story of the imminent invasion of the island of Heligoland by a Roman fleet and the miraculous intervention of a wild storm which throws the ships on the rocks and saves the islanders. According to Ringer, Silberstein's 'storm-battered North Sea rocks' were a 'timeless symbol of the unified German nation which had finally come into existence in 1870'.[37] Bruckner's setting has that 'primitive' grandeur reminiscent of parts of the Te Deum and Psalm 150. Passages of a traditional cast intermingle with 'progressive' elements (bold voice-leading, advanced chromatic harmony, arresting orchestral colour) and the work has a symphonic feel which links it to the Eighth and Ninth Symphonies. It is on a much larger canvas than *Germanenzug* but a number of internal motivic connections guarantee overall unity. Critical reaction to the première was mixed, the most frequent criticism being that, while the orchestral depiction of the tempestuous elements was successful, the voices were over-stretched.[38]

The songs

If *Helgoland* represents Bruckner at his most 'massive' in terms of combined choral and orchestral forces, the handful of songs show a much more intimate and even less well-known side of the composer. With one exception they were all written before his move to Vienna and betoken an acquaintance with the Lied repertoire of Mendelssohn and Schubert.

Only one of the songs composed in the St. Florian period has survived in complete form. The voice part of 'Mild wie Bäche' (WAB 138; c. 1845) is complete but the piano part is sketched in only a few places. In 'Wie des Bächleins Silberquelle' (*Duetto*) (WAB 137; c. 1845) for two sopranos and piano, the voice parts are again complete but there is no piano accompaniment apart from a few bass notes. The Mendelssohnian 'Frühlingslied' (WAB 68; 1851), a setting of a poem by Heine, was dedicated to Aloisia, Michael Bogner's daughter, described by Bruckner as a 'blossoming spring rose'.[39] During the St. Florian years, Bruckner also arranged folksongs for voice and piano accompaniment for Aloisia.

The dating of all four songs Bruckner composed during the Linz period is uncertain. On 30 October 1858, the composer wrote to Rudolf Weinwurm that he had written 'a little song'.[40] Although Max Auer surmised that this was a reference to 'Wie bist du, Frühling, gut und treu' (WAB 58), a setting of five verses from Oskar von Redwitz's *Amaranths Waldeslieder* intended for one of Mayr's musical evenings at St. Florian, Angela Pachovsky considers that it was probably composed in 1856 as Bruckner's 'farewell present to his music-loving patron on leaving St. Florian abbey'.[41] Far superior in its word-setting and use of the piano is 'Im April' (WAB 75), a setting of words by Emanuel Geibel which Bruckner conceived in the early 1860s and dedicated to Helene

Hofmann, one of his piano pupils. In the longer second half of the song Bruckner uses a sudden dynamic and harmonic contrast to underline the poet's frustration in not being able to find the appropriate sonority to capture the 'atmosphere of the April evening'. In his discussion of 'Mein Herz und deine Stimme' (WAB 79), a setting of a poem by Platen, and 'Herbstkummer', WAB 72, a setting of a poem by Ernst, Auer remarks that 'both songs have only curiosity value' and casts doubts on the authenticity of the former which was dedicated to Pauline Hofmann, Helene's sister.[42] Walther Dürr was more inclined to accept it as genuine Bruckner, however, and argued that it was firmly in the tradition of the Romantic Lied. Bruckner took care to provide an interpretation which does justice to its mood and imagery and preserves an equal balance between poem, vocal melody, and piano accompaniment.[43] The date of 'Herbstkummer' (April 1864) is corroborated by stylistic features such as a more mature grasp of harmony, careful integration of voice and accompaniment, and judicious use of word-painting, no doubt the result of experience gained in his studies with Kitzler (for whom Bruckner had already completed a number of song exercises between Christmas 1861 and August 1862; they range from incomplete sketches to complete compositions and are contained in the *Kitzler Studienbuch*). We return finally to the patriotic theme. In the early 1880s when Bruckner composed 'Volkslied' (WAB 94) as his competition entry for a 'hymn for the German people of Austria', he submitted his manuscript in two forms, one for unaccompanied male voices, the other for voice with suitably hymn-like piano accompaniment.[44]

Conclusion

Bruckner's songs show a grasp of the medium but, like his piano and organ music, were occasional compositions written for others and displaying only occasionally the spark of greatness which was to illuminate much of his mature sacred and symphonic oeuvre. The secular choral works, the patriotic ones in particular, were extremely successful and popular during Bruckner's lifetime and for several years after his death. Stylistically, not least in the frequent use of atmospheric 'humming voices', they are 'locked into' and very much part of the nineteenth-century German choral tradition and are rarely performed today. Nevertheless, they provide us with a fascinating glimpse of the less serious side of the composer and enable us to experience many of the grand gestures of the symphonies on a miniature scale.

PART THREE

The symphonist

7 The Brucknerian symphony: an overview

JOHN WILLIAMSON

Types, characteristics, and schemas

In a study of the symphony published in the 1960s, Bruckner was subjected to a unique treatment. In place of the consideration of whole works applied to other composers, Deryck Cooke described a 'composite' Bruckner symphony: the Adagio of the Seventh, the Scherzo of the Eighth, and the outer movements of the Third (thereby providing the opportunity to demonstrate the phenomenon of thematic linkage). The strategy was rather clever: by accepting 'a grain of truth' in the hoary old idea that Bruckner wrote the same symphony nine times, Cooke demonstrated the variety of 'characteristics' that existed within movement 'types'.[1] Since then, the same strategy has appeared in different contexts, though the question of the 'schema' behind Bruckner's symphonies has never entirely been resolved, apart from the firm adherence to four movements. The question affects form far more than other aspect of Bruckner's works, and will be considered in detail in Chapter 12. Nonetheless, attempts to define the 'essence' of Bruckner the symphonist have also tended to involve the taxonomy of a fairly narrow collection of characteristics and influences (the contrast between formal schema and characteristics is developed further in Chapter 13 by Margaret Notley).

These may be melodic, in which context the famous Bruckner rhythm (♩♩ ♪♪ or ♪♪ ♩♩) immediately comes to mind, occurring as it does in most of the symphonies from the Second onwards. Yet even so instantly recognizable a rhythmic tic can be used with great variety: melodically, as a brass signal (as it first appears with a significant modification in the Second – ♪♪♪), as a string ostinato (as in the Sixth, once more modified – ♪ ♫). Characteristics may be technical or procedural, such as the high incidence of quasi-religious counterpoint that finds a particular climax in the Fifth. A further category is the use of folk characteristics from Austria and the Danubian area in general, particularly in the Trio sections of Scherzos. Such features are not unique to Bruckner, and can often be compared with other composers such as Schubert, but they are at the foreground in his style to a degree that is unusual and striking. Collectively they tend to place Bruckner's music somewhat apart from what might loosely be called the 'modernism' of his own time (Liszt and Wagner) and of the succeeding age.

In addition, there are characteristics that seem to stem from modern Wagnerian practice but which, on closer inspection, reveal themselves to be so modified as to render the comparison meaningless. The famous tremolo passages that open several symphonies and symphonic allegros (and the ostinato variants found at the start of the Third and Sixth) do not sound conspicuously similar to the Wagnerian 'ex nihilo' opening (as in *Lohengrin* or *Das Rheingold*).[2] Investigation of the phenomenon of tremolo in Bruckner in general has played down 'dramaturgical refinement' in favour of specific musical functions: the tremolo of development, as at the start of the Fourth or Ninth, where thematic material is born out of nothing, or of registral change, as in the introduction of the first movement of the Fifth (bars 31–55 and beyond). Related phenomena can be found in the orchestral religious music (notably the setting of 'Et resurrexit' in the F minor Mass) and may even infiltrate a chamber work (the beginning of the Finale of the String Quintet). Whatever their provenance, Bruckner fashioned something original from them that again sets him slightly apart from the currents of his time.[3]

Anachronisms

That such features exceed the symphonic and encroach upon the style of the orchestral choral music suggests a further dimension to the peculiarities of Bruckner's output: the notion of his orchestral works as 'mass-symphonies'. The ramifications of this reach far beyond mere notes into questions relating to 'absolute music' in more than one sense (as pursued in Chapter 9). The resemblance of certain figures in the religious works to similar ideas and motives in the symphonies raises the question whether a specifically 'religious' content is transferred. Although there will be more extensive discussion of this below in Chapters 8 and 9, it is worth noting that even purely musical discussion of Bruckner's symphonies can hardly avoid the world of the church, even if limited to the possible influence of organ registration on his orchestration (see Chapter 11). Once it proceeds beyond that, then the issue opens into such cases as the quotations from mass movements in the symphonies (notably the Second) and from the 'Non confundar' of the Te Deum in the Adagio of the Seventh. At such points discussion can hover uncertainly on the border of ancient and modern: 'The eternity that Bruckner intimates in the Adagio of the Seventh does not mean that world behind and beyond criticized by Nietzsche but the culmination of this world, the "new heaven and the new earth" that music promises according to the evidence of Romanticism.'[4] To believe in this interpretation is to accept a modernist (because Nietzschean) Bruckner in spite of Bruckner's ignorance

Example 7.1   Symphony No. 3 (1873), II, bars 13–15

of Nietzsche. It also flies in the face of traditional interpretations of the composer that rested content with Schopenhauer as philosophical background (as noted by Christa Brüstle in Chapter 16).

To view Bruckner in the light of a coming musical modernism, as a forerunner of Schoenberg even in the limited sense of a vehicle for the ideas of Sechter, also runs into problems with the manner in which his melodic style relates to models taken from the church.[5] This is not simply a matter of echoes of specific works as discussed by many Bruckneri-ans. Obvious archaisms such as the 'Marian' cadence discerned in the slow movement of the Third also do not tell the whole story (see Example 7.1).[6] Where a sacred choral work such as the Te Deum is concerned, it is truer to speak of a thread of unison, Gregorian-like melody that expands and contracts texturally and is decorated by an orchestral pseudo-polyphony rather than the real thing.[7] In this context 'anachronism' is fundamental to style.

Such phenomena are not unknown in the symphonies, often during the elaborated (or double) unisons that function as third or 'closing' theme group in outer movements. To speak of these as being in some sense related to the 'Gregorian' substrata of the Te Deum is not implausible. Bruckner is quite capable of placing such writing in close juxtaposition with an altogether different type of material (e.g. the folk-like); what matters is the maintenance of the underlying monody. Thus from the earliest version of the Third's opening movement (1873), the closing theme group of the exposition (bars 205–84) involved a unison theme in regular minims decorated by octave statements of the 'Bruckner rhythm'. The presence of chromatic inflections in the line cannot be attributable to any single mode but guarantees a restless tone to the underlying solid rhythmic movement that is then fragmented by trumpet fanfares on a diminished seventh (bar 213). The tension generated by the alteration of unison and accompanied fanfare results in a chorale-like figure that fills out the steady minim melody with a more elaborate pseudo-polyphony (bars 235–45). The history of this passage in revision (1877) is of the further elaboration of the chorale by the introduction of a new and distinctive cadence and continuation (bars 205–9). The illusion of a solidly harmonized chorale tune conceals the monodic inspiration of the passage. At the similar moment in the first movement of the Eighth, a much more sophisticated elaborated unison still falls back on the sudden intrusion of a diminished seventh (1890: bars 97–102), while in the Finale, yet another elaborated unison alternates with fully harmonized chorale-like phrases (1890: bars 135–66). At least one writer speaks of a synthesis of traditional and contemporary elements in relation to the church music, but the symphonies seem capable of bearing a similar interpretation.[8] A strong sense of monody (whether sacred or folk-like) underpins Bruckner's use of modern harmony.

Cathedrals and counterpoint

The presence of such underlying monody suggests a possible link between Bruckner and the historicism that manifested itself in his age in other, mainly visual arts. At first sight this flies in the face of Carl Dahlhaus' perception that, apart from a few weak cases, music as a whole was relatively untouched by the historicism that reigned unchallenged in nineteenth-century architecture.[9] Yet few accounts of Bruckner's music avoid reference to styles from history (often wrenched out of any strictly musical context), with the suggestion that Bruckner's personality is to be enlightened by his relationship to them. It is evident nowadays that much of the talk about '"Baroque" or "Gothic structure"' and 'the great pathos of Baroque music' belongs among the clichés of Bruckner perception, but even those that so argue concede that the circumstances of his education at St. Florian made it probable that echoes of earlier historical periods would be important for Bruckner.[10] The perception of continuity between Bruckner the composer of religious choral music and the symphonist, to the point of using 'mass-symphonies' as a positive value judgement (as Werner Notter has pointed out), is closely related to this.[11] In such a context, to speak of historicism rather than mysticism is at least to keep one's feet on the ground of the late nineteenth-century context.

However clichéd talk of the 'Baroque' might be, it is a pointer to certain matter-of-fact aspects that remain of interest to Brucknerians: monumentality, quasi-sacred polyphony, organ-like instrumentation. Such characteristics remain factors in all attempts to define Bruckner's style. The challenge has always been to encompass its contradictions without surrendering to eclecticism. Constantin Floros has defined it in a little collection of propositions originally written in the 1980s. His list of influences embraces the 'archaic' in Palestrina and Giovanni Gabrieli, the 'modern' in Wagner, Berlioz, and Liszt; the symphonic in Beethoven, and the Austrian Schubert.[12] As is related in Chapter 16, several of the names in this list feature in the writings of other Brucknerians for reasons that have less to do with the composer than with the construction of an image. Floros reminds us that there remain specifically musical elements to the comparisons.

It is not necessary to elevate the homophonic and contrapuntal aspects of Bruckner's music into 'two principles' symbolized by Beethoven and Bach as in Halm's writings. The coexistence of sonata form with fugue, for instance, had continued fruitfully from Haydn until Bruckner's younger contemporaries such as Mahler and beyond. Interpretations of this have varied, ranging from the equation of counterpoint and humour in Viennese Classicism and in Mahler to the perception that fugato was a vehicle of intensification and *crescendo* in such symphonists as Berlioz and Liszt. These aspects are present in Bruckner, where they have been problematized by talk of the opposition of sectional sonata form and Baroque *Fortspinnung* (defined as monothematic and lacking in periodicity); yet the most thoroughgoing analyst of Bruckner's use of fugue can point directly to parallels (unison figures, brass rhythmic monotones, pauses, block contrasts of instrumental groups) with Mozart's use of fugue in the last movement of Symphony No. 41 that suggest not a problem, rather a domestication of counterpoint within sonata form in the century before Bruckner wrote his Fifth Symphony.[13]

There is, however, a qualitative difference between the cases of Mozart and Bruckner that is partly a matter of technique, partly of tone. The Finale of the Fifth Symphony illustrates the similarities and the contrasts. The presentation of the fugue subject in the clarinet is humorous, particularly in its contrast with the opening string polyphony. Once heard in these tones the fugue subject never quite throws off the impression of irreverence, particularly in the manic repetitions that offset the choral theme in the development. Yet its combination of wide leaps with a narrow semitonal motion anticipates the fugue subject of Psalm 150, which urges, 'Alles was Odem hat, lobe den Herrn!' This fusion of contrasting tones helps to explain why Bruckner became a symphonist rather than remained a composer of church music. In a similar manner Mozart in his symphony (and in the G major Quartet K. 387) fused the appearance of archaic polyphony with the sound of the opera orchestra.

The difference lies in the relative degrees of integration pursued and achieved. Whereas Mozart infiltrated contrapuntal elements into all sectional areas of the exposition in the Finale of the 'Jupiter', Bruckner presents fugue, song theme, massive unison with 'stormy' accompaniment, and chorale scrolled off by the famous pauses. This is not to deny that there may be contrapuntal inflection to the lyrical second subject, for instance, but to note that it is of a different kind, relying on the proliferation of motivic detail (as at bar 67 where Bruckner asks all three strands to 'stand out'; the texture is all foreground). Analysts have long agonized over this method of construction. If counterpoint is the technical aspect of the 'Baroque' in Bruckner, then the isolated, 'monumental' blocks are the metaphorical, prompting talk of cathedrals in sound.

Within the Fifth's Finale, there is little doubt that the process of contrapuntal intensification goes hand in hand with the evolution of a more continuous musical construction from the isolated blocks. This is first achieved by fugal exposition (bars 223–37) on the chorale theme, which grows through stretto into a combination of the original fugue theme with the chorale (bar 270). Throughout the many ramifications of this section, the opening phrase of the chorale achieves a dominance which was already latent in the whole tune. There Bruckner presented three loud and tonally varied statements of one phrase, interspersed with echoes that struggle to evolve into a sequence (bars 186–9). For contrast there is one quiet phrase in the brass; but it is indicative of Bruckner's overall sense of growth and change that it supplants the final statement of the main phrase during the coda (bars 607–14). The succession of keys and cadence points, not to mention the pizzicato strings' surreptitious 'correction' of the brass from G minor to E♭ major (bars 192–3), suggests that chorale is present here not as traditional form or genre but as topic. It has enough tonal mobility and motivic extension to be ready for symphonic and fugal development.

At the height of the latter, Bruckner presents a combination of old-fashioned 'madrigalian' treatment of the chorale with a key scheme that suggests the mobility of symphonic development while clinging on to the tonic with an un-symphonic obstinacy (B♭ major arrives in bars 270, 350, and 374). Such a tonal structure is not uncommon in Bruckner's movements in sonata form (as in the first movement of the Third), and here it is a product of the nesting of contrapuntal structures within a symphonic context. Counterpoint has the function of a double intensification. Fugal chorale fantasia blends into a *crescendo* that prepares the fugato on the combined themes. Though it threatens to expire prematurely before bar 350, the violent reassertion of the tonic revivifies the fugato for a further *crescendo* to the largest climax (at bar 374). Fugal intensification thus not merely reconstructs the idea of development; it transforms the notion of recapitulation (which of the three returns is the reprise?). Quasi-Baroque procedures in Bruckner thus cease to resemble the examples of Viennese Classicism at the point where they radically restructure form.

The image of the 'Baroque' or 'Gothic' cathedral is also a yardstick of the scale of the sound with its many contrasts between extremes, found at its simplest in the echoing strains of the chorale itself. Bruckner scholarship has sometimes been so intrigued with this that it has failed to see it in its nineteenth-century context, alongside those few historicist examples that Dahlhaus permitted. When Brucknerians recovered the scale of his early knowledge of Mendelssohn, they were handed a key as yet barely used to rediscovering the manner in which Bruckner had integrated church polyphony with the modern orchestra after the manner of such historicizing works as *St Paul*.[14]

Beethoven

To turn to the influence of Beethoven on Bruckner is to move to a somewhat different level of perception. Whereas the Baroque in a late nineteenth-century composer represents a possible 'anachronism', Beethoven remained a permanent feature of the symphonic landscape. Much analysis of his influence on Bruckner tends to remain at the level of reminiscence: the nature of his symphonic openings, for instance, which probably prompted Hanslick's memorably silly image of Beethoven's Ninth Symphony beneath the horses' hooves of the Valkyrie in Bruckner's Third. Some penetrating comments have been made at the level of formal types and expressive intention in recent years, though this has tended to take the presence of Beethoven in Bruckner's music as a given (if not as a relic of the claims of Halm, Kurth, and others).[15]

Deeper insight is to be found in an essay by Ludwig Finscher in which he demonstrates the degree to which Bruckner's First Symphony in C minor follows patterns derived from Beethoven's Fifth in the same key, composing out the transition from minor to major with its 'stylized semantic implications' and incorporating a slow movement in A♭ major; the legacy of the Beethovenian model includes the style of thematic working in the outer movements and the tone of the last: 'One will not easily find a second symphonic movement in Bruckner that so splendidly, yet also so traditionally, makes use of the struggling [*agonisch*] character of thematic work since Beethoven and the idea of the work, the breakthrough to C major.'[16] There is a reservation in that sentiment that is explained by Finscher's conclusion that the First is a 'secular' outsider among Bruckner's generally 'sacred' symphonies. It is not necessary to accept this entirely to subscribe to the notion that the Beethovenian influence was mediated in more complex and diffuse ways in later works, though the 'programme' of struggle and apotheosis remains, albeit transformed, in other symphonies (notably the Third, Eighth, and – according to his intentions – Ninth). This is the essential background for the specific features that might be described as Beethovenian: the 'ex nihilo' opening, the intensifying ostinati of the codas in the opening movements of the Second, Third, and Fifth Symphonies that recall Beethoven's

Ninth, the review in 'quotation marks' of music from earlier movements as in the finales of the Third (1873) and Fifth, the modified rondo but with development rather than variations in the slow movements. Less clear in character are the thematic reprises in the finales that are part of the culminating process: these seem to belong rather to the aftermath of Beethoven. Yet they are not full-scale Lisztian transformations but musical icons that signify the conclusion of a more complex process. When the main theme of the first movement of the Sixth Symphony returns at the end of the Finale, the mere brandishing of its head motive announces a musical fulfilment that is acted out on many dimensions besides the thematic and motivic.

Wagner

The most vexatious aspect of Bruckner's style is its relationship to Wagner. As with several matters mentioned here, this goes beyond purely musical influence to raise issues that impinge on Bruckner's personality and aesthetic. That the writing of symphonies ran counter to the picture of music history that Wagner held throughout much of his career is a truism; from a Bayreuth perspective it should have been as much a 'heresy' as Bruckner's departure from the world of church music.[17] The analyst is left with the principal theory that Bruckner's debt to Wagner was essentially in harmony. To consider this may involve reinterpretation of those passages that seem inflected by the archaic. In a particularly virtuosic article, Graham Phipps considered the idea of 'church style' in the first movement of the Seventh Symphony, noting that 'modal characteristics' could derive from certain tonal and harmonic traits in Wagner which were then cross-fertilized by specifically Brucknerian thematic material. The complete lack of adequate criteria to confirm that these traits are 'quotations' (why does Bruckner bury them in subordinate parts?) does not refute his argument as a whole.[18]

The Brucknerian who despairs of saying anything truly meaningful or original about Bruckner's debt to Wagner is confronted with the problem that there are so many different images of Wagner on which to draw; he is too protean for simple musical classification. To claim that Bruckner's style clamps a four-square periodicity on 'endless melody' is to overlook those many passages in Wagner that follow similar strategies (the 'Liebestod' manages to be both 'infinite' and to grow from two-bar phrases). Comparison with one possible Wagner quotation in the 1873 version of the Third Symphony reveals certain striking differences, not so much in the use of chromaticism as in the way that Bruckner allows a greater degree of prolongation of diatonic moments (see Example 7.2). Although this evocation of the 'Magic Sleep' motif from *Die Walküre* (see Example 7.3) resembles

Example 7.2   Symphony No. 3 (1873), I, bars 479–502

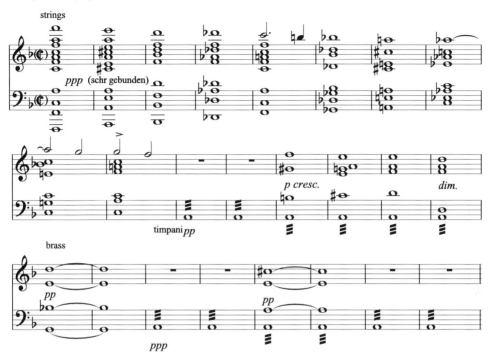

its model in side-slipping chromaticism allied to third motion in the bass, there are much clearer diatonic landmarks such as the subdominant in bar 481, the return of the local tonic (F major) in bar 483, and the pedals on the dominants of F and D minor. Part of the relative stiffness of this passage (which may explain why Bruckner eventually cut it) comes from its strong sense of what is tonally appropriate at this point in a symphony. If Wagner is protean, Bruckner remains fairly circumscribed in his appreciation of how recapitulations are prepared. Later he grew much freer in his use of such chromatic resources without abandoning completely his faith in tonic and dominant pedals as means of anchoring chromaticism. The Scherzo of the Ninth derives much of its force from deployment of chromatic resources first without, then with, tonic pedal.

In assessing the degree to which Wagner's harmony influenced Bruckner, it is important to balance this by consideration of the aspects that create chromatic enrichment by more Schubertian methods. Thus in the swaying folk-like Trio of the Second Symphony the choice of subsidiary keys within a traditional C major tonic–dominant pattern is clearly Schubertian: E major, the Phrygian Db major, and B major (related by third to the dominant of C, and also the dominant of E). Schubertian also is the way in which each region is prolonged by mostly diatonic phrases. Although this section of the

Example 7.3 *Die Walküre*, 'Magic Sleep'

Example 7.4 Symphony No. 6, III, Trio, bars 1–9

Second is relatively simple in tone, similar sections in later symphonies take up tonal relationships by third more thoroughly (A♭ and E majors in the Eighth) without discarding the fundamentally diatonic material, while the Trio of the Sixth is an extended game with the Schubertian German sixth (see Example 7.4).[19]

Tone

Discussion of Bruckner's music inevitably circles round the symphony. His largest religious works are often discussed from a 'symphonic' perspective, his most substantial chamber work is scrutinized for symphonic characteristics. Close inspection of the String Quintet has suggested that its symphonic characteristics are matters of 'tone' and 'foreground' rather than an exact relationship to symphonic characteristics.[20] It also reveals that much that is 'schematic' about Bruckner's type of symphony could be transformed within the sphere of chamber music. Thus the much-discussed tripartite exposition is still present in the Quintet's first movement, but in surprising form. Uniquely in Bruckner's mature instrumental works, the movement is in triple time with a first subject involving contrast between soft and loud material, but the 'ex nihilo' opening is abandoned for the sake of a chamber texture that diffidently inserts contrapuntal detail into a well-formed melody; unlike the mainly quadratic constructions that Bruckner used as themes in his symphonic movements, subtle overlaps and extensions generate a ten-bar period before the louder idea brings a note of classical regularity both in phrase structure and ornamentation. The second subject is not scrolled off from the first by a pause, nor is it a typical *Gesangsthema*, but it exhausts the possibilities of a number of rococo figures that climax in a unison passage. There are still changes of 'register', but their impact is of dynamic rather than tone colour, and the unison figures are more elaborate. Of the 'three-key exposition' described in Chapter 10 by Korstvedt, elements remain, since the second group is tonally mobile, and the final section, which recalls the loud material of the first subject in characteristic fashion, flirts with F♯ major, before the addition of a Schubertian A♭ pulls the music via a German sixth into the dominant, C major. In the closing bars of the exposition, echoing fragments provide clearer reminiscences of the tone of the Brucknerian symphony than the themes themselves.

Not the least curious moment is the opening of the development. At this point, Bruckner's outer movements almost invariably fall into a brooding quiet in which motivic fragments or simple rhythmic recollections refer to earlier thematic events. In the Quintet, he brings back fragments of the opening theme but disturbs its momentum with recitative-like passages for first violin and first viola. That Bruckner's orchestra often declaims against a sombre backcloth at this point in his symphonies is clear from such moments as the horn at the start of the development in the first movement of all three versions of the Third, the cellos at bar 177 in the Finale of the Sixth, and the melancholy tuba in the first movement of the Eighth. Even small details, such as the emphatic horn echo of the scherzo theme at bars 234–5 of the Finale of the Eighth (1890), have a rhetorical purpose, as they attempt to convey a content too full for mere notes. None of these instances gives quite such a clear example of instrumental oratory as the solos in the quintet; the melodic style of the opening of the movement leaps beyond its bounds to embrace the unison material of the second group. A surprisingly modern operatic dimension appears briefly, as though the writing of chamber music had peeled away a layer of Bruckner's tone to leave its technical correlative in an unusually bright glare.

Elsewhere surprises are fewer. The Scherzo possesses both the forward impetus and the quadratic structure that are characteristic of the symphonic equivalents, but with occasional hemiola effects and expansion. Thus the main theme at the opening creates an initial eight-bar period out of two four-bar phrases. The expected balancing eight-bar period, however, is expanded to twelve bars, thereby upsetting symmetry while retaining quadratic uniformity. This is a different kind of irregularity from that found in many of the early Bruckner symphonic scherzos, but is a clear model for a mature example such as that of the Seventh Symphony, which begins after a four-bar ostinato with a theme that expands an eight-bar period to sixteen by sequential extension of one idea.[21] The Trio confirms that in Bruckner it is a place for construction in tone-colour even in a chamber work: the bald juxtaposition of Ländler melody with pizzicato is comparable to the equivalent moment in the Sixth Symphony, where pizzicato and horns compete on the same rhythmic figure.

The tone and characteristics of the Brucknerian scherzo, which remain relatively fixed in spite of the interesting fluctuations according to period, thus carry over from symphony to chamber music. If the instrumental recitative of the first movement suggests Liszt at some distance, then the style of the Scherzo has been compared to a combination of Beethoven for his rhythmic drive and Schubert for his integration of popular Austrian dance idioms with the forms and procedures of 'high' art. The picture of the 'Austrian' Bruckner depends heavily upon comparison with Schubert. It is not simply a matter of popular idioms, there are the factors detailed by Floros: monumental construction, three theme complexes, tonal layout of the expositions, the 'song periods'.[22] In this context much that might seem discordant in the attempted reconciling of anachronistic and modern comes together on a nineteenth-century Austrian basis.

Even the harmony of the Quintet's Adagio encroaches upon Schubertian procedures when textures change at the prompting of a German sixth (bars 34–5), or when sequential patterns revolve around the rise of a third in the bass (bars 47–50). This is hardly surprising given the manner in which hymnal textures and Schubert's characteristic tonal procedures came together in songs like 'Das Wirtshaus' and 'Die Nebensonnen' and provided one model for the early Brucknerian Adagio in the Second and Third Symphonies. Such details had been absorbed into the common practice of tonality by Bruckner's day, however, as comparison with Brahms richly illustrates. Between them and the idea of a monumental layout interpretable as Schubertian 'heavenly length', there lie so many discrepancies that to speak of a common Austrian tone misses the distance that Bruckner travelled from Biedermeier to the verges of the modernism of the 1890s. If we are to understand Bruckner as an Austrian symphonist, it is necessary to see him within an age at once more characterized by a ritualized splendour and worship of the powerful and monumental in the past and present. That may be a crude estimate of Bruckner's relationship to his own time, but it is more truthful than the viewpoint that would see him in the timeless perspective of a mystical peasant.

8 Bruckner's symphonies – a reinterpretation: the dialectic of darkness and light

DEREK B. SCOTT

This chapter attempts to tease out some of the extra-musical meanings in Bruckner's symphonies by seeking to understand how the sacred character of his music is constructed, and how religious thought, especially relating to the dualism darkness/light, may have influenced Bruckner's compositional practice. It is well known that both light and darkness have important sacred connotations. Light is associated with goodness, morality, and salvation. In contrast, darkness has connotations of immorality (especially lust), evil, and hell. Bruckner's early familiarity with conventions for signifying light can be seen in the Offertory of his Requiem of 1849. Immediately following an agitated setting of 'ne absorbeat eas tartarus, ne cadant in obscurum', the C minor of 'tartarus' is exchanged for C major for the words 'sed signifer sanctus Michael repraesentet eas in lucem sanctam'. A similar change from minor to major occurs at the word 'Lux' in the Agnus Dei of the same work.

Life is associated with light – 'the light of life'[1] – as death is with darkness (the 'shadow of death' being a common image).[2] We find associations of C minor with death in the 'funeral marches' in the slow movements of the Fourth and the Sixth (its third theme). We can be certain about what the climax of the Adagio of the Seventh represented for Bruckner, since the 'Non confundar' theme of his Te Deum is quoted, and he described the beginning of the coda as 'funeral music for the Master'.[3] Here, the C major climax has connotations of 'lux sancta', the holy light of salvation for the believer (the divine response to the Te Deum words 'In te, Domine, speravi'). The use of low and high pitch as signifiers of life and death is evident in Bruckner's Masses, in each of which the words 'Judicare vivos et mortuos' are set with a high pitch for 'living' and a low pitch for 'dead'. That was how Beethoven treated them in his *Missa solemnis*, Haydn in his 'Nelson' Mass, and Schubert in his A♭ Mass of 1822 and, therefore, we can locate the historical specificity of Bruckner's musical signs. One would expect to find this feature in most eighteenth- and nineteenth-century Masses, but not in earlier Masses; indeed, William Byrd's Mass for four voices rises in pitch at the word 'mortuos'. The formative influence on Bruckner's semiotic markings was Austrian church music and the works of the Viennese classical composers. He became familiar with Mozart's Masses and Haydn's *Creation* during the year (1835–6) spent with his relation and godfather Johann Baptist Weiss, organist at Hörsching. His compositions rely on our knowledge of a sacred music paradigm, so that we recognize, say, the use of a chorale-like theme, a *Marienkadenz*, and other signs. The urge to quote his own liturgical music in his symphonies functions as a means of asserting a unitary sacred paradigm for his compositions. These self-quotations cover his entire symphonic career: for example, he quotes the 'miserere' of his early D minor Mass in bars 181–4 of the Adagio of his final symphony.

According to the Bible, darkness existed *before* God created light, and after creating light, God 'divided the light from the darkness'.[4] It was the latter image that Michelangelo placed on the ceiling of the Sistine Chapel immediately above the altar; it is the birth of form. Bruckner's tremolando beginnings have often been interpreted as birth tropes: August Halm remarks, 'we think we are inhaling something like the breath of creation, when we are enveloped in the first tones of his Seventh, Ninth, or Fourth Symphonies', and Derek Watson writes of 'the evocation of creation itself' in these beginnings.[5]

Max Auer's description of the openings of most Bruckner symphonies as 'an awakening from unconsciousness and darkness to light and clarity' could also be applied to most of his codas.[6] These are especially helpful for showing the appropriateness of the darkness/light trope, being tonally static. Robert Simpson comments that most of Bruckner's ultimate passages open 'in darkness'.[7] They then move from darkness to light, but it is not achieved, as in the Hegelian dialectic, through struggle and reconciliation; thus, the end is only a contingent victory. There can be no reconciliation of contradictions, since light cannot be reconciled with darkness.

The peculiarly non-muscular character of Bruckner's dialectic is in some ways epitomized by the lack of struggle between the polka theme and the chorale theme in the Finale of his Third Symphony. Here, again, a Hegelian dialectic cannot work because there can be no reconciliation between life and death.[8] More of a conflict *could* have been suggested; we have only to think of the third movement of Mahler's First Symphony. Yet, this polka-chorale, rather than signifying life struggling against death, seems to suggest the non-dialectical interpretation, 'In the midst of life we are in death.'[9]

In attempting to understand Bruckner's compositional process, we should note that the initial term of the opposition light/darkness both implies and is privileged over the other: darkness is absence of light; light is not absence of darkness.[10] Although light/darkness is not itself a metaphysical opposition (since darkness does differ *physically* from light), its connotations, with the exception of life/death, are metaphysical: for example, night can suggest the feminine, lust, and evil. Therefore, it offers itself up to Jacques

Derrida's deconstruction, which is concerned with demonstrating the priv-ileging of one term over another in metaphysical oppositions.[11] Moreover, light/darkness is metaphysical in Bruckner, because it exists only as *represen-tation*. Meaning in Bruckner is created by differing and deferring (Derrida's *différance*): a musical illustration of this is that minor does not simply differ from major; it is governed by major. Therefore the minor opening of the Third Symphony is not mistaken for the dominant term of the opposition major/minor; we know major will triumph, though its triumph is deferred. Minor is *always* the antithesis – but not a true antithesis, because Bruckner privileges major over minor. In Bruckner's music, *major is the command-ing term for ideological and not structural reasons*: major connotes light and minor connotes darkness; or, we might say, minor is a lack of major, as dark-ness is a lack of light. There is no structural reason why minor should not command major: to take an example from another composer, in Mahler's Sixth Symphony all light is extinguished (adumbrated early on by the tonic major triad's turn to tonic minor).

Apocalyptic vision in Bruckner's music

I now wish to argue that Bruckner's treatment of structure can often be understood as a process of revelation, thereby presenting us with a musical form of apocalyptic vision. Consider, for example, the unexpected revealing of the tonic at the point of recapitulation in the first movement of the Seventh Symphony (see Example 8.1), or the slow unveiling of the tonic in the first movement recapitulation of the Eighth (in both cases effected without strug-gle or drama). Also, consider Simpson's description of the Finale of that work as the 'cathedral' Bruckner has been trying to envisage during the course of the Symphony: 'One by one the impediments have been removed, until the image is clearly revealed.'[12] Liddell and Scott's *Greek–English Lexicon* gives 'an uncovering, (revelation N.T.)' as its definition of 'αποκαλυψις.[13] Again, an analogy may be found with Bruckner's formal method: Simpson described Bruckner's music as having a tendency 'to remove, one by one, dis-rupting or distracting elements, to seem to uncover at length a last stratum of calm contemplative thought'.[14] Ernst Bloch maintained that, in Bruck-ner's finales, 'the listener is released from the pressure of the temporal world in a contemplative review of the passions, territories and the established primary colour of the whole performance, in the expectation of visionary prospects and with the consciousness of standing at the birthplace of that which is lyrically essential in the symphony'.[15]

Instead of Beethoven's version of the Hegelian dialectic in his sonata form movements, where there is dramatic conflict of key and material in

Example 8.1 Symphony No. 7, I, bars 275–82

the exposition, struggle in the development section, and reconciliation in the recapitulation, Bruckner's dialectic of darkness and light involves slow discovery rather than muscular striving, and resolution without reconciliation. For, while we do have opposing forces, there is no sense of Hegel's 'inadequate thesis' v. 'inadequate antithesis' reaching finally a higher reconciling synthesis or sublation (*Aufhebung*) that preserves what is rational in them and cancels out the irrational. As an illustration of Hegelian sublation applied to sonata form, here is Rose Rosengard Subotnik explaining the reconciliation of dialectical opposites in middle-period Beethoven: 'through the recapitulation the subject seems not only to bring together within itself, but actually to derive from within itself, the principles of dynamic development (historical change) and fixed, eternal order (unchangeable identity) and to synthesize the two into a higher level of reality'.[16] In the dialectic of darkness and light we cannot move towards this higher synthesis. Apocalyptic literature emphasized the dualism of good and evil, gave structure to the notion of Heaven and Hell, and created the idea of the 'final judgement'. Good cannot achieve a higher synthesis with evil, nor Heaven with Hell; thus, the very existence of a dialectical conflict is questioned. This also holds for darkness and light: as stated earlier, darkness is understood as absence of light *and not vice-versa*. The first theme of Bruckner's Third does not undergo a tonal struggle to become 'light'; light (in the form of major tonality) is merely absent from it until the end of the Symphony. Changing the order in which major and minor appear makes no difference: in Bruckner's Seventh, where the opening theme is major, we do not interpret the dark inverted minor form of the theme midway through the movement as dominant, because we do not perceive a lack, a desire for darkness, in its major form.

Ernst Bloch expresses concern about the 'profound problem... of the musical finale as *happy ending*' in Bruckner and Beethoven. While agreeing that 'Climax and resolution are necessary', he insists that 'Through darkness to light!' or the joyous ending 'does not stem from the music-making itself in an inexorable way'. As I have argued, there is no innately musical logic for Bruckner's Third to end in D major rather than D minor. Bloch is looking for an inner human essence making itself felt in the musical processes themselves, so that joy is achieved by the work itself and not just by the will of the composer: he speaks of 'a birth of faith out of music, coming from the quietest, innermost, farthest depths of the musician's soul' which could 'finally strike up the "Sed signifer sanctus Michael"'.[17] But there *is* no inexorable logic about darkness moving to light; and in the Christian religion movement from darkness to light is interpreted precisely as a matter of free will. Bloch's search for deeper unity and organic growth in music is motivated by his need to find logical explanations for what is happening on the surface. Today, we must recognize that postmodernist theory, poststructuralism, and deconstruction have strongly challenged notions of organic unity and the composer's expressive presence within his/her music. Concern with 'deep structure' in Bruckner, and the presence of multiple versions of his music, gives rise to something similar to demands for the 'Director's cut' in film – the Haas editions are just such an attempt to provide the originary, univocal creations of the 'master artist'. It is instructive to read Rose Rosengard Subotnik on Adorno's opinion that exaggeration enters Beethoven's preparations for recapitulation as he begins to realize that 'the principle of reprise... arises from no logical necessity within the subject'.[18] She explains: 'By contrast with logical implication, as embodied in the syllogism, musical implication, as Adorno understands it to occur in the classical style, is a temporal rather than a formal process... musical implication makes itself fully known only in terms of an actual and hence subsequent resolution.'[19]

In Bruckner, imbalance is created between tonal forces without the sense of physical struggle found in Beethoven. Simpson remarks of the first movement of Bruckner's Seventh: 'Throughout the whole first part of the movement B major takes over, as it were, by stealth, in a manner remote from the muscular action of sonata.'[20] I would argue that this is why the metaphors of darkness and light so often work in Bruckner – because darkness does not *struggle* to become light. Instead, night is either *gradually transformed* into day, or a light *suddenly shines* in the darkness. The inversion of the main theme in the C minor middle section of this movement (bars 233–6) may constitute a moment of crisis, but it is not generated as part of a process of tonal tension and release. As a result, no stability is achieved when the home key is reached at the start of the recapitulation. While the C minor passage may readily be interpreted as the dark antithesis of the movement's opening (this key carrying, as it does, connotations of death), it should be emphasized that *inversion* itself does not work as an opposite in musical semantics. When the 'Miserere' motive from the Gloria of the D minor Mass appears in inverted form in the Adagio of the Ninth (the A♭ theme at bar 45), it does not become 'Jubilate'. Notice, also, that when the fugue subject of Bruckner's Psalm 150 is inverted it is still sung to the same words. The inverted theme in the Seventh Symphony *does* work as an opposite, however, because musical *descent* has been established by convention as an opposite to *ascent* in music of this style and period, and the inversion of this theme produces an unwavering descent.

Since many musicologists have commented on the gendered character of nineteenth-century sonata structures, we should consider the applicability of such ideas to Bruckner. Susan McClary summarizes the argument, thus:

> In sonata, the principal key/theme clearly occupies the narrative position of masculine protagonist; and while the less dynamic second key/theme is *necessary* to the sonata or tonal plot (without this foil or obstacle, there is no story), it serves the narrative function of the feminine Other. Moreover, satisfactory resolution – the ending always generically guaranteed in advance by tonality and sonata procedure – demands the containment of whatever is semiotically or structurally marked as 'feminine', whether a second theme or simply a non-tonic key area.[21]

McClary is discussing what she regards as a typical sonata narrative and what she describes elsewhere as 'tonal striving, climax, and closure'.[22] Bruckner's climaxes, however, are not really reached by tonal striving – we remarked upon its absence in discussing the Seventh Symphony's first movement above. There is more in the way of tonal *balancing* in Bruckner. I am referring here to balanced tonal masses rather than a balance of power. In a rudimentary musical structure, for example, a move from tonic to dominant may be balanced by a flat-side move to the subdominant. This does not mean that the tonic does not remain the commanding tonal area; the tonic chord was the *Generalissimus* for Bruckner.[23] Constantin Floros has remarked: 'For all Bruckner's modulatory flexibility, the harmonic design is always lucid and methodical.'[24] Equal attention is devoted to balancing his phrase structure, building short blocks into huge formal designs.[25]

Transfiguration of themes

I am not the first to recognize the appropriateness of the word 'transfigure' to Bruckner's music. Crawford Howie claims, 'In no other settings of the Mass is one so aware of the transfiguration of the contrite mood of the opening Kyrie into the confident mood of the final "Dona nobis pacem".'[26] Erwin Doernberg speaks of 'two delicately transfigured greetings from the Eighth and Seventh Symphonies' at the close of the Adagio of the Ninth.[27] As long ago as 1907, Willibald Kähler described the Adagio of the Eighth as 'solemnly transfigurative'.[28] I wish to use 'transfigure' in a more specific sense, however, in what I have to say below. By describing any theme or motive as 'transfigured', I mean that it acquires a new 'radiance' while its rhythmic identity remains unchanged.[29] This radiance may be created by an alteration from minor to major, from low to high pitch, or from chromatic to diatonic, and in each of these cases a change in texture is usually involved. Examples are found as early as the coda to the G minor Overture (1863) and, in this piece, the 'transfiguring' may derive from Beethoven. Just before the coda of the first movement of Beethoven's Ninth (bars 469–76), the development's minor fugue subject (bars 218–23) changes to major, resembling a procedure adopted in Bruckner's Overture.

Beethoven's coda, however, reasserts darkness, and nowhere else does the light shine upon this theme nor upon any of his dark themes. To have concluded his Ninth Symphony with a loud tonic major version of the first subject of the first movement, as Bruckner does in his Third, would have been out of the question. A resolution in Beethoven's dialectic has to be reached by agreement, even if this can only be attained by bitter struggle. In contrast, Bruckner often presents a sudden outright victory, but with a sense that the conflict may recommence. Sometimes, a theme seems to epitomize *lux in tenebris*: the revelation of the final bars of the Third, for example, is that the trumpet theme has from the beginning been designed for transfiguration by the tonic major chord (it is accomplished by the alteration of a single note). Light is absent at first, but destined to shine in the darkness at the end. I think the most likely prototype for this type of Brucknerian transfiguration occurs at the end of Wagner's *Der fliegende Holländer*, where the Dutchman and Senta appear as 'verklärte Gestalten' (transfigured forms) as they ascend to heaven. The Dutchman's motive is lit by major harmony without any change to its melodic structure, thus

Example 8.2   The Flying Dutchman's motive (a) at the beginning and (b) at the end of the opera

(a)

(b)

demonstrating a remarkable resemblance to what happens in Bruckner's Third Symphony (see Examples 8.2 and 8.3).[30]

Bruckner does not transform his themes by changing tempo, metre, and rhythm (like, say, Liszt in *Tasso*); he transfigures them by changing pitches and harmony. Carl Dahlhaus remarks that 'Bruckner's symphonic style … is primarily rhythmic rather than diastematic, and thus seems to stand the usual hierarchy of tonal properties on its head.'[31] When Bruckner changes the pitch structure (the diastematic structure) of his motives, 'there is no need to search for an overriding thematic process to legitimize the change' as one would seek to do with Brahms.[32] In certain cases, pitch is undoubtedly important: inversions, for example, are not accidents. However, Bruckner does not conform to the musical logic of the Brahmsian 'developing variation' for which pitch structure is the crucial parameter. Bruckner, it may be noted, uses inversion, augmentation, diminution, but not retrograde, which drastically affects rhythm.

Let us examine various kinds of transfigurations in the later symphonies. In the coda of the first movement of the Sixth, the theme that, for Simpson, originally heaved 'darkly in the depths', now 'rises and falls like some great ship, the water illuminated in superb hues as the sun rises, at last bursting

Example 8.3   (a) The opening and (b) the closing theme of Bruckner's Symphony No. 3

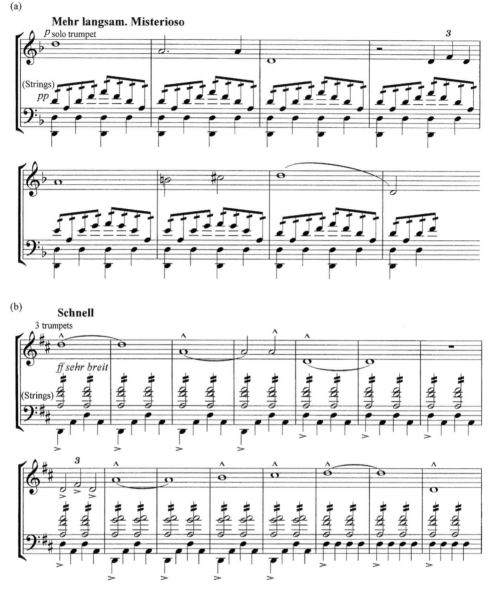

clear in the sky'.[33] The theme is here transfigured by an alteration in shape, a transposition upwards in pitch, 'glowing' brass timbre and a new accompaniment of religiously symbolic plagal harmony. At the close of the symphony, the theme is transfigured by a change from Phrygian mode to diatonic major while, above it, the string figure from bars 29–30 of the Finale returns transfigured by a change from chromaticism to diatonicism. These changes conform to my earlier definition of transfiguration as a process in which rhythmic identity is retained while other parameters are altered in a way that marks them semiotically as 'elevated', 'glowing', and so forth.

Watson speaks of the 'grim darkness' of the C minor inverted statement of the main theme in the first movement of the Seventh, which is in marked contrast to the close of the movement, when E major 'shines forth'.[34] A parallel may be found in Raphael's *Transfiguration* (1517–20), in the Vatican Museum, Rome. This painting, which Bruckner may well have known, is based on St Matthew's description of Christ's transfiguration: 'his face did shine as the sun, and his raiment was white as the light'.[35] It is interpreted by the art historian Linda Murray as follows: 'The contrast between the divine radiance of the vision and earthly confusion and sorrow, between the means of salvation in which one must believe rather than just witness, and the blindness and suffering of unregenerate human nature, made insensible of its state by possession of sin, seems to be the programme behind this work.'[36] Raphael depicts a light/darkness opposition, which Murray reads metaphorically as 'vision' and 'blindness'. The clear-cut division into faith and sin would no doubt have appealed to Bruckner.

The Eighth Symphony contains some of the most remarkable examples of Bruckner's technique of thematic transfiguration. The main motive of the first movement is identical in rhythm to the first subject in the opening movement of Beethoven's Ninth, as Doernberg points out.[37] This is more than simple coincidence for, although they have only rhythm in common, this is the crucial parameter for Bruckner. The motive is, in fact, restricted to a single pitch for what Bruckner described as the 'annunciation of death', but is transfigured as a C major broken chord at the Symphony's close. The 'annunciation of death' is followed by what Bruckner called the *Totenuhr*. Rather than 'hour of death', this refers to the *Klopfkäfer* (knocking beetle), whose sound was a sign, in folklore, for impending death.[38] The negative impact of the ending of the first movement is counterbalanced by the extremely positive effect of four simultaneous thematic transfigurations at the symphony's close. Moreover, the transfigured main themes from each movement are joined by a fifth transfiguration: it is of a figure which appeared in C minor at the beginning of the coda and now resounds in C major. After the first performance of the Eighth, no wonder Hugo Wolf felt impelled to write that it was 'an absolute victory of light over darkness'.[39]

Plateaus of intensity

Bruckner's music presents us with plateaus of intensity rather than orgasmic releases. His method of breaking off, replacing, then reinstating is not the typical tonal process of tension and relaxation. Because there is no reconciliation in Bruckner's dialectic, the resolution of conflict needs massive emphasis, and yet may still be heard as uncertain, conditional, abrupt. In a commentary on John 1: 1–5, A. E. Brooke explains that in men 'life takes the higher form of "light", moral and spiritual life' of which God is the source, and that the 'fight between this light and its opposite, the moral darkness of evil, has always been going on, and the light has never been conquered'.[40] The phrase *lux in tenebris* affirms that light has never been conquered – but, then, neither has darkness. Perhaps all climaxes for Bruckner are contingent until the *tuba mirum* sounds for Judgement Day. Until then, darkness cannot be completely and forever vanquished by light. The fact that darkness so often returns at the beginnings of his codas shows the provisional nature of his climaxes. If brightness can be eclipsed at this late stage, what sense of finality is really achieved in the concluding blaze of sound? Bruckner seeks a spiritual closure in his codas, but it is never more than provisionally attained, because any sense of a *telos* (or final goal) has been displaced by a multiplicity of break-flows and reversals.

For Watson, the C major climax of the slow movement of the Seventh is 'a most wonderful letting in of the light'.[41] Yet, in the bar prior to this blaze of light, we are poised on the dominant of C♯ minor, the movement's tonic. Halfway through this bar, the dominant harmony is interpreted enharmonically as a German sixth in C major/minor, facilitating an abrupt shift of tonal direction. The massive C major climax in this C♯ minor movement satisfies an *ideological*, not a *structural* need. Its meaning must be sought in an intertextual field of reference; it is not to be found embodied in an autonomous compositional logic. The climax of the Adagio of the original Eighth was also C major, a key that had already been loudly proclaimed in this first version at the end of the first movement. It may be that Bruckner resited this climax tonally to avoid resemblance with its predecessor. However, like Watson, I am inclined to assume that when Bruckner revised the loud C major ending of the first movement, he changed the climax of the Adagio for the same reason, to maximize the impact of the C major climax to the Finale. Watson is surely wrong, however, to claim that the original first movement ending 'weakens the overall tonal pattern'.[42] The revised ending is also in C major, although it may not feel much like it (and the last nine bars are hollow fifths). The devout Bruckner could not allow what he himself termed, with its religious connotations, an 'annunciation of death' to be followed by a nihilistic minor conclusion as Tchaikovsky or Mahler might have done. In the original version it is the *triumphal impact* of C major at the symphony's conclusion that is weakened, not the symphony's overall tonal pattern.

Bruckner's main climaxes may resonate darkly as *quantus tremor, dies irae*, or the 'shadow of death', or they may blaze radiantly as *rex gloriae, Gloria/Hosanna in excelsis*, or *lux sancta*. The Finale of the Fifth, which Simpson labelled 'one of the greatest climaxes in symphonic music', is a climax of the *Gloria/Hosanna* type.[43] The first fugue subject is three bars long, like that which Bruckner later gave to the words 'Alles was Odem hat' in Psalm 150, and the two are clearly related. There are no erotic 'Tristan' climaxes in Bruckner; he builds climaxes not with 'yearning' appoggiaturas, but by accretion of motives – and his climaxes end far too abruptly. While a tragic climax, complete with 'aching' or 'despairing' appoggiaturas sometimes occurs (for instance, the Adagio of the Eighth, bars 125–8, 1890 version), it is never the movement's, or symphony's, *main* climax. Bruckner avoids the heroic climax, too, and this is not to be put down solely to an absence of percussion and martial rhythmic figures. The difference between Brucknerian transfigurations and heroic transformations of material can be understood clearly by studying the endings of Liszt's *Tasso* and *Les Préludes*. Eero Tarasti comments that the 'fanfare theme' of *Les Préludes* 'moves in the Beethovenian tonality of triumph, C major but whose dotted rhythmic figure, the unison sound of heavy wind instruments, cellos and basses as well as plagal harmonies give this theme an ideal and sublime hero-mythical quality typical of Liszt'.[44] It was not inappropriately used many years ago as incidental music to the American film serial *Flash Gordon Conquers the Universe*. Simpson declares that the typical Bruckner Finale is 'not really a summing-up, despite the immense climaxes that end the Fifth and Eighth symphonies. Such climaxes, far from being driven by the accumulated energy of a vividly muscular process (as in a classical symphony) or by the warring of emotive elements (as in the purely romantic work), are rather the final intensification of an essence.'[45] For Cooke, too, a Bruckner Finale is not 'the culminating high point of the symphony'; its function is rather to 'simply ratify the world of the first three movements on a larger scale'.[46] Simpson's and Cooke's comments provide evidence for my contention that it is more appropriate to speak of plateaus in Bruckner's music rather than peaks. Evidence, in the shape of performance, can be found to support this interpretation – I am thinking, especially, of Sergiu Celibidache and the Münchner Philharmoniker. The typical Bruckner climax is attained as a plateau of intensity, as distinct from the more usual nineteenth-century process of arsis, climax, and catharsis. The various stages of Bruckner's formal process, states Cooke, 'are not offered as dynamic phases of a drama, but as so many different viewpoints from which to absorb the basic material'.[47]

Gregory Bateson's idea of a 'plateau of intensity' which he finds, for example, in Balinese culture, has been taken up by Gilles Deleuze and Félix Guattari.[48] They explain this plateau as 'a continuous, self-vibrating region of intensities whose development avoids any orientation toward a culmination point or external end'.[49] The idea leads them to envisage a book which, instead of chapters having culmination and termination points, is composed of 'plateaus that communicate with one another across microfissures'.[50] The

Bible might already be thought to approach this description, and so do Bruckner's non-culminative and fissured structures.[51] Heinrich Schenker complained that Bruckner's musical thought 'admits no inner need for a middle, a beginning, or even an end';[52] and a later music analyst, Derrick Puffett, commented on 'determinedly non-functional (dysfunctional?) harmony' in the Adagio of the Ninth Symphony.[53] The parallel should not be overdone: Deleuze and Guattari have a much freer assemblage in mind than a Bruckner symphony; but let us explore further. By 'plateau', they explain that they mean 'any multiplicity connected to other multiplicities by superficial underground stems in such a way as to form or extend a rhizome'.[54] Cooke's 'ratifying on a larger scale' would suggest just such an extension. Furthermore, Simpson insists, 'The massive endings of all Bruckner's symphonies are (with the exception of that of the Fifth) not really culminative in the old sense; they are formal intensifications that blaze with calm.'[55]

Simpson contrasts Beethoven's review of previous themes in the Finale of his Ninth as a means of 'discovering' the Joy theme, with Bruckner's reminiscing in the Finale of his Third (1873 version). He also remarks of the introduction to the Fifth's Finale : 'Bruckner recalls the old themes because it is an effective way of discussing how to get back to B♭ after all that D minor. There is no question of rejecting the themes.'[56] Again, this is contrary to Beethoven's Ninth, and supports the 'plateau of intensity' argument. Watson suggests that the return of opening themes at the ends of the symphonies has its roots in the traditional practice of concluding Masses with reference to thematic material of the Kyrie, a feature common to Bruckner's Masses.[57] This would explain the reminiscing feel to Bruckner's quotations in finales.

I have argued that the Bruckner climax is provisional, and would suggest that the lack of synthesis in his work is made evident by the lack of, or difficulties in obtaining, closure. Darkness keeps returning. For example, after the climax at letter F in the Finale of the Second Symphony, there is an abrupt silence, then a *pp* quotation (bar 200, Haas edition) from the Kyrie of the F minor Mass (bar 122 onwards) and the exposition concludes in this mood (with a plagal cadence). The Kyrie is quoted again (bar 547, Haas edition) shortly before the coda; it is again *pp* following an *fff* climax and eight unexpectedly quiet intervening bars. The coda itself fails to achieve closure at its first attempt. I cannot agree, therefore, with Newlin's view that 'Bruckner's ideal finale is one in which all that has happened in the preceding movements is synthesized', and that such a synthesis 'is symbolized in the citation of themes from previous sections of the work'.[58] In the closing bars of the Sixth, two themes from the Finale are presented simultaneously with a transfigured version of the main theme of the opening movement, yet Simpson remarks, rightly it seems to me, on its inconclusiveness. The 'nocturnal mystery'[59] with which the Finale opens has passed, and 'the A major sun is high in the sky', but the ending 'leaves dark questions unanswered'.[60] I assume he has in mind the gestures towards B♭ minor at letter X and at bar 397, which are too close to the movement's end for comfort. Ernst Kurth notes perceptively that harmonic and instrumental darkenings frequently occur 'at the moment of achieved apexes' in Bruckner's music.[61] He sees it as symptomatic of Bruckner's anxiety in the midst of exuberance. On the other hand, exuberance can be found in the midst of anxiety. Doernberg remarks of the end of the Second Symphony: 'when a defiant C minor ending seems inevitable, there is a striking change to the major and the symphony ends with positive confidence'.[62] Confidence, however, is never secure. Bryan Gilliam writes of the first movement of the Eighth: 'as Bruckner originally conceived it, the movement's chief dramatic event was a final presentation of the tonally ambiguous opening theme – at the very end of the coda – now resonantly clarified into an unambiguous tonal context'.[63] Indeed, the coda of the first version concludes with seventeen loud bars of C major. Gilliam claims that Bruckner 'clearly intended the coda as an apotheosis';[64] therefore, the revision 'represents a fundamental change from his original structural concept'.[65] One might also add that it represents a fundamental change of mood. Bruckner, from the G minor Overture on,[66] is always at his least secure when trying to attain closure, which is why his music lends substance to Deleuze and Guattari's claim that 'musical form, right down to its ruptures and proliferations, is comparable to a weed, a rhizome'.[67]

Doernberg, commenting on the climax of the Adagio of the Ninth, remarks that 'No solution is offered to the paroxysm of dissonance and restlessness.'[68] The music is shattered at this point; yet, it revives. Like Deleuze and Guattari's rhizome, it 'may be broken, shattered at a given spot, but it will start up again on one of its old lines, or on new lines'.[69] Examples are legion in his symphonies: at letter N in the first movement of the Eighth (after the third *fff* statement of the main theme) the music splinters into fragments, but then begins to reconstruct itself; at letter D in the Finale of the Eighth, the music starts up on new lines after having broken off (at I, and between P and T, there are other examples).[70]

Conclusion

It has not been my intention to argue that Bruckner's music is solely about darkness and light; neither has it been my contention that Bruckner's music is sacred to the exclusion of all else. Constantin Floros sums up the contradictory elements embraced in the cosmos of the Bruckner symphony as 'the sacred and profane, the ceremonial and the intimate, religious and romantic, drama and lyricism, march and funeral march, the *Ländler* and the chorale'.[71] Ländler rhythms can be found in the Scherzos of the Third and Fifth Symphonies. Bruckner was once in demand as a fiddler at village dances, loved dancing himself, and wrote dance music for piano. He was disappointed in love many times, and was far from uninterested in romance. His love interests probably spilled over into his songs and piano music, for example, 'Mein Herz und deine Stimme' and *Steiermärker*). He referred to his First Symphony as ' 's kecke Beserl' which, according to Newlin, was 'a favourite expression of Viennese students designating a bold young girl'.[72] Ludwig Finscher regards this symphony as a secular work in contrast to 'die Nullte' (Symphony No. 0) which conforms to the sacred paradigm.[73] Bruckner often described a lyrical second group of themes in his scores as *Gesangsthema* or *Gesangsperiode,* and it is possible that 'feminine' connotations may be found here. Ludwig Wittgenstein considered this section of a Bruckner symphony the 'wife' to the 'husband' of the first subject.[74] Nevertheless, it is important to recognize a distinction between a gendered theme and a gendered sonata structure. To use Tarasti's semantic vocabulary, there is a sacred isotopy in Bruckner's music into which other mythical semes merge. In the Fourth, it could be argued that the nature-mythical and the pastoral dominate; in this work Martin Pulbrook claims that there is evidence of Bruckner's making a conscious effort to move away from 'specifically religious inspiration'.[75]

I have argued that darkness and light proves to be a productive trope for understanding certain structural and ideological processes in his music; and this is partly, of course, because darkness and light are themselves not just about darkness and light. Both terms are rich in the connotations, especially of a religious kind, that were deep concerns of the composer. The darkness and light trope reveals Bruckner to be a man of religious doubt. The blaze of light following the repetitions of the 'Non confundar in aeternam' theme in the Adagio of his Seventh Symphony turns quickly to darkness: three bars after a massive climactic assertion of C major (bars 177–82) we are cast into a despondent C♯ minor. Bruckner cannot be sure whether he will be confounded or not. His friend and ex-pupil Carl Hruby claimed that he was 'a perfect example of speculative Christianity: he wanted to be insured against every eventuality'.[76] Two years before his death, his private diaries reveal him meditating on the words of the anatomist Hyrtl: 'Is that which Faith calls the immortal soul of man only an organic reaction of the brain?'[77] Enormous imaginative richness and variety of detail can be encompassed in a journey from darkness to light. For further exemplification of the variety of possibilities available, one has only to compare Bruckner's symphonies with the darkness-to-light journeys of the Second, Fifth and

Seventh Symphonies of the temperamentally very different Mahler. Newlin suggests that 'certain stylistic traits' are persistent in all Bruckner's symphonies, and may be thought of as symptomatic of a 'higher unity among the works'.[78] It is, perhaps, the reason a light/darkness trope works so consistently. It is the case, sadly, that Bruckner has even been pilloried in terms of darkness and light: Hanslick, after the first Viennese performance of the Seventh in 1886, complained, 'in between the lightnings are interminable stretches of darkness'.[79]

9 Programme symphony and absolute music

JOHN WILLIAMSON

The quarter century in which Bruckner composed his first symphonies contained no shortage of symphonies in general, and they exhibit considerable diversity of genre and style but they have largely not survived in the concert hall: although there remain many good reasons for claiming the symphony as the central genre of instrumental music in the nineteenth century, the years 1850–75 constitute a period richer in historical themes than in major works. Of 507 symphonic works considered in a recent survey, some have survived though overshadowed by their composer's later output (e.g. the first five symphonies of Dvořák). Others have lived on as rare examples of the genre from composers whose career flourished in other fields (e.g. Smetana's 'Triumphal' Symphony). Symphonists who have been rediscovered in the age of recording include the underrated Gernsheim, while Gade and Raff serve as examples of prolific composers who have clung on tenuously to experience intermittent modest revivals.[1] The vast majority belong in the category of 'forgotten symphonies' discussed in another recently published thesis on 'epigonality' in the symphony.[2]

The influence of Liszt seems reflected in the large number of programmatic works: symphonies, symphonic poems, and a host of intermediate genres such as the symphonic fantasy and overture-symphony. Closer inspection, however, discourages viewing the programmatic phenomenon uniformly as a monument to the triumph of the New German School. Among composers with a biographical link to Weimar is Raff, who composed programme symphonies that show little formal or procedural resemblance to Liszt; Draeseke serves as an example of a composer of symphonic poems who later turned to older concepts of the 'characteristic' symphony with few claims to the rhetoric of the 'poetic' espoused by Liszt.[3]

This diversity extended to the manner in which programme symphonies were disseminated: 'In the Gewandhaus, Liszt was practically boycotted; whoever wanted to have a responsible say in the party conflict had to visit the Euterpe Concert Society. In comparison no justification was evidently needed for the performance of programme symphonies by the likes of Rheinberger, Abert, Hiller, or Rubinstein even in the renowned institutions such as the Gewandhaus or Cologne's Gürzenich Concerts.'[4] This should serve as a caution in considering the historical significance of Bruckner's attitude towards the programmatic.

Whether Bruckner can in any strict sense be said to have composed 'programme symphonies' is contentious. There is a long tradition of regarding his symphonies as 'absolute music', defined in ways that are not simply to be seen in opposition to programme music or as related to Hanslick's aesthetics; the most complex example of this is Ernst Kurth's attempt to define Bruckner's symphonies as 'absolute' in a double sense: as expression of an 'absolute' and as 'detached from song'; more recently Carl Dahlhaus has provided a restatement of the view that Bruckner was a composer of 'absolute music'.[5]

In spite of this the issue of programmes has never entirely been banished from Bruckner studies. This is not simply a matter of anecdotes or the interpretations of commentators. Constantin Floros, the champion of the view that Bruckner created programme music in the Fourth and Eighth Symphonies, speaks in terms that suggest the expounding of a canonical text. Yet the programmes themselves are hardly sustained enough to survive without interpretation and Floros justified his efforts by reference to the Lisztian variety of symphonic poetry and to the Wagnerian music drama, viewing these and Berlioz as the realization of the 'New German School' that was dreamt of in mid-century Weimar.[6] This is far from necessary.

Bruckner certainly supplied enough programmatic hints about these symphonies to construct narratives. Even the subtitle 'Romantic' attached to the Fourth in itself permits more or less legitimate speculation. As distinguished a Bruckner scholar as Leopold Nowak displayed a degree of ambivalence on the matter: 'The blending of poetry and music in instrumental music was alien to Bruckner. He was a lifelong artist of absolute music, organ, and orchestra. Even the Fourth Symphony is in its basic structure of classical form'; he acknowledged, however, that the Scherzo of the Fourth is an 'example of real programme music in Bruckner' and relaxed into a variety of programmatic hermeneutics when discussing the rest of the symphony.[7]

Something similar occurred to Walter Wiora, who, beginning with hunt and dance in the Scherzo, went on to describe the Fourth as a whole in relation to 'the Romanesque fantasy landscape of the "wood"' and noted that it was the only Bruckner symphony 'in which he approached the idea of programme music for which Beethoven had supplied a model in his "Pastoral"'. This comment at once distances the Fourth to some extent from the religious traits that Wiora saw in the other symphonies. But Wiora is also prepared to make a similar distinction to that of Nowak about the Fourth's Scherzo. He noted that there was a 'reverence' in Bruckner's feeling for nature but that it was distinct from the religious sense to be found in the majority of his symphonies; yet even passages touched by the sense of natural phenomena 'often reach into the sphere of the numinous' in cases such as the unison theme from the Fourth's Finale or 'the mysterious beginning of the development' in the first movement.[8] In these circumstances it is legitimate to consider how far Bruckner's explanations of the contents of two of his symphonies express some elements of their content.

The programme for the Fourth Symphony can be collated from Bruckner's explanations to various friends, with some corroboration from his correspondence. References to it as a 'Romantic' symphony occur as early as 1874 and 1876 and are thus associated with the earliest version.[9] Particular weight has been placed on Bernhard Deubler's account communicated by Theodor Helm (who thought all such explanations should be taken 'cum grano salis'):

> Mediaeval city – Daybreak – Morning calls sound from the city towers – the gates open – On proud horses the knights burst out into the open, the magic of nature envelops them – forest murmurs – bird song – and so the Romantic picture develops further . . .

Elsewhere Helm clarified the bird song as the 'twittering' of a titmouse, citing violin motives from the second theme group of the first movement (bar 75 of the 1878–80 version) set against 'the particular feeling of happiness . . . at being able to hear such friendly voices of nature in the wood' in the violas.[10]

The strongest evidence for taking this seriously comes less from such comments as 'Jagdthema' (hunting theme), 'Tanzweise während der Mahlzeit auf der Jagd' (dance tune during the lunch break while hunting), or 'Volksfest' (people's festival) on autograph material for the 1878 Scherzo and Finale than from letters to Hermann Levi (8 December 1884) and Paul Heyse (22 December 1890). The first refers to 'the Romantic Fourth in E♭', recommends the 'first and third movements' and notes: 'In the first movement after a full night's sleep the day is announced by the horn, 2nd movement song, 3rd movement hunting trio, musical entertainment of the hunters in the wood.'[11] According to the second, 'In the first movement of the "Romantic" Fourth Symphony the intention is to depict the horn that proclaims the day from the town hall! Then life goes on; in the *Gesangsperiode* the theme is the song of the great tit *Zizipe*. 2nd movement: song, prayer, serenade. 3rd: hunt and in the Trio how a barrel-organ plays during the midday meal in the forest.'[12]

The persistence with which Bruckner refers to the various elements in these accounts suggests that they indeed reflect something of Bruckner's own thinking. From this recognition two directions lead to full-blown hermeneutics. There are those that pursue the notion of a 'Romantic' symphony from the viewpoint of *Naturromantik* as opposed to Floros' own tendency to read 'Romantic' as belonging to a mystical-religious ethos with a symbolic narrative. The 'mystical-religious' and nature are admittedly both connected intimately with German Romanticism. Whether Romanticism stands for 'an indistinct symbolic reinterpretation of Catholicism', or is the product of 'the knightly spirit and the crusades' as 'children of the Christian', it is not absolutely clear to what degree the programmatic hints about the 'Romantic' Symphony sustain that degree of poetic intensity.[13]

One of the problems with the programme of the Fourth is the lack of reference to the Finale, since the hint contained in the title 'Volksfest' seems to belong only to the Finale of 1878, while the description of the opening as 'Regenwetter' equally clearly belongs to 1874; for the third Finale completed in 1880, it is necessary to fall back on Bruckner anecdotes about the 'swansong of Romanticism' or theories of the 'terrors of nature' as 'storms of the soul'.[14] A similar sense of incompleteness haunts the Eighth Symphony's programme, though to a lesser degree. Only three movements are represented in the letter to Weingartner of 27 January 1891 that establishes the narrative. Since the omission is the Adagio, the longest and most affecting movement, the programme steers the listener down channels that are not entirely consistent with the apocalyptic terms in which this work is sometimes described.[15]

> In the first movement the trumpet and horn passage from the rhythm of the theme is *the proclamation of death*, which enters sporadically ever stronger and finally very strong, at the close: resignation.
>
> Scherzo: main theme: called 'deutscher Michel'; in the second part the rascal wants to sleep and dreamily doesn't find his little song; finally it plaintively turns itself upside down.
>
> Finale. Our Emperor at that time received the visit of the Tsars in Olmütz; hence strings: ride of the Cossacks; brass: martial music; trumpets: fanfare as their majesties meet. Finally *all* themes; (comic), just as in *Tannhäuser* in the second act the king comes, so, as *der deutsche Michel* arrives from his journey, everything is already brilliant.
>
> In the Finale too there is the death march and then (brass) transfiguration.[16]

As Korstvedt notes, this programme is an interesting and not entirely convincing combination of elements that are opportunistic on the one hand and deeply rooted on the other. Among the latter are the references to *der deutsche Michael* and the meeting of the three emperors, both of which are mentioned by Bruckner's acquaintances and in his letters.[17] But in addition to these there are further programmatic hints reported by Bruckner intimates, but supposedly in the composer's own words, relating to the first movement ...

> That is the death watch beetle... that ticks implacably, without let-up, until everything is over...!
>
> Thus it is when someone is dying, and opposite hangs the clock, which, while his life draws to an end – keeps on beating regularly: tick, tock, tick, tock...[18]

...and to the slow movement: 'There I have gazed too deeply into a maiden's eyes.'[19]

The last example is a useful demonstration of how a seemingly authentic (though undeniably banal) clue can be jettisoned in the face of received ideas as to the contents of Bruckner's symphonies. Hardly a commentator pays it serious attention apart from Thomas Röder's comment that it 'fits reasonably into the context of the...affinity of religious and subtly erotic tones'.[20] The slow movement evokes from most writers the idea of the 'sublime' (best represented by Korstvedt) or of religious ecstasy. This agrees with the notion of Bruckner's music as manifestation of the absolute in the first sense noted by Kurth. But the second sense is not far removed and enters the picture in Eckstein's description of the composition of the Adagio.

Bruckner apparently resisted the inclusion of harps although there were examples in Liszt because they suggested 'tone-painting, programme music, symphonic poems, but not real symphonies in the strict sense'. When the harps were finally included, Eckstein surrendered to the sense of the transcendental (albeit in Bruckner's performance at the piano):

> Deeply shaken I listened to the solemn entry of the three [sic] harps, which spread their magic sounds over the solemn choir of the multiply divided strings and seemed thus to lift the entire movement above everything earthly.[21]

The harps are rescued from the Lisztian tradition for a symphony that is absolute both in being non-programmatic and in moving the listener to fantasize about the absolute.

If interpretations of the slow movement have stressed the numinous, 'German Michael' has proved more ambivalent, with both a religious dimension (most simply denoted in Floros' reminder that Michael was Bruckner's patron saint) and a German national element expressed most trenchantly by Albrecht Dümling as '"Germany awake!" composed out'.[22] To draw this into the web of the Romantic mystical and sublime sometimes required a degree of ideological cloudiness satirized in an earlier age by Heine in *Die romantische Schule*: 'When German patriotism and nationality finally triumphed, there also triumphed the folksy-German-Christian-Romantic school, the "new-German-religious-patriotic art". Napoleon the great classicist, as classical as Alexander and Caesar, collapsed to the floor and Herren August Wilhelm and Friedrich Schlegel, the little Romantics...rose as victors.'[23]

That patriotic readings of the Eighth were particularly characteristic of the Nazi period lends retrospective force to Heine's irony and to Bruckner's remark that the 'German Michael' was meant as 'no joke'.[24]

Writers who stress the 'absolute musician' in Bruckner and those who take the programmes rather more seriously tend to unite, at least as far as the Eighth in concerned, in the same interpretative stream. Differences tend to arise over the ways in which patriotic and religious elements are combined, and Korstvedt gives an interesting demonstration of the ways in which a modern post-semiotic ear listens to categories such as the 'sublime' with an aesthetic or historical, rather than a metaphysical, sensibility. The case of the Fourth is rather different, as might almost be predicted from the many-layered connotations of 'Romantic'.

That continuity exists between Bruckner's various comments on the Fourth and an interpretative (as opposed to an exegetic) tradition can be demonstrated from the views of that most committed of hermeneutic analysts Hermann Kretzschmar.[25] The Fourth is a '"forest symphony", but is of far greater profundity than the familiar one by Raff, which displays a *galant* French vein of Romanticism'. Kretzschmar (like some of Bruckner's contemporaries) has in mind a forest at once Germanic, pagan, but religious in feeling and 'ceremonious exaltation'.[26] The profundity is explicitly religious:

> Bruckner, like the pagans of ancient Germany, performs his religious rituals in the forest. He processes through the avenues of lofty tree trunks, in his mind the lines of the poet: 'Thou hast built up thine own pillars and founded thy temple.' His thoughts have gone back to those long-gone times when we Germans were still a forest folk; and the forest was the most magnificent church, the most splendid cathedral, that the lord of all worlds had built with his own hands. The forest inspires the composer with deeply religious feeling.

Kretzschmar is thus able to establish a programme that takes elements of Bruckner's various hints but knits them into a tighter narrative than those stemming from Bruckner and with a controlling ideology. 'Joy of nature' unites with priestly exaltation (the dialogue of horn with woodwind near the start of the first movement is priest with congregational responses). Bruckner's reference to 'song, prayer, serenade' in the slow movement (which plausibly describes the thematic events at bars 3, 25, and 51), is turned into a funeral march (with the forest as 'a comforter in time of sorrow'), 'chorale singing', and the 'grief-laden voice'. The Finale begins with 'mist and twilight', passes through 'the terror of the forest, the woods at night and in storms, their sombre and ghostly character', and a second theme that 'transports us into times long past, perhaps to childhood days'. The goal, reached through 'wonderful, supernatural apparitions', is Wagnerian:

'We hear the transformation motif from the *Ring of the Nibelung*, and the Romantic Symphony closes with the strains of the Fire Music.'

The invocation of Wagner is of particular interest because it comes at the point where the mystery achieves fulfilment. It is a metaphor for something that is not intrinsically Wagnerian or even musical. This is its chief disagreement with Floros. For him it is necessary to invoke the further spirits of Berlioz and Liszt and specific works, and to construct an elaborate parallel between the programme and Wagnerian operas, specifically *Lohengrin* and *Siegfried*, the latter a particularly contrived business since only by invoking its second act can bird song and forest murmurs be grafted on to the mystical and knightly tableau of the first act of the former. Bruckner's programme is purged of elements such as 'serenade', with its decidedly secular connotations: 'it would be perfectly horrible if Bruckner's alleged explanation, "In the second movement an infatuated youth wants to climb through his sweetheart's window, but isn't allowed in", were really true and to be taken seriously'.[27] By different directions, Kretzschmar and Floros reach solemn interpretations that stress the religious and banish the evidence of robustly 'natural' Romanticism to the lower classes in the hunting field. Where Bruckner's comments let Floros down, interpretation is ready in the form of reference to his chosen composers, as when the idea of the slow movement as a song is simply swept aside by invocation of the opening theme as a 'Pilgrim's March' in the style of *Harold en Italie*. What is intended in Berlioz as partly picturesque (but hardly generic), partly alienating (to the watching Harold), is rescued for a programme that fails to define the nature of its religious imagery. Then, too, there is the question of whether the viola theme should be read as frustrated serenade (after the manner of Rellstab), as the plucked string accompaniment and Schubertian tonal structure with internal cadences on the flat side might suggest, or as chorale; the mystical-religious tendency in Floros of necessity rejects the former; he sees 'confusion' where a semiotician might read 'disjunction'.[28]

Essentially this is an interpretative undertaking that has marginal significance to Bruckner's matter-of-fact comments. It is unnecessary to make Bruckner out to be a Lisztian or Wagnerian symphonist with boosted religious dimension. It is a simpler matter to see this as an aspect of Bruckner interpretation in the light of a tradition that is far from uniquely German; it is notably represented in Chateaubriand by a famous passage. The Gothic cathedral as the casting in stone of the forest, with its shadows and secrets, expresses a similar 'religious horror' and mystery. The forest murmurs, the thunder and the wind, live on in the organ and the bells, while 'the birds themselves seem to confuse them and adopt them for the trees of their forest'.[29]

This Romantic view of Gothic, scarcely to be seen in Bruckner's various picturesque descriptions, seizes upon the Fourth Symphony whether in the name of the absolute or of the programmatic. That it is effectively an interpretation rather than an exposition of something intrinsic to the music is suggested strongly by the results of Floros' application of his method to works for which only tenuous hints survive, most notably the Ninth Symphony.[30] When considering the clue provided by Bruckner to Helm, that the tuba chorale in that symphony's Adagio represented a 'farewell to life', Floros constructs a narrative that notes a similar comment about the opening of the movement, pursues a 'religious meaning', and finds a resolution in the comment of the 'absolute' Kurth that the ending is a 'process of dissolution'.[31]

The technical correlative to the hermeneutic narrative is the quotation. Floros' method largely depends on the identification of semantic units in the form of quotations from works whose 'meaning' is known, but Bruckner's use of quotations has been much reappraised in recent years. The most questionable area of this technique relates to the supposed references to other composers since Bruckner's self-quotations are usually relatively unmistakable or at least easily assimilated to his highly concentrated style. Where references to predecessors or contemporaries are concerned, complications arise that are related to formal or stylistic aspects of his works. That this is a subject that affects other nineteenth-century symphonists is evident from the recent appearance of a published thesis that deals with the phenomenon in the large.[32] There, the two composers most affected are Bruckner and Mahler. In the case of the latter, quotation is often seen as an aspect of the critical mentality that has been widely discerned in the composer. Bruckner's case is more complex, since it is possible to see elements of homage, thematic transformation, and contrapuntal combination in his quotations, all of which can impinge on the semantic level. To invoke a purely semantic interpretation, however, assumes mistakenly that musical quotation invariably infers a transfer of meaning from one work to another.

Against this, there is the citation of *Tristan und Isolde* at bar 463 in the 1873 version of the Third Symphony (see Example 9.1). The 'white-note' presentation of the motif, the leading role of the woodwind, and the timpani pedal suggest that the reference is to a seven-bar enclave in Act II after the entry of Mark and Melot (see Example 9.2). Even casual inspection reveals that Bruckner has carried out a transformation with a definite purpose. By reducing the weight of the orchestra, by eliminating string tremolo, and by replacing two repeated notes in the main motif with a single tied note, Bruckner reveals the general topos of which Wagner's idea is a radical reworking. It returns to its origin, a standard figure of Fuxian counterpoint,

Example 9.1 Symphony No. 3 (1873), I, bars 463–70

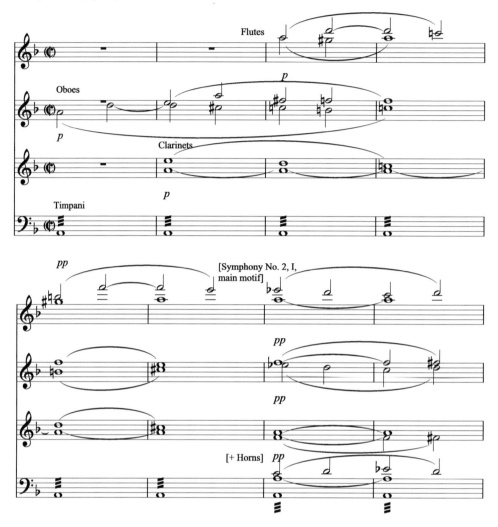

particularly amenable to treatment by suspension; in place of Wagner's melodic presentation, Bruckner uses stretto, thus turning music-dramatic motif into pseudo-antique polyphony. How convincing is it to argue that something of its Wagnerian origins remains?[33] The placing of it immediately before a self-quotation (from the Second Symphony) and a much clearer reference to a motif from *Die Walküre* (Examples 7.2 and 7.3), and the situation of the whole complex immediately before the reprise emphasizes the singularity of this moment, but it is Wagner musically transformed into something un-Wagnerian rather than a 'message' from his world. The cases of quotation in the works considered by Floros should therefore be considered very cautiously.

Example 9.2 *Tristan und Isolde*, Act II, Scene 3, bars 27–33

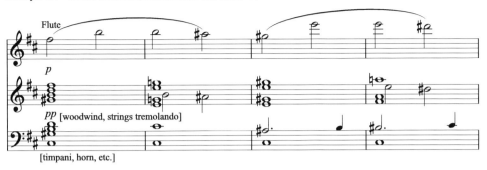

This has all been recognized clearly by Floros' critics, who have noted his tendency to unsubstantiated hypothesis, narrow definition of absolute music, refusal to allow formal elements to enter into the picture, and willingness to elevate figures common to several composers into strictly defined semantic units.[34] Of the last the most frequent is the transforming of the melodic-contrapuntal figure best known from the Finale of Mozart's Symphony No. 41 via Liszt's *Hunnenschlacht* and *Legende von der heiligen Elisabeth* into the 'musical symbol of the cross'; of this, which he finds in the Eighth Symphony, it can only be said that there are cases that seem convincing, and others that do not; arguments about its validity also enter into at least one attempt to refute Floros' theories.[35] Above all, the question of Bruckner's quotations has avoided the mechanics by which his music 'can mean', an idea traceable to Peter Gülke's writings on the composer; when Bruckner quotes from, or even unconsciously alludes to, Wagner, there is a case for agreeing with Hinrichsen that it is not a matter of a 'vocabulary function' but of a 'novel tonal language…and of its connecting place in the light of his own compositional technique…the state of development of Bruckner's harmony at the time of the Third and Fourth Symphonies'.[36] Even talk of *Lohengrin* and *Siegfried* might relate more to Bruckner's reception of Wagner's influence than to a subscription to the ethos of the works.

In criticizing the view of Bruckner as composer of programme music, it is only partly a matter of objecting to Floros' techniques of analysis. To criticize his point of view is to reject the manner in which his approach yields a uniformly romantic-religious result, by different means but with similar results to Kretzschmar; to criticize is to share in that desire to 'remove a little false incense from Bruckner', to uncover something of that representative of 'the uncertainty of modern man' that more recently has been claimed for him; the use that has been made of Bruckner's programmes has been as problematic ideologically as Thomas Röder has pointed out in the case of the Eighth, where the 'boastful tone' of the programme itself exposes a disturbing dimension to the music, notably in the elevation of the common units of musical construction into the 'mighty coup' of the typical Brucknerian climax.[37]

What then is the significance of Bruckner's programmes? Carl Dahlhaus has attempted to reclaim Bruckner (specifically the Eighth Symphony) for 'absolute music' by severing the links between programmes and 'biographical genesis' on the one hand and aesthetic value on the other.[38] Curiously this endeavour, which is entirely of a piece with Dahlhaus' long and distinguished career, is drawn back to Wagner. Exponents of the programmatic and the absolute standpoints both take Bruckner back to the stage of being a symphonic demonstration of ideas found in the development of music drama. Dahlhaus' essay restates a position found throughout his writings, that ultimately Wagner in the 1870s came to regard dramatic action as commentary on music in accordance with his interpretation of Schopenhauer's aesthetic. When Bruckner listened to Wagner's operas 'abstractly', he was acting out an important truth that Wagner had grasped about his own music. There is a curious disagreement between Dahlhaus and Floros here that circles round the familiar picture of the naïve peasant Bruckner. To make him a vehicle for quasi-Lisztian programmes expressing a half-Wagnerian, half-religious content, Floros must question Bruckner's alleged lack of interest in literature and philosophy, while covering himself against the charge of lack of evidence by invoking Kurth's distinction between *Bildung* and intelligence. To Dahlhaus, on the other hand, what Bruckner might have read is immaterial; in listening to Wagner, 'in which Schopenhauer's metaphysics had taken sounding form', Bruckner partook of the 'ideological substance of an epoch'. In short, Bruckner's symphonies do not express extra-musical ideas; they acquire a 'metaphysics of absolute music' in which they then participate.[39] One does not have to be a convinced opponent of the idea of a *Zeitgeist* to feel that music is performing a mission that is as much mystification as Kretzschmar's fantasies of a German Romantic religion. On the other hand, when Dahlhaus claims that programme music is at bottom nothing but absolute music, he is expressing in an aphoristic way the notions, common to Liszt, Bruckner, and Strauss, that musical coherence is not determined by programmes, that musical works yield interpretations but do not illustrate things.

To make any sense of Bruckner's willingness to offer programmatic explanations of his symphonies, it is better to return briefly to the comparison that Kretzschmar raised only to cast aside in his discussion of the Fourth, Raff's Third Symphony, 'Im Walde' of 1869. One of its composer's most attractive and melodious works, it prefigures Bruckner's Fourth above all in the elemental simplicity of its opening, where horn calls echo against string background (and also in the existence of programmatic information, both as titles and as unpublished narrative). If there is a difference in conception, it has little to do with French and German conceptions of Romanticism. Raff's subtitles suggest the 'Impressions and Feelings' of day, to which the horn responds with a morning call that stresses the interval of a fourth, scarcely less elemental than the fifth with which Bruckner's horn calls out from the top of the city's towers. Raff's unpublished programme includes the metaphor of the Gothic cathedral with the usual images almost as a reflex action.[40] The main differences between the two openings comprise the more elaborate string figuration and the clearly introductory status of Raff's horn motif, which occurs twice before pushing on to a rising theme (again rather as in Bruckner). In the Mendelssohnian tradition to which Raff (in spite of all Lisztian associations) still belonged, the 'elemental' motif is subservient to the creation of the well-made melody; Bruckner creates his melodic paragraphs out of hypnotic repetitions of the elemental motif. In Raff, such details add to the sense of the picturesque and the characteristic (viewed as a repertory of appropriate musical 'topics'), whereas with Bruckner, the horn-call topos takes over the continuity to the extent that accompaniment dwindles to tremolo.

As Raff progresses, the work leaves behind the dreaming of the slow movement and the dryads' dance of the Scherzo. The Finale evokes night, the terror of which Kretzschmar speaks in Bruckner, a wild hunt with 'Frau Holle' and Wotan, leading to daybreak. As Mendelssohnian melody starts to seem inadequate, Raff's music comes to resemble that string of genre pictures that Wiegandt also finds in his later symphonies.[41] In short, the characteristics of a nature picture replace the trappings of the post-Beethovenian symphony. With Bruckner, the elements of the 'characteristic' are more firmly etched in the various programme hints than in the unfolding course and continuity of the work itself. Indeed the idea of a string of genre pictures is applied by Floros precisely to the programme of the Fourth Symphony, not the symphony itself.[42] Even the discontinuities of its various Finales have tended to be explained as developing technique rather than in pictorial terms. Where they have not in the more recent Bruckner literature, the language of the 'characteristic' or the 'semiotic' has tended to look behind concepts of programmatic and absolute. Meaning in Bruckner has come to signify the analytical legitimation of interpretation by the investigation of topics, 'expressive genres', ironic 'tropes', and 'conjectural' interpretation of 'formal-tonal event[s] in programmatic-rhetorical terms'.[43] 'Absolute music' in this context is merely the background continuity against which a reborn hermeneutics plays itself out. The language of such interpretations does not renounce the images of transcendence and religion.[44] The exhausted categories of nineteenth-century debate about programme music, however, should finally be left behind.

10 Bruckner editions: the revolution revisited

BENJAMIN M. KORSTVEDT

Textual matters loom large with Bruckner. Not only have they been considered and reconsidered by generations of Bruckner scholars, but anyone, professional, student, or amateur, approaching this repertory soon runs into the 'Bruckner problem'.[1] Put simply, many of Bruckner's works exist in multiple versions and editions, some of which are clearly authentic, some of which are now known to be not authentic, and some of which are of unclear or disputed authenticity. The existence of multiple versions of Bruckner's symphonies goes back to the composer's time; as is well known, he prepared more than one version of several of his works and the published texts of most of his works deviate in some way or another from his manuscript scores.

Currently the study and performance of Bruckner's works are ordinarily based on a fairly well-defined canon of versions drawn from the Bruckner *Gesamtausgabe*, the now nearly complete critical edition of Bruckner's works primarily edited by Leopold Nowak. For several symphonies, notably the Second, Fourth, Seventh, and Eighth, some conductors and critics prefer the somewhat different scores edited by Robert Haas, who directed the first collected edition in the 1930s and 1940s. Nowak's and Haas' scores alike are based principally on Bruckner's autograph manuscript scores and, with a few exceptions – most importantly, Haas' editions of the Second and Eighth Symphonies – are examples of sound editorial methodology.[2]

Alongside this group of regularly used versions stand a number of other versions, which we tend to see as variants of the now usual versions. These are encountered among the volumes of the *Gesamtausgabe* itself, in old scores found in libraries and antiquarians, on pioneering recordings of recently published scores of early versions (by Eliahu Inbal and Georg Tintner, among others), on some historical recordings that preserve older practices (most famously those by Hans Knappertsbusch), and occasionally in the concert hall. These variant texts fall into two distinct categories: early versions that were precursors of the familiar later versions and revised versions published during the composer's lifetime or shortly thereafter. The First, Second, Third, Fourth, and Eighth Symphonies were revised by Bruckner before publication and often even before performance, and the early versions of these works have been published in modern editions. Bruckner's revisions were concentrated in two periods of time: the late 1870s when the First through Fourth Symphonies were revised, and the years between 1887 through 1891 when the First, Third, and Fourth were all revised again and the newly composed Eighth Symphony was reworked. The motivations for these revisions were several. The Third, Fourth, and Eighth Symphonies were all first revised before they were performed, partly because of changing compositional conceptions and partly to ameliorate anticipated problems in performance; in withdrawing the first version of the Fourth Symphony Bruckner referred to 'difficult, unplayable violin figures in the Adagio' and instrumentation 'that was too unsettled and overladen' in some places.[3] Many revisions made in the 1870s also reflect Bruckner's desire to 'regulate' rhythmically the periodic structures of his music, and those of the late 1880s contain alterations of voice-leading to expunge hidden parallel octaves and fifths.[4]

The editing, publication, and elucidation of these early versions are among the most salient accomplishments of modern Bruckner scholarship. In the 1930s Haas prepared versions of previously unpublished, and effectively unknown, versions of the First, Fourth, and Fifth Symphonies, as did Alfred Orel with the Ninth Symphony. In the 1970s Leopold Nowak produced editions of early versions of the Third, Fourth, and Eighth Symphonies; more recently John Phillips published a critical edition of the extant sources of the incomplete score of the Finale of the Ninth Symphony and soon William Carragan will publish an edition of the earliest version of the Second Symphony.[5] Furthermore, the early versions have generated a substantial body of criticism that addresses their import in relation to Bruckner's compositional methods and his evolving approach to symphonic form.[6]

The second major category of variant versions consists of the texts of the symphonies that were published during the composer's lifetime or shortly after. Seven of the symphonies were published before Bruckner's death in 1896; the Sixth was not published until 1899 and the unfinished Ninth appeared in 1903 in an edition prepared by Ferdinand Löwe (see Table 10.1). The texts of these so-called 'Erstdruckfassungen' or 'first published versions' (literally 'first printed versions') in varying degree incorporate orchestral retouching, alterations in phrasing, articulation, and dynamics, and added tempo and expression markings.[7] The score of the Eighth has a cut of six bars and a two-bar insertion in the Finale and, like several other symphonies, it contains suggestions for optional cuts (marked 'Vi-de'). In the first published versions of the Fourth and Fifth Symphonies the da capo restatement of the Scherzo movement is shortened. The first published scores of the First, Second, Third (both the 1879 publication and the 1890), Sixth, Seventh, and Eighth Symphonies do not comprise full-fledged versions in their own right, but are variants of versions transmitted by manuscript scores and now published in the *Gesamtausgabe*. The first published version of the

Table 10.1 *Early publications of Bruckner's major works*

Date	Work[a]	Publisher	Location
1864	*Germanenzug*	Josef Kränzl	Ried
1879	Third Symphony (1877 version)	Theodor Rättig	Vienna
1884	String Quintet	Albert J. Gutmann	Vienna
1885	Seventh Symphony	Albert J. Gutmann	Vienna
1885	Te Deum	Theodor Rättig	Vienna
1889/90	Fourth Symphony (1888 version)	Albert J. Gutmann	Vienna
1890	Third Symphony (1889 version)	Theodor Rättig	Vienna
1892	Second Symphony	Ludwig Doblinger	Vienna
1892	Psalm 150	Ludwig Doblinger	Vienna
1892	D minor Mass	Johann Gross	Innsbruck
1892	Eighth Symphony	Schlesinger/Haslinger	Berlin and Vienna
1893	First Symphony (Vienna version)	Ludwig Doblinger	Vienna
1893	*Helgoland*[b]	Ludwig Doblinger	Vienna
1894	F minor Mass (ed. Schalk)	Ludwig Doblinger	Vienna
1896	Fifth Symphony (ed. Schalk)	Ludwig Doblinger	Vienna
1896	E minor Mass	Ludwig Doblinger	Vienna
1899	Sixth Symphony	Ludwig Doblinger	Vienna
1903	Ninth Symphony (ed. Löwe)	Ludwig Doblinger	Vienna

[a] Smaller choral works are not included.
[b] Vocal score published in 1893. The full score first published in 1899.

Sources
Uwe Harten (ed.), *Anton Bruckner: ein Handbuch* (Salzburg, 1996).
Paul Hawkshaw, 'Bruckner, (Joseph) Anton', Works List in *The New Grove Dictionary of Music and Musicians*, 2nd edn, ed. Stanley Sadie and John Tyrrell, 29 vols. (London and New York, 2001), vol. IV, pp. 476–84.
Nigel Simeone, 'Bruckner's Publishers, 1865–1938', *Brio* 36 (1999), 19–38.
Alexander Weinman, 'Anton Bruckner und seine Verleger', in *Bruckner-Studien: Leopold Nowak zum 60. Geburtstag*, ed. Franz Grasberger (Vienna, 1965), 121–38.

Fourth Symphony, with its modest but significant formal modifications in the last two movements, constitutes a distinct version, which is now generally accepted as authentic (an edition of which will soon be published in the *Gesamtausgabe*).[8] The most extreme changes are found in the posthumous edition of the Ninth Symphony, in which the orchestral textures were thoroughly revamped by Löwe (the score was not cut), and in the Fifth Symphony, which in addition to reworked orchestration includes two large cuts in the Finale and a recasting of the final coda. Although the Fifth was performed and published in 1894–5, it is now clear that that publication was revised by Franz and Joseph Schalk largely without Bruckner's participation or awareness of what was being done. (Bruckner did make some revisions between the finalization of the first version in 1878 and Schalk's reworking, but their extent and significance have not been fully clarified.)

In contrast to the straightforward ways in which scholars have handled the early versions, the reception of the first published versions has been complex, contentious, and difficult. It has become traditional to regard these scores as essentially inauthentic, if not outright corruptions of Bruckner's intended texts. By the middle of the twentieth century this judgement had become a basic premise shared by scholars, performers, and enthusiasts alike, and the first published versions fell into disrepute and out of use, replaced by modern scores transmitting what are commonly, if imprecisely, described as Bruckner's 'original versions', a term used to identify texts derived from Bruckner's manuscript scores, which are claimed as the only authentic expressions of his artistic vision.[9] These matters are ordinarily explained quite simply in terms of authenticity and inauthenticity. For example, Deryck Cooke, whose writings on the 'Bruckner problem' were tremendously influential for English-speaking Brucknerians, wrote that with the Second Symphony, we are faced with a simple 'choice between the original version and the revised version; and only one decision seems possible'.[10] Despite their long familiarity, such formulations are misjudged if not actually mistaken, and their prevalence has constrained the emergence of a more critical and historically complete view of the texts of Bruckner's symphonies. Above all, the idea that the main issue is one of simple authenticity is too limiting to encompass the real textual complexities of Bruckner's music.

The seeds of the Bruckner problem lie in Bruckner's own processes of composition and revision, the ways in which his scores were brought to publication, and the nature of the extant sources of his works. Bruckner revised many of his works extensively and often over relatively long periods of time. On various occasions he sought advice about revisions, which he heeded or not as he saw fit. Many manuscript scores of his works are preserved, and these often present a complicated picture to modern-day scholars. The processes by which his works were published in his lifetime were often rather involved and not always straightforward. In addition, the particular directions in which Bruckner scholarship developed in the twentieth century decisively shaped modern perceptions of the issues at stake and the ways in which the discourse about them is framed. The most influential, and in many ways the most radical, work in this area was done in the 1930s and 1940s by Robert Haas in conjunction with the preparation of the first collected edition of Bruckner's works. Haas and his colleagues, including Max Auer, Alfred Orel, and Fritz Oeser, set out to publish *'for the first time the texts determined by Bruckner'*.[11] How successfully and appropriately they accomplished this task may be questioned, but it cannot be doubted that their work effectively reshaped the canon of Bruckner's symphonies and revolutionized understanding of the textual issues attending them.

The revolution in Bruckner editing

Serious concern with editorial problems in Bruckner's symphonies arose in the decade following the First World War. In 1919 the German conductor Georg Göhler decried the poor quality of the then-available editions of

Table 10.2 *Publication of the Bruckner* Gesamtausgabe, *1930–44*

Volume	Title	Editor	Date of publication
15	Requiem d-Moll, Missa Solemnis b-Moll	Haas	1934[a]
9	IX. Symphonie d-Moll	Orel	1934
11	Vier Orchesterstücke	Orel	1934[b]
1	I. Symphonie c-Moll, Wiener (1890/91) Fassung und Linzer (1865/66) Fassung	Haas	1935[c]
6	VI. Symphonie A-Dur	Haas	1935
5	V. Symphonie B-Dur	Haas	1935
4	IV. Symphonie Es-Dur, Fassung von 1878 mit dem Finale von 1880. Finale von 1878	Haas	1936[d]
2	II. Symphonie c-Moll	Haas	1938
8	VIII. Symphonie c-Moll	Haas	1939[e]
12	Messe in e-Moll	Haas/Nowak	1940[e]
12	Messe in f-Moll	Haas	1944[e]
6	VII. Symphonie E-Dur	Haas	1944[e]

[a] Unless otherwise noted, all scores were published in large-format conductor's score, study score, and orchestral parts. All of the volumes that appeared before 1939 were also published in a 'scholarly edition', a folio including the full score and critical apparatus. Source reports for the later volumes were never completed.
[b] This volume was labelled 'Band 11, Sonderdruck daraus' because it contained the partial contents of a larger volume planned to contain Bruckner's early orchestral works, String Quintet, and small instrumental pieces.
[c] The Vienna version was not made available in study score, conductor's score or orchestral parts.
[d] This volume was labelled '4. Band, 1. Teil'. A second part containing the score of the first version of the Fourth Symphony (1874) was planned but not completed.
[e] No 'scholarly edition' of this score was produced. It was published only as a study score and as a conductor's score without critical apparatus.

Bruckner's music in a polemical article.[12] Göhler did not work from a direct knowledge of Bruckner's manuscripts, but was alarmed by prevalent errors and discrepancies in the published orchestral score, piano score, and orchestral parts of the Sixth Symphony. What was needed, Göhler argued, was a 'definitive, rigorous scholarly edition of Bruckner's scores' that reflected 'what Bruckner himself had originally written'. The Austrian musicologist Alfred Orel promptly confirmed that it was well-known in 'musicological circles' that significant differences existed between printed versions and autograph manuscripts of Bruckner's symphonies, and agreed that a 'stringent critical edition of the works of Anton Bruckner that contains authentic texts based on the master's manuscripts is urgently needed'.[13] Despite these calls by Orel and Göhler, it was not until 1927, with the founding of the Internationale Bruckner Gesellschaft, that concrete steps were taken towards a new Bruckner edition. The Bruckner Gesellschaft included among its main goals the publication of a critical edition of Bruckner's complete works, and over the course of the next decade and a half twelve volumes were published, most of them edited by Robert Haas (see Table 10.2).

The initial impetus behind the *Gesamtausgabe* may have been the desire to replace the error-ridden editions of Bruckner's symphonies then in circulation with 'error-free practical editions', yet in the end it came to have a scope undoubtedly greater than could have been foreseen in 1927, let alone 1919. Ultimately it led to the determination that only Bruckner's unpublished manuscript scores, not the first published versions, could be accepted as authentic. This conclusion emerged incrementally. The series began with works that presented relatively straightforward editorial choices before moving on to knottier cases, and as the text-critical problems faced by the editors of the *Gesamtausgabe* grew increasingly difficult, their solutions grew increasingly radical.

The first five volumes of the *Gesamtausgabe* contain works that had not been published in Bruckner's lifetime, with the sole exception of the Vienna version of the First Symphony. With these works, including the posthumously published Sixth and Ninth Symphonies, there was no question about the primacy of autograph manuscript sources. Orel's edition of the Ninth Symphony was of pivotal significance. In this case, a previously unknown original version, which differed markedly from the then-familiar score edited after Bruckner's death by Löwe, did exist, and its publication must have been a revelation. The rather sensational way in which this score was introduced – at a special concert that juxtaposed Löwe's edition and the original version before an invited audience – and the often overeager promotion, which occasionally verged on sloganeering, of the original version as the unveiling of the 'true Bruckner' after long obscurity, proved to be symptomatic of future developments.

The next two volumes of the *Gesamtausgabe*, those containing the Fifth and the Fourth Symphonies, raised different and more difficult questions, and the ways in which these problems were handled were to prove lastingly significant. Both symphonies had been published during Bruckner's lifetime and were important repertory pieces; Haas' new editions, particularly that of the Fifth, presented these works in a form that differed dramatically from the guise in which they had been known and admired for some four decades. The publication of the Fifth Symphony in 1935 was supported by a vigorous and occasionally extravagant critical campaign, waged largely by Haas and Auer, president of the Internationale Bruckner Gesellschaft. This campaign sought to discredit the published version of the symphony as an 'inauthentic' version prepared behind Bruckner's back, and urged its replacement by Haas' new 'authentic' score. Similar critical support had been offered for the new editions of the Sixth and Ninth Symphonies, but these cases had been much less contentious because the questions of authenticity they posed were much clearer. The new edition of the Fifth Symphony, however, sparked a heated dispute in the musical community about the relative merits of the two competing versions of the symphony. Ultimately, Haas' claim that the first published version was not authentic carried the day. Postwar scholarship supports this view, but in the 1930s its acceptance was due at least as much to support by the National Socialist cultural establishment and the emotional appeal of the resurrection of a suppressed text of a great German master as to its scholarly or musical merits. The legitimization of the new edition of the Fifth Symphony as the only indisputably authentic text seems to have strengthened Haas' resolve to replace all of the first published versions, most of which were far less clearly 'inauthentic' than was that of the Fifth Symphony, with editions of the 'original versions'. Haas' consolidation of power and the increasing rigidity of his editorial position led Orel to break with him. Orel objected to Haas' methodology and his approach to the first published versions; he specifically contested Haas' rejection of the 1888 version of the Fourth Symphony. In 1936 Orel published a lengthy article arguing for a less categorical approach and shortly thereafter was removed from the editorial board of the *Gesamtausgabe*.[14]

The third and, as it transpired, final phase of the *Gesamtausgabe* consisted of five volumes: the Second, Eighth, and Seventh Symphonies and the Masses in E minor and F minor. All of these volumes, like the two preceding volumes, contained works that had been published in Bruckner's lifetime. Again, Haas rejected the versions published in the 1880s and 1890s in favour of texts derived from earlier manuscript sources. Now the *Gesamtausgabe* went forward virtually without opposition; the climate in the Third Reich was hardly favourable for open, critical discussion of the Bruckner problem, particularly after Goebbels' infamous pronouncement at the ceremony installing a bust of Bruckner in Walhalla (a shrine to German culture built by Ludwig I in the 1840s later appropriated by the Nazis) in June 1937 that 'the Führer and his government consider it their honourable duty' to promote and disseminate Bruckner's 'precious legacy' and therefore they 'have decided to make a substantial annual contribution to the Internationale Bruckner Gesellschaft for the editing of the original versions of his symphonies'.[15]

The final volumes of Haas' *Gesamtausgabe* witnessed a decline in the quality and integrity of his editing; as Leopold Nowak wrote, 'with the Second Symphony…Haas set out on a path that proved to be disastrous for the subsequent works he edited'.[16] In his editions of the Seventh and, especially, the Second and Eighth Symphonies Haas went beyond the limits of scholarly responsibility in his pursuit of new texts that differed from the first published versions. He attempted to recover an early version of the Seventh Symphony, largely by deciphering earlier readings of passages that Bruckner had revised in the manuscript and by omitting the famous entrance of cymbal, triangle, and timpani in the Adagio that he implausibly deemed to have been later cancelled by Bruckner.[17] In his editions of the Second and Eighth Symphonies, Haas conflated discrete texts and actually reworked details of some brief passages himself without signalling this fact to users of the edition.[18] The Second Symphony was the last for which

Haas prepared a critical report, and the lack of documentation for the four volumes published in 1939–44 long obscured the sometimes extreme nature of Haas' editorial choices. Following the German defeat, Haas, who had been a member of the Nazi party, was removed as editor of the *Gesamtausgabe* and replaced by Leopold Nowak, who then held the position until his death in 1991.

Haas' editorial work has been subject to some revision, most importantly by Nowak, who rectified Haas' dubious editorial decisions in the Second, Seventh, and Eighth Symphonies in producing new editions that more accurately represented the texts of Bruckner's manuscript scores. He also supplemented Haas' work by preparing editions of early versions of the Third, Fourth, and Eighth Symphonies. Although Haas' editions are no longer universally accepted, his basic premise that Bruckner's autograph manuscripts alone represent the 'real Bruckner' is still an article of faith for many Brucknerians, as is the belief that the composer's works were generally subjected to unwanted, ill-advised, clandestine, and even coercive editing before publication and that therefore the first published versions cannot be accepted as authentic.[19]

Reassessing Haas' project and its ramifications

Although substantial objections to central aspects of Haas' position have been raised periodically since the 1930s, beginning with Orel, they have remained largely on the margins until quite recently.[20] Only in the last decade or so has new scholarship modifying and even contesting the traditional wisdom begun to emerge and gain credence.[21] In particular, several scholars have seriously re-evaluated the broad dismissive judgement of the first published versions, including its genealogy, its historical justification, and its continued validity in an era in which the theory and practice of textual criticism have evolved substantially.[22] This reassessment has several aspects.

First, our knowledge of the manuscript and printed sources of Bruckner's works has advanced greatly in the past half century. Numerous manuscript sources, primarily copy scores with or without emendations in Bruckner's hand, have emerged since the 1930s, and some of these are crucial in understanding some of the first published versions. To take one prominent case, the score used to prepare the first edition of the Fourth Symphony emerged after Haas' edition of this symphony was finished.[23] This score, which was copied by Löwe and the Schalk brothers and contains extensive revision in Bruckner's hand, makes it clear that Bruckner was fully involved in the composition of the printed text. In addition, general understanding of the sources of Bruckner's works has been greatly aided by the appearance of new and revised critical reports detailing autograph manuscripts, copy scores, printed scores, variant readings, and other pertinent information about several of the *Gesamtausgabe* editions. These include updated reports prepared in the 1980s by Nowak for the Fifth and Sixth Symphonies, and new reports on the Third and Ninth Symphonies. Those on the First, Second, Fourth, and Seventh Symphonies as well as the F minor Mass are underway, but the Eighth Symphony, in many ways the most complicated case of all, is still awaited.[24]

The biographical explanations that have been offered in defence of the rejection of the published versions seem less persuasive today than they did a generation or two ago. Not only is there far less acceptance of legendary characterizations of Bruckner as an insecure, easily manipulated figure, but some of the specific claims made in support of Haas' contentions are now known to be false. It is not true, as Haas claimed, that at the time the Fifth Symphony was published Bruckner was under the sway of 'sanctions' threatened by the Schalks and Löwe.[25] We know now that Hermann Levi's rejection of the first version of the Eighth Symphony in 1887 came too late to motivate Bruckner's decision to revise the Fourth Symphony. Nor is it true, as Hans Redlich and Cooke asserted, that Bruckner made a fresh copy of the 1880 version of the Fourth Symphony in 1890 as a 'silent protest' against the first published version.[26] Systematic study of the correspondence of Bruckner, the Schalk brothers, and others has, however, lent clear support to the idea that several works published in 1893 and after were subject to covert, unauthorized revision. Paul Hawkshaw wrote of 'Bruckner's loss of control over the publication process' of the Fifth Symphony and the F minor Mass.[27] The circumstances surrounding the publication of several other works – notably the First, Second, and Eighth Symphonies – are widely considered suspicious, but much remains unclear about the circumstances of these editions.

Bruckner's famous bequest, stipulated in his will and testament dated 10 November 1893, of the 'original manuscripts' of his major works to the Hofbibliothek in Vienna (now the Österreichische Nationalbibliothek) may well have been prompted by the unauthorized revision of the F minor Mass. The will states that the firm of Joseph Eberle 'shall be authorized to borrow from the Imperial and Royal Hofbibliothek for a reasonable period of time the manuscripts of the compositions it publishes', notably the First, Second, Fifth, and Sixth Symphonies, Psalm 150, and the Masses in E minor and F minor. This stipulation often has been claimed as an indication that Bruckner did not accept the first published versions of these works, thereby giving future editors licence, or even the imperative, to replace these texts with editions derived from the bequeathed scores.[28] The will clearly does instruct that the Fifth and Sixth Symphonies and the E minor Mass, which were the works in question still unpublished in November 1893, should be published from the bequeathed manuscripts (which did not happen); broader readings of the will that extend similar coverage to other works, even to those published by other firms, are open to question.

It has long been recognized that Haas' work and its reception in the Third Reich were deeply politicized; however, many Bruckner scholars and critics, especially English-speaking ones, long remained rather oblivious to the ideological aspects of Haas' project. Mid-century Anglo-American ideals of scholarly objectivity, which tended to see textual criticism as an essentially 'positivistic' pursuit not much implicated in ideology, may paradoxically have made it hard to see how ideological Haas' work actually was. It was not until the 1990s, after poststructuralism and critical theory had focused attention on the ideological dimensions of all sorts of scholarship and cultural work, that several scholars returned to question how ideology and politics affected the substance of Haas' text-critical work.

Deciphering the ways in which the relatively abstract and largely apolitical work of a musical editor ramifies the influence of ideology is a complex task and certainly not one amenable to easy answers, yet it is clear that ideological and political forces impinged in several ways on the development and reception of the first Bruckner *Gesamtausgabe*. Over time external forces seem to have conspired to overdetermine the rejection of the first published versions and fuel the pursuit of new 'original versions'. For example, Christa Brüstle has documented previously unrecognized ways in which concerns about copyright impinged on Haas' editorial determinations. From quite early in the publication of the *Gesamtausgabe*, Universal-Edition, which held copyrights on all previously published scores of Bruckner's symphonies, contested the legitimacy of copyrighting Haas' 'original versions' as new, independent texts. Following a series of legal actions in 1936–8, Haas was left having to 'manoeuvre his editions through various legal opinions'. In the end, he was not permitted to claim copyright on versions that Bruckner had published or performed or those that had been published posthumously and was 'compelled therefore', as Brüstle explained, 'to edit "versions" that concurred with neither the Universal-Edition scores nor Bruckner's own'.[29] This stricture must have greatly inhibited Haas. His editions of the Second, Seventh, and Eighth Symphonies – in which he pursued questionable editorial decisions to produce new textual readings – may in part be products of these constraints.

Ideology worked in more abstract ways to influence the course of the edition as well. The belief that the *Gesamtausgabe* represented 'a liberation of the true symphonic will of the master' and thus helped the regeneration of the works of an unfairly beset German master must have resonated with the Nazi ethos.[30] Likewise, the express interest in recovering and restoring the pure, 'original versions' of Bruckner symphonies, freed from the foreign elements and textual contaminants, echoes other, far more sinister, Nazi practices. Anti-Semitism emerged palpably in the eagerness of Haas and other commentators to implicate Jews and Jewish firms (Levi, Löwe, Dessoff, Universal-Edition, the 'Jewish press') as culprits. Haas himself described his work in terms of cultural politics; he reported that he had personally told Goebbels immediately after the *Anschluss* that 'the spirit of this *Gesamtausgabe* with its plan, determined by me from the beginning, has differentiated itself so profoundly from the usual liberalistic habits of musical philology that it inevitably aroused the strongest Jewish objections and opposition'.[31] Politics also played an important role in the legitimization of Haas' work as well; not only was open debate of the Bruckner problem largely stifled in the Third Reich from the late 1930s, but Haas was very willing to employ political advantage in this and other matters, ranging from obtaining manuscripts to disenfranchising opponents.[32] In the end, careful and thorough study of these aspects of Haas' project can only undermine confidence in its commitment to reasonable standards of scholarly rigour.[33]

The purposes of critiquing Haas' project in these ways should not be misunderstood. Surely the point is not, as has been suggested, to oppose the *Gesamtausgabe*, or to suggest that Haas' work must be jettisoned wholesale.[34] Nor is it a matter of exposing, let alone sensationalizing, the political past of Haas or other Bruckner scholars; the Nazi affiliations of Haas, Orel, and several others are well known and the political slant of much writing about the *Gesamtausgabe*, and much else about Bruckner, during that era is painfully evident. Nor is it a matter, as Günter Brosche explained, of 'de-Nazifying' Bruckner, who was dead long before the Nazi movement began its rise to power and who, moreover, was a man who had nothing to do with any 'murderous ideology'.[35] The productive purposes of the critical analysis of the ideology of the first Bruckner *Gesamtausgabe* are twofold. First, it documents an important chapter in the history of musical scholarship in Nazi Germany, a topic of considerable import in its own right. Secondly, since the standard accounts of the text-critical problems of Bruckner's works remain deeply indebted to Haas, the realization of how his work and the acceptance of it were affected by the ideological and political circumstances of his times has direct relevance for current and future developments in this field. It should encourage an acute analysis of his text-critical judgements, especially in areas where the external impingements were most intense and compromising, notably those relating to the judgement of the first published versions. The ramifications of this are important. The belief in the inauthenticity of the first published versions of Bruckner's works, and the imperative instead to use, value, and believe in authentic, 'original versions', has come to function as a mythology. The term mythology here does not necessarily imply untruth; quite the opposite, for, as Garry Wills wrote, 'a myth does not take hold without expressing many truths – misleading truths, usually, but important ones', including 'truth to the demand for some control over complex realities'.[36] Functional myths tend to elude our awareness; as Stephen H. Daniel suggested, 'myths become effective, then, for the same reason that they fail to remain myths: Insofar as they provide the basis for organizing experience, they become incorporated into the discursive practices of a community and thus are no longer viewed as source expressions of meaning...'.[37] As the contingencies that shaped the origins of the received view of the 'Bruckner problem' come clearly into view, it begins to lose its transparency and the ability of interpretative paradigms derived from it begin to lose their ability to provide effective 'control over complex realities'.

The first published versions: towards a new paradigm

The possibility of readmitting the first published versions of the Bruckner symphonies to serious consideration poses some difficult and perhaps not finally soluble problems. The most basic problem is this: it seems quite clear that most if not all of the first published versions contain some emendations, revisions, and additions that were made by others, with or without Bruckner's approval and authorization; yet a historically and critically grounded comprehension of Bruckner's music and its significance can hardly afford to dismiss these editions out of hand, even if they contain some elements that did not originate directly from the composer. Most of them were performed and published with the composer's evident approval, and some are based on revised texts that the composer intended to supersede earlier versions.

First, some important distinctions need to be drawn. The first published versions of the Fifth and Ninth symphonies as well as the F minor Mass certainly contain extensive modifications and additions made without Bruckner's approval, participation, or knowledge. The text of the Sixth Symphony as published in 1899 does too, but here the changes are less profound. These texts are not then 'authentic' *per se*, but may hold interest as reflections of turn-of-the-twentieth-century conceptions of Bruckner's music and its performance. The published versions of the Third (both the 1879 and 1890 versions), Fourth, and Seventh Symphonies (and possibly the Quintet) are at the other end of the spectrum; these are authentic versions prepared, supervised, and authorized by Bruckner. They do contain some elements that did not originate from the composer, but especially in the light of his publication of them, this is not enough reason to reject them. The remaining symphonies, the First, Second, and Eighth, fall into something of a grey area: they differ in certain ways from the readings of Bruckner's last manuscript scores and certainly contain some external editorial emendations (in the tempo and performance markings and occasional instrumental retouching) yet they were published with Bruckner's apparent approval. (More study is needed here; one of the negative effects of the vigorous rejection of the first published versions has been to discourage serious research into these texts.) In the absence of any extraordinary mitigating circumstances, such as those of the Fifth Symphony, it is hard to justify simple rejection of texts published during Bruckner's lifetime. To do so in the name of honouring the composer's 'real intentions' runs the risk of contradicting his own actions and defeating his own meticulous pre-publication decisions.

A crucial issue in developing a coherent critical interpretation of these texts is making sense of their authorship, especially its collaborative dimensions. It is helpful to gauge how unusual they are in this regard. Seen against the ways in which contemporary composers handled the final revisions and editing of published musical texts, the editorial alterations found in the first published versions of Bruckner's works appear unusually pronounced; yet they do not stand out as essentially aberrant. Published musical texts ordinarily contain changes not found in a composer's raw manuscript score, whether these derive from the proving and refining of the musical text in performance or from the processes of editing, copying, and engraving. For example, as Robert Pascall has shown, Brahms often made revisions and emendation to his works in the engraver's score, in proof, or even in his personal copies of published scores; Brahms himself stated that with the Haydn Variations (Op. 56a), 'it is not the manuscript that is definitive but rather the engraved score, which I myself have corrected'.[38] Not all of such changes, even those that are ordinarily considered authentic, necessarily originate directly from the author's written script or even were made at his express direction. A remarkable case is the score of Verdi's *Falstaff* (1893). James Hepokoski argued that 'we grossly misunderstand the multi-layered reality' of this text if we approach it with a narrow 'concern for Verdi's intentions alone'.[39] The published text, for example, contains bowing markings and, very possibly, substantial revision of the string writing that was the work of the leader of La Scala's orchestra; although these changes are not found in Verdi's autograph scores, he knew about this work and 'all the available evidence suggests that he welcomed it'.[40] For these and related reasons, Hepokoski concluded that 'the autograph score was not produced to serve as the final court of appeal in editorial questions'; rather it was a step – the single most important one, to be sure – in a process that aimed ultimately to produce a final, edited, published text, and therefore the autograph manuscript could not properly be the 'preferred principal source' for a modern critical edition of the opera.[41] It is not appropriate to draw easy parallels between the published texts of Bruckner's symphonies and the text-critical problems stemming from their production and those of Brahms, let alone with a work as heterogeneous as a Verdi opera; yet these examples offer pause for thought about the propriety of a notion of textual authenticity that regards the composer's autograph, especially one superseded by a published edition, as the pre-eminent or even exclusive source.

Reconceptualizing authorship and authenticity – matters at the heart of the Bruckner problem – have been vibrant issues in the fields of literary scholarship and textual criticism for some two decades. The notion of authorship as an ideally isolated, essentially inner process, which has been called the 'Romantic ideology of authorship', has been subject to important critique.[42] In particular, textual critics have argued that authorship inevitably includes collaborative elements; this is doubly true of works written and produced in modern print-based cultures. In the age of print, it is argued, authorial intention ordinarily includes the intention to publish, and this entails an expectation that certain types of textual changes – notably typographic standardization and notational completion – would take place in the publishing process.[43] Indeed published texts often stand as the first fully completed notation of a work; as Donald Reimann wrote, 'unlike earlier scribal manuscripts (which were themselves the published works), modern holographs or transcriptions by amanuenses … were intended merely as way-stations to the printed texts'.[44] This applies to musical works as well. Writing about Brahms' works, Pascall made the point that it is in the nature of an engraved score to differ from a composer's manuscript notation in certain ways, since it was part of an engraver's task not simply to reproduce the manuscript text but also to 'regulate and amplify signs according to the then current compositional practice'.[45]

Many critics see the social dimensions of publication as important sources of meaning. Jerome McGann argued famously that textual authority does not derive from 'authorial intention' narrowly defined; but rather 'the concept of authorial intention only comes into force for criticism when (paradoxically) the artist's work begins to engage with social structures and functions'.[46] Thus, although published texts may commonly be considered less authoritative than manuscript sources, published texts carry levels of meaning absent from unpublished manuscripts; the decision by Bruckner, or any author, to publish a particular version of one of his works endows that text with a certain authority, as do the ways in which a published text enters into the meaningful discourses of audiences, critics, and performers. A text-critical approach responsive to social, collaborative models of authorship and textual meaning, as James Grier wrote, 'transforms the process of editing from a psychological endeavor (in which the editor attempts to determine the author's intention) into a historical undertaking' in which 'the editor assesses the value of [the] evidence against the background of the larger historical context in which the piece was created'.[47] This can be particularly helpful with Bruckner because claims about his true, inner wishes have often been used to deny the authority of the first published versions and to trump, legitimately or not, the development of more complex answers that are more strongly historical and contextual.

One of the most important contexts for music is of course performance, and it is in conjunction with issues of performance that the first published versions have clear pertinence. As a rule, these scores, which formed the sole basis for Bruckner performance traditions for several decades, contain more extensive and more detailed marking of tempo, dynamics, and expression than do Bruckner's manuscript scores (and the modern editions based on them). Connections between these new markings and the experience of performance are manifest. With only a few exceptions (the Ninth Symphony and the outer movements of the Sixth were not performed during Bruckner's lifetime, and the Eighth was published before its first performance), Bruckner's symphonies were performed before publication and these performances, not surprisingly, provided the opportunity to emend, correct, and even complete the notation of performance markings. In 1884 in anticipation of the premiere of the Seventh Symphony in Leipzig, Bruckner twice wrote to the conductor Arthur Nikisch regarding the notation of tempi. On 5 July he wrote: 'Schalk and Löwe have just played the Finale of the Seventh Symphony for me on two pianos, and I see that I may have selected too quick a tempo. I am convinced that the tempo must be very moderate and that tempo changes are often required.'[48] In a letter dated 5 November, Bruckner reiterated that 'many important things as well as frequent tempo modifications are not marked in the score'.[49] The score of the symphony was emended before publication, not in Bruckner's hand, to contain several notated tempo changes, which seem designed to spell out some of these tempo modifications. It is possible to trace in other symphonies a similar process of emendation and clarification of tempo and other markings during rehearsal and after first performances.[50] Often these markings are not present in the 'original versions', i.e. the autograph manuscripts.

The value and meaning of these performance indications is naturally open to interpretation. No one can claim that these scores (or indeed any other scores) preserve Bruckner's interpretation of a symphony in all of its details; yet, they are a potentially very rich resource for the interpretation of Bruckner's music. The scores of some of the 'original versions' do not clearly delineate large-scale tempo schemes and often the first published versions contain markings that can help clarify things. To take one instructive example, the outer movements of the original version of the Sixth Symphony, which were never brought to performance in Bruckner's lifetime, contain an incomplete, ambiguous series of tempo markings, and the 'obstinate adherence' to them, as Peter Gülke put it, 'leads to a dead end'.[51] The first published version indicates defined tempi for each of the three theme groups in the first movement of the Sixth; but in the original version the markings are ambiguous: either the third theme group of the first movement should be taken at different tempi in the exposition and the recapitulation (as Nowak's text seems to imply); or, following Haas or Nowak to the letter, the slower tempo marked for the second theme group should be held through the development section and for most of the coda.[52] Several musicians and scholars have turned to the first published versions in considering these and similar interpretative problems and found that the tempo markings of these scores can facilitate the sensible organization of Bruckner's symphonic structures and their component parts in performance.[53]

The first published versions are also intriguing because of the ways in which their tempo and performance markings, and even their orchestral modifications, contrast and conflict with the ways Bruckner symphonies are now typically performed. The confluence of modern, relatively literal approaches to musical notation and to the realization of tempi in particular, and the sparse tempo indications characteristic of the critical editions of Bruckner's symphonies (reflecting those in Bruckner's autograph manuscripts), have encouraged performances that attain a degree of sonic monumentality and marmoreal grandeur that seems quite incompatible with the much more mercurial, dramatically labile picture presented by the first printed versions and supported by what we know generally about performance styles from around 1900.[54] The aims of historically and contextually informed approaches to musical performance are not just the achievement of historical authenticity or the recreation of a composer's original conception, but also the stimulation of new, musically compelling performances. Here the first printed versions should have something to say. Precisely because of the fascinating difference (even strangeness) of their flow of accelerandos and ritenutos, the Wagnerian vocabulary of their tempo markings, and their detailed dynamic shadings, the critical reading and performance of these texts may productively challenge our traditions of performance and our assumptions of how Bruckner should and could sound.[55]

The pursuit of the original texts of Bruckner's works has unquestionably underwritten, and continues to underwrite, a great deal of important research that greatly enriches our understanding of this music. We would be incomparably poorer without the critical editions of the early versions that are now available, and it would be impossible to understand Bruckner's art and career adequately without a clear picture of the complex patterns of his revisions and a sense of how they interlocked with his efforts to bring his scores successfully to performance and publication. Yet, concern about textual authenticity, especially if framed too facilely, becomes counter-productive when it unduly inhibits or even forecloses other critical and interpretative approaches. Myths, if not outright misconceptions, growing from the discourse about the inauthenticity of the first published versions have, for example, sedimented themselves widely across many areas of Bruckner reception, from biography to style criticism to performance practices. Narrow, dogmatic approaches to the 'Bruckner problem' have long obstructed serious, reasonable engagement with the texts of the first published versions. It can only be beneficial that this is gradually beginning to change. To do full justice to the 'Bruckner problem' surely means testing our understanding of these texts, their authorship, their authenticity, and their musical meanings against the fullness of the existing documentary and contextual evidence, and simultaneously to judge this evidence (and our reading of it) against our conceptualizations of authorship and authenticity. Some preliminary steps in this direction have already been taken and while it is still unclear exactly where this process will lead, it may well become an important avenue for the continued renewal of the study, performance, and understanding of Bruckner's music.

11 Bruckner and the symphony orchestra

JULIAN HORTON

Two views on the nature and derivation of Bruckner's orchestral practices have predominated. In the early part of the twentieth century, the prevailing attitude styled Bruckner as a Wagnerian symphonist, and thus characterized his orchestration as a (more or less successful) imitation of Wagner's instrumental textures. With the publication in the 1930s and 1940s of the complete edition under Robert Haas, this view proved hard to sustain, relying as it did on the first published editions, the orchestration of which was often changed, to overtly Wagnerian ends, and without Bruckner's consent. The Wagnerian interpretation consequently ceded to an 'organistic' conception: orchestral technique was conditioned above all by the composer's long association with the organ loft.

Opinions on this matter crystallized in the mid-1930s, in a debate between Max Auer, then president of the Bruckner Gesellschaft, and the theorist and analyst Alfred Lorenz.[1] Auer presented perhaps the classic formulation of the organistic view. The basis of his attitude was a belief in the importance of formative musical experience: whatever subsequent influences Bruckner accrued, his aural imagination was crucially formed during his period of employment at the monastery of St. Florian, and afterwards as organist of Linz Cathedral.[2] His concept of orchestration was therefore predicated on the soundworld of the organ and its technical possibilities. The link between the organ and orchestration was located in the resemblance of Bruckner's way of constructing orchestral texture to the technique of organ registration, a connection mediated by the composer's predilection for keyboard improvisation. In short, Bruckner's material, devised at the organ, required an orchestral technique that reflected its instrumental origins.

For Auer, the organistic nature of Bruckner's orchestration took two basic forms. Primarily, he considered the orchestral groups to be treated in the manner of the 'basic tone-colours' (*Grundfarben*) of the organ, which Bruckner imitated by opposing discrete blocks of orchestral sound.[3] Auer cited the first appearance of the chorale melody in the Finale of the Fifth Symphony as an example of this technique.[4] Strains of the chorale are presented successively in the different orchestral groups, their textural distinctness articulated by sharp changes of dynamic. Such oppositions were considered by Auer to be inconceivable apart from an experience of the organ, both in terms of their sonorous characteristic and their dynamic effect.[5] The correspondence with registration also has a linear aspect. Textures that mix rather than oppose orchestral sonorities were considered to arise from the practice of combining stops from the organ's vocal groups. Auer contended that Bruckner's practice in this respect clarified a key feature of the history of orchestration. The development of organ voicing had close ties with the development of orchestration itself; the former effectively reflected the latter.

For Lorenz, by contrast, the opposition of orchestral groups, which he called the *Gruppenprinzip*, had nothing to do with organ registration, either historically or specifically in Bruckner's case. Rather, it derived originally from the instrumentation of the Baroque concerto grosso, having its origins in the *ripieno–concertante* distinction, and was standardized as the solo–tutti division in classical orchestration.[6] Such practices were therefore not only the province of Bruckner's music, or generally of composers who had a pedagogical or practical link with the organ. The *Gruppenprinzip* and its alternative, the *Mischungsprinzip* (mixture principle), were basic textural procedures in the western canon. Lorenz traced their use not only in Bruckner's symphonies, but also in Handel's *Music for the Royal Fireworks*, in symphonies by Haydn, Mozart, and Beethoven, and in Wagner's *Tristan*, *Parsifal*, and *Götterdämmerung*. The net effect of this argument was to produce a shift from a sacred to a secular orientation. Whereas Auer ultimately grounded Bruckner in his church-music background, Lorenz placed him directly in the line of development from Bach through Beethoven to Wagner. This reorientation consequently reconstrued Bruckner as a Wagnerian symphonist. In an interpretative turn that resonated with contemporary National Socialist views, Lorenz perceived the reception of Wagner as the catalysing influence of Bruckner's symphonic ambition, and therefore as the key factor in conditioning his orchestral soundworld: 'the gift of genius must often be awakened by external impetus... Wagner was, and remains, the rouser of Bruckner's sublime genius'.[7]

Whilst debate about the Wagnerian character of Bruckner's orchestration has persisted in Germany and Austria, in the English-language literature the idea that Bruckner conceived of orchestral texture in organistic terms has virtually become a truism.[8] Sometimes this association was unequivocally pejorative. Gerald Abraham deployed it to offset Bruckner's orchestration negatively against that of Brahms: 'the effect [of Brahms' orchestration] is produced not by the unpleasant "organ registration" scoring of actual organists such as Bruckner and Franck, which is merely bad orchestration and does not even sound like an organ, but by skilful disposition of his instruments'.[9] Successive contributors to the *Grove Dictionary* have reiterated the idea, albeit in more positive terms. As early as 1927, Alfred Einstein commented on 'Bruckner's instrumentation after the manner of organ registration', and in 1954 the point was made again by Hans Redlich: 'Bruckner's orchestration can no longer be called Wagnerian, now that the publication of the original versions has revealed its basically organ-like texture.'[10] The view has been reproduced in a more less unvaried form by Donald Jay Grout, Deryck Cooke, Denis Arnold, Derek Watson, and Hans-Hubert Schönzeler, amongst others.[11]

In Germany and Austria, this debate carried political overtones that had little influence on the Anglophone literature. The question of whether Bruckner was a church composer writing away from the Wagnerian mainstream or a Wagnerian symphonist at the heart of the Austro-German canon became enmeshed in the politics of the Third Reich, largely to the detriment of the former view.[12] The dissociation of Bruckner from his background in church music accorded with the interpretative strategies of Nazi propaganda, which lionized Bruckner, whilst either conveniently overlooking or flatly denying his fervent Catholicism. The connotations of the epithet 'organist-composer' were consequently not palatable to the Nazi regime, which preferred to see in Bruckner's music a reflection of its own atavistic, quasi-pagan religious stance. As is well known, Lorenz was much involved with the discourse of Nazi cultural politics; his pro-Wagnerian, anti-clerical stance on this matter is part of a wider trope of political appropriation, a context from which Auer was also far from detached.[13]

Political sensitivities aside, the argument about the relationship between Bruckner's orchestration and the organ is worth reviving at least because it generates theoretical problems that have since received scant attention. To begin with, Lorenz was right to point out that the instrumental habits traditionally classified as organistic in Bruckner's music are endemic to the Austro-German repertoire at least from the high Baroque onwards. As a result, the classification 'organistic' becomes meaningless as a way of differentiating Bruckner's orchestral practice; if it derives from the pervasiveness of the 'group principle', it could be applied to any composer of orchestral music from Handel to Mahler. Auer's counter-argument, that the development of orchestral technique is reflected in the disposition of organ registration, generalizes the matter to a point where it loses any clear definition, being simply a theory of orchestration in general that tells us little about Bruckner's orchestral technique in particular. To overcome this difficulty, we would need to show how Bruckner's orchestration is linked specifically to his experience as an organist over and above the broader correspondence between the development of the organ and the development of orchestral technique; such a study has not as yet been undertaken.

The biographical evidence in support of Auer's view is also less than convincing. The so-called *Kitzler Studienbuch*, which documents

Bruckner's training in orchestration and composition under Otto Kitzler during the 1860s, supplies evidence of a formative didactic experience of which Auer does not take account, and which was essentially separate from his duties as an organist. The orchestral exercises from this period, most significantly the F minor Symphony and the G minor Overture, make clear that his studies were directed towards emulating the symphonic composers of the early nineteenth century.[14] The orchestration of the Symphony in F minor of 1863 takes Mendelssohn and (especially in the last movement) Schumann as a model. The orchestral style of this work is still very much apparent in the Masses in D minor and F minor, and in the First Symphony. If we wished to uphold Auer's opinions, we would at the very least have to show that there is a complete break between the Mendelssohnian influences of the *Studienbuch* works and their near successors and the instrumentation of the mature symphonies. Simple detection of examples of the *Gruppenprinzip* would not achieve this, since they are also readily available in the F minor Symphony.[15] Auer's emphasis on the organ as a formative influence is consequently hard to sustain. Bruckner purposely studied orchestration as part of a separate course of free composition; there is no reason to suspect that these studies had any less of an impact on his orchestration than other practical or didactic experiences from the Linz years or before. Remarks to the effect that Bruckner always had the organ of St. Florian in his mind when constructing orchestral textures are hermeneutic impositions that are scarcely grounded in hard biographical evidence.

Furthermore, statements about Bruckner's orchestration are infrequently supported by detailed analysis; certainly, analysis has not as yet been deployed systematically to the end of developing a general picture of Bruckner's instrumentation and its structural implications. Ernst Kurth's dense pre-war study, although very much concerned with the structural functions of orchestral texture, suffered from the substantial drawback of relying on the first published editions, which deviate most consistently from the manuscripts of the Bruckner bequest in matters of orchestration. Moreover, Kurth sought to demonstrate a psychoanalytical and ultimately metaphysical point in his work, to which end the question of orchestration definitely functioned as a contributory means. An extended study treating Bruckner's orchestration as an analytical end in itself remains to be written.

Analysis: the first movement of the Sixth Symphony

The first movement of the Sixth Symphony provides a clear analytical model through which many of the issues raised above might be clarified. The first theme group in the exposition divides into two sections, each of which can be described as a sentence, comprising statement and complementary repetition (bars 1–14 and 25–36), elaboration (bars 15–18 and 37–40) and liquidation (bars 19–24 and 41–8). This passage demonstrates immediately the problems of characterizing Bruckner's orchestration in terms of any clear-cut deployment of the group principle. With the single exception of the final six bars, the excerpt makes no use of this technique. Consistently, the instrumental division of labour between melody and accompaniment involves either the distribution of these roles within a single instrumental group, or the mixture of instrumental sonorities. Thus the statement and complementary repetition in bars 1–14 allocates the accompaniment to upper strings, and divides the theme between lower strings and horns. In the elaboration, the role of the horns is taken over by the flutes and oboes, and in the liquidation the ascending clarinet line is initially doubled by the first trumpet. The principles of mixture and distribution within a single orchestral group also govern the tutti restatement of the sentence in bars 25–48: in the statement and elaboration the theme is allocated to upper winds, brass and violins, the accompaniment to lower strings and (initially) timpani.

Two textural devices are at work in this passage, which are apparent in Bruckner's orchestration at least from the Third Symphony onwards, and which have nothing to do with any overtly 'organistic' concept of instrumentation. This is first of all (as Lorenz rightly observed) the tutti–solo distinction: the alternation of passages deploying the full ensemble and passages isolating individual groups or mixtures of groups. Group and mixture principles may both be applied freely within this distinction; the example under consideration mostly favours mixture. In this respect, the orchestration, as Lorenz also observed, stands within the tradition of Germanic music from the Baroque concerto grosso, through the Classical orchestra to the instrumentation of Beethoven, Schubert, Schumann, and Mendelssohn; in other words, within the repertoire of orchestral music from which Bruckner absorbed his orchestral technique under the tutelage of Kitzler. The orchestration departs from this lineage in its application of a second device: a stratified notion of texture based on the addition and subtraction of instrumental layers, or 'strata'.[16] Frequently strata are characterized by discrete rhythmic identities. As a result, the texture often comprises a counterpoint of rhythmically distinct levels, which fill in a rhythmic space between two durational extremes. Throughout this movement, and in the mature symphonies in general, this technique prevails regardless of whether the orchestration involves the group or mixture principles.

Only two strata are present in bars 1–24; from bar 25 the bassoon semibreves add a third.[17] The structure of the group is articulated by varied application of the devices defined above. On the largest scale, the two sections

Table 11.1 *Symphony No. 6, I, second theme group, synopsis of form*

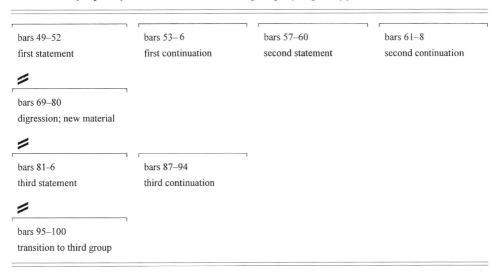

| bars 49–52 | bars 53–6 | bars 57–60 | bars 61–8 |
| first statement | first continuation | second statement | second continuation |

| bars 69–80 |
| digression; new material |

| bars 81–6 | bars 87–94 |
| third statement | third continuation |

| bars 95–100 |
| transition to third group |

are differentiated by a shift from solo to tutti, along with a loose inversion of the instrumental distribution of strata: the accompaniment passes from upper strings to lower strings; the theme vice versa. The thematic stratum participates in an ongoing motivic process that facilitates this inversion. In bars 1–24, the rhythmic values of the stratum successively contract until they equal those of the accompaniment. This involves a simultaneous rise in tessitura, and with it a transference of the thematic stratum from lower strings to trumpets and clarinets. The shift of the theme into the violins at bar 25 constitutes the next stage of this ascent.

The stratification of texture is more complex in the second group. Whereas the first-theme group originally contained two strata (melody and accompaniment) to which a simple third was added, in the second group strata are successively accumulated and removed, and no less than three strata are present at any one time. The group is organized around three statements of the subject, in bars 49–52, 57–60 and 81–7 respectively, to which varied continuations are appended. Bars 69–80 punctuate the structure with fresh material, and bars 94–100 function as a transition to the third group (see Table 11.1). In each statement, the quantity of strata is increased: from three to four in bars 57–60; from four to six in bars 83–6 (see Example 11.1). The first continuation, bars 53–6, expands the texture of the statement to four strata, whilst the second, bars 61–8, retains the stratification of the preceding statement, but varies the texture by means of the mixture principle, doubling the second violins with the first clarinet. In contrast, the quantity of strata is reduced both in the digression of bars 69–80 and in the third continuation, bars 87–94. The transition then accumulates strata to

Example 11.1   Symphony No. 6, I, 2nd theme group, distribution of strata

statement 1 bar 49

strings alone

continuation 1 bar 53   **statement 2 bar 57**

continuation 2 bar 61

Example 11.1   (*cont.*)

statement 3 bar 81

digression bar 69

bar 77

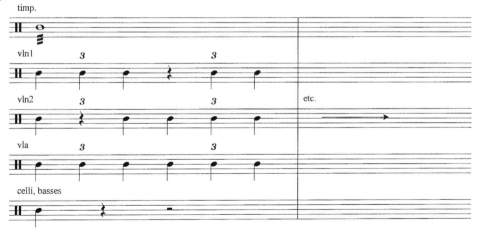

Example 11.1   (*cont.*)

a point of maximum density for the group: seven layers are present, filling out a rhythmic space from tremolandi in the second violins and violas to tied semibreves in the horns.

The mixture principle is deployed consistently in the second theme group. Both the first and second continuations augment the texture through the doubling of wind and strings; in the third statement two of the strata are doubled in the same manner. Mixture also predominates in bars 69–72, where the bass line is taken by the fourth horn and the cellos, and the upper parts are shared between oboes, flutes, and horns. In the transition to the third group, two of the strata are doubled, by clarinets and cellos, and by violas and horns respectively. The tutti–solo distinction also plays a key role in articulating structure. The two points of maximum density with respect to stratification, the third statement of the theme and the transition, also tend most closely towards a tutti texture. On the other hand, the gestural low points of the group, the first statement and the end of the digression, confine the strata to strings alone, with the single addition of the timpani pedal in the latter example. The group principle is only clearly employed in bars 89–94, where the material passes successively through wind, violins, and lower strings.

The third group is similarly defined by a process of adding and subtracting strata. This takes place in three stages (see Example 11.2). The tutti

Example 11.2   Symphony No. 6, I, 3rd theme group, distribution of strata

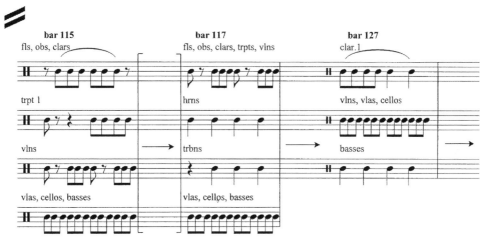

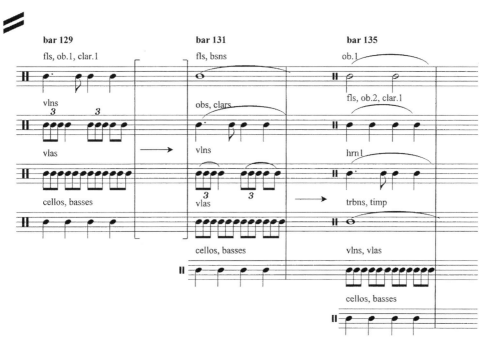

Example 11.2   (*cont.*)

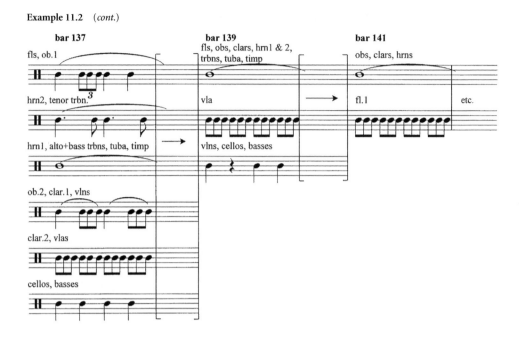

passage in bars 101–10 yields two strata in bars 101–4, and only a single octave line in bars 105–10. Strata start to accumulate from bar 111, building from two in bar 111 to four in bars 117–20, and then to thin out after the climax, reducing to three by bars 127–8. The closing section of the exposition in bars 129–44 exhibits a similar process: the texture expands to five strata in bars 133–4, and to six in bars 135–6. Layers are progressively stripped away after the resolution to E in bar 137, until only a single flute line remains in bars 143–4.

The group principle is applied more extensively in the third group than in the preceding material. The gradual intensification in bars 111–16 unambiguously divides strata between orchestral groups, the upper woodwind taking the melodic line, the strings taking the accompaniment, and the brass freely imitating the winds at a bar's distance. Similarly, bars 129 and 130 commence the closing section by setting three strata in the strings against one in the winds. Yet on the whole mixture remains the predominant technique. In the tutti of bars 101–4 the sustained E in the upper voice is shared by the flutes, first oboe, second clarinet, horns, first trumpet, and first violins, and the third theme itself is given to the remaining parts. Bars 105–10 naturally employ mixture, being a tutti single line. And although strata often occur in only a single instrumental group after bar 111, the instrumentation is not exclusively conceived in this way. Even in bars 133–6, in which distinct material appears superficially to be allocated discretely to the orchestral families, mixture is present, the viola line being doubled by the second clarinet.

Like the two preceding theme groups, the third group is also defined by a characteristic distribution of tutti and solo passages. Each of the three main structural downbeats is marked by a tutti texture: bars 101–10, in effect the climactic moment of the form to this point; bars 117–21; and bars 137–41, at the point of resolution to E major. Unlike the first theme group, where the stratification remains invariant despite the shift from solo to tutti, the quantity of strata increases with each tutti in the third group. This fact indicates a consistent property of the texture: there is no necessary correspondence between density of stratification and tutti scoring.

Analysis of the exposition in this way emphasizes these basic points. The prevalence of an 'organistic' orchestration based on the group principle is not borne out by the analytical evidence. Bruckner to a large extent favours mixture, and when he does employ grouping it can hardly be considered a uniquely Brucknerian device, standing as it does within the broader tutti–solo distinction in a way that resembles much of the orchestral practice of Austro-German composers at least from Beethoven onwards. The distinctive feature of Bruckner's textures is their linear, rather than their vertical, characteristics: the tendency either to vary the orchestration of a consistently stratified texture, or to accumulate and subtract strata. This technique is not extraneous to the form-defining functions of thematic and tonal process. Rather, each subject group is defined additionally by a particular distribution of strata, and this in turn is articulated by the way Bruckner deploys orchestral techniques within a theme group.

As a result, the development is concerned not only with the thematic and tonal elements of the exposition, but also with its characteristic textural devices. In this respect, it has two main functions: the combination or juxtaposition of strata from different theme groups; progression towards a return of the first-theme texture at the start of the exposition. This takes place in four stages: bars 145–58, 159–82, 183–94, and 195–208.

In the first section, material is juxtaposed from the third and second theme groups respectively. These references are often as much a matter of texture as of strict thematic reprise. Thus although the crotchet triplets in the lower strings in bars 147–54 are a loose inversion of the bass line of the second theme, development is equally a function of the varied textural context: an expansion from pizzicato basses and cellos in the exposition to divided lower strings as a whole in this instance. The orchestration of this section relies largely, but again not exclusively, on the group principle. In bars 145 and 146, the two triplet strata in the strings are set against sustained semibreves in the bassoons; in bars 147–50, distinct strata are allocated to lower strings and horns. In the same way, the embellishing triplet figures in bars 151–4 appear only in the flutes and clarinets, and when the material of bars 145–6 returns in transposition in bars 154–5, the original orchestration is retained. Two examples of mixture occur in this passage: the internal part of bars 151–4 alternates between bassoons and horns; the triplet figures in bars 157 and 158 are present in violas and clarinet.

In contrast, the second section is occupied with the combination, rather than juxtaposition, of strata from the respective theme groups. Five strata are present between bars 159 and 182, and the texture expands from two to four strata in bars 183–94 (see Example 11.3a). Again, development is a matter of texture as well as thematic process in this section. The entry of the first theme variant over the triplet figure from the third group at bar 159 is not only a thematic combination; it also situates these ideas within a new instrumental context derived from a conflation of previously separate textural characteristics. Bars 183–94 effect a process of motivic 'mutation' (see Example 11.3b), which also transforms the texture of bars 159–82 into that of bar 195 onwards. The triplet stratum and overlaid dotted figure derived from bars 15 and 16 of the first theme gradually coalesce into the first theme accompaniment, which enters as a single stratum from bar 195. This transition introduces a new developmental textural strategy: two separate strata are subsequently fused into a single stratum.

Bars 159–82 betray both group and mixture principles. The free inversions of the first theme introduced from bar 159 are consistently doubled between flutes, first violins, and violas, augmented from bar 175 by the addition of trumpets. The remaining strata deploy the group principle. The free imitations of the first theme introduced at the half bar are taken by woodwind alone, the strings supply the triplet stratum, and the first horn supplies an elaborative internal voice. The group principle also accounts for bars 183–6, but from bar 187 the stratum bearing the dotted figure becomes mixed, accumulating woodwind over sustained viola repetitions. The other three strata between bars 189 and 194 occupy discrete orchestral groups: horns; violins; cellos and basses.

The final section of the development functions both as false recapitulation and retransition. From bar 195 the texture is reduced to three strata, and again both group and mixture principles are apparent. On the largest scale, the passage divides predominantly into two group sonorities: a thematic stratum in the brass and winds, containing the first theme; an accompanimental stratum in the strings. At the same time, the thematic stratum is itself an example of mixture. The sustained bassoon part forms a separate stratum throughout, except in bar 201, where the second bassoon momentarily doubles the bass tuba. Even in a passage as apparently indebted to the juxtaposition of group sonorities as this, characterization of the orchestration entirely in terms of the group principle is inadequate.

Example 11.3a   Symphony No. 6, I, Development, bars 159–95

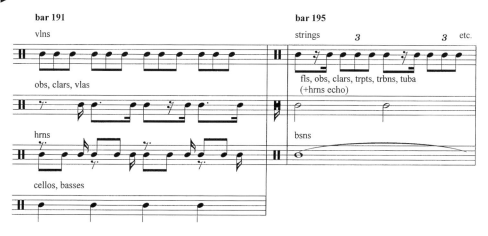

Example 11.3b   Symphony No. 6, I, Development, bars 183–95, motivic process

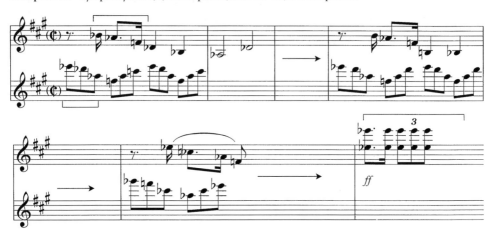

In contrast with the exposition, where each theme group is allotted a distinct arrangement of tutti–solo alternations, the development unfolds a clear progression from solo to tutti scoring, in two dynamic waves, to use Kurth's term. The first wave culminates in bars 175–82, at the end of a progressive expansion from the solo flute line concluding the exposition to a texture comprising woodwind without bassoons, two horns, trumpets, and strings. The second wave encompasses the transition, false recapitulation, and the true reprise of the first theme, which is the first full tutti since the exposition. Once more, orchestration performs a key structural function, defining the recapitulation as the goal of a textural process.

The textural and instrumental characteristics of the recapitulation differ most strongly from those of the exposition in the reprise of the first theme group. This is above all a product of the reversal of tutti and solo statements. The tutti statement occurs first, and this establishes the beginning of the recapitulation as the structural highpoint of the entire movement thus far. The reversal also situates the reprise of the first theme as a whole within a larger dynamic arch, which peaks at bar 209 and subsides before the return of the second subject. The stratification of texture is also revised. In the tutti statement (bars 209–28), the thematic stratum now appears in the brass alone, and the accompaniment is given to strings and woodwind. In the solo statement, flutes and oboes introduce a third stratum which occupies a rhythmic middleground between theme and accompaniment (see Example 11.4). The applied instrumental techniques are also varied. The tutti retains the combination of mixture and grouping, but moves the mixed stratum from theme to accompaniment. The solo passage relies entirely on grouping; even when, at bar 241, the theme is transferred from cellos and basses to trumpet, grouping prevails. Progression from tutti to solo moreover involves

Example 11.4 Symphony No. 6, 1, Recapitulation, bars 229–32

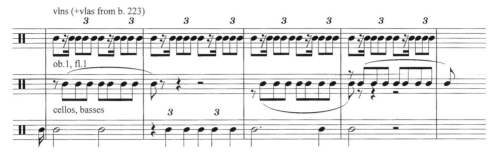

a process of textural liquidation reflecting the thematic liquidation at the end of each section. The thinning of orchestral texture in bars 222–8 prepares the ensuing solo texture, in a way that parallels the reduction of the thematic material at this point to repetitions of a single residual motive.

Allowing for the shortening of the recapitulated second theme group – the central digression is truncated and the transition to the third group is removed – the texture and instrumentation of the group largely follows its exposition form. A rhythmically imitative horn stratum is added to the first and second statements, and an extra trombone stratum to the third statement; otherwise the distribution of strata is unchanged. The orchestration is only slightly revised. The woodwind embellishments of the second continuation, bars 257–64, are varied, and the quaver triplet stratum in the third statement, bars 269–74, is now given to the violas rather than the second clarinet, which doubles the theme. The most substantial variation appears in the third continuation, bars 274–84, which employ mixture rather than grouping.

The texture of the third theme group is likewise largely unvaried. Notwithstanding the replacement of the closing section with a four-bar link to the coda in bars 305–8, the orchestration betrays only two significant amendments: the doubling of the trombone stratum at the climax in bars 302 and 303 by bassoons and the second clarinet; the introduction of a new stratum in the trumpets and first and second horns.

Stratification is applied most expansively in the coda. Consistently, the texture comprises strata that fill in the rhythmic space between two extremes. In bars 309–36 five strata can be identified (see Example 11.5), the rhythmic space between the second violin tremolandi and the tied trombone semibreves being occupied by crotchet pulses in the cellos and basses, quaver triplets in the first violins and violas, and a thematic stratum containing the first theme in the woodwind and horns. The group principle prevails as far as bar 318; from bar 319 the texture becomes more complex. The thematic stratum is now passed, in imitative two-bar phrases, between mixed orchestral groupings: oboes and horns, joined from bar 321 by the first

Example 11.5   Symphony No. 6, I, Coda, distribution of strata

clarinet, are answered by the first bassoon and second and third trumpets in combination. The stratum carried by the trombones is also augmented by the remaining brass from bar 319. As is the case in bars 195–208, so here also a broad opposition of string sonority on the one hand and brass and wind on the other conceals details that rely on the mixture principle. Grouping is however deployed unambiguously in bars 329–36, the winds being removed entirely fom the texture.

From bar 337, the quantity of strata increases to six. Example 11.5 also shows that the way in which rhythmic space is occupied also changes from this point. The cellos and basses accelerate to repeated quavers, and a new stratum is introduced in the form of an augmentation of the first theme accompaniment. The overlaying of mixture and grouping returns from this point. The thematic stratum is now passed between the trumpets and horns, doubled with the bassoons and oboes respectively, and the new stratum is shared between flutes, clarinets, and third and fourth horns. Adherence to the group principle breaks down further in bars 345–8. For the first time in the coda, the strings, winds, and brass are mixed. The first theme accompaniment, now rhythmically contracted to its original form, appears not only in the full upper winds, but in bars 345 and 347 in the second violins. Similarly, the viola tremolando now becomes thematic, doubling the first theme material in the trumpets and bass trombone, and the sustained chords are taken by bassoons as well as trumpets, trombones, and tuba. In the aftermath of this climax, the pervasiveness of mixture recedes. Only one doubling remains, in the horns and violas; the distinction between brass chords and string accompanimental figures is preserved. Thus far, the coda betrays a clear structural process, based on two ideas: the accumulation of strata towards the climax in bars 345–8; the gradual replacement of grouping with mixture.

In the closing cadential section from bar 353 to the end, five strata are consistently present, and the interaction of mixture and grouping changes again. On the one hand, the brass takes up the first theme as a distinct group; on the other hand, the first theme accompanimental figure is now taken *en masse* by the upper winds, timpani, second violins, cellos, and basses. Three strata are allocated within groups that are mixed in other strata: the violins persist alone with the quaver triplets; the violas continue with tremolando; the bassoons maintain sustained semibreves.

Conclusions

Three essential points arise from collating the evidence of this analysis and placing the distribution of strata and instrumental techniques within a synopsis of the form (see Table 11.2). First, the group principle is by no means the rule in this movement; on the contrary, Bruckner turns the interaction of grouping and mixture into a structural procedure, moving between the two in a way that both characterizes the individual subject groups and supplies a textural process in the development and coda.

Table 11.2 *Summary of analysis*

Bars	Number of strata	Instrumentation of strata	Tutti/solo
First theme group			
1–14	2	1: vlns, vlas from b. 7	solo
		2: cellos, basses, hrn 1	
15–18	2	1: vlns, vlas	solo
		2: cellos, basses + fl. & ob. echo	
19–24	2	1: vlns, vlas	solo
		2: clar. 1, trpt. 1	
25–36	3	1: vlas, cellos, basses	tutti
		2: vlns, fls., obs., clars., brass	
		3: bsns	
37–40	3	1: vlas, cellos, basses	tutti
		2: vlns, fls., obs., clars., trpts, trbns (+echo in hrn 1, 2)	
		3: bsns, hrn 3, 4	
41–8	2	1: vlns, vlas	solo
		2: cellos, hrn 1, 2 + ob. echo (bb. 41–2); clar. 1, ob. 1 (bb. 43–6); fl. 1 (bb. 47–8)	
Second theme group			
49–52	3	1: vln 1	solo
		2: vln 2, vlas	
		3: cellos, basses	
53–6	4	1: vln 1, ob. 1 + hrn echo, fl. 1 from b. 55	solo
		2: vln 2	
		3: vlas, clars.	
		4: cellos, basses	
57–60	4 (4th enters in b. 59)	1: vln 1	solo
		2: vln 2, vlas, ob. 1 in bb. 57–8	
		3: cellos, basses	
		4: vlas	
61–8	4	1: vln 1 + hrn 1 at half bar	solo
		2: vln 2, clar. 1; 3: vlas	
		4: cellos, basses	
69–72	3	1: obs., fls. from b. 71	solo
		2: hrns	
		3: hrn 4, cellos	
73–4	2	1: vlns	solo
		2: timp.	
75–6	3	1: vln 1, vlas	solo
		2: vln 2	
		3: timp.	
77–80	5	1: vln 1	solo
		2: vln 2	
		3: vlas	
		4: cellos, basses	
		5: timp.	
81–2	4	1: vlns, vlas, fls., ob. 1, clar. 1	tutti
		2: clar. 2	
		3: hrns	
		4: cellos, basses	
83–6	6	1: vln 1, vlas, fls., ob. 1, clar. 1	tutti
		2: clar. 2	
		3: vln 2	
		4: trpt 2, ob. 2	
		5: trpt 1 & 3	
		6: cellos, basses	
87–8	4	1: vln 1	solo
		2: vln 2	
		3: vlas	
		4: hrns	

Table 11.2 (*cont.*)

Bars	Number of strata	Instrumentation of strata	Tutti/solo
89–94	3	1: fl. 1 (bb. 89–90), vln 1 (bb. 91–2), vlas (bb. 93–4) 2: clar. 1 (bb. 89–90), vln 2 (bb. 91–2), cellos (bb. 93–4) 3: basses	solo
95–100	7	1: fl. 1 + fl. 2, obs. from b. 97 2: vln 1 3: clars., cellos 4: vln 2 5: vlas 6: hrns 1, 2 (+3, 4 from b. 99) 7: basses	solo
Third theme group			
101–4	2	1: vln 1, fls., ob. 1, clar. 2, hrns, trpt 1 2: ob. 2, clar. 1, bsns, vln 2, vlas, cellos, basses	tutti
105–10	1	—	tutti
111–14	2	1: fls., obs., clars. (+ trpt echo) 2: strings	solo
115–16	4	1: fls., obs., clars. 2: trpt 1 3: vlns 4: vlas, cellos, basses	solo
117–21	4	1: fls., obs., clars., vlns, trpts 2: hrns 3: trbns 4: vlas, cellos, basses	tutti
121–4	4	strings alone	solo
125–6	4	1: clar. 1, hrn 1 alternating 2: vln 1, vla 3: vln 2 4: cellos, basses	solo
127–8	3	1: clar. 1 2: vlns, vlas, cellos 3: basses	solo
129–30	4	1: fls., ob. 1, clar. 1 2: vlns 3: vlas 4: cellos, basses	solo
131–2	5	1: fls., bsns 2: obs., clars. 3: vlns 4: vlas 5: cellos, basses	solo
133–6	6	1: ob. 1 2: fls., ob. 2, clar. 1 3: hrn 1 4: trbns, timp. 5: vlns, vlas 6: cellos, basses	tutti
137–8	6	1: fls., ob. 1 2: hrn 2, tenor trbn 3: hrn 1, alto + bass trbns, tuba, timp. 4: ob. 2, clar. 1, vlns 5: clar. 2, vlas 6: cellos, basses	tutti
139–40	3	1: fls., obs., clars., hrns 1 & 2, trbns, tuba, timp. 2: vla 3: vlns, cellos, basses	tutti
141–2	2	1: obs., clars., hrns 2: fl. 1	solo
143–4	1	fl. 1	solo

(*cont.*)

Table 11.2 (*cont.*)

Bars	Number of strata	Instrumentation of strata	Tutti/solo
Development			
145–6	3	1: bsns	solo
		2: vln 1	
		3: vln 2	
147–50	3	1: hrns 1 & 2	solo
		2: vlas, cellos (div.)	
		3: celli (div.), basses	
151–4	4	1: fl. 1, clars.	solo
		2: bsn 1, hrn 1 alternating	
		3: vlas	
		4: cellos, basses	
155–6	3	1: bsns	solo
		2: vln 1	
		3: vln 2	
157–8	2	1: trbns	solo
		2: vlas, clar. 1	
159–82	5	1: fls., vln 1, vlas (trpts added from b. 174)	solo
		2: obs., clars.	
		3: bsn 1 (omitted from b. 169)	
		4: hrn 1	
		5: vln 2, cellos, basses	
183–8	2	1: vlns	solo
		2: hrn 1 + trpt echo; clars., vlas from b. 187	
189–90	5	1: vlns	solo
		2: obs., clars., vlas	
		3: bsns	
		4: hrns 1, 2	
		5: cellos, basses	
191–4	4	1: vlns	solo
		2: obs., clars., vlas	
		3: hrns	
		4: cellos, basses	
195–208	3	1: strings	tutti
		2: brass, fls., obs., clars.	
		3: bsns	
Recapitulation – first theme group			
209–18	3	1: strings, fls., obs., clars., timp. until b. 212	tutti
		2: brass	
		3: bsns	
219–22	3	1: strings, fls., obs., clars.	tutti
		2: brass	
		3: bsns, hrns 3, 4	
223–8	2	1: vlns	solo
		2: hrns, vlas, cellos (bb. 223–4); clar. 1, ob. 1, fl. 1 (bb. 225–8)	
229–44	3	1: vlns, vlas from b. 233	solo
		2: ob. 1, fl. 1	
		3: cellos, basses; trpt 1 from b. 241	
Recapitulation – second theme group			
245–8	3	Strings, hrn 1 echo of vln 1	solo
249–52	4	1: vln 1, ob. 1 + trpt echo, fl. 1 from b. 251	solo
		2: vln 2	
		3: vlas, clars.	
		4: cellos, basses	
253–6	4 (4th enters in b. 255)	strings, ob. 1 in bb. 253–4, + hrn echo of vln 1	solo
257–64	5	1: vln 1	solo
		2: vln 2, ob. 1, fl. 1 from b. 261	
		3: clar. 1	
		4: vlas	
		5: cellos, basses	

Table 11.2 (*cont.*)

Bars	Number of strata	Instrumentation of strata	Tutti/solo
265–8	3	1: obs., fls. from b. 267 2: hrns 3: hrn 4, cellos	solo
269–70	4	1: vlns, fls., ob. 1, clars. 2: vlas 3: hrns, ob. 2 4: cellos, basses	tutti
271–2	6	1: vln 1 + 2 (div.), fls., clars. 2: vlas 3: vln 2 (div.) 4: trpt 2, obs. 5: trpt 1 & 3 6: bsns, cellos, basses	tutti
273–4	5	1: vln 1 + 2 (div.), ob. 1, clars., hrn 1 & 2, trpt 2 & 3 2: vln 2 (div.), fls., ob. 2 3: vlas 4: trbns 5: bsns, cellos, basses	tutti
275–6	3	1: vln 1 2: vln 2 3: hrn 3 & 4	solo
277–8	4	1: vlas 2: cellos, clar. 1 3: bsns 4: basses	solo
279–80	3	1: vln 1 2: vln 2 3: basses	solo
281–4	4	1: vlas, clar. 1 in bb. 281–2 2: cellos 3: fl. 1 4: basses	solo
Recapitulation – third theme group			
285–8	2	1: vln 1, fls., ob. 1, clar. 2, hrns, trpt 1 2: ob. 2, clar. 1, bsns, vln 2, vlas, cellos, basses	tutti
289–94	1	—	tutti
295–8	3	1: ob. 1, clars., echo in bsn 1, fls. 2: hrn 3 3: strings	solo
299–300	5	1: obs., clars. 2: vlns 3: vlas, cellos, basses 4: trbns, tuba, hrn 3 5: hrn 1	solo
301–4	4	1: vlns, fls., ob. 1, clar. 1 2: trpts, hrn 1 & 2 3: ob. 2, clar. 2, bsns, hrn 3 & 4, trbns, tuba 4: vlas, cellos, basses	tutti
305–8	4	1: vln 1, ob. 1, clar. 1 2: vln 2 3: vlas, cellos 4: basses	solo
Coda			
309–16	5	1: ob. 1, hrn 1 & 2, clar. 1 from b. 313 2: trbns 3: vln 1, vlas 4: vln 2 5: cellos, basses	solo

(*cont.*)

Table 11.2 (*cont.*)

Bars	Number of strata	Instrumentation of strata	Tutti/solo
317–28	5	1: ob. 1, hrn 1, clar. 1 alternating with trpt 2 & 3, bsn 1 2: trpt 1, trbns, hrn 3 & 4 3: vln 1, vlas 4: vln 2 5: cellos, basses	solo
329–36	5	1: hrns 2: vlns 3: vlas; 4: trpt 1, tbns 5: cellos, basses	solo
337–44	6	1: fls., clars., hrn 3 & 4 2: bsns, trpt 2 & 3 alternating with obs., hrn 1 & 2 3: trpt 1, trbns 4: vlns 5: vlas 6: cellos, basses	tutti
345–8	6	1: fls., obs., clars., vln 2 in bb. 345 & 347 2: trpt 2 & 3, hrn 4 from b. 346, bass trbn 3: bsns, hrn 1, 2 & 3 (hrn 4 in b. 345 only), trpt 1, alto & tenor trbns, tuba 4: vln 1, vln 2 in bb. 346 & 348 5: vlas 6: cellos, basses	tutti
349–52	6	1: hrn 1 2: trpt 1, trbns 3: vln 1 4: vln 2 5: vlas 6: cellos	solo
353–69	5	1: brass 2: bsns 3: vln 1 4: vlas 5: fls., obs., clars., timp., vln 2, cellos, basses	tutti

Secondly, these techniques operate within a general distinction between tutti and solo that is endemic to the Austro-German symphonic tradition. This distinction also has a structural function. The location of formal 'apices', as Ernst Kurth described them, around which the form appears to revolve, is consistently articulated by motion towards, and away from, tutti passages.[18] All the important structural downbeats are emphasized in this way, perhaps most effectively the point of recapitulation, where the true return of the first theme is marked by the addition of the timpani, the only instrument absent from the preceding texture.

Thirdly, Bruckner's orchestration is distinctive chiefly for its deployment of the stratification technique. The *Gruppenprinzip* and *Mischungsprinzip* are put to the end of developing an essentially linear concept of orchestral texture, which has an analogous function to tonality and theme within the sonata structure: the form is driven by textural contrasts that derive from the characteristic distribution of strata. Processes of stratification occur both within the individual theme groups and spanning larger regions of music, and involve either a progressive accumulation of strata, the point of maximum density falling at a structural apex, or else an 'emptying out' of texture, where layers are subsumed into more massive group sonorities, as is the case at the point of recapitulation. It is stratification above all that sets Bruckner's orchestration apart from that of his contemporaries. Certainly, the device is not a prominent characteristic of Brahms' orchestration, and notwithstanding the kind of spatial effects used in the *Vorspiel* of *Das Rheingold*, it was also not widely deployed by Wagner. It is primarily in this respect that Lorenz's analysis is misleading. The association of Bruckner and Wagner arose, one suspects, more from political motivations than from a clear assessment of the analytical evidence.

The stratification technique is by no means limited to the first movement of the Sixth Symphony; it pervades the symphonies at least from the Third onwards. Brief comparison of passages from the F minor 'Student' Symphony and the First, Second, and Third Symphonies makes clear the extent to which Bruckner's orchestration changes as this concept is introduced. At the opening of the Finale of the 'Student' Symphony the texture is conceived vertically. Even when more than one voice is present, as in bars 9–15, the instrumentation nevertheless aims at defining vertical sonorities at a given point (see Example 11.6). Generally, these sonorities are centred on the string group, the other instruments either augmenting or temporarily replacing the strings as the focus of the texture.

Broadly similar techniques are employed in the Finale of the First: particularly in bars 1–8, the brass and winds present a basic textural framework which the strings elaborate. At the same time, an embryonic stratification process is apparent. From bars 9–21, the texture comprises layers of rhythmically distinct material, which are specific to instrumental groups, although the strata are less clearly defined than those observed in the Sixth Symphony. The idea is more fully developed in the opening of the Second Symphony. Here, strata are given much more distinctive rhythmic identities: in bars 12–15, the upper strings have quaver triplets, the cellos supply dotted rhythms, the lower winds sustain semibreves and the upper winds occupy the rhythmic middleground between upper and lower strings with continuous quavers (see Example 11.7). The trumpet entry in bars 20 and 21 provides a further level of complexity, through the addition of the dotted duplet-triplet figure.

The technique comes fully to fruition at the start of the Third Symphony (see Example 11.8). The opening trumpet theme inhabits a rhythmic middleground between the sustained drone fifths of the woodwind and the layers of rhythmic detail building up in the strings. In contrast with Example 11.7, in which no more than four strata are present at any one time, six strata are evident in this passage, each conveying a clearly defined rhythmic pattern. More generally, in the Second Symphony stratification still coexists with

Example 11.6 Symphony in F minor, IV, bars 9 (with upbeat) – 15

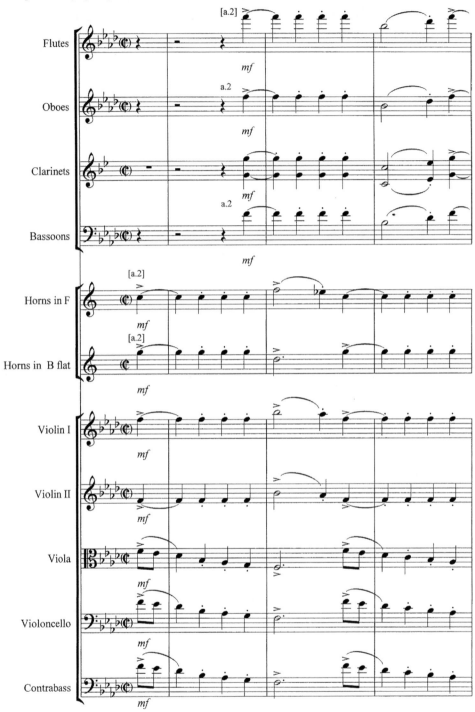

Example 11.6   (*cont.*)

Example 11.7   Symphony No. 2, I, bars 12–21

Example 11.8   Symphony No. 3, I, bars 1–14

Example 11.8 (*cont.*)

Example 11.8   *(cont.)*

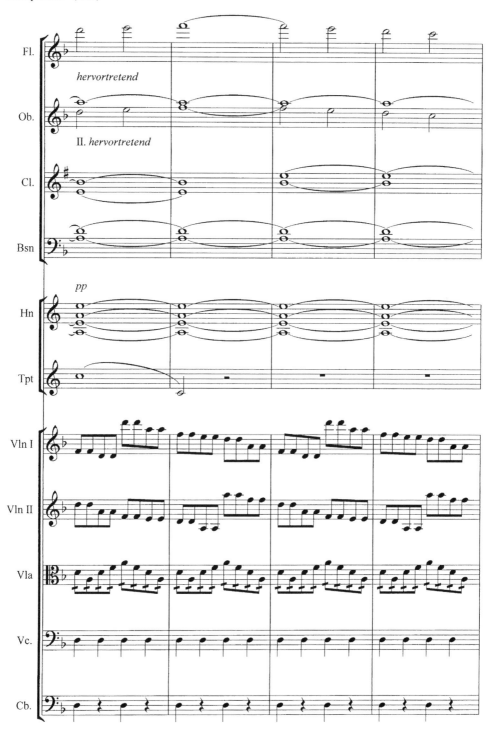

elements of the older textural principle (see for example bars 151–60 in the first movement); in the Third Symphony the procedures observed in the Sixth Symphony are much more consistently basic to the texture. For example, the climax of the passage of which Example 11.7 constitutes the beginning – bars 37–40 in the 1873 version and 31–3 in the 1877 and 1889 versions – affords a classic instance of the textural emptying out observed at key points in the first movement of the Sixth Symphony, the accumulated layers of material coalescing into a huge unison theme for full orchestra.

This comparison clarifies the essential difference between the earlier and later orchestral styles: in the earlier music, the tutti is an augmentation of the material presented in the string group; in the later music, it is the focal point of a stratification process, which is not necessarily centred on the strings. The most consistent use of stratification appears in Bruckner's adagios, of which that of the Third Symphony in its 1873 version again constitutes a *locus classicus*, although it is also to an extent prefigured by the Adagio of the Second Symphony. In all Bruckner's subsequent slow movements, increasingly dense levels of rhythmic diminution are overlaid on to a first theme, contrasting an unvaried second theme which functions as a texturally static interlude.

The most obvious precedent for this technique is not the practice of organ improvisation or registration. Rather, it most readily resembles a contrapuntal principle, in particular species counterpoint. The layering of texture according to the accumulation of rhythmically distinct strata is redolent of the layering of diminutions over a *cantus firmus*. This observation allows a historical location of Bruckner's instrumentation that the organistic perspective does not permit. In effect, Bruckner anchors an essentially modernistic technique in a strict compositional principle. The novel idea of organizing material in a sonata form around processes of stratification is grounded in a theoretically permissible device: the species model of musical texture. In this way, the music embodies a dialectic of innovation and tradition that Bruckner has sought to synthesize into a coherent symphonic style. This style therefore does not stand apart from the Beethovenian mainstream, as commentators have habitually claimed.[19] The preoccupation with grounding progressive tendencies in classical or pre-classical norms is a primary motivating feature of nineteenth-century symphonic composition in general, apparent equally in Mendelssohn's conflation of post-Beethovenian formal and thematic strategies with Bachian influences in the Second Symphony, or in Brahms' simultaneous application of late nineteenth-century harmony, developing variation, passacaglia, and Baroque quotation in the Finale of the Fourth Symphony. In Bruckner, as in Brahms and Mendelssohn, the coexistence of these elements amounts to a compositional manifestation of the dialectic of enlightenment. Bruckner's symphonies differ from those of his contemporaries and predecessors in the nineteenth century only in the details of his response to this imperative.

The species model also has biographical resonances. In his teaching and in his own pedagogical development, Bruckner was consistently careful to distinguish between strict and free composition, and between theory and practice, in a way that has often encouraged parallels with Baroque rather than nineteenth-century musical attitudes.[20] Yet in an important sense this is not a complete representation of Bruckner's musical mentality. Rather, in free composition, he sought to ground his modernistic impulses in textural, structural, and theoretical devices that could be taken as strict, artificial, or traditional procedures that have been revised to accommodate new musical materials. The opposition of strict and free reasserts itself within Bruckner's works, almost as if the music should reveal the artifice that grants permission for the overlaid harmonic, thematic, and textural innovations. The concept of stratification is a clear example of this. Bruckner employs an archaic contrapuntal device as a textural principle, which in turn forms the basis of a highly original notion of orchestration and its formal function.

We are perhaps now in a position to follow a middle path between the respective views of Auer and Lorenz. On the one hand, it seems clear that Auer's belief in the role of the organ as a pervasive formative influence relies on connections that are less than secure. On the other hand, Lorenz's contextualization of the question of orchestration as a facet of the Wagnerian influence is excessive, and ignores the ways in which Bruckner's instrumentation is evidently distinct from that of Wagner. We can also draw productively on both positions. Lorenz's use of the group and mixture principles, and the tutti–solo distinction, as analytical categories is apposite, and links Bruckner with a symphonic lineage that is detrimentally marginalized by the organistic view. At the same time, isolation of species counterpoint as a model for orchestral texture permits, to an extent, a re-engagement with Auer's attitude. Relation of Bruckner's music to a notion of Baroque technical authority has strong resonances with the idea that his symphonic style is linked to church music and its performance traditions.

Paul Hawkshaw's recent observation that textual research in Bruckner scholarship needs to proceed carefully, work by work, and with patient attention to detail also holds true for the study of orchestration.[21] Generally, statements have been made without the benefit of a systematic survey of Bruckner's instrumentation, or a consideration of its analytical implications. Realistically, this study would require the systematic analysis of all Bruckner's major orchestral works, isolating precisely how the principles of grouping and mixture are employed, and the textural and structural ends to which they are put, a project which clearly exceeds the scope of this study. In the absence of such a survey, misconceptions have proliferated that have little basis in analytical evidence.

12 Between formlessness and formality: aspects of Bruckner's approach to symphonic form

BENJAMIN M. KORSTVEDT

In memoriam Eugene K. Wolf (1939–2002)

There is something sphinx-like about Bruckner's musical forms. They can seem neat and traditional at one moment, but at the next appear free and unconventional. This duality is evident in the rather disparate interpretations, ranging from the accusation of 'formlessness' to the claim that Bruckner's symphonies represent a pinnacle in the evolution of musical form, that have been offered, discussed, and elaborated from the nineteenth century onward.

A prevalent early judgement found Bruckner's music 'formless'. This concern was first raised after the composer conducted the Second Symphony on 26 October 1873. A. W. Ambros, staking out what was to become a familiar position, wrote that instead of exhibiting, as expected, a 'firmly joined musical structure [*festgefügte musikalische Tektonik*]' the symphony drove the listener to 'breathlessness' by presenting a series of 'tonal shapes [*Tongebilde*] wilfully strung one after another'.[1] Throughout the 1880s the notion that Bruckner's symphonies were chaotic in form percolated through antagonistic reviews, most importantly in those by Hanslick, Kalbeck, and Gustav Dömpke. Dömpke, for example, opened his review of the Viennese première of the Seventh Symphony with the assertion 'Bruckner lacks the feel for the primary elements of musical formal shape, for the coherence of a series of melodic and harmonic component parts.'[2] Even observers sympathetic to Bruckner's music were occasionally puzzled by his forms; Hugo Wolf referred to a certain 'formlessness' that haunted the symphonies despite their 'originality, grandeur, power, imagination and invention'.[3] The durability of this notion is reflected by the publication in 1902 of a brief essay entitled 'Is Bruckner Formless?'[4] As late as 1925 Hans Alfred Grunsky published a lengthy analytical defence of Bruckner's 'immortal masterworks' against the 'accusation of musical formlessness'.[5] What exactly the term 'formless' meant was never made entirely clear. It undoubtedly referred in part to matters – including novelties of harmony, syntax, and motivic work – that are not aspects of 'form' in the modern sense, as well as to Bruckner's divergence from conventional *Formenlehre* paradigms. It is noteworthy that each of the Bruckner symphonies best known in the nineteenth century (the last revised versions of the Third and

Fourth, and the Seventh) has a Finale that is strikingly unconventional in form.[6]

Other observers felt that Bruckner's symphonies were all too formal in their reliance on traditional symphonic models, both in their four-movement schemes and in the sonata form of individual movements. This claim particularly worried the young Wagnerians who advocated Bruckner's cause. Wagnerian formal doctrine placed great value on the ideal of organic form, and held that the symphony and especially the conventional forms associated with the genre were no longer vital. As Christian von Ehrenfels put it, Wagner's achievement was not to destroy musical form, as his critics claimed, but to demolish the continued validity of musical 'templates'.[7] Thus Rudolf Louis' observation in 1893 that Bruckner was 'all but slavish' in his use of conventional symphonic forms was meant to censure Bruckner both aesthetically and historically.[8] The difficulty of reconciling this view with an essential approval of Bruckner's works is apparent in August Göllerich's assertion (offered in an address about Bruckner on the occasion of the seventy-first anniversary of Wagner's birth!) that it was only because Bruckner was 'so intrinsically deep and richly talented, so German and therefore so specifically a musician ... that he is satisfied with the outward form of the symphony'.[9] Early twentieth-century critics echoed this view, but with subtly changed emphasis. In 1921 Franz Schalk wrote that 'nothing is more primitive than Brucknerian form ... Bruckner fabricated a very simple schema for his movements, and never speculated about it and held to it regularly in all of his symphonies'.[10] This sweeping overstatement, which certainly feels like criticism, rings strangely coming from an active proponent of Bruckner's symphonies. While it may have been intended simply to counter the idea that Bruckner was 'formless', it also probably reflected the changing politics of musical form in the early twentieth century, when Bruckner, no longer avant-garde and provocative, was increasingly positioned against the perceived scourge of the New Music and its 'formless' atonal tendencies.

August Halm and Ernst Kurth, two great Bruckner champions of the early twentieth century, developed a rather different view of his form and its historical significance. Halm claimed Bruckner's symphonic art as a synthesis of the two preceding musical 'cultures', the 'culture of the theme' epitomized by the fugal art of Bach and the 'culture of form' consummated in Beethoven's sonatas. 'A third culture of music ... is to be expected', he wrote, and 'it will be a complete culture of music for the first time ... I see it germinating ... in Anton Bruckner's symphonies.'[11] Kurth, whose work is related to Halm's in important ways, famously explained Bruckner's form not as a matter of static architecture but as the outward manifestation of metaphysical energy unfolding in series of dynamic waves. He argued that

Bruckner was a '*Dynamiker* of form' who 'snatched back the concept of form from one-sided rigidity and revived it' and was able to 'renew not form but forming [*das Formen*]'.[12] As historical prophecy such views do not hold up well – Bruckner had relatively little direct influence on succeeding generations of composers – yet they do focus worthwhile attention on the undeniable fluidity of Bruckner's music.

That the form of Bruckner's symphonies has generated such a range of contradictory interpretations is not explainable merely as the reflection of differences of opinion or even of different systems of evaluation; it stems ultimately from the originality and complexity of Bruckner's approach to the integration of symphonic form and content. Each of these lines of interpretation is partial, yet each fixes on something significant. Indeed much of the inner tension of Bruckner's symphonic project emerges from delicate balances: between a commitment to the structural grandeur of symphonic sonata form and an expressive agenda rooted in a vocabulary of advanced chromatic harmony, between tradition and innovation, between form as scheme and as dynamic process, between general and particular. Any successful criticism of these works needs to encompass the interrelationships of these elements and address the critical issues that bear on them and their interpretation. The goal of this essay is to consider and elucidate Bruckner's approach to form, specifically symphonic sonata form, by focusing on several of its crucial patterns and procedures, including the structure of the exposition, methods of recapitulation, and the interaction of form and content.

Bruckner's formal schema

In the latter half of the twentieth century several German scholars returned to the question of the schematicism of Bruckner's form. In the first edition of *Die Musik in Geschichte und Gegenwart* Friedrich Blume, explicitly echoing Franz Schalk, asserted that Bruckner's symphonies represent a series of 'increasingly emphatic and gripping solutions' to one basic problem and are fundamentally alike in their forms and patterns, that his themes bear great 'family resemblance', and that he relied upon a single basic schema in creating his symphonies.[13] Blume broached two related yet distinct points. The first is the suggestion that Bruckner's symphonies are essentially similar and exhibit little development over the course of his career, a notion that may not be entirely baseless, but is easily overemphasized and has been by various authorities (unfortunately including some of the most widely used American music history textbooks).[14] Seen from afar, the likenesses among Bruckner's symphonies can impress, but as one begins to grasp them as a series of individual works Bruckner's approach to form begins to reveal some striking lines of development. This evolution is most evident between Bruckner's two major periods of symphonic composition. The first of these (1872–6) produced the Second to Fifth Symphonies in their earliest versions. The second, which followed several years devoted to revising these works and extended until the late 1880s, produced a second group, comprising the Sixth to Eighth Symphonies, as well as the String Quintet. A second wave of revisions followed in the years around 1890, associated with the publication of several of the symphonies, notably the First, Third, Fourth, and Eighth.[15] The Ninth Symphony, begun in the late 1880s but left with the Finale unfinished at the composer's death, stands somewhat alone in time and, to some extent, in style. As will become clear, several aspects of Bruckner's approach to form underwent a significant change between the symphonies written in the 1870s and those from the 1880s.

Blume's second point, which has received some worthwhile attention in the analytical literature, is that 'a single basic schema' underlies Bruckner's forms.[16] While it is entirely possible to overstate the regularity and formality of Bruckner's forms, there is a whiff of schematicism about them. His symphonies are all based on the standard four-movement scheme; his Scherzos use the standard three-part form with trio and da capo; the structure of his outer movements is derived from the Classical pattern of exposition–development–recapitulation; his expositions present the structural oppositions basic to sonata form, namely the polarity of tonic and dominant keys and the presentation of distinct contrasting thematic ideas; his development sections elaborate material presented in the exposition and pursue a modulatory harmonic course; and his recapitulations restate the movement's themes and resolve into the tonic key. All of this is clearly laid out, perhaps too clearly at times, so that there is a hint of stiffness or formality to Bruckner's sonata form. Yet Bruckner's forms are not, in the end, very conventional: the key schemes in both the expositions and the recapitulations are often out of the ordinary (see Table 12.1) and the balance of the various sections of sonata form is very different from that of the Viennese classics; in particular, Bruckner gives both the second theme group and the closing material much greater space and attention than was traditional. And in several movements, Bruckner deviated substantially from classical forms, as in the unconventional layout of some Finales (notably in the Sixth and Seventh Symphonies and the Quintet) or in the intercutting of development and reprise in the first movement of the Ninth.

Moreover, as Wolfram Steinbeck emphasized, despite his 'broad brushstrokes', 'in no way did Bruckner fill out a learned, abstract, "ready-made" form-schema'.[17] Bruckner often worked out, especially in his later works,

Table 12.1 *Key schemes in Bruckner's sonata-form movements*

	1st. mvt.						4th. mvt.					
	expo.			recap.			expo.			recap.		
theme groups	A	B	C	A	B	C	A	B	C	A	B	C
Sym. 1	c	Eb	Eb	c	C	c	c	c	Eb	c	a	C
'Nullte'	d	A	F	d	D	D	d	C	F	c	d	d(D)*
Sym. 2	c	Eb	Eb→G	c	C	c	c	A→Eb	Eb	c	C	c
Sym. 3[a]	d	F	F	d	D	d	d	F#→F	Db(F)†	d	Ab→A	B(D)*
Sym. 4[b]	Eb	Db	Bb	Eb	B	Eb	bb→Eb	c→C	bb	eb	f#→D	eb(Eb)*
Quintet	F	C	C(F#)C	F	Db	F(B)F	Gb	f	E	—	Db	F
Sym. 5[c]	bb	F	Db (F)†	bb	g	Eb (Bb)*	Bb	Db	Bb	Bb	F	Bb
Sym. 6	A	e	C(E)†	Eb→A	f#	D→E(A)*	A	C	C→E	A	A	C(A)*
Sym. 7	E	B	b	E	e	G(E)*	E	Ab	a	b[d]	C	E
Sym. 8[e]	c	G	Eb	→(c)	Bb	c	→c	Ab/f	eb	→c	Ab/f	c(C)*
Sym. 9	d	A	d(F)†	d	D	b→d	G→d	G	E	d	G	D

* This key is achieved only in the coda.
† This key is achieved only in the codetta.
[a] 1873 version
[b] 1880 version
[c] Slow introductions not included
[d] The recapitulation is reversed, beginning with the C theme and ending with the A theme.
[e] 1890 version

a subtle balance between formal convention and creative idiosyncrasy. A striking example is the arrival of the second theme group of the first movement of the Fourth Symphony (bars 75ff.), which is preceded by a rather formal arrival on the dominant of Bb, the expected dominant key (Tovey described it as 'stiff' and 'archaic');[18] yet following a momentary pause, the theme group begins resolutely in the remote key of Db. In the recapitulation, where things presumably ought to be 'set right' tonally, the second theme group appears, again following a similar cadence on the tonic triad of Eb, in the key of B major (= Cb) (bars 437ff.).

An even more important point is that Bruckner's forms are not schematic in the usual sense of the term. Carl Dahlhaus defined a schematic form as one 'sustained exclusively by the quality of the initial idea, the individual character of which compensated for the conventionality of the overall outline'.[19] In Bruckner, form emphatically does not serve merely to provide a frame for melodic content; rather the overall architecture is supported by the careful construction of key schemes and the strategic deployment of cadential progressions. This is evident in the care with which Bruckner arrays the keys in which material is restated in the second half of movements: e.g. the cadential passage that ends the slow introduction of the first movement of the Fifth Symphony on the dominant of the mediant returns on the home dominant to introduce the recapitulation (bars 347–62). He also made considerable use of well-articulated cadential progressions to define formally decisive junctures. In the earlier symphonies these signal themselves very clearly with a strong IV–V motion in the bass and/or a prominent

4–3 suspension on the dominant. In the 'Nullte' Symphony and the Second the coda of the Finale is announced by a compact decisive cadence of this sort, as is the final section of the coda in the Finale of the Third Symphony. In the first movements of the Second, Third, and Fourth the recapitulation is prefaced by an elongated version of the same basic progression. In the later symphonies cadential progression of this type are used to assert tonal goals somewhat more fluidly, often in the context of a chromatic, locally unstable harmonic medium, a practice reminiscent of that used in Wagner's mature works. For example, in the opening thematic statement in the first movement of the Eighth, an unresolved IV–V progression in C minor (bars 20–1) is important in establishing the tonal centre of a passage that starts far from the tonic. Similar progressions cadencing in secondary keys stabilize the second group (bars 71–3) and prepare the closing group (bars 89–97). In the first movement of the Ninth Symphony, this tendency is reduced to its essence in the coda, where a massively primal unison assertion of the pitches G and A prepares the final tonic D minor (bars 549–51).

The three-part exposition

The form of Bruckner's expositions is highly characteristic. Described simply, his expositions consist of three distinct sections: a primary thematic area that essays the tonic key, a lyrical second group, or, in Bruckner's terminology, the *Gesangsperiode*, and a closing group. Each of these sections is well marked and usually rather self-contained; often they comprise multipartite paragraphs in and of themselves. Bruckner provides little formal transitional music to bridge the sectional divides. In addition to the essential differences in thematic content and tonality, each section is, as a rule, quite distinct in mood, tone, rhythm, tempo (including in a number of movements, beginning with the Finale of the Third, a broadening of the basic tempo for the second theme group), texture, and orchestration.

Bruckner was quite consistent in his expositions, and it is possible to describe the characteristic traits of each of the three sections. The first group presents the primary thematic material, which may be based on a short motivic idea (as in the opening movements of the Second, Fourth, Sixth, and Eighth) or on a more complete, closed melodic theme (the first movement of the Seventh is the greatest example). In first movements, the primary theme group begins *piano* before presenting a contrastingly louder section, whether a *fortissimo* counterstatement as in the Fifth to Eighth, or with the introduction of complementary material at the crest of an intensifying *Steigerung* (build-up) as in the Third, Fourth, or Ninth. Generally Finales begin similarly, but several do begin forcefully straightaway (notably the First, Third, and Eighth).

Bruckner's *Gesangsperioden* are, as the term suggests, songful, flowing in motion, less insistent though often richly contrapuntal in texture, with orchestration that favours strings and woodwinds. Often the thematic material is a double-theme of some type, either a two-part contrapuntal complex (as in the opening movements of the first four symphonies) or the simultaneous presentation of two fairly distinct musical ideas, as in the well-known combination of polka and chorale in the Finale of the Third. A Brucknerian *Gesangsperiode* is considerably larger in size than a typical second theme group; indeed several are developed ternary forms in their own right. This tendency is strongest in his later works; in the first movements of the Sixth and the Seventh the second theme group is a complex rounded structure of some fifty bars covering considerable harmonic ground.

The concluding third theme group rounds off the exposition by returning to a mood closer to that of the opening group: the orchestration is full, the weight of the brass more evident, and in movements with a slower *Gesangsperiode*, the tempo returns to that of the opening material. Sometimes the thematic material feels akin to the primary theme, sometimes not. Often the closing group is based on some sort of grand *unisono* scoring; striking examples include the searing syncopated string unisons in the Finale of the Third and the enriched unison writing in the opening movements of the Sixth and the Eighth. The exposition closes with a quiet lyrical codetta, whose mood carries across the double bar into the beginning of the development section, blurring the division between the exposition and the development section and often giving rise to some of the most soulful music in the movement. See, for example, how Bruckner handles this juncture in the first movements of the Sixth, Seventh, and Eighth, and also in the Finale of the Fifth. With the exception of two apprentice works, the F minor Symphony of 1863 and the 1862 String Quartet, none of Bruckner's expositions is marked with a repeat sign.

Halm provided descriptions of the musical nature of each of the three theme groups that, although rather old-fashioned in tone, are trenchantly metaphorical. The first theme group is the 'dramatic group'; it exhibits 'the will to consequence' and 'the spirit of the future'. The *Gesangsperiode* in contrast is 'idyllic or lyric': 'its melodic self-sufficiency gives a feeling of the present... Here we no longer feel the passage of time, yet we sense within an urge forward.' The third group returns the music to directed action, but is more 'relaxed' than the first group. It is not 'fed by the conflict of opposites', rather the musical impulse is now unitary as 'gathered energy frees itself' and 'recovers' to yield basic triadic and stepwise progressions.[20]

Once he struck upon this tripartite plan in the First Symphony, Bruckner held to it consistently, both across his career and in the revision of individual symphonies; even in the most extensively revised movements – notably the outer movements of the Third, Fourth, and Eighth Symphonies – the form of the exposition remained relatively unchanged. It is not a mere coincidence that Bruckner's first maturity, from his arrival in Vienna up to the completion of the Fifth Symphony, coincided with the crystallization of the three-part exposition. His method of exposition is conditioned by his overall approach to sonata form; conversely, the larger patterns of his movements, especially those of the recapitulation, depend on possibilities that arise from the nature of his expositions. In addition, the structure of Bruckner's expositions underwrites many of the most striking characteristics of his music including its richness of thematic material, the great contrasts that arise from the juxtaposition and working-out of several well-marked thematic ideas, and a pronounced expansion of the formal and temporal dimensions.

Bruckner's threefold exposition is indebted to the music of previous generations. Beethoven and Schubert fairly often made use of a closing group with a clear thematic profile, and, as John Williamson pointed out, 'that the closing section of a sonata-form exposition may make reference to the first subject is a procedure as old as Mozart. The so-called third subject in Bruckner is merely an expansion of this tendency.'[21] Schubert's fondness for lyrically expansive and self-contained second theme areas made a deep impression on Bruckner. Bruckner's expositions also clearly participate in a nineteenth-century tendency to expand the tonal scheme of sonata-form expositions to include a third key; these so-called 'three-key expositions' are found often in the works of Beethoven, Schubert, Schumann, Mendelssohn, Brahms, and other Romantic composers, and the roots of this procedure have been traced back to Haydn, Mozart, and other late eighteenth-century composers.[22] Bruckner's employment of these structures pursued many of the advantages adduced by James Webster in his important essay on three-key expositions of Schubert and Brahms, notably the possibility of integrating 'lyrical themes, quasi-closed forms, remote keys, and the double second group' into 'a coherent large sonata-form exposition'.[23] Despite a certain similarity of aim, Bruckner's recasting of the classical exposition is in several ways more radical. In contrast to Brahms' ideal of meticulously crafted transitions, Bruckner's desire to emphasize contrast led him to minimize transitional sections. In Bruckner's expositions theme groups usually follow each other quite directly, without much mediating material, and when transitional sections do appear, they are limited to a few bars of dominant preparation and often even this is suppressed (precedents may be found in the opening movements of Beethoven's Fifth and Schubert's 'Unfinished', which limit themselves to a brusque transition between the first and second theme groups). The most significant morphological difference in Bruckner's expositions is the expansion and elevation of the third group into a fully fledged unit on a par with the first and second groups. This process anchored both ends of the exposition, freeing the *Gesangsperiode* to evolve into a characteristically extensive and musically replete section. Also, since a main function of the third group was to secure and define the key of the dominant or, in some minor-key movements, the relative major, the *Gesangsperiode* was relieved of one of the traditional function of a second theme group, the establishment of the exposition's second structural key. Bruckner was happy to take full advantage of this latitude, especially from the Third Symphony on; the key schemes of his expositions, or more precisely of his second theme groups, are often very rich and wide-ranging.

The expansion of the exposition, and therefore the recapitulation as well, obviously contributes to the splendid expansiveness of Bruckner's symphonies. Simply enlarging the theme groups, especially the second and third, serves to extend the duration of a movement. Of even more importance perhaps, are the grand contrasts created by the markedly different patterns of musical motion of the primary and closing groups, on one hand, and the *Gesangsperioden* on the other. These contribute greatly to Bruckner's impressively extensive feeling of time; as Tovey wrote about Beethoven's Ninth Symphony, 'the enlargement of time-scale is not a matter of total length; it is a matter of contrasts in movement'.[24] Bruckner symphonies expound and glorify such contrasts.

Also, and this should be emphasized, Bruckner's symphonies do contain musical elements that cut across formal divisions, counteracting any latent tendency to stasis inherent to his architectonic schemas. The most important of these are Bruckner's famous *Steigerungen*, intensifying passages that build climactically by means of *crescendo*, rhythmic compression, and (often) rising linear motion and harmonic tension.[25] Sometimes such passages remain neatly within the bounds of a formal section, as for example near the end of the primary theme area in the 1880 Finale of the Fourth Symphony (bars 50–92) or in the first movement opening theme group in the Third and the Ninth. When coordinated with the end of a formal section, a *Steigerung* can emphasize its integrity; the best example might be the forceful and prolonged dominant preparation that ushers in the closing group in the first movement of the Seventh (bars 103–22). More often, however, Bruckner's *Steigerungen* refuse to accede neatly to formal schemes. An early instance is found in the first movement of the First Symphony when a sudden, sharp intensification leads to an abrupt, unexpected thematic outburst near the end of the exposition (from bar 78 in the Linz version). Another striking destabilizing *Steigerung* occurs near the end of the first movement of the Eighth; it builds to a seething peak of intensity and rapidly collapses into the tautly quiet coda. And in several of his later symphonies Bruckner artfully deployed gestures of this sort in conjunction with the process of recapitulation.

A number of other gestures are characteristic of Bruckner's symphonic forms. These include the grandly sweeping tuttis that surge forward in several first movement development sections (see the Fourth Symphony at bar 253 or the Fifth at bar 283), sudden momentary lyrical outbursts (as in the *Gesangsperiode* in the first movement of the Ninth at bar 123), and the peremptory return of the tonic in the development section of the first movements of the Third, Fourth, and Ninth Symphonies. The most important of these gestures may be sudden local tonal shifts based on half-step progressions, examples of which can be found across Bruckner's symphonic career: these shifts are similar to what Adorno described as Mahler's 'macrological' progressions that, in their brusqueness, create broad patterns of 'light and shadow . . . foreground and depth'.[26] In Bruckner, such progressions do occur between abutting formal sections, a usage that seems more conventionally Romantic, if unusual in symphonic music. A good example is the appearance of the *Gesangsperiode* in the Finale of the Second Symphony in the key of A major following a firm arrival on the dominant of D♭ major (at bar 76). More characteristically, though, these macrological shifts occur within theme groups and in development sections, as in the finale of the First at bar 134, the middle of the *Gesangsperiode* of the first movement of the Third (bar 147 of the 1873 version), the finale of the Sixth at bar 151, and in the opening theme group of the Ninth, where the shift from D minor to E♭ is integral to the thematic concept.

Gestures of quotation and recall

One of Bruckner's most characteristic formal procedures is the use of various gestures of thematic quotation or recall, and these too are coordinated in various ways with formal architecture. Several types of quotation, differing in placement, material, and method, can be discerned. In the Second Symphony and in the early version of the Third Bruckner introduces quotations from outside the work. These gestures appear between formal units and thus outside the main structural argument of the movement (making it easy for Bruckner to remove them in later versions). In the Second material directly derived from Bruckner's F minor Mass is quoted in the slow movement (bars 138–40 and 180–3 of the Nowak edition) and in the Finale (bars 200–9 and 547–56), and a motive reminiscent of *Rienzi* is presented near the end of the third theme group of the first movement (bars 163–76 and 460–79). The first movement of the 1873 version of the Third Symphony, as is well known, includes several clear evocations of Wagner: the 'Liebestod' motive from *Tristan* appears in bars 463–8 and the 'Magic Sleep Music' from *Die Walküre* is paraphrased in bars 479–88 (the opening theme of the Second appears between these Wagner allusions). Leaving aside the thorny questions about the possible semantic and/or programmatic meanings of these quotations, the form of these gestures, which marks the quoted material as something extrinsic, is itself significant.[27]

Most of Bruckner's gestures of quotation are cyclical; they recall material presented earlier in the symphony. The Second, Third, Fourth, and, even more dramatically, Fifth Symphonies include in their final movements clear reminiscences of themes from preceding movements. In the earliest versions of the Second and the Third principal motives from earlier movements are presented in a quiet interstice before the final phase of the coda. In the Fourth (1880 and 1888 versions), these allusions are less formal: the first movement's main motive is dramatically recalled at the culmination of the opening theme group (at bar 79) and the Scherzo is invoked both in the opening group (bars 29–42) and near the end of the development (bars 360–70). The Finale of the Fifth Symphony opens with a passage surely modelled on Beethoven's Ninth that reviews the main themes of the slow introduction, the first movement, and the Adagio. In his later works, as his feeling for form became more fluid, Bruckner largely abandoned this sort of formalized quotation, and he removed most of them from the revised versions of the Second and Third Symphonies. From the Sixth Symphony onwards another type of thematic recall is pre-eminent, an apotheosizing statement of the main theme of the first movement (usually in a stabilized form) late in the Finale. This is held back until the conclusive period of the coda in the Sixth and the Seventh, on the model of the Finale of the Third. In the Eighth, as in the Fifth, Bruckner brings the opening theme back somewhat earlier (bars 619–23 of the 1890 version, just before the coda) and then crowns the work with its famous triple thematic overlay in the final pages, just as the Fifth culminates in a chorale with the head motive of the first movement deployed contrapuntally as a countersubject.

Recapitulation

It is in the recapitulation, which is both the crucial and the most problematic element of sonata form, that Bruckner breaks most decisively with formal convention. The 'metaphysics of return', to borrow James Buhler's apposite formulation, is essential to the traditional aesthetic of sonata form; return, as formalized by the process of recapitulation, 'carries the heavy burden not only of creating musical time but also of engendering and thus making possible the totality of the work', and it 'thus possesses a metaphysical import that brings into existence the appearance of the properly musical'.[28] It is appropriate, then, that the recapitulation of the exposition's thematic material, beginning with the 'simultaneous return' of both primary theme and tonic key at the end of the development section, has been described as 'the central structural event, distinguishing sonata form from all others that begin with an exposition ... Neither a simple restatement of the main theme alone, nor a simple return to the tonic alone, has the intense impact of this simultaneous return.'[29] A complementary notion of recapitulation places special emphasis on the so-called 'sonata principle': the exposition, with its tonicization of the dominant (or relative key) and presentation of a second theme group in the new key, establishes a 'large-scale dissonance' that the recapitulation then resolves by reprising the 'material played outside of the tonic (i.e., the second group)' in the tonic key.[30] Bruckner's recapitulations pay court to both of these principles, the 'double return' and the resolving restatement of the second (and third) groups in the body of the recapitulation; yet they tend to avoid simple fulfilment of them, especially in the later symphonies. The gestures and pattern of recapitulations grow increasingly complex and Bruckner was at pains, especially in his finales, to postpone full resolution and tonal completion until late in the movement. The ways in which Bruckner accomplished this repay careful attention, both because of their musical interest and because they involve an aesthetically fraught structural juncture.

In his earlier symphonies, up to the Fourth, Bruckner's handling of the initial portion of his recapitulations is quite regular, with the reprise beginning with a 'simultaneous return' prepared by a dominant preparation. In first movements the development section comes to rest on the dominant, whereupon the recapitulation begins quietly in the tonic, as did the exposition. In the First and Second Symphonies, the recapitulation of the Finale begins forcefully with the main theme arriving at the peak of a prolonged, gathering dominant preparation. However, the ways in which Bruckner recapitulates the second and third theme groups in these works is somewhat more unusual. The task of recapitulating this material is made more complicated by the structure of the exposition, with the presence of a definite third theme group and often a third key area; since these comprise the 'material played outside of the tonic' in the exposition their restatement is crucial to fulfilment of the sonata principle. In the first movements of these symphonies Bruckner restates this material quite conventionally, with some important exceptions in the First Symphony (where the great trombone theme from the exposition (bars 94ff. in the Linz version) is simply absent) and the Fourth Symphony (a work in E♭ major in which the *Gesangsperiode* first appears in D♭ major and is restated in B major). The key schemes of the recapitulation of the Finales of the Third and Fourth display great latitude. The Finale of the Third in D minor has a second theme group that in the exposition begins firmly in F♯ major before making its way to the expected F major. In the recapitulation (1873 and 1877), this section begins in A♭ before arriving in A major, a key much closer to the tonic, yet not *the* tonic, as formal convention would seem to require. (In the 1889 version A major is all but eliminated at this point.) This is followed by a blazing restatement of the closing theme group on B♭, which circles closer to the tonic, but hardly fulfils the conventions of the sonata principle. The tonic of D minor arrives only in the coda. In both the 1874 and the 1878 versions of the Finale of the Fourth Symphony, which is in E♭, the second theme group first appears in C and is recapitulated in D, and this pattern persists with modification in the two later versions of the movement (1880 and 1888) as well.

Bruckner's methods of recapitulation evolved substantially in the late 1870s. The turning point seems to have occurred with the Fifth Symphony (composed in 1875–6 and reworked through 1878) and the recomposition of the Finale of the Fourth Symphony (1879–80). In these works new strategies emerge, especially around the juncture at the beginning of the recapitulation. In the first movement of the Fifth, the recapitulation arrives with a *fortissimo* announcement of the head motive of the main theme on the tonic, B♭ major. This 'simultaneous return' differs from the commencement of the exposition in several ways: it does away with the *piano* statement of the theme that opens the Allegro and the recapitulation is set up by sixteen strong bars of dominant preparation, while in the exposition the main theme emerges from the slow introduction that ends with a powerful sounding of the dominant of D minor. Both of these modifications serve to increase the impact of the thematic reprise; yet in the recapitulation, the main theme group, which is harmonically unstable, is truncated to a mere eighteen bars and quickly slides to the dominant of G minor, in which key the *Gesangsperiode* is restated.

The 1880 Finale of the Fourth (the version commonly performed today) handles the start of the recapitulation so freely that the boundary marking its beginning is blurred: the development section dissolves into a mysterious passage, based on the inversion of the movement's main theme, of great harmonic subtlety (with prominent use of an augmented triad) that hovers around the dominant of D minor before settling to dwell quietly on the home dominant (bars 351–82). Following a long bar of near silence, a prominent motive from the primary theme group is announced *fortissimo* in a massive tutti that begins on the tonic E♭ (in bar 383) but immediately begins to move harmonically and soon subsides on the dominant of F♯ minor. The restatement of the complete two-part *Gesangsperiode* begins in F♯ minor and moves to D major. In the 1888 version of this movement, the *fortissimo* passage from bar 383 is removed and the reprise of the first part of the *Gesangsperiode* begins in D minor, not F♯ minor, preceding the second part of the *Gesangsperiode* in D major. (Interestingly, the 1888 changes bring the key scheme of this portion of reprise closer to the form it had in the 1874 and 1878 versions of the movement.) The third theme group, elements of which were handled at length in the development section, is merely hinted at before the coda begins with a transformed variant of the material that had opened the movement, now transposed from B♭ minor to the tonic minor.

In both of these movements Bruckner splits the various components of the process of recapitulation – dominant preparation, thematic and tonal return, restatement of the second and third theme groups in the tonic key or not – and doles them out in ways that do not follow the usual patterns or structural conventions. These manipulations serve to postpone the achievement of full structural closure until late in the movement, often not until the final phase of the coda.

Bruckner carries this process further in his final group of symphonies. The first movements of the Sixth and the Eighth both do several things worthy of special note. Both symphonies, like the Fifth, begin with an initial *piano* statement of the main theme that is balanced by an immediate *forte* counterstatement; in both recapitulations, however, Bruckner (again as in the Fifth) begins the recapitulation with a shattering *fortissimo* thematic statement that dramatizes the moment of arrival. Each of these arrivals is emphatically prepared by a propulsive dominant preparation, neither of which, remarkably, is rooted on the home dominant; moreover, neither recapitulation begins firmly in the tonic key, thus contesting the central norm of symphonic recapitulation. In the Sixth (in the key of A) the reprise of the main theme is prefaced by a dissonant sonority on the dominant of E♭ minor, which ushers in a reprise of the innately mobile primary theme beginning on E♭ and quickly moving through A (the tonic) to C♯. The *Gesangsperiode*, which appeared in E minor in the exposition, in recapitulated in F♯ minor.[31]

In the Eighth (in C minor), Bruckner also actively destabilizes the tonality at the start of the recapitulation. As the home dominant begins to gather itself in preparation, the harmony slips to the dominant of B♭ minor (bars 217–24) and the music drives forward to a massive announcement based on the primary theme at its original pitch level. The main theme, which is chromatically inflected, tends to veer away from the tonic key, and here Bruckner maximizes this tendency by driving the music through a series of sequential statements. Some bars later, a second statement of the main theme appears in something like the tonic, but with a richly dissonant Neapolitan overlay (bars 283ff.). With the return of the second theme group held to the relative major, it is not until the reprise of the third theme group that the tonic key is finally secured.[32]

Bruckner's handling of the recapitulation in the first movement of the Seventh Symphony in E major is equally sophisticated, but is necessarily treated differently because the primary theme is based on an inherently stable arpeggiation of the tonic triad. The process of reprise begins, after some sixty-five bars of development, as the music comes to hover on a quiet G major triad (bars 229–32). Suddenly a grandiose statement by the full orchestra of the head motive of the main theme in inversion rings out in C minor. Because of its force, this gesture feels like the start of a recapitulation, yet it is so palpably remote from the tonic key that it clearly cannot be the real thing. After sixteen bars of this, the first clause of the main theme, still in C minor, is restated in its original form with its first few bars surrounded by canonic entries of its head motive in both prime and inverted forms. This entire twelve-bar unit is then repeated, transposed up a step to D minor. If this pattern were to be repeated, we would land on E minor, the tonic minor, but Bruckner tinkers with its continuation to deflect the music to the dominant seventh of Ab. Here the clustering canonic entries of the head motive return, only to give way abruptly after four bars to a radiant and still E major and the restatement of the complete primary theme, which is sounded, as on the opening pages, by the cellos with doubling first by a single horn and then the clarinets. Unlike the exposition, though, the theme is here mirrored by the simultaneous sounding of its ornamented inversion in the first violin and flutes. Following an extraordinarily elliptical transition (bars 303–18), the *Gesangsperiode* is restated beginning in the tonic. This harmonically mobile theme group inevitably unfolds through a range of flat-side harmonies and leads to a restatement of the third theme group that wholly avoids E. It is not until the coda, then, that E is finally established by the sort of firm, if not yet decisive, cadential motion that was so pointedly absent at the return of either the first or second theme group. In this movement, then, Bruckner effectively deconstructs the process of recapitulation and individually distributes its various thematic, tonal, and gestural elements.

Form and content: incongruence?

Despite the undeniable presence of a number of formal conventions and patterns derived from standard sonata form, Bruckner's symphonies do not feel terribly classical or traditional. A number of critics have described a tension or imbalance between the outward trappings of sonata form and the specific content and style of Bruckner's music. During Bruckner's lifetime, Rudolf Louis referred to the 'incongruence between form and content' in Bruckner.[33] In the 1960s Werner Korte suggested that the influence of

Formenlehre led Bruckner into the 'cardinal sin' of 'regarding "form" and "content" as two separate matters'.[34] Roughly similar sentiments became quite prevalent in British Bruckner criticism. Tovey bluntly asserted that 'the fundamental mistake of Bruckner was in associating his Wagnerian style with sonata form at all'.[35] Robert Simpson, who like Tovey admired Bruckner's music, in discussing the first movement of the Seventh referred to 'the gulf between sonata principles and those obeyed by Bruckner', a sentiment that recurs several other times in his writings.[36]

This line of criticism connects with several aesthetic positions. One is the familiar sense that the classical equilibrium of form and content, of part and whole, was increasingly lost in the course of the nineteenth century. In the Romantic era, as Edward Cone put it, composers treated sonata form 'no longer as a principle, but as a "form"'. Thus composers from 'Chopin to Bruckner and beyond, dutifully try, in individual ways, to force intractable material into an unyielding mould'.[37] In a similar vein, Roger Sessions wrote that Romantic composers increasingly emphasized 'the individual detail' at the expense of 'synthesis, the real essence of musical form', such that in Wagnerian music 'musical coherence is there, to be sure – but in a passive sense'.[38] These judgements assume an ideal of musical form as organic, a belief that musical form should arise, or grow, by inner processes, not external conventions or patterns. Charles Rosen identified as a hallmark of classical form the 'sense that the movement, the development, and the dramatic course of a work all can be found latent in the material [and] that this material can be made to release its charged force so that the music . . . is literally impelled from within'.[39] Bruckner's music is hard to accommodate within this organicist aesthetic, notwithstanding Kurth's Herculean – and often truly perceptive – efforts in this direction; it is not seamless music that seems to germinate effortlessly, nor is it free from traces of schematicism. Bruckner, it seems fair to conclude, was less concerned with formal organicism than many of his critics; he was also out of step with Wagner, who placed great emphasis on the significance of organic structures and the escape from artistic conventions. Perhaps Bruckner's non-organic sense of form reaches back to the Latin Mass, highly conventionalized both as a text and as a musical genre, that was such an important presence in his musical world, especially in his formative years.

Many of the musical ends Bruckner pursued – powerful expressions of contrast, lyrical and harmonic intensity, and epic grandeur – could not be achieved easily or naturally within more 'organic' forms. It may be that one of Bruckner's basic insights was to accept that musical form was to some extent, in Dahlhaus' terms, 'a system of formal relations' – in other words, something in dialogue with conventional patterns and schemes – and not to insist that form must appear as the result of 'organic' unfolding of the possibilities latent in motivic and thematic kernels.[40] Bruckner was thus responding to a tension emerging from the historical condition of the symphony and of musical language itself in the final decades of the nineteenth century. The advanced chromatic and motivic techniques of the time were not easily adaptable to the purposes of traditionally conceived symphonic forms, which had originally developed out of a much more basic harmonic vocabulary. Bruckner's schematic formal approach responded to this condition; the solidity of its larger architecture allowed the accommodation of a complex tonal and motivic vocabulary within a firmly drawn symphonic structure.

Bruckner's use of harmonic and motivic devices that were stylistically progressive, and thus by the standards of the time broadly Wagnerian, is probably the source for the idea bluntly expressed by Hanslick that a basic 'peculiarity' of Bruckner's symphonies was his 'importing Wagner's dramatic style into the symphony'.[41] The particular formation of Viennese musical politics certainly coloured Hanslick's view, yet scholars such as Tovey have shared it and not without musical justification. Guido Adler, who studied under both Hanslick and Bruckner, wrote that Bruckner 'transferred idiosyncratically the motivic workmanship of the musical drama to his themes and thematic treatment'.[42] Adler did not explain how this influence manifested itself, but its effect is clearly to be felt in Bruckner's preference for plastic, well-characterized, fragmentary, and often chromatic and/or harmonically unstable thematic ideas (e.g. the opening themes of the Second, Sixth, and Eighth Symphonies) that are presented very clearly and often immediately developed into paragraphs that tend to avoid the grammatical conventions of classical periodic phrase structure; thus, as Blume wrote, Bruckner worked 'with brisk, energy-laden motifs each of which is developed within itself... out of this motivic work grows an extensive thematic complex that in itself forms a tense and firm symphonic unit'.[43] Consider the opening pages of the Fourth Symphony: a simple motive based on a dotted rhythm and the interval of a fifth is introduced by a solo horn (instrumental timbre is here thematic, as in many Wagnerian leitmotifs) and is repeated, first by the horn and later by upper woodwinds and the horn in dialogue, in a series of increasingly evolved variants before giving way to a new motive (in the 'Bruckner rhythm', bars 43ff.) and at last reaching a structural cadence (bar 51). Harmonically this passage, which sets wind and horn firmly in relief against a continuous tremolando background played by the strings, derives less from the syntax of common-practice chord progression than from harmonic motion around sustained pedal tones (the tonic is sounded by the cellos and/or the violas through bar 32) leavened by sudden enharmonic shifts (for example, in bars 29–35 where a C minor sixth chord moves to a D♭ minor sixth followed by a second inversion triad of A). It is followed by a counterstatement based on variants of the rhythmic motive introduced in bar 43 that differs markedly from the opening paragraph in character, sonority, and rhythmic structure but is similar to it in its smart progression through some remote harmonic regions (from C♭ to A♭ minor via an augmented sixth on F♭, bars 59–65) before defining a firm tonal goal (the dominant of the dominant). Adler suggested that Bruckner's manner of motivic treatment may have 'exercised a loosening influence on his thematic work [and] on the sequence and juxtaposition of groups within movement-sections', and wondered whether 'the manner in which his ideas were handled was an essential component of his design'.[44] These observations are not, of course, mutually exclusive. The inherent richness of many of Bruckner's thematic ideas and their treatment serve direct expressive purposes, yet the solid and often fairly closed paragraphs they engender foreclose the possibility of a smoothly connected overall structure emerging seamlessly from thematic-motivic work; instead, they necessitated forms that had exposed seams and palpable 'edges and corners'. Thus with Bruckner, the larger connections become evident 'only by grasping the complete structure'.[45]

As Dahlhaus pointed out, in the wake of the 'crisis' of symphonic form in the mid-nineteenth century 'the connection between syntactic structure and formal function that existed in classical sonata form was sundered'.[46] The effect of this disruption – or perhaps better, a response to possibilities arising from it – is evident in Bruckner's coordination of function and gesture; many of his theme groups make use of syntactic features – sequence, roving chromatic harmony, motivic evolution, *Steigerungen* – that were traditionally devices of development, not exposition. As a critical category, 'form' (and therefore 'formlessness') indexes more than morphology; it also encompasses the intelligibility of the work (heard against the horizon of tradition) and the interplay of thematic content, formal design, and generic expectation. Bruckner's novel approach to the coordination of the elements contributed to the nineteenth-century perception that his music was formless. This is evident in comments made by Theodor Helm in 1896, who stated that Bruckner's music could 'immediately alienate those unprepared listeners who cannot let go of strict classical formal notions. Specifically, Bruckner was fond of elaborating the second and third themes of his first movements just as extensively as his main theme, and of spinning out these subsidiary ideas at length before returning to the main theme. This hinders the impression of unity on first hearing…'[47] The infusion of 'developmental' devices into areas devoted to thematic exposition, and in turn recapitulation, is facilitated by the schematic aspects of Bruckner's conception of form, which makes possible the structural balancing of large sections regardless of their content and apparent function and which also ameliorates the importance of thematic antagonism as a generative force of sonata form. The thematic contrasts in Bruckner are great – often greater than anything to be found in Mozart, Brahms, Schumann, and even Beethoven – but the contrasting themes rarely interact with each other in the ways that they do in the work of other, more 'organic' composers. Perhaps it is that Bruckner's contrasts are so sharply drawn and preserved throughout the course of a work that the individual parts remain too autonomous to submit easily to the impression of seamless formal totality.

Epilogue: form, fragment, and feeling

Some of Bruckner's most moving and affecting pages – for me these include the C minor passage that opens the *Gesangsperiode* of the Finale of the Fourth Symphony, the mosaic-like second theme group in the first movement of the Sixth, the poignantly plain melody sung by the Wagner tubas in the Adagio of the Eighth (bars 67–70, 1890 version) and a moment of passionate arioso in the Finale of that symphony (at letter T) – have an odd self-sufficiency; they seem to exist microcosmically in the larger universe of the symphony. With this, these passages aspire to the condition of the 'Romantic Fragment', a term recently introduced to the criticism of nineteenth-century music by Charles Rosen. In Rosen's formulation, a fragment of this type is 'imperfect and yet complete' and 'is, or should be, a finished form: it is the content that is incomplete – or, rather, that develops further with each reading'.[48] 'The Romantic Fragment', he elaborates, 'is, therefore, a closed structure, but its closure is a formality: it may be separated from the rest of the universe, but it implies the existence of what is outside of itself not by reference but by its instability'.[49] It might seem odd to apply a formal notion derived from *Lieder* and character pieces to monumental symphonies; yet because of the 'formality' of Bruckner's forms certain episodes, especially *Gesangsperioden*, achieve a sheltered isolation somewhat akin to the uneasy autonomy of a song in a song cycle. And because they are self-subsisting units whose meaning, but not form, 'develops further with each reading' Bruckner's theme groups can return essentially unchanged, if often tonally alienated, yet still with new meaning in the recapitulation.

Edward Said responded to Bruckner's distinctive patterns of repetition and change. Before quoting the *Gesangsperiode* of the first movement of the Ninth, he speculated that the value of musical elaboration is not necessarily its achievement of 'finished perfection', but 'that the essence of the elaboration can be transformative and reflective, that it can occur slowly not only because we affirm and reaffirm its repetition, its meandering course, but also because it too seems to be about the same process, the way, for example, there is something both reflective and circular – without regard for impressive development – in the leisurely, majestic unfolding of Bruckner's Ninth Symphony'.[50] Perhaps these ideas can help us perceive the larger patterns of meaning in Bruckner's form. The pacing, the majesty, the reflection, the circling, the repetition that occur within individual movements and across Bruckner's symphonic oeuvre can, evidently, be objectionable to some; yet it is by them that Bruckner's music wins some of its greatest and most humane expression.

13 Formal process as spiritual progress: the symphonic slow movements

MARGARET NOTLEY

Notions of genre have a stubborn persistence. As recently as 1950, Bernhard Paumgartner wrote of the symphony's continuing significance, in the 'post-war cultural confusion' of his own time, as 'a monumental art performed by a multitude of players before a still greater multitude of listeners'. The concept of symphonic monumentality – sometimes interpreted as having to do with the sheer magnitude of a work but more complex than that, as we shall see – has special relevance to Bruckner, as do other assumptions about genre that come up in Paumgartner's remarks. After having separated musical genres into the communal and the purely private (the latter exemplified by the lullaby), he divided communal music into three basic categories and then asserted that the various movements within the symphony showed the imprint of all three. That is to say, Paumgartner discerned traces of primordial communal functions in each type of symphonic movement: of martial or of ceremonial state music in the first, of dance music in the minuet or scherzo and also in the finale. And in the 'emotional significance' of the slow movement he heard a residue of the sounds and spirit of music used in religious rites.[1]

Nowhere has the connection between the genre of the symphonic slow movement, in particular the symphonic Adagio, and religious experience been noted more often, it seems, than in treatments of Bruckner's lifework. August Halm, for example, called the Adagio not just the 'central movement' but the 'shrine' in his symphonies, adding that this had nothing to do with whether the character of the melodies sounds 'ritualistically religious'. He wrote that Bruckner was in fact as likely to place a melody reminiscent 'of the chorale or even of chant or the hymn' in an opening movement or finale as in an Adagio. What Halm saw as of primary importance was that 'for the construction of the Adagio he established a more regular rule – thus, more or less a ritual'.[2]

In stressing both the assumed spiritual essence and basically predictable course of the symphonic slow movements, Halm brought together two of the most prominent themes in the reception of those works. Critics have often attributed the predictability of Bruckner's slow movements to a schematic approach to large-scale form, but this observation does not hold up under scrutiny. On the other hand, he does repeatedly use an array of smaller-scale formal patterns, textures, and other musical topoi with more or less stable meaning. Working these into his slow movements in a variety of ways, he appears to tell a similar story over and over again: one of spiritual development towards an ultimate state of acceptance or even transfiguration. Technical procedures that seem significant for particular movements or groups of movements have suggested the topical arrangement in this essay.[3]

Unending melody and the Adagio of Bruckner's First Symphony

By the time that Bruckner started to compose symphonies in the 1860s, the genre of the Adagio had already become associated with religious experience and therefore begun to rise in status. His Adagios would come to seem the most perfect distillation of that conception of the genre because of his compositional affinity for slow movements but also his personal piety and continuing ties to the Catholic Church. In technical terms, the increased stature of the slow movement that Bruckner inherited appears largely to have resulted from types of phrase-structure that made it sound as eloquent as the outer movements. A number of Wagnerites, in particular, saw certain classical slow movements as having anticipated their Master's ideal of *unendliche Melodie*, seeming to offer a glimpse of the beyond by suggesting eternity. And they considered the valued melodic constructions to have reached a zenith in instrumental music in the Adagios of Beethoven's so-called third period: for example, the Cavatina of the String Quartet in B♭ major (Op. 130) and the slow movements of the 'Hammerclavier' Sonata and Ninth Symphony.[4]

Critics have frequently linked Bruckner's typical practice of alternating two broad thematic groups, a putative source of the ritualistic inevitability noted by Halm, to Beethoven's procedures in the Adagio of his Ninth Symphony. But many late nineteenth-century musicians appear to have regarded the quality of individual themes and the means for simulating melodic endlessness as more significant than fixed formal patterns (or inventive deviations from them). In any case, as we shall see, Bruckner never adopted the double-variation shape usually discerned in the Adagio of Beethoven's Ninth. Matters of melodic style offer other, possibly more meaningful, connections between the symphonic slow movements of the two composers. The opening themes of Bruckner's slow movements often bear a resemblance to themes that Beethoven wrote for the same position. Moreover, Bruckner at times cultivated phrase-structures and other stylistic/formal strategies reminiscent of those that underlie Beethovenian unending melody, which in the earlier master's symphonic slow movements found its most celebrated expression in the Ninth.

Elements in the Adagio of Beethoven's Ninth that serve to move the music forward 'endlessly' include the spinning-out of figures in the second theme and in the variations of the first. The tentative introductory bars in the wind and the overlapping or echoing insertions between apparently more fundamental phrases of the opening theme also promote the desired effect. By softening any underlying symmetry, as well as obscuring the beginnings and endings of phrases, these 'added' bars help support an illusion of ongoing melodic process that may override expected points of structural articulation: the hallmark of *unendliche Melodie*.[5] Unending melody does not appear in a single voice; rather, it arises from a compelling interweaving of voices such as Beethoven composed in this Adagio. Throughout this movement, furthermore, cadences tend to fall on weak beats. And the thematic statements themselves, the variations of them, the brief interlude (bars 83–98), and most of the coda achieve no closure, but instead always lead on through various deceptive resolutions to the next formal section.

Some of the same strategies are apparent in the slow movement of Bruckner's First Symphony (which is not to say that Beethoven's Ninth provided a direct model for it). Formally this Adagio, divisible without much effort into three sections since there is a change of both metre and tempo for the central one, may bear the least resemblance to the Adagio of Beethoven's Ninth of any of Bruckner's slow movements. But in it Bruckner has used melodic and phrase-structural techniques similar to those evident in Beethoven's Adagio. Indeed, Bruckner takes the idea of a hesitant beginning much further in his Adagio: neither the correct placement of downbeats nor the key (Ab major) is discernible for some time, the former becoming apparent in bar 9 and the latter in bar 19. A theme does not start to take shape until even later, though thematic fragments begin to form in bars 19ff. With the appearance of a fully-fledged theme over a Bb triad at the upbeat to bar 31 – the local tonic eventually turns out to be Eb major – comes the initial culminating point in the movement. Here as elsewhere, the treatment of cadences satisfies the most obvious condition of melodic endlessness, for the theme (bars 30–43) and the first large formal section as a whole do not achieve closure. At the juncture between the opening and central sections (bars 43–4), as in a number of other critical passages, diminished seventh chords smooth the connections.

Like the theme in the first section, the central section is in Eb but, with its short phrases and, in part, staccato articulation – along with its contrasting tempo and metre – stylistically distinct. The manner in which Bruckner handles the transition between the central section and the return of the opening supports Ernst Kurth's observation that in unending melody, certain types of motives (*Entwicklungsmotive*) result from the process of development rather than providing the impetus for it.[6] Towards the end of the central section, the spinning-out of derived motives of this sort begins in the first violins (bar 91), continuing over a prolonged dominant seventh of E♭ until characteristic motives from the central section in other voices disappear (bars 93–9). The figuration still does not stop as motives and diminished seventh chords from the opening begin to resurface (bars 100ff.) and the metre becomes uncertain. (The metre must change back from 3/4 to common time, but when the first section begins again, in bar 115, the correct placement of downbeats is immediately clear; the obscuring of the metre has taken place in the preceding transitional passage.) As in the Adagio of Beethoven's Ninth, figuration furthers the illusion of melodic endlessness.

For the reprise Bruckner adjusted the relative weight of the components within the initial thematic complex so that the movement's second point of culmination does not occur, like the first, at the beginning of the 'true' theme (here at the upbeat to bar 141), but rather at its close in bar 158. For now the theme does conclude with a perfect cadence, in A♭ major. Theodor Helm, who reviewed the first performance of the Vienna version of Bruckner's First in 1891, wrote that the ending of the Adagio seemed 'to soar upward into heaven itself', adding that 'a deeper, more significant Adagio had not been written since Beethoven'.[7] A melodic process underlies the unfolding aural image of uncertainty, change, and eventual transfiguration.

Images of ceremony and transcendence in the Andantes

Is it possible or even desirable to extricate Bruckner's slow movements from otherworldly associations? After World War II, as Walter Wiora has written, there may have been a backlash against hermeneutics in work on Bruckner, as in other areas of musical scholarship.[8] If so, a number of more recent monographs and articles suggest that musicologists have become comfortable again with questions of interpretation. Resuming a type of earlier criticism cultivated extensively by Kurth, these writers – most notably Wiora himself – have catalogued a repertory of religious topoi that Bruckner used repeatedly in his compositions and especially in his slow movements.

Quotation, including self-quotation, in particular of liturgical compositions, constitutes one category of such signs. Related to this are apparent, but less direct references to passages with spiritual connotations in the works of other composers: for example, the 'otherworldly' figuration for solo violin that Beethoven introduced into the Benedictus of the *Missa solemnis*.[9]

A recurring topos that seems to have had personal meaning for Bruckner involved the use of extremes in register, perhaps to bring to mind the enormity of the universe. These musical signs also encompass the hymn- or chant-like melodies and chorale textures referred to by Halm. Other referential devices include trombone choirs in the style of funereal equali, the steady andante pace of a religious procession, and chains of suspensions or passages of quasi-modal writing that recall early church music.[10]

Choosing certain of these musical images – chains of suspensions, for instance, or a sign that has to do with basic melodic material, such as a theme evocative of a type of church music – sets in motion a succession of events. For example, the overriding topos in the Andante of Bruckner's Fourth Symphony, a religious procession – whether associated with a funeral, since it is in C minor, or with some other ceremony – pervades the entire composition, determining its gait and much of how it otherwise, so to speak, moves forward.

Other topoi seem more spatial than temporal in nature. How, then, did Bruckner coordinate momentary effects, such as the orchestrational devices that use musical space to evoke vastness and thus eternity, with a melodic style (*unendliche Melodie*) that likewise creates an image of the beyond, but through temporal means? After his First Symphony, Bruckner never again composed a slow movement as a single unbroken process. In the later slow movements, the reappearance of the opening phrases of his themes initiates new stages of melodic elaboration, whereas spatial symbols often served to articulate the end of a thematic statement or phase of development.

As a work that calls to mind a religious procession, the Andante of the Fourth Symphony may of necessity involve more repetition than the other slow movements: the very act of repeating appropriate themes suggests ceremonial walking. Most of the transitional passages between thematic statements, including the 'extra' bars at the end of statements of the first theme, use topoi of the types described above. After the second statement of the first theme, for example, a succession of related signs – chorale texture (bars 25–40), quasi-modal harmony (bars 33–40), and a chain of suspensions (bars 41–5) – effects most of the transition to the second theme, which begins in bar 51. And a dramatic use of musical space – a descent in register from the flutes through the various other wind and brass instruments to the lowest range of the bass tuba and contrabasses – connects the second statement of the second theme to the final, much elaborated and intensified appearance of the first theme (bars 187–92).

The Andante, in A♭ major, from Bruckner's Second Symphony provides further examples of both ongoing melodic processes and discrete signs that convey a sense of endlessness. For example, a bar-long chord for all four horns plus trombone trio – the latter instruments, according to Kurth, a central symbol for Bruckner of 'primordial darkness' and 'religious sublimity'[11] – punctuates the end of statements of the second theme in F minor and then B♭ minor (bars 34–47, 107–20). Following the second statement, Bruckner varies and develops the theme, leading to motives (bars 138–9) that recall a passage in the Benedictus of his Mass in F minor; the movement as a whole will culminate in a full quotation of the same phrase.

In the first theme Wiora considers Bruckner to have drawn on the 'solemn Adagio of Viennese Classicism' – as exemplified by the slow movement of Beethoven's Ninth – in the 'quiet, slow motion in duple metre, the gentle contours of the cantilena', and the resulting affect.[12] As in most of the slow movements, the first theme appears in three increasingly long versions (bars 1–16, 70–99, 149–84, in the Nowak edition) before a final brief reference to it in the coda. Bruckner lengthens the second occurrence of this theme through an internal expansion after the first four bars. A spatial sign, in this case an isolated flute figure in bar 87, marks the end of the expansion, followed by a more or less unaltered restatement of bars 5–16 in bars 88–99.

The final version of the first theme not only is the longest but also goes the furthest afield harmonically and motivically. In an even more protracted developmental expansion (bars 153–67), the theme again begins to diverge from the opening version after four bars. Although the statement of the theme resumes with the fifth bar, 'visionary' chromaticism not explainable by inherited norms of harmonic logic (bars 168–71) now distorts it, and the theme begins to fragment, getting no further than the tenth bar of the original version (bars 172–9). For the ultimate goals are the quotation from Bruckner's Mass in F minor (Nowak, bars 180–3), a reference to the opening theme (bars 184–90), and an allusion to the topos of otherworldly figuration (bars 190–8).

Repeated mention of topoi here may bring to mind well-established traditions having to do with techniques of a specifically musical rhetoric. Like the frequently encountered trope of a symphony as a speech to a large group of listeners, these traditions are based on a pervasive metaphor of music as language. Beyond that, the idea of musical rhetoric implies an aesthetic that is directed towards audience reception, and this, as we shall see, is in accord with the late nineteenth-century concept of symphonic monumentality.

Symphonic monumentality and Bruckner's Adagios

Slow movements may well have been understood to express or even to evoke religious experience before the late nineteenth century, but that view of the genre does not appear to have been much disseminated in print before then. The connection between symphonic slow movements and spirituality does, however, seem to have played a central role in a 'cult of Classicism' that developed concomitantly with a rejection of Romanticism after mid-century.[13] Various sources from the late nineteenth and first half of the twentieth centuries suggest widespread acceptance of a narrative of musical (and cultural) decline after Beethoven: many observers of Austro-German music worlds seem to have regarded Romanticism as having signalled a precipitous falling-off of compositional aspirations and accomplishments. Because these writers valorized Classicism at the expense of Romanticism, they viewed Beethoven's cultivation of classical genres, of necessity, as free of any Romantic tendencies. As another corollary, Brahms the symphonist was considered to have continued the lesser Romantic tradition of Schumann and Mendelssohn in the second half of the century, whereas Bruckner was seen as having renewed the great Beethovenian tradition.

Now to observe, as Reinhold Brinkmann did in a recent monograph on Brahms' Second Symphony, that the inner movements of Romantic symphonies tend to be 'character pieces of "medium" dimensions and weight' is one thing.[14] To devalue Schumann's symphonic slow movements as 'charming character pieces rather than spiritual revelations' – the latter of course exemplified by the Adagios of Beethoven and Bruckner – as the musicologist Walther Vetter did in the early 1940s, is another matter.[15] More than a half-century after the fact, Vetter's comments echoed positive reactions to the first performances of Bruckner's Seventh Symphony in 1885. These remarks, for instance, had appeared at that time in a Munich newspaper: 'No song without words inflated to an Adagio, no elfin dance to a Scherzo', followed by a seemingly inevitable comparison of Bruckner's Adagio and Scherzo to inner movements by Beethoven.[16] (Mendelssohn is the obvious target in this case.) Behind such observations lies not only a narrative of decline and eventual renewal, but also an aesthetics based on essentialist ideas of genre: for why must a symphonic slow movement not resemble a character piece?

For those who accepted that aesthetics, the answer would be that a lyrical character piece and song-without-words texture are suitable only for self-expression and that a symphony must seem to express the sentiments of a group.[17] Without subscribing to the exclusionary perspective evident in much writing about Bruckner, one can reconstruct its foundations, at which point the concept of monumentality becomes crucial. In commentary from the late nineteenth and early twentieth centuries on symphonies, 'monumentality' at times functioned as an opposing term to 'Romanticism'. In the context of genre aesthetics, this key word, which often suggested not just grandeur but also the suprapersonal and even more precisely a communal quasi-religious experience, had particular pertinence to the symphonic slow movement. Stated in the lofty idealist language of the time, 'all of humanity' should seem to be making music in a performance of a symphonic slow movement, and it should allow a group intuition of the Absolute: content and reception are related facets of this widely held aesthetics of the symphony.[18]

In a frequently cited passage from the late eighteenth century, Heinrich Koch had likened the symphony to the chorus in vocal music, which 'has as its purpose to express the feelings of a whole multitude of people'.[19] Early accounts of the genre such as Koch's formed a foundation for late nineteenth-century ideas concerning not only appropriate content but also the expected impact on the listener. And, indeed, symphonic monumentality is not dissimilar to the late eighteenth-century aesthetic of the symphonic sublime.[20] New in the late nineteenth century is the emphasis on slow movements and the extension to those movements of stylistic expectations earlier reserved for opening Allegros. For late eighteenth-century treatments of the symphony had linked the sublime, associated above all with first movements, to melodic structures that created an impression of apparently limitless forward motion. With reference to slow movements in the nineteenth century, as we have seen, *unendliche Melodie* conveyed a related concept.

Unending melody is not, however, invariably tied to monumentality: the Cavatina from Beethoven's String Quartet in Bb (Op. 130), for instance, exemplifies the former but not the latter. What, then, are the defining features of musical monumentality? Arnold Schering wrote an essay on that topic, with special reference to Bach and Handel, first published in 1934. Schering stressed the importance of a style suitable for performance in a large space and, as a consequence, of clarity, simplicity, and a grand line, the 'predominance of simple but full harmonies and a certain splendour and power of sound'. He also emphasized the need for composers to make visible the rules that govern the disposition of their works: 'The more sections and groups are sharply marked and a continuous constructive principle becomes perceptible, the greater the impact.' In line with this last observation comes the heightened significance of techniques such as fugue, basso ostinato, and chains of sequences, which 'because of their objective character are easily exploited for monumental effects'.[21] These particular techniques, it may be noted, can also create an impression of melodic endlessness. With respect to the content of a monumental work – recalling traditional ideas about the symphony – 'the personal, the subjective must disappear so that the universal can come to light'.[22] (The overt subjectivity of expression in the Cavatina eliminates it from the category of the monumental.) Like the visual arts, moreover, music had developed a network of images associated with monumentality, some of which we have already observed in

Bruckner's slow movements: 'Gregorian chant or Evangelical chorale, characteristic uses of instrumental and thematic symbolism, special measures for the contrapuntal-constructive arrangement of sound masses, spatial-acoustic effects, etc.'.[23]

Taking Schering's discussion as a point of departure, what features might be said to contribute to a presumed monumental effect in the Adagio of Beethoven's Ninth, the work to which Bruckner's Adagios are most frequently compared? A list might include the unadorned solemnity of the first theme, the relative harmonic simplicity throughout, the long line achieved through overriding forward motion, and the alternation of two distinct themes and variation of the first of these as an evident constructive principle.

In Bruckner's slow movements, as has already been noted, appearances of (usually) two alternating themes likewise demarcate large formal sections. An initial so-called A section in a slow movement by Bruckner, however, fulfils functions of thematic statement, transition, and, increasingly, also development that had tended to be compartmentalized in the late eighteenth-century schemata used by Beethoven. (Deceptive cadences effect the modulation at the end of each section in the Adagio of his Ninth Symphony.) As a result, subsequent A sections by Bruckner cannot easily vary the first statement – though he attempted to do this in early versions of the Third Symphony's Adagio. Rather than retaining the phrase-structure and length of the initial thematic complex in the A sections that follow, he introduces procedures, most notably sequences, that alter and inevitably expand the shape – as we have seen, for example, in the Andante of the Second Symphony. Schering had cited the sequence for its 'objective character', but a rising sequence set as a *crescendo* can have a powerful impact.[24] With respect to concerns of both audience reception and content, the sequence is thus well suited to the monumental symphony.

Sequential *Steigerungen* (intensifications) nonetheless had limited applications in symphonic slow movements before Bruckner. They do not, for instance, appear in the Adagio of Beethoven's Ninth, which remains lyrical throughout. And when Mozart uses the *crescendo* in the sonata-form slow movement of the 'Jupiter' Symphony, it emphasizes, and the sequences effect, modulations in the transition and development sections; intensifications in general serve to underscore functions of transition and development in movements based on late eighteenth-century schemata. Just as Bruckner increasingly mixed formal functions within sections, he also introduced *Steigerungen* even into the initial A section.

Although the treatment of monumentality here has focused for the most part on matters of reception, trends in Bruckner's compositional approach suggest that he strove for ever more impressive effects. After the slow movements of the First and Second Symphonies, lyricism seems to have been less important than grandeur to him. The Adagio of the Sixth, the most songful and understated and also the shortest of the later slow movements, provides a revealing exception to this trend. For in this, the slow movement by him most unambiguously in sonata form, Bruckner used intensifications to underscore his adaptation of the schema, based on the three-key-expositional approach associated with Schubert. Rising sequences appear in the development (bars 77–84), of course. In a reversal of traditional practice, however, he keeps transitional passages at a low dynamic level while designing each of the first two themes around a modulating intensification. The first theme, in F minor, takes shape as a rising sequence (bars 5–6, 7–8, 9–10), the objectivity of this technique and of the walking bass line counteracting the lyric plaintiveness of the oboe melody. A quiet transition (bars 18–24) completes the modulation to the secondary key, E major. Within the second theme, another intensification (bars 33–41) emphasizes the move from E major to a long but subdued pedal on the dominant of C (C minor will be the third key). Both thematic intensifications reappear in the recapitulation (bars 97–112, 121–9), the first one dramatically expanded. At the end of each of Bruckner's minor-mode slow movements, a change to the parallel major key suggests an improved spiritual condition; here this takes place in a hushed coda.

In the other later Adagios his concern with symphonic monumentality and the problems that it presents in slow movements becomes evident. One problem that crystallized in the four versions of the Third Symphony's Adagio (completed respectively in 1873, 1876, 1877, and 1889) had to do with writing an initial section of sufficient length and weight for the scale of his ambitions. Although Bruckner substantially shortened the third and fourth versions of this Adagio – the 1873 version was 278 bars, the 1889 version 222 bars long – the first section grew from thirty-two to forty bars in length. The original A section began with eight bars composed in the manner of what Wiora called the 'solemn Adagio of Viennese Classicism'. After this appeared a patchwork of three short intensifications (bars 9–13, 16–17, 20–4) separated by so-called 'Marian' cadences (see Example 7.1), followed by a passage recalling the Prelude to *Tristan und Isolde* that finally effected a modulation. Except for a few details mostly concerning orchestration, the opening eight bars remained unchanged throughout the different versions. But already in the 1876 revisions, Bruckner lengthened the first two *Steigerungen* to eight and four bars respectively; in the final two versions he lengthened the first intensification to twelve bars and came up with more convincing figuration for it.

During various phases of revision, he tried different types of intensifying figures to surround later appearances of A material. For the third and fourth versions he reduced the number of sections (not including the coda) from seven (A B C B′ A′ B″ A″) to five (A B C B′ A′), while increasing the focus both within each section and from one section to the next. In the final version he also eliminated later references to the *misterioso* chorale theme (C), concentrating allusions to this type of group song into one section. The appearance and ensuing elaboration of this theme more clearly became the centre of the movement, and he made this section and each of the succeeding two sections lead to ever stronger climaxes.

Even more than the Adagio of Bruckner's Third, that of the Fifth Symphony stands out as a model of musical monumentality, remarkable for the sheer vastness of its scale and also for its reliance on sequences. The opening texture might almost seem to recall that of a song without words, but Bruckner has already planted the beginnings of the sequential writing that will pervade the movement in the bass line (bars 1–3) and in the oboe melody itself (bar 7). Bare sequences, unmistakably objective in expression, appear throughout the movement, allowing him to write a slow movement of unprecedented length yet composed of only five sections in a pattern (A B A′ B′ A″) that he would draw on in his final three monumental Adagios.

The Adagio of the Fifth Symphony offers a study in sequential writing. Many of the sequences descend by step with no change in dynamics, creating no sense of urgency but rather seeming to imply the possibility of an unending cycle. Wiora cites one of these passages (bars 145ff.), which appears towards the end of B′, as signifying 'infinity of space and time'.[25] As usual, rising sequences have an exciting effect and, for example, bring the end of A′ (bars 97–9) to a climax. After a general pause, the section comes to a close with a use of high and low registers and rhythmic augmentation that again seems to suggest infinity. It is only fitting that a sequential passage from the beginning (bars 11–12) should be transformed into the high point of the movement. This brief passage becomes a magnificent rising chorale (bars 169–71, 187–9), a suitable invocation of a symbolic song texture at the culmination of a landmark in the monumental Adagio.

Themes and redemption in the final three symphonic Adagios

Bruckner had inherited a wealth of both phrase-structural possibilities and discrete musical signs from which to choose in composing his symphonic slow movements. But a composer's own themes had always been privileged over elements at the disposal of any musician working within the same tradition. For reasons that are not hard to fathom, a theme had long been seen as the purest and most direct expression of a composer's subjectivity. This may account in part for why the fate of the theme – how it is developed, whether it returns, and if so, whether it comes back unchanged – could be made to seem a consequential matter.

Because Bruckner intertwined functions of statement, elaboration, and transition in the initial thematic complexes of his final three symphonic Adagios, however, determining the limits of the actual 'theme' poses a problem. Bars 1–9 of the Adagio of the Seventh Symphony apparently constitute its first theme, since they provide the material that is developed in the A' and A'' sections and the two phrases in those nine bars return several times, both separately and together. (Another passage from A does come back in the coda.) In the Adagio of the Eighth Symphony, the immediate – if condensed and otherwise somewhat altered – repetition of eighteen of the opening twenty-eight bars establishes the importance of *all* of the elements therein. For in this Adagio the thematic complex A consists entirely of those two lengthy statements. Repetition likewise establishes bars 1–8 in the Adagio of the Ninth Symphony as the first theme. In this movement the opening eight bars are repeated at the beginning of A' and then restated in an exact sequence (bars 77–92). The theme does not return in A'' – for semantically crucial reasons, as we shall see – but extended passages from elsewhere in the thematic complex do come back.

In these late Adagios, along with choices of intervals and contours, striking uses of harmony, texture, and orchestration contribute to the unmistakable particularity of the themes. Bruckner thus turned the timbre of the tuba quintet into a significant thematic element in the Adagio of the Seventh Symphony, which led Vetter to distinguish between 'tutti tubas' and 'Adagio tubas'. While the five instruments function as 'tutti tubas' in the movement's first climax (bars 27–9), for example, they appear as 'Adagio tubas' in the opening four-bar phrase. Drawing on a kind of language often encountered in discussions of Adagios, especially those by Bruckner, he called such use of the instruments the 'incarnation of the deepest Adagio feeling of the slow movement'. And he wrote that 'the particularity of the quintet's softly powerful, dark sound brought out and elevated the composer's most solemnly ceremonial inspirations'.[26]

Vetter's distinction between 'tutti tubas' and 'Adagio tubas' offers a key to understanding the movement. After the first high point, Bruckner used tubas to complete the tutti only at the climax of each of the other A sections (bars 127–31, 177–82). 'Adagio tubas' appear infrequently, as well: at the beginning of each A section, and also at the end of the initial thematic complex (bars 33–6), their darkness creating a foil for the lyricism of B. The tubas rest in B, a three-part so-called song form (bars 37–44, 45–52, 53–66).

About B, 'a music full of light and of mild enticement', Kurth wrote that it could offer 'only a dreamlike image of redemption', for 'the all-overpowering experience of redemption' would not occur until the end.[27] Much of the significance of B′ (bars 133–56) derives from its incompleteness: after a rhetorical pause in bar 148, it becomes apparent that the third part of the form has been suppressed because the idyll cannot continue and that critical events will occur in A″, which follows shortly thereafter.

'Adagio tubas' reappear in the first four bars of A″ of course, but also in a rising sequence (bars 164–72) that Wolfram Steinbeck has linked to such passages as the climax of the Adagio in the Fifth Symphony and ultimately the 'Dona nobis pacem' of the Mass in D minor.[28] The tubas emerge from the final tutti to bring A″ to a close in C♯ minor (bars 185–93). Inevitably, the tubas must take the lead in the change of mode that occurs in the coda: the tenor tubas state the opening motive over a C♯ major triad (bars 207–10) before withdrawing into the background with the rest of the quintet and ceding the more active role to the horns. The dissolution of a thematic element into general sound will become an even more meaningful event in the Adagio of the Ninth.

Like the tubas in the Seventh Symphony, harps have overt symbolic value in the Adagio of the Eighth, which is in D♭ major. As was noted, A consists of two statements of the same materials, each of which itself comprises a pair of open-ended themes. The second theme (bars 21–8, 39–46) features another of the significant ascending passages noted by Steinbeck, which leads to a glimpse of heaven: harps playing a series of plagal progressions. The harps then rest until the end of A″. Throughout all of A′ and most of A″ Bruckner draws on only part of the first theme, holding in reserve its high point (bars 15–20, 33–8) as well as the second theme in its entirety. The culmination of the first theme reappears at a climactic moment in A″ (bars 209–11), but more development follows. When the figure comes back a second time, rhythmically augmented (bars 239–43), it is in the movement's only true tutti – that is, with the harps included. This time the figure leads to the rest of the first theme and also the complete second theme, with harps. For the opening thematic complex had concluded in a celestial vision, a telos appropriate for the movement as a whole.

For the Adagio of the Ninth, Bruckner came up with a different approach centred on progressively dissolving themes. This Adagio, like that of the First Symphony, strives towards an unambiguous statement of the tonic triad. In the earlier movement, the securing of the tonic coincided with the reprise of the theme from the initial complex. But in the Adagio of the Ninth, there is no clear statement of the tonic until thematic material has disappeared.

Extreme dissonance and chromaticism, with traditional associations of suffering and sorrow, mark bars 1–4 of the first theme, while bars 5–7 are set as a diatonic rising line in E-Mixolydian. The initial thematic complex also includes an intensification based on the opening motive (bars 9–16) and an extended high point (bars 17–24). As the field of sound fades, a diffuse brass chorale is heard (bars 29–44) before the entrance of B. While the lyricism and three-part shape of this thematic group might at first make it seem to resemble, for example, B in the Adagio of the Seventh Symphony, this group and its parts appear less complete.

Themes begin to disintegrate after the sequential presentation of the first theme in so-called A′, which resembles a development section more than the corresponding passages of the earlier Adagios in its length and in its recollection and working of elements from both A and B. Through this section, as Kurth notes, the Adagio might be understood as a sonata-form movement.[29] But the process of dissolution increases, as pure sound comes to seem more and more of the essence. Only the first part of the original group reappears in B′, rhythmically augmented (bars 173–86). A massive *Steigerung*, based on motives from B, leads thereafter to the return not of the first theme, but rather of the first intensification (bars 207ff.) and another chorale (for winds and horns this time, bars 219–30): these materials, not the theme, represent the initial complex. Release finally comes in the coda with its sustained E major triad (bars 231–43).

In keeping with the philosophical tradition that links themes with subjectivity, Steinbeck suggests that the opposition between thematic and non-thematic elements is dialectical. From this perspective the disappearance of thematic material into general orchestral sound that typically occurs at the end of a finale – his example is Beethoven's Ninth – can be seen as another facet of the monumental symphony.[30] Bruckner likewise eliminated themes in the Adagio of his own Ninth Symphony, which became the finale, creating the effect of dissolving all ties to this world, according to Kurth.[31]

For the first theme in each of the slow movements is not only an expression of Bruckner's individuality but also the protagonist in the events suggested in them. He builds both thematic and non-thematic elements into powerful sequential intensifications. In the Adagios of the Seventh and Eighth Symphonies a reference to or return of a thematic element after the highest peak signals the impending completion of formal and semantic processes. And in the Adagio of the Ninth the utter dissolution of thematic elements takes on extraordinary meaning.

Bruckner's introduction of awe-inspiring intensifications, previously restricted for the most part to the outer movements of symphonies, may constitute his most significant technical contribution to the genre of the

Adagio. In conjunction with a system of musical signs, both inherited and particular to himself, his use of this constructive device permitted effects of a grandeur not possible before in a slow movement. That the resulting dialectic between thematic and non-thematic elements also allowed him to intimate spiritual experience of an extreme loftiness should not be overlooked in any consideration of the materials that he received and of his own personal achievements in the genre of the symphonic Adagio.

14 Bruckner and harmony

KEVIN SWINDEN

Analysts of late nineteenth-century chromatic harmony must often reconcile both the conservative and progressive aspects of the music. On the one hand, the music has a venerable history to which it is indebted; on the other, musical works are subject to the creativity of individual musical voices, with resultant effect on tonal relations. This situation presents a problem that is perhaps more difficult than a first glance might suggest. In deference to its history, a sensitive analyst might opt to mimic the historical process by applying tried-and-true analytical techniques that have served so well for earlier musical styles. An equally sensitive analyst may be drawn to the opposite pole; in an effort to capture the music's forward-looking, individual nature, an analyst may apply newer methodologies, adapting them to account for the music's veiled tonality.

Certainly, it is a truism that an analytical methodology will return results that betray its bias. For example, Edward Laufer accounts for many of Bruckner's bold harmonic progressions by illustrating how a traditional classical model might be distorted to produce the end result.[1] One of the techniques that Laufer insightfully asserts to be typically Brucknerian is 'elision', the process whereby a composer omits essential voices in a texture that provide the understood consonant support for a prolongation. The musical texture present is shown to take its meaning from a set of passing tones originating in a traditional, yet unstated harmonic model. Thus, Laufer's analytical technique is used to normalize Bruckner's composition to a classical model.

From the other direction, recent work deriving from the theories of Hugo Riemann has painted the music with a new brush. At its heart, neo-Riemannian theory deals with transformational processes in the music. Here, the presence of a tonic is virtually irrelevant, as a transformation applies to collections of actual notes, regardless of their tonal affinity, or (and this is where neo-Riemannian theory may have its greatest pay-off) the lack thereof. Of course, there is also a great deal of music that cannot be explained by neo-Riemannian methods at its current stage of development.

Not only do neo-Riemannian transformational methods often neglect passages that are straightforward and plainly functional (though neo-Riemannian theory has never set out to explain them anew) but also other passages that are grounded more firmly on transformational voice-leading than on traditional progressions of functional harmony. Thus there emerges a musical environment that is impervious in part to both traditional theories and techniques of the new transformational models, but where each analytical method may go a great distance to fill the gaps left by the other.

In this essay, I will adopt a method that borrows freely from the traditional and new approaches to nineteenth-century music, and attempt to bridge the methodologies through the musical regions that they govern. In this context, a region may be the result of Schoenbergian vagrant chords that articulate a transient key, it may be more akin to a Schenkerian prolongation, or more generally, it may be an area governed by a particular harmonic function, following Charles J. Smith's analytical methods.[2] Whatever the case, the formal meaning of a passage is thus separated from the *technique* employed to articulate it.

This essay is divided into two large sections. The first section is devoted to ideas of extended functionality in chromatic music, focusing on specific chromatic dominants that must be understood if one is to navigate Bruckner's late style successfully. While it would be clearly impossible, and indeed of questionable profit, to attempt to itemize every possible chord that Bruckner might employ, there are a few essentials that must be addressed. The second large section is devoted to passages that lie squarely outside functional harmony on the surface – passages that are based on voice-leading transformations rather than the obvious movement of fundamental basses or functional progression. While each section may display a bias towards ideas of harmonic function, I hope that the presentation here is adaptable to many modes of analysis, and may be profitably incorporated by students from many schools of analytical thought.

Extended functionality

Before it is possible to consider Bruckner's music in terms of any theory of harmonic function, it seems necessary to comment on several elements of extended functionality that are found regularly in Bruckner's music. While it may not be possible (or even desirable) to classify every Brucknerian peculiarity, there are a few that warrant initial comment. Bruckner is particularly fond of major triads and dominant seventh sonorities built on the leading-note and the mediant of a key. That is, the VII and VII[7] chords have a clear pedigree in Bruckner's music, alongside their diatonic cousins.[3] Likewise, chromatic mediants III and III[7] join the ranks of the strong, key-defining progressions.

While it is difficult to define an authentic origin for the use of VII^7 and III^7 chords as dominants, there are two explanations that seem reasonable and cover both cases. Charles J. Smith suggests: 'By the end of the century, any sonority that is traditionally associated with the dominant function has become plausible as a functioning dominant – in any key to which it contains a leading tone. In other words, all four dominant sevenths and all four half-diminished sevenths that contain B can be used as dominants of C.'[4] Thus, VII^7 and III^7 are admitted as dominants; by extension, their associated triads may reasonably enter into play. Daniel Harrison explains a VII chord as a dominant by first recognizing the functional power of the leading-note, and that scale step $\sharp\hat{4}$ is a fifth projected upward from it, what he terms the 'ambassador to the [functional] agent'.[5] Thus, when $\sharp\hat{4}$ is not functioning in its normal role as a dominant-of-the-dominant, it may serve to discharge primary dominant function as the upper-fifth projection from the leading-note.[6] Harrison's deconstruction of III^7 would require that the functional potential of each constituent scale-step be analysed in its context; in this case, III^7 contains the dominant agent and associate (scale steps $\hat{7}$ and $\hat{2}$ respectively) which probably tip the scale towards dominant function.

Bruckner's music abounds with clear instances of VII chords discharging dominant function on to relative tonics. That the relationship VII^7–I has a diatonic basis in the progression V^7–$\flat$VI is, in part, what makes the progression VII^7–I such a colourful, if not disorienting, progression. While such progressions may appear as interrupted cadences in Bruckner's music, the listener must also be prepared to recognize and understand that the progression might also be a type of authentic cadence VII^7–I.

A passage from the first movement of Bruckner's Seventh Symphony illustrates how Bruckner uses VII^7 as a chord that may stand in for a diatonic V^7. At rehearsal letter I (bar 185) Bruckner introduces the second theme of the symphony in its mirror inversion. This passage serves as the model for the ensuing music, and places the relevant VII^7 chord into context. Bars 185–8 present this descending theme in the key of D minor with a progression that moves from tonic to the dominant (V^7 of D), and resolves deceptively to a D$\sharp^{\circ 4}_3$ chord (see Example 14.1). The following four bars (bars 189–92) restate this mirror inversion in the key of E minor against the uninverted form in the bass. This creates a somewhat richer, though structurally unchanged harmonization. It is enough to say at this point that this double presentation of the theme is twice associated as beginning with a local tonic triad. This interpretation cannot help but affect our perception of the following statements.

A third statement of the theme begins at bar 193 in F$\sharp$ minor (see Example 14.2). At the fourth bar (bar 196), instead of the expected vii$^{\circ 4}_3$/ii, a $\flat$III$^6_5$

Example 14.1   Symphony No. 7, I, bars 185–92

chord is now used to deceptively resolve V^7 of F♯ minor, and through a chromatic voice-exchange, B minor is subsequently tonicized. The theme appears in two-bar fragments in bars 197–8 and 199–200, all in the key of B minor, although the eventual goal of the passage (E) is anticipated at 199 when the second fragment appears on the subdominant.

At bar 200, a C♯ major triad is introduced as a secondary dominant of V, and confirmed when the bass passes through the seventh, B. Instead of the expected F♯ dominant chord, Bruckner substitutes an A♯^{7} chord – VII^7 of B stands in for V^7. The passage continues as a somewhat skewed circle of fifths as the A♯^{7} chord moves by fifth to D♯^{7}, which finally resolves to an E major triad in bar 203 (VII^7 to I). Thus, VII^7 chords are used back-to-back: once to substitute for V^7 following its dominant; then to resolve directly to the tonic through a chain of dominants.

The passage just discussed has shown a few features that are noteworthy in terms of a study of Bruckner's harmony in general. Apart from showing a relatively clear case where Bruckner uses VII^7 as viable chromatic dominant, the technique displayed is typical of his music. First, complete thematic units are placed in chromatic sequence, ascending by major seconds. The connection between such thematic blocks is frequently functional, but in this case, Bruckner clearly separates the thematic units through a

Example 14.2 Symphony No. 7, I, bars 193–203

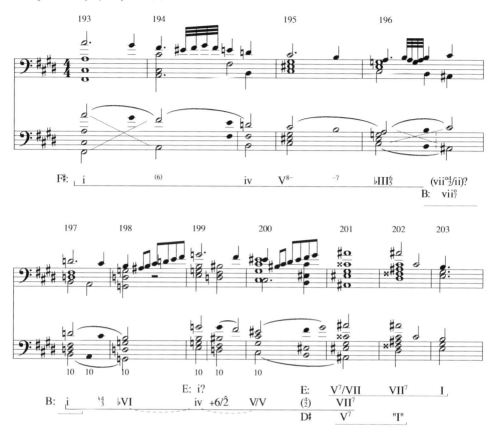

register contrast, two beats of silence, and by placing the D♯$^{°7}$ chord in its $\frac{4}{3}$ inversion.

The passage also demonstrates the technique whereby a relatively simple model is followed by increasingly complex statements that maintain the same essential harmonic structure. The theme is then fragmented and given the most complex harmonic structure of the passage, which ultimately resolves with the introduction of a new thematic block. When examining Bruckner's harmony, it is essential to study the entire thematic block as an evolving unit, as clues will invariably be given to explain the most difficult harmonic moments.

In the Third Symphony, the passage at bars 39–45 presents a harmonically closed phrase in D minor, based principally on a circle-of-fifths progression where a VII^7 chord is used to pull the progression prematurely back to the tonic (see Example 14.3).

A tonic-to-dominant declamatory gesture begins the passage in D minor. A gesture in rhythmic diminution follows, articulating a major tonic (understood as V/iv) moving to an embellished dominant seventh chord on

Example 14.3   Symphony No. 3, I, bars 39–45

the subdominant, V^7/♭VII. The chain of dominants continues after three beats of silence, as expected, to a first-inversion C major triad, V^6/♭III. Instead of continuing to ♭III, this dominant resolves deceptively to ♭VI of ♭III (D♭ major), the enharmonic equivalent of VII in D minor. However, despite this surprising manoeuvre, Bruckner shows no intent to modulate, as D♭ is respelled to C♯ while the melodic F moves to E, supported by a V^7 chord of D minor. Thus, VII^7 dissolves into the diatonic dominant seventh, which then resolves immediately back to the tonic, D minor.

While another reading might cast the C major triad in this passage as VII^6 of D♭, tonicizing the VII chord of the local key, the circle of fifths is too tangible to ignore. Therefore, the D♭ triad is more convincingly understood as a deceptive resolution, standing in for an F chord. (Of course, the F chord we would have expected is F major, while Bruckner supplies an interrupted cadence in F minor.)

A final example will suffice to demonstrate Bruckner's use of VII^7 as a typical dominant chord. Returning to the first movement of the

Example 14.4   Symphony No. 7, I, bars 39–51

Seventh Symphony, the harmonically open phrase at bars 39–50 prepares a modulation from E major to B major, with a substantial expansion of the subdominant A major *en route* (see Example 14.4).

The passage begins on an E major triad and descends by thirds, tonicizing C♯ minor and A major with a regular harmonic rhythm in minims. Once A major is established in bar 41, Bruckner tonicizes a D♭ major triad with a C dominant seventh chord, an applied VII⁷ of D♭. On beat three of bar 42, Bruckner moves to an A♭ dominant seventh chord, which is approached as though it were V⁷ of D♭. This A♭ dominant seventh chord then resolves to an

A major triad, as VII⁷/IV to IV in the key of E. The subdominant is tonicized twice more in succession before the tonicizing of a passing dominant chord on the way to four bars of a prolonged German augmented sixth chord. These four bars anticipate the B major triad in bar 51, which serves as the local tonic for the next section of the symphony. Thus, Bruckner uses secondary VII⁷ chords as tonicizing gestures in a manner that is exactly analogous to secondary V⁶₅ chords.

Mediant chords have long been the bane of functional theories, never fitting neatly into one of the three primary functional categories (I, IV, and V). While in many cases, the status of the mediant is certainly unclear, filling the space between stronger functional anchors, there are instances where the mediant is used in a manner that is in some sense, key defining. In particular, Bruckner uses the major triad or seventh chord on scale degree 3̂ with an uncommon regularity, and in contexts that suggest he used it to stand in for diatonic dominant chords. Characteristic Brucknerian uses of III or III⁷ chords that emulate typical placements of diatonic dominant chords include (i) the mediant as a half-cadence and (ii) the mediant used to expand a local tonic harmony. Instances of the flat-mediant used in a similar manner are also found; see Example 14.13 below for a particularly interesting occurrence.

In the second movement of the Sixth Symphony, Bruckner writes a passage that uses a III triad and a III⁷ chord as key-defining objects. After a plagal expansion of tonic harmony in the key of E major at bars 25–30, Bruckner uses two bars of an A♭ major triad (an enharmonically spelled III triad) to continue the expansion of the E major triad over a I–III–I bass line (see Example 14.5). Immediately following, a G♯ dominant seventh chord is explicitly used (spelled as G♯ this time), and is itself expanded with a neighbouring A♯ minor seventh chord before deceptively resolving to ♭VI⁶ of E (a C major triad). This C major triad becomes a local tonic chord, retrospectively painting the G♯⁷ chord as an inverted German augmented sixth resolving plagally to its tonic in the key of C, in which the music remains until the half-cadence in bar 41.

In a harmonically unstable passage in the Eighth Symphony at bars 301–2, Bruckner prolongs a III⁷ chord in a very brief tonicization of E♭ minor (see Example 14.6). Following a brief tonicization of F minor, Bruckner moves to a G⁷ chord, approached as a secondary V⁷/V. However, the key of C never fully materializes, and instead, the G⁷ chord resolves into an E♭ minor triad in bar 303. Thus, the expanded G⁷ harmony resolves to E♭ as III⁷ to tonic.

Obviously, it is not possible to make a blanket statement that every instance of the major mediant implies dominant function, as an example from Bruckner's song 'Herbstkummer' will attest (see Example 14.7). The passage

Example 14.5 Symphony No. 6, II, bars 31–7

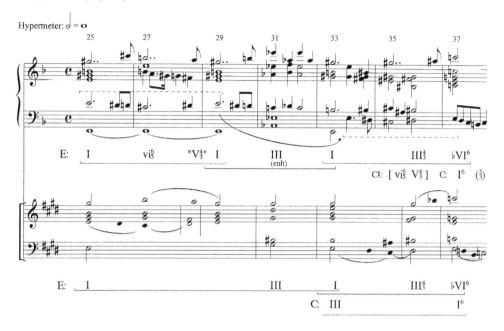

Example 14.6 Symphony No. 8, I, bars 299–303

beginning at bar 24 of the song is in E major; bars 24–5 establish the tonic and subsequently prolong the dominant in outer-voice counterpoint of descending parallel sixths. The final chord in bar 25 is a III$^6_5$ chord, approached from a secondary dominant of V, and in this context clearly stands in for the dominant. However, the progression that follows recasts this III$^6_5$ chord by moving to a ♭VII$^4_2$ chord, exploiting the common tones F♯ and C (scale steps $\hat{2}$ and ♭$\hat{6}$ in E major). A passing A♯ intensifies the motion towards scale

Example 14.7 'Herbstkummer', bars 24–8

step $\hat{5}$ and the arrival of an embellished dominant. This dominant then sets up a perfect authentic cadence in E. Thus Bruckner realizes the subdominant potential of scale steps $\hat{2}$ and $\flat\hat{6}$ in the III^7 chord in this context.[7]

These few preceding examples suffice to demonstrate that Bruckner's music is not impervious to functional analysis, just because the functional relationships can, at times, be complex. Especially regarding VII and III harmonies, the student of Bruckner's music is well advised to admit these chords into the realm of 'that which is to be expected', rather than placing them squarely in the 'unusual or extraordinary' category. Particularly regarding the III^7 chords, however, functionality must be critically examined as its constituent scale steps might imbue the chord with at least two meanings. As III^7 bears the $\hat{2}$ /$b\hat{6}$ tritone, it might prepare chords either of dominant or of tonic function.

Beyond the functional

Straightforward or extended functionality is only one aspect of Bruckner's harmonic language. To see the full picture, we must remember that Bruckner was also a student of motivic composition, where musical lines and patterns are also seamlessly woven into the musical fabric alongside functional anchors. The following section will examine moments in Bruckner's harmony where functionality is suspended, as a chord or progression is projected through some form of tangible or repeating harmonic pattern.

Consider a well-known passage from Chopin's Prelude in C minor, op. 28 no. 20 to illustrate this technique. The first bar presents a perfectly functional progression in C minor, i–iv–V^7–i. The second bar gives exactly the same progression in the flat submediant, and the third bar begins an expansion of the dominant seventh chord. In this way, a single functional pattern is used to prolong the tonic, followed by the flat submediant, *en route* to the dominant; it is fair to say that these patterns project single statements of the tonic and the flat submediant in a large-scale progression i–bVI–V. This design is remarkably simple to construct and explain, in large part because the patterns themselves are closed functional progressions, beginning and ending with the local tonicized triad. In this way, the connection from any chord to the next makes perfectly good functional sense.

Consider a similar situation, where the tonicized chords each project a harmonically *open* progression in their local keys. In this hypothetical example the chord-to-chord connections between the tonicized chords may not be functional, yet the strong diatonic anchors keep the passage understandable. When this general technique is coupled with Bruckner's harmonic language, employing more colourful and dramatic progressions, the results can be most interesting.

In the fourth movement of his Sixth Symphony, Bruckner begins the second theme group in C major, the relative major to the opening key of the movement. The second theme group begins at bar 65; the main thematic portion has regular four-bar periodicity, divided into two parallel periods of eight bars each. This section will focus on a developmental passage that follows these two periods, which begins at bar 81. As the passage is based on the material of the first period, I shall begin the discussion by considering its relationship to the harmonic design of the theme itself.

Example 14.8 Symphony No. 6, IV, bars 81–4

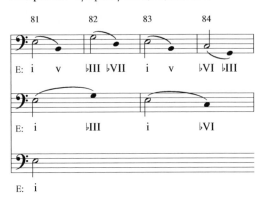

Bars 65–8 present a harmonically open phrase, ending on a weakly tonicized dominant chord; the parallel phrase states the same basic idea in bars 69–70, followed by a contrasting idea that tonicizes the submediant, and ends on a half-cadence in that key.[8] The presentation of this period gives a clear impression of the first phrase cut off in mid-stroke on the dominant, followed by a second phrase that reattempts the progression, completing the intended harmonic statement [I–V] – [vi–III].[9] (I shall use the brackets here to assist the reader to conceptualize the pairs of chords together.) To understand the developmental passage that begins at bar 81, I shall describe this progression as a single statement of a tonic harmony, reinforced by a projection a third below, with each of these chords strengthened by their fifth-related triads. Thus, in this context I am placing the tonic chord at the top of a three-tiered hierarchy, followed by the submediant, with the two dominant chords V and III used to strengthen each.

Bruckner uses the material from bars 65–72 as the basis for a developmental passage in bars 81–8, beginning in the key of E minor. E minor is initially established in the basic idea of an antecedent phrase by reversing the direction of the projection from tonic, projecting a i–V progression first from the tonic, and then from ♭III (G major) with the progression [i–v] – [♭III–♭VII]. The contrasting idea in bars 83–4 restores the original direction of the projection (recast into the minor mode) moving from E minor to C major, with each chord followed by its fifth-related triad, [i–v] – [♭VI–♭III]. In this way, there is an intricate web of functional relationships, all held in the orbit of E minor. C major in the contrasting idea answers the motion towards G major in the basic idea; that same G major in the basic idea itself prepares the dominant of C major that ends the passage. All the while, each idea is heard as a projection of the E minor tonic; this hierarchical structure is graphed above (see Example 14.8).

Now we enter deep water. Bars 85 and 87 replicate the voicing of bars 81 and 82, thereby also replicating the initial upward projection of

Example 14.9   Symphony No. 6, IV, bars 85–8

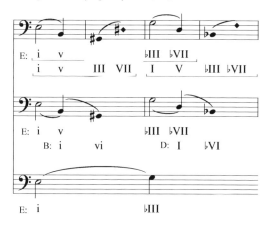

[i–v] – [♭III–♭VII]. However, bar 86 interrupts the progress of this projection, and inserts a [i–V] progression in G♯ minor. Similarly, in bar 88, the [♭III–♭VII] progression is followed by a [I–V] progression in B♭ major. These added progressions add another layer to the hierarchy. The G♯ minor progression appears as a lower minor third projection from the B minor chord (the second chord of the [i–v] pair in E minor); the B♭ major progression appears as a lower major third projection from the D major triad (the second chord of the [♭III–♭VII] pair.) These extra progressions also might be compared to the first chord of each pair; G♯ minor is the upper major third to E minor, and B♭ major is the upper minor third to G major. These relationships are graphed above (see Example 14.9).

With all these pieces of the puzzle in place, it is clear that the developmental passage at bars 81–8 is not primarily guided by clear functional harmony. The process at work here is a pattern-transformation, governed by the gravity of E minor, but bearing little resemblance to a traditional expression of that key. The process is a matter of using a strong, tangible progression (a fifth relationship) to reinforce individual chords, and to move that pattern around in a network of third relations. However far from home the passage may wander, it is fundamentally an expression of E minor.

In a similar manner, secondary dominant chords embellish a descending sequence in the Seventh Symphony at bars 51–9 in such a way that the surface progression complicates a more straightforward underlying harmonic motion (see Example 14.10.)

The passage from bar 51 of the Seventh Symphony begins with a typical harmonic gesture: I–i–♭VI, supporting an ascending scalar melody. A descending sequence follows immediately, articulating tonicized major triads on B♭, A♭, and G♭ at bars 54–9. These chords serve to expand dominant function in B major. The arrival of V⁶ of B is delayed through a sequence that moves from VII⁶ of B (A♯ major, spelled here as B♭ major) through

Example 14.10 Symphony No. 7, I, bars 51–9

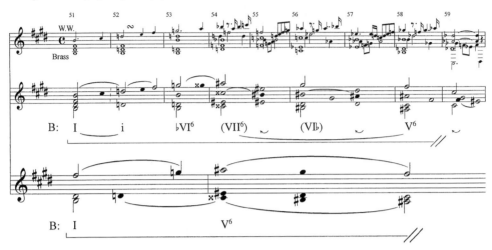

a passing VI⁶ harmony (G♯ major, spelled as A♭) on the way to V⁶ of B
(F♯ major, spelled as G♭). To complicate the passage, Bruckner follows tonicized chord with its dominant, and suspends an unresolved fourth over
V-of-VII and V-of-VI; the suspension resolves on the final chord of the passage in bar 59, V⁴⁻³-of-V. This final chord (V-of-V) is then used as a tonic to
begin a restatement of the passage at bars 51–9, recast with some harmonic
embellishment, with the original melody placed in the lowest voice in bars
59–68. Example 14.10 graphs the passage at bars 51–9, showing the essential structure of the passage as an elaboration of I–♭VI⁶–V⁶. Once again,
Bruckner uses a familiar harmonic pattern (a relative I⁶–V progression) as
a block to express single harmonies (in this case, each local I⁶ chord), creating a surface harmonic progression that is far more complicated than its
structural underpinning. To understand the passage, we must recognize the
motion of the blocks, rather than the motion of the surface harmonies.

Harmonic progressions that arise strictly from voice-leading manoeu-
vres are also ripe for study in Bruckner's works. While several such patterns
have received enough attention to warrant special names (such as the omnibus progression or a hexatonic cycle), other patterns exist that clearly
behave in a similar fashion, without adherence to such strictly defined
models.

In its classic form, the chromatic omnibus expands a dominant seventh
chord through a chromatic voice-exchange between scale-steps $\hat{5}$ and $\hat{7}$,
while scale-steps $\hat{2}$ and $\hat{4}$ remain stationary.[10] In practice, Yellin, Telesco,
and Wason all admit many variants of the classic omnibus as well as the
Vogler omnibus (the same technique applied to a fully diminished seventh
chord), so long as the basic principles of chromatic contrary motion are
maintained (see Example 14.11).

Example 14.11   The omnibus progression

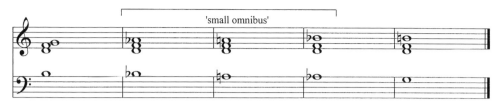

Example 14.12   Symphony No. 7, I, bars 70–3

Telesco also admits what she describes as the small omnibus, a three-chord pattern where a chromatic voice-exchange occurs between scale-steps $\hat{5}$ and $\hat{4}$ of a dominant seventh chord, placing a non-functional minor $^6_4$ chord in between.[11] This progression is an extrapolation of the middle three chords of the full five-chord classic omnibus. A small omnibus is found in the first movement of Bruckner's Seventh Symphony, from bars 69–72 (see Example 14.12), as a reharmonization of the melody shown above in Example 14.10.[12]

A particularly interesting aspect of this occurrence of the small omnibus is how Bruckner continues the passage. The dominant $^4_2$ chord in bar 72 resolves deceptively to a diminished seventh chord (with the anticipated bass scale-step $\hat{3}$) which moves to scale-step $\flat\hat{3}$ to form a root-position seventh chord on the flat-mediant on the third beat of bar 73. Three passing harmonies intervene, and at bar 76, the same flat-mediant seventh chord appears in $^4_2$ inversion, which resolves to a C major tonic triad at bar 78. Given

Example 14.13 Symphony No. 7, I, bars 73–8

these anchors, it is easy to see the inner three harmonies as an elaboration of the small omnibus; rather than remaining completely stationary, the other voices move by half-steps to support the ascending scalar melody that is so prominent in this section of the symphony (see Example 14.13). In this instance, it is noteworthy that Bruckner uses a technique associated with expanding the dominant on a dominant-substitute, ♭III⁷.

Yellin has already shown an instance of a variant of the classic omnibus in the Scherzo of the Seventh Symphony.[13] However, an omnibus progression also forms the basis of the opening to the first movement of Bruckner's Ninth Symphony (see Example 14.14).

The opening eighteen bars of the Ninth Symphony gradually expose the D minor tonic triad of the movement. The first harmonic motion away from D minor takes the form of a chromatic expansion away from the pitch D, to a major second D♭–E♭, anticipating the voice-leading of the omnibus progression that follows. A B♭ is added to the harmony in an ascending arpeggiation, implying what could be an E♭$^4_2$ chord, which resolves to a C♭ major triad in bar 21. If we hypothesize for the moment that the E♭$^4_2$ chord is a dominant of A♭, a standard resolution would be to a chord with that root, perhaps an A♭$^6_5$ chord. If that A♭$^6_5$ chord is assumed (with a textbook resolution of the notes of the E♭$^4_2$ present), the A♭$^6_5$ chord would then initiate a clear variant of a complete classic omnibus, keeping the

Example 14.14 Symphony No. 9, I, bars 19–26

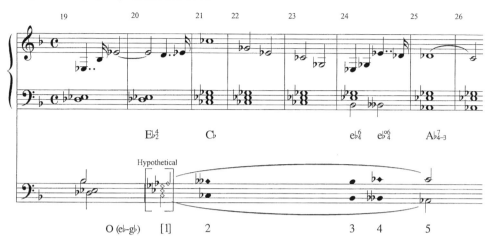

common-tone pair E♭ and G♭ stationary throughout the passage, and only slightly altering two of the chords. Chord 2 of the omnibus omits the seventh of the chord, substituting a C♭ major triad in bar 21 instead of the expected C♭ dominant seventh chord; chord 4 omits the root of the expected C♭⁴₃ chord, producing an E♭ diminished ⁶₄ chord. Chords 3 and 5 appear exactly as the classic omnibus progression would demand – the expected E♭ minor ⁶₄ and A♭⁷ chord respectively. In example 14.14, the diamond-shaped note-heads represent the pitches that are expected in the classic omnibus, but which Bruckner omits here.

In recent years, Richard Cohn has examined hexatonic cycles in nineteenth-century music; it is clear that Bruckner was aware of the potential of such cycles in their complcte form, as well as using the parsimonious voice-leading of these cycles in modulatory contexts.[14]

In the first movement of Bruckner's Fifth Symphony, bars 83–5, there is an interesting use of an almost-complete hexatonic cycle. In this instance, the cycle is interrupted to maintain a functional dominant-to-tonic discharge at its conclusion through the chromatic mediant relationship of III to I, omitting the E minor triad that would otherwise complete the cycle. In context, the entire cycle as presented is a prolongation of the C major triad that frames it, even though the cycle itself cannot properly be said to function entirely in the key of C major (see Example 14.15). After the C major triad is prolonged through the hexatonic cycle, the progression concludes with a half cadence on a dominant VII triad.

Bruckner also uses fragments of hexatonic cycles to accomplish abrupt and distant modulations, smoothed over by the parsimonious voice-leading associated with these models. In the first movement of the Sixth Symphony,

Example 14.15 Symphony No. 5, I, bars 83–8 (strings only)

Example 14.16 Symphony No. 6, I, bars 195–209

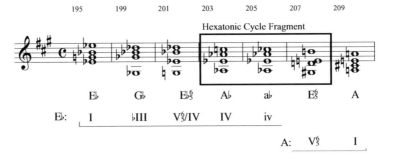

Bruckner modulates between bars 195–209 from E♭ major to the distant key of A major. From the E♭ major tonic triad in bar 195, Bruckner tonicizes the subdominant, A♭ major, which arrives at bar 203. At this point, the hexatonic cycle fragment begins. A♭ major becomes A♭ minor by a single semitone move (C to C♭) in bar 205. The chromatic pitches are respelled as another single semitone moves from E♭ to E and a seventh is added to the chord, to produce a dominant $^6_5$ chord on a bass G♯, the V$^6_5$ chord of A major, which arrives in bar 209. Thus, while the modulation is distant, the voice-leading applied to accomplish the change is maximally smooth, and follows the same pattern as Cohn's hexatonic cycle. The orchestral texture through this passage is thick, articulating block chords in the 'Bruckner-rhythm' that characterizes the movement, supporting a reprise of the first theme of the symphony. The example above abbreviates the passage, showing only the summarized block chord changes (see Example 14.16).

Example 14.17 'Herbstkummer', bars 10–14

A characteristic feature of the hexatonic cycle is its parsimonious voice-leading, where a single pitch moves by a single semitone to produce recognizable harmonic triads. This technique, clearly, is applicable to passages that may not have the tidy cyclic properties associated with the hexatonic cycle, but which nevertheless belong in the same broad category. Bars 10–14 of 'Herbstkummer' provide just such an example (see Example 14.17). The song begins in E minor and the harmony is diatonic in that key up to bar 11. In bar 12, the melody reaches a local climax, supported by a 'root-position' German augmented sixth chord (Gr^7) that dissolves into a first-inversion supertonic half-diminished seventh chord through a two-octave bass arpeggiation. In the following two bars (13–14), the seventh of the chord (E) remains stationary while the remaining three voices each move up a half-step, one at a time. In this manner, Bruckner produces a Fr^6_5, Gr^7, V^6_5/V in turn, at which point all three voices move back to the their original position, to the $ii^{ø6}_5$ chord.[15]

Cohn (2000) shares a private correspondence from Jack Douthett, in which Douthett proposes modelling the hexatonic cycle with binary numbers. In this model, each triad factor has a lower pitch (0) and a higher pitch (1) which toggle as needed to produce the cycle. In this manner, a hexatonic cycle might be represented as a binary three-numeral set representing triads from the bottom note to the top thus: <1,0,0>, <1,0,1>, <0,0,1>, <0,1,1>, <0,1,0>, <1,1,0>, returning to <1,0,0> to complete the cycle.[16]

Table 14.1 *Binary mapping for hexatonic cycle and in 'Herbstkummer'*

Pitch class	binary		Hexatonic cycle: c <1,0,0>
B	0		C <1,1,0>
C		1	e <0,1,0>
Eb	0		E <0,1,1>
E		1	ab <0,0,1>
G	0		Ab <1,0,1>
Ab		1	c <1,0,0> ...
			Cycle:
F♯	0		F♯^{7} <0,0,0,1>
G		1	Fr^{+6} <0,1,0,1>
A	0		C7 <1,1,0,1>
A♯		1	A♯^{o7} <1,1,1,1>
C	0		F♯^{7} <0,1,1,1>
C♯		1	F♯^{7} <0,0,0,1> ...
Eb	0		
E		1	

(In a hexatonic cycle, the augmented triad formations <1,1,1> and <0,0,0> do not participate in the progression; see Table 14.1.) The example from 'Herbstkummer' above might also be modelled similarly, with the seventh of the chord locked into the <1> position permanently.[17] The lower triad of the chord would then take a similar form to a hexatonic cycle. In this instance, the <0,0,0> position of the lower three factors is a diminished triad, with the whole complex progressing thus: <0,0,0,1>, <0,1,0,1>, <1,1,0,1>, <1,1,1,1>, <0,1,1,1>, at which point the remaining members toggle back to <0,0,0,1> simultaneously. (The choice to model these chords beginning with a root-position seventh chord has no bearing on the principle underlying the model.)

In functional terms, passages such as this are best understood as a progression that prolongs the framing chords. In this instance, the choice to hold the E stationary makes good functional sense, as this pitch holds the passage in the orbit of the key of E minor, within a prolongation of chords with subdominant function.

Omnibus progressions and hexatonic cycles are specific patterns of chords and transformations. The technique shared by these patterns is their parsimonious voice-leading while holding common tones, kaleidoscopically changing the harmonic colour while keeping a passage firmly grounded in an expansion of a particular harmony. Focusing on the technique rather than the defined patterns, we can find many more passages in Bruckner's music that rely on subtle changes that may take the harmony far afield, but which nevertheless remain grounded by a particular chord or harmonic function. One such example is found in the first movement of the Eighth

Example 14.18 Symphony No. 8, I, bars 31–41

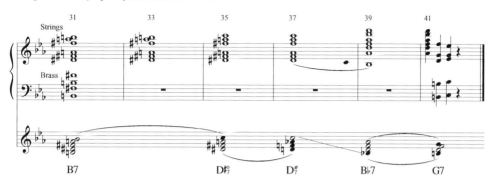

Symphony, where Bruckner expands a chromatic dominant of C minor (see Example 14.18) using this kaleidoscopic technique.

In bar 27 of the first movement of the Eighth symphony, Bruckner arrives on a C minor tonic triad; in bars 29–30, the melody arpeggiates through E♭ and B♭ against upper-octave Gs before arriving at a thickly scored B dominant seventh chord (VII^7 of C). From bar 31 to bar 41, parsimonious voice-leading shifts the harmony through recognizable, although contextually non-functional chords, ultimately transforming VII^7 of C into V$^6_5$ of C in bar 40. Along the way, the passage passes through D♯$^{\circ 7}$, D$^{\varnothing 7}$, and B♭^{7} chords, presenting an elaborate expansion of the framing dominant chords of the passage. Upon reaching the V$^6_5$ chord in bar 41, the passage gives way to a harmonic sequence that is easily recognizable in the key of C minor.

To accomplish this manoeuvre, the D♯/F♯ pair shifts down a semitone to D/F at bar 37. In some way, these two notes share the behaviour of the common tones associated with the omnibus progression or hexatonic cycles – the stabilizing pitches that move together when necessary in order to accomplish the change from VII^7 to V$^6_5$. If this fudge-factor is accepted, the remaining voices behave precisely as the related techniques – with single pitches moving stepwise to effect colour changes. B^7 is transformed to D♯$^{\circ 7}$ by the semitone motion of B-to-C; A then moves to A♭ in bar 37 (coinciding with the moment that the D♯/F♯ pair slide down to D/F) producing D$^{\varnothing 7}$; the C moves to B♭ in bar 39 to produce the B♭^{7} chord. Finally, in bar 41, B♭ and A♭ contract to B and G, producing the first inversion G^7 chord. Thus, the B in bar 37 follows a chromatic double-neighbour line to bar 41 (B–C–B♭–B); the A in bar 31 moves chromatically through A♭ to G, and the D♯/F♯ pair slide down a semitone to D/F. Clearly this seems far removed from an omnibus or a hexatonic cycle, but the essential idea is retained – and it is the idea that seems so crucial to navigating Bruckner's harmony – not every chord change should be read as an element of harmonic progression. Small chromatic moves in Bruckner's music often return to their point of origin, or move to a functionally similar goal (as in this case), and the intermediary chords are of little functional consequence in the whole passage. Here, Bruckner expands a functional region (dominant) through chords that just happen to result because the voice-leading is happening slowly enough that the listener registers every subtle colour along the way.

In his *Katechismus der Musik*, Hugo Riemann describes a triadic progression – C major–E major–A major – as a modulatory third progression from C to A major.[18] Riemann credits cohesion in this passage to the root motion, C–E–A (which in this instance is the same as the bass-line), and states that this root motion in some way articulates an A minor triad, even though no such chord is explicitly present. David Kopp observes: 'This concept of the horizontalization of a triad in the bass serving as the framework for a progression of chords built atop each chord member is unquestionably a type of composing-out, even though none of the chords actually present in this progression are themselves prolonged.'[19] In Bruckner's late music, this idea is significant and merits exploration, although the bass-line horizontalizations to which Kopp refers are not necessarily such simple triadic shapes.

The Adagio movement from Bruckner's Ninth Symphony contains a convincing example of this phenomenon, where Bruckner uses a harmonic sequence with an irregular intervallic projection to articulate, of all things, a 'Tristan' progression. Immediately after the opening thematic statement, a transitional passage begins at bar 9. A series of dominant seventh sonorities, each in $\frac{4}{3}$ inversion, appear in bars 9, 11, 13, and 15, over a rising bass-line G, B♭, C♯, and F (therefore, with roots of C, E♭, F♯, and B♭ respectively; for our present purpose, however, we shall focus on the bass scale-steps). In the even-numbered bars, Bruckner places embellishing chords whose bass tones move by semitone into these structural dominant seventh sonorities. In the first instance, bars 10–11 may be read as an inverted German augmented sixth chord resolving to V$_3^4$ in the local key of A♭; bars 12–13 repeat this progression in the key of B. The fourth dominant seventh sonority (the B♭ chord) is embellished with a common-tone diminished seventh chord. In bar 16, Bruckner places a vii°^{7} that tonicizes the fully orchestrated F♯ dominant seventh chord that is prolonged over the following eight bars, and is clearly the tonal goal of the transition passage at bars 9–16. Thus, embellishing chords direct our attention to four inverted dominant seventh sonorities over a rising bass-line of G, B♭, C♯, and F. Each of these chords is in the service of preparing the arrival of the bombastic F♯ dominant seventh chord in the key of B. Of course, this progression is the 'Tristan' progression transposed up a tone from Wagner's initial statement of it in his opera. To further support this reading, the only common tone shared

Example 14.19   Symphony No. 9, III, bars 9–17

Horizontalized Tristan Sixth

by the principal dominant seventh sonorities is A♯ (or its enharmonic, B♭), echoing the common-tone scale-step $\hat{7}$ that makes Wagner's 'Tristan' progression so poignant. A harmonic summary of this passage is given above (see Example 14.19).

Conclusions

As should be evident to any reader with a passing knowledge of Bruckner's music, there is clearly a great body of his work that demonstrates harmony and progressions of a more 'traditional' nature – passages clearly grounded in the Classical/Early Romantic tradition he inherited. In the foregoing essay, I have attempted to highlight those passages and techniques that behave in different, less orthodox ways. To believe that all of Bruckner's harmony is tranformationally based rather than functional, or that every key or chord must also have a hidden structural agenda, would be to miss the point entirely. Bruckner's particular creative genius was one that succeeded in smoothly integrating those passages of traditional functional harmony with passages driven by other forces.

PART FOUR

Reception

15 Conductors and Bruckner

JOHN WILLIAMSON

Maestros, mystics, and monuments

In the Linz Bruckner Symposium of 1982, specifically devoted to interpretation, Daniel Barenboim gave a lecture whose title, 'Mystische Erfahrung', is symptomatic of the celebrity conductor's relationship to the cult of the mystic Bruckner.[1] In an extreme form it can be seen in the publicity for the appearance of Celibidache's Munich recordings of Bruckner in *Music Theory Online*. The writer took pains to link 'the last surviving great genius of conducting' to 'an entirely new and extremely moving Bruckner'. The reminiscences of a member of the Munich Philharmonic detailed the maestro's unusually protracted tempi, extreme demands on players, and the level of abuse that accompanied them. The interpretations, at which people wept openly, were 'more than mere music', and 'clothed the soul of the listener' like 'running water'. When not screaming abuse at violinists, Celibidache was a nice man who loved dogs.[2]

A strange Bruckner did indeed emerge, characterized by a breadth of tempo that at times verged on the eccentric. Such passages as the extraordinarily slow coda to the Fourth Symphony's Finale presented a vision that seemed to represent the maestro cult's rage at the lack of truly creative powers.[3] Against this there were moments, and indeed whole movements, that illuminated Bruckner's ideas. Comparison of these eccentric performances with those from his earlier Stuttgart years suggested that extreme breadth came late to Celibidache's Bruckner; in this he played out another element of the maestro cult, the 'Olympian' wisdom that comes to conductors with age in the form of increasingly slower tempi. Such a version of the cult seems to hover perpetually around Bruckner performance.

This factor inevitably complicates any attempt to establish the performance style of Bruckner symphonies according to epoch. Karl Böhm's recordings of the Fourth Symphony illustrate the changes that can come over an interpretation with the passage of time, but leave open the extent to which these reflect the taste of the age. In the live performance of 1936 with the Sächsische Staatskapelle, he showed himself in the first movement at least already partly a literalist, adding little to the score apart from a few small expressive touches, some deriving from the Schalk score.[4] In the *crescendo* beginning at bar 43, he is more inclined to inflect the 'Bruckner rhythm' with the *marcato* slowing-down that does not appear in the score until a few bars later. In both exposition and recapitulation, he lingers on the unaccompanied line for cellos (bars 105–7 and 467–9), which on the second occasion becomes a transition to the mysterious little episode in bars 469–74, a fleeting shadow on an uncomplicated reading; as a result he is more or less forced to adopt Schalk's later recommendation of 'Belebend'. At bar 209, the dialogue of the flute and clarinet calls for a light delay, while the return to the recapitulation is shaped by a ritenuto from bar 356, reflecting the 'Immer ruhiger' in the Schalk score of 1888. Some of these and similar moments are so imperceptible as to be almost subliminal (e.g. the accelerando into the *fff* at bar 253).

Over a quarter of a century later, Böhm's recording with the Vienna Philharmonic Orchestra does not make many significant changes to his interpretation, which still sets a basic speed and then allows the music to unfold naturally.[5] The basic tempo, however, is held back by an initially barely perceptible margin. The inflections which added interest to the earlier account tend to sink into the new broadening; what felt like subtle shadings in 1936 become less noticeable, and the pleasantly natural quality of the reading drifts imperceptibly towards the 'mystical'. Yet the change is not enough to confirm that the pre-war reading was part of a radically different performing style.

This comparison serves to impose some caution on some of the claims in *The Musical Quarterly* in 1996 on performance practice. Thus Korstvedt described a modern performance style characterized by monumentality and severity, while Botstein heard 'a sombre dour and frightening dimension' that served to turn a wider audience away.[6] Botstein had little doubt that this had much to do with the maestro cult. His remedy, a 'Schubertian Bruckner, fleet in pacing, lyrical, flexible, and transparent in timbre', accords with phenomena analysed by Richard Taruskin: a recognizably modern preoccupation with lightweight performance, a call to resurrect a more 'authentic' past, and the debunking of the 'sublime'.[7] Nonetheless Korstvedt reinforced Botstein's argument with greater moderation. For him the modern approach to Bruckner was at one with the 'mystic' construct, counselling a return to dramatic ebb and flow through subtleties of tempo change and refined shadings of dynamics, the approach in Jochum, Furtwängler, Knappertsbusch, Horenstein, and Schuricht.[8]

Paradigm shifts in interpretation

Performance of Bruckner may have grown monumental but categorizing it remains a subjective business. It is worth recalling the sane remarks of Constantin Floros, who reviewed the history of Bruckner performance in the same symposium that contained Barenboim's essay. He dismissed much of the conventional wisdom about the disciples' scores by maintaining that they 'do not sound more "Wagnerian" than the originals, but less "Brucknerian", i.e. more conventional'; nevertheless they had 'left behind deep tracks'.[9] By comparing various approaches to the first movements of the Fifth and Seventh Symphonies, he suggested that the tempo inflections of the first published scores had been cleared away in the *Gesamtausgabe* but remained indispensable to conductors. In effect he answered Harry Halbreich's question, whether a unified tempo was needed in Bruckner, with a resounding negative and had no difficulty in finding corroboration in the composer's letters.[10]

The continuing influence of the disciples' suggestions can indeed be heard in the first movement of Böhm's remarkable live recording of the Seventh from 1948, where an initially broad tempo suggests the modern monumental school.[11] From the famous *Steigerung* to the third theme, however, a subjectively changing succession of tempi includes a deliberately dance-like four-in-the-bar for the third theme, a broadening for the brass fanfares, and different speeds for each change in the development. Here truly is a mercurial approach to Bruckner that sacrifices the 'absolute' to drama based on the first published edition of the score. That it comes from the 'classicist' Böhm is all the more remarkable.

That this was not the only way to play the movement was certainly apparent a few years later in Hans Rosbaud's much more unified account. What is also striking is its similarity in general shape to a recent recording. Nikolaus Harnoncourt's reading of the Seventh Symphony is notably leaner and more dynamic than the accounts of a contemporary such as Rattle.[12] The approach adopted in the first two movements at least may stem from a conductor steeped in early music, but it could almost come from a fifties modernist such as Rosbaud. Nonetheless, behind the similarities in tempo between the two readings, Rosbaud is decidedly more interventionist in terms of accentuation and building of climaxes than the early music specialist with the Vienna Philharmonic; he represents a halfway house between Böhm and Harnoncourt. This matters particularly at the start of the Adagio, where Bruckner's thematic writing is so unusual. By constructing the opening section from 'a series of segments' of differing motivic provenance, Bruckner invited the kind of powerful intervention that Rosbaud brings to articulation, clearly climaxing in the *sforzando* markings in the brass.[13] Harnoncourt seems to be less convinced that such weight of tone should be necessary. That the two approaches should coincide in tempo and be drifting towards a rapprochement in other matters, however, would not surprise a diligent reader of Taruskin. The growth of the monumental tradition with its unified tempi is thus not entirely a reflection of superstars such as Karajan and Giulini. The preference for restricting tempo fluctuations was

Table 15.1 *Symphony No. 5, I, selected markings*

Bar		Nowak	Schalk
31	*Steigerung*	Bewegter (im künftigen Allegro-Tempo)	Allmählich bewegter
51	1st subject	Allegro	Allegro (mässig)
101	2nd subject		Langsamer, 4/4
177	3rd subject + 16		Allmählich belebend
199	Unison motif		Tempo 1 (Allegro)
217	Textural change		Etwas langsamer
220			poco rall.
283	A minor		Etwas langsamer (4/4)
303	B♭ major		Noch breiter
325	Head motif, 2nd subject		sehr ruhig
377	Approach to . . .		beruhigend
381	2nd subject		Wieder langsamer
493	Stretta		Beschleunigtes Hauptzeitmaass

a reflection of trends of the fifties and in time came to a surprising accommodation with the early music movement.

Style and editions: the Fifth Symphony revisited

In his essay, Floros laid out the manner in which the 1896 score of the Fifth Symphony augmented the bald impression of the *Gesamtausgabe*. The passage of twenty years and the rush of new and reissued historical recordings have provided the opportunity to return to this and consider how modern taste has changed.

Many of the conductor's problems in the first movement reside in the fact that although the time signature is alla breve, the sensation of four beats to the bar can be established in the steady rhythm of the opening. A similar problem occurs whenever the introductory material returns, even before the retransition, where the restatement of a fragment of the introduction involves no notated change from the main Allegro. The Allegro itself poses the more general question of how to cope with different thematic types within an apparently unified structure. A main theme of restless character (justifying the alla breve marking) yields to a quasi-chorale in violins with pizzicato string accompaniment. The latter characteristically sprouts more elaborate continuations that counsel a slower pace. The subsequent woodwind melody (bar 161) is more forthright without necessarily encouraging a rapid pace, but this third group rises to a much more energetic dotted quaver figure. To judge by recorded performances, few conductors believe that a single tempo embraces all three types. The Schalk edition published in 1896 rationalizes this by markings that may well correspond to general perceptions as to how Bruckner's 'fantastic' structure should cohere. Floros lists these in a table that is adapted here (see Table 15.1).[14]

Table 15.2 *Symphony No. 5, I, selected timings*

Jochum, Concertgebouw Orchestra, 1964*	Philips 464 693–2	21.06
Furtwängler, Berlin Philharmonic Orchestra, 1942*	DG 427 774–2	18.56
Horenstein, BBC Symphony Orchestra, 1971*	BBCL 4033–2	19.20
Botstein, London Philharmonic Orchestra, 1998	Telarc CD-80509	16.24

* = live performance

Cumulatively these markings introduce an ebb and flow into the picture, confirming that the theme groups should be differentiated by tempo and metre. Elsewhere the suggestions underline changes of material and register. It is entirely natural that someone should have revived this version as a matter of historical curiosity. In choosing to record it, Leon Botstein followed his own call for a pre-monumental Bruckner cleansed of the performing styles that have grown up since the introduction of the first *Gesamtausgabe*. Comparison with conductors who have used either *Gesamtausgabe*, however, reveals a more complex picture that reflects their knowledge of the disciples' versions as well as their commitment to the 'originals'. Table 15.2 presents Botstein and a group of Bruckner 'specialists' of an older generation, all captured in live performances; although both Jascha Horenstein and Eugen Jochum were in the later stages of their career when these performances took place, there is reason for believing them characteristic of their approach in general.[15]

All are substantially slower than Botstein, who alone attempts a sense of alla breve in the introduction's Adagio with surprising success. The supposedly 'inspirational' Jochum reveals a preoccupation with continuity in that he employs an element of metrical modulation to hold together the climax of the introduction and the succeeding Allegro: the crotchet of the former virtually becomes the minim of the latter.[16] In anticipation of this, he employs a suddenly faster pace at the *Steigerung* at bar 31 rather than the Schalks' accelerando, resembling Horenstein who does not come so close to metrical modulation but still sees the need to establish a relationship between bars 31 and 51. Thus far they present Bruckner very much in a modern spirit, with minimal deformation of continuity by expressive interjection.

Botstein's observance of the acceleration at bar 31 is rather chaste, avoiding any suggestion of hysterical over-excitement. In this he resembles Furtwängler, who speeds up moderately during the *Steigerung*, fails to return to the original tempo at the chorale-climax, and avoids the suggestion of a metrical relationship between Adagio and Allegro. Botstein and Furtwängler can hardly be said to resemble each other in any deeper sense. Furtwängler is unique among this group in a command of rubato remarkable for one whose stick technique was often thought eccentric. Both in the introduction and in the acceleration of the coda (from bar 453), he cultivated a style that renders pulse uncertain and naturally results in accelerations of a subtle and initially imperceptible kind. In sustained paragraphs such as the second subject, a sense of rubato within the phrase is all-pervasive. He represents a dynamic style of conducting that is hard to find among modern Brucknerians, certainly not in the revisionist Botstein.

What stands out from the three older conductors' performances is the degree to which they are implicitly aware of the tempo fluctuations that Schalk made literal. They retain these, however, within their own individual approach. Thus the slowing down at the second subject is observed by all three, but Horenstein almost maintains the illusion that the pulse is alla breve, whereas Furtwängler has an altogether more expressive agenda. If Botstein resembles anyone here, it is Horenstein. The acceleration within the third group is also to be observed in most cases (the exception is Horenstein). With Jochum and Botstein, it is delayed from bar 177 until bar 190 or 193 and neither conductor truly achieves a Tempo 1 at bar 199. Nor does Botstein underscore the proposed easing at bar 217 to any marked degree, which is more noticeable in Jochum. The familiar impulsive Jochum seems to be more recognizable once the traps of the introduction are past. Furtwängler stands out again by beginning the acceleration before bar 177 and comes closer than the others to achieving the sense of alla breve at 199. If Horenstein is a founder of the modern school of Bruckner conducting, Furtwängler is the protagonist of an older style. For all his use of the Schalk score and deliberate avoidance of severity, Botstein tends at times towards the inflexible.

Metrical modulation becomes a concern again during the alternation of Allegro and Adagio at the start of the development, where Botstein establishes a relationship between the tempo in which he ended the exposition and the returning introduction. This explains why no such procedure was possible earlier in the movement; the faster speed of the first subject theme requires a sudden plunge forward at bars 243 and 261. The slowing-down advocated by the Schalk score at bar 283 is observed by Jochum, Horenstein (less noticeably), and Botstein, who better suggests a pulse in four. None is particularly willing to observe the further easing at bar 303, not even for the sake of cleaner brass double-tonguing. The change of texture and material at bar 325 is an altogether different matter. Jochum makes a lot of this, almost suggesting the original tempo of the second subject, and in this he is followed by Botstein, who also allows a substantial *Luftpause* before the horns begin their chorale-phrase. He then takes the suggestion in the Schalk score of an acceleration and rallentando in bars 333–6 very literally.

Table 15.3 *Symphony No. 5, I, selected timings (cont.)*

Haitink, Vienna Philharmonic Orchestra, 1988	Philips 422 342–2	21.10
Dohnányi, Cleveland Orchestra, 1993	Decca 433 318–2	19.41
Abbado, Vienna Philharmonic Orchestra, 1993*	DG 445 879–2	19.33
Wand, Berlin Philharmonic Orchestra, 1996*	RCA 09026 68503 2	21.30

* = live peformance(s)

Furtwängler shows a more subtly modulated approach to this that seems to grow naturally out of his conducting style. The effect that Botstein pursues is a slightly exaggerated version of something that was second nature to Furtwängler. This perception persists until the end, where lack of technique leads Botstein not to the gradual accelerando of the final *stretta* but to a sudden gear-change. Both Jochum and Horenstein resist acceleration at this point, having already made their push forward from the slower tempo of the second and third themes at the start of the coda (bar 453).

If a 'non-monumental' approach to Bruckner is required, then it seems more obvious in Furtwängler. This particular performance in wartime is by no means the only way in which he conducted Bruckner, but it does represent a manner that has since yielded to literalism, which is a component of the monumental style if not the whole story. This can be confirmed by considering four performances later than Floros' comparison, some studio, others 'live', though compiled in at least one case over several concerts (see Table 15.3).

Dohnányi manages to combine metrical modulation with tempo fluctuations that suggest familiarity with the Schalk version; thus he slows, if not quite to four-in-the-bar, at the second subject, accelerates in four-bar units from bar 177, and begins his speeding-up in the coda at bar 453, with slightly unsettling effect on the Cleveland Orchestra's ensemble. At bar 325, his use of a *Luftpause* points to a tendency found in other modern conductors to slow for the horns' legato presentation of the chorale-phrase but not for the staccato version in woodwind a few bars later, which remains in time to the extent of rejecting Schalk's suggested acceleration and slowing-down. Dohnányi's performance is similar in timing and general characteristics to that of Abbado; but the latter seems less carefully planned in the introduction, failing to arrive at the 'original' tempo at the chorale climax (like Furtwängler), and slowing more markedly at the second subject.

A more truly monumental approach comes with Haitink and Wand, whose longer timings reflect an initial Allegro that hovers on the edge of four rather than alla breve as marked. As a result, the easing of tempo for the second subject leads to a clear quadruple pulse. Wand was in advanced old age when he made this in many ways impressive recording and his style of rubato, like that of many another ageing maestro, was towards rallentando. The broadenings suggested by Schalk in the development become imperceptible parts of a more general slowing-down that reaches a climax in the brutal unisons of bars 319–24. This is not combined with the suggested rubato in bars 333–6, however, and the feeling is not of fluctuation of tempo but of a certain emphatic grandeur. In this he resembles Haitink, who is more aware of metrical modulation to link sections and combines this with a literal approach to the markings of the *Gesamtausgabe*. Although they take much the same time over this movement as Jochum, they seem to resemble less his approach than the more generalized breadth represented in Bruckner performance by Karajan.

The impact of the first versions

The rivalry between 'Haas' and 'Nowak' that dogged Bruckner performance in the sixties and seventies eventually gave way to the realization that in the case of three symphonies early versions were available that rendered Bruckner interpretation more complicated. Although conductors have been relatively slow to take up these versions, enough performances now exist on record to make comparisons possible. Table 15.4 provides a selection of recordings of the Eighth that overlaps with that of Korstvedt, whose goal is to assess fluctuations within a single stretch of music; this table attempts a brief 'global' assessment reflected in the crude medium of performance timings.[17] It also reflects the dominance of Haas versions among conductors of the last two decades. The resurgence of the 1890 version may possibly be seen in the recent recordings by Harnoncourt and Chailly.

That the monumental approach should be represented at its most extreme by Tintner is characteristic of his cycle (whose critical acceptance would seem to reflect the style's triumph). His unified tempi are sufficiently slow, however, as to suggest that a non-interventionist approach is more truly to be observed in the uncontroversial Inbal. What is altogether more striking is that Giulini, conducting a score considerably shorter in terms of bars, should take longer over the slow movement than everyone except Tintner. In the Finale, Karajan is noticeably slow, but his 1958 recording is a landmark in the evolution of the monumental approach to which even he never aspired in subsequent recordings. Few performances of the 'originals' approach in concentrated fire and intensity Knappertsbusch's reading with the 1892 score.

If there is a consensus for a *via media* (and these timings do not reflect the many fascinating differences in details), it seems to lie in the area inhabited

Table 15.4 *Symphony No. 8, selected timings*

Version	Conductor	Recording	I	II	III	IV
1887	Inbal	Teldec, 8.44293 243 791-2	14.01	13.25	26.46	21.08
	Tintner	Naxos, 8.554215-16	17.41	15.14	31.10	25.10
1890	Jochum	EMI, 7243 5 73827 2 4	13.55	14.00	27.24	20.46
	Giulini	DG, 445 529-2	17.07	16.25	29.24	24.36
	Harnoncourt	Teldec, 8573-81037-2	16.25	14.19	27.22	24.32
	Chailly	Decca, 466 653-2	16.05	14.59	25.29	22.06
1892	Knappertsbusch	Orfeo, C577 021 B	12.31	13.01	21.59	22.08
Composite	Schuricht	IMG, 7243 5 75130 2 9	15.40	14.08	21.46	19.46
Haas	Furtwängler	Testament, SBT 1143	15.58	14.23	25.27	22.58
	Karajan	EMI, 7243 5 66109 2 7	17.05	16.01	27.38	26.12
	Horenstein	BBC, BBCL 4017-2	15.45	15.03	25.52	25.22
	Wand	EMI (deutsche Harmonia Mundi), CDS 7 47749 8	15.48	15.04	26.10	24.24
	Dohnányi	Decca, 443 753-2	16.16	13.53	29.02	22.59
	Haitink	Philips, 446 659-2	16.48	15.04	27.26	23.47
	Boulez	DG, 459 678-2	15.08	13.39	24.52	22.19
	Wand	RCA, 74321 82866 2	17.03	16.07	27.36	26.21

by Schuricht, Furtwängler, Horenstein, and the younger Wand. There are fluctuations in individual movements and at times they are approached by others, but they form an interesting group combining some of Korstvedt's chosen models in 1996 and a leading exponent of the 'sombre'. The two conductors who have chosen the 1887 score seem to represent approaches that lie apart from the consensus, but in opposite directions. The noticeably faster approach to the first movement by Inbal may well reflect a perception that the loud ending in the major favours less portentous dwelling on the great highpoints of the score, while the lack of a truly melodic paragraph in the 1887 Trio may account for changed emphases there. Yet Inbal is not distinctive enough to represent a 'Schubertian' rethinking (which is difficult to imagine for this of all Bruckner's symphonies), while Tintner suggests that a generalized preoccupation with breadth and solemnity has the capacity to overwhelm the relative novelty of the version.

Korstvedt is quite clear that there is a distinct group of conductors who remain influenced by the 1892 score in matters of tempo and expression, and that both Furtwängler and Schuricht fall into it. His test sample is the *Steigerung* between bars 583 and 646 in the Finale, and its crux is whether the climactic entrance of the first movement's main theme is taken on the 'crest of a wave' at full speed (after the 1892 model) or at a steady tempo in line with current expectations, possibly even with a broadening. The Wand performance that he considers is fourteen years older than the 1979 recording that I have listed. Then he tended towards the excitable though with only marginal fluctuations, in confirmation that his reading later underwent considerable change. Horenstein, on the other hand, is typical of the modern approach, possibly one of its founders. Among more recent exponents whom Korstvedt does not consider, Boulez and Chailly are firm modernists (though both still convey a sense of mounting excitement by articulation and control of dynamics). The disappointment is that Harnoncourt proves the pedant, following the letter of the Nowak score with a marked slowing down for the whole section, a dogged insistence on the 'nicht gebunden' quality to the playing, and a sudden leap forward at Tempo I in accordance with the Nowak score at bar 623 (the 1892 score's 'a tempo' is surely correct in spirit here). The style of performance favoured in varying degrees by Schuricht, Furtwängler, and Knappertsbusch is truly dead in recent readings.

Of the devotees of the 1887 score, Inbal begins swiftly and preserves momentum at the climax. But the 1887 score differs in a striking detail, the *diminuendo* in bar 672 (1890: bar 622). This makes the slowing-down marked at this point in all scores (including the 'zurückhaltend' of 1892) more understandable. Tintner, whose slow general pace seems less obtrusive here than in the Adagio, also takes a reasonably literal approach that is more monumental than Inbal but accurately catches the combination of *diminuendo* and easing that is so striking a feature of the version. That the 'langsam' of this bar makes sense in relation to 1887, while the 'zurückhaltend' of 1892 is really what is applicable in all other versions is a not unreasonable conclusion. To this extent, knowledge of the 1887 scores brings a degree of insight into performance of other versions.

Early version, early music

Although conductors from the early music movement have tackled Bruckner with traditional orchestras as in the case of Harnoncourt, there have been relatively few attempts to perform his symphonies with period instruments. A notable exception is Roger Norrington, whose recording of the Third Symphony with his London Classical Players followed his performances of Wagner and Brahms with period instruments and balance of forces. The documentation that accompanied the recording is lacking in details of what kinds of instruments were employed by comparison with the information that was supplied in the crusading days of 'authentic' instruments (but that sort of precise registration of maker and year has never been a characteristic of Norrington's approach). Perhaps such precision is unnecessary, particularly in the strings, where Norrington concedes that 'gut upper strings' constitute the 'only difference'. Woodwind and brass are more interesting, and while the sleeve note rests content with noting the lack of 'supercharged' qualities familiar from the present, this presumably means the same kind of instruments that Norrington describes in his account of 'Performing Brahms', with the Viennese oboe, the 'more delicate' valve horn

Table 15.5 *Symphony No. 3, I (1873),*
selected timings

Inbal, RSOF, 1983	Teldec 8.42922 ZK	24.00
Norrington, LCP, 1996	EMI 5 56167 2	18.48
Tintner, RSNO, 1998	Naxos 8.553454	30.34

in F, the darker trumpet in F, and trombones without the pronounced bell flaring and larger bore of the late twentieth century. The number and balance of the strings, the layout with violins on either side of the conductor, and the style, which banishes vibrato to the distant 1920s, are all cited as goals in creating the hypothetical sound of the Third Symphony in 1873, when it was written but not performed; Norrington, uncomfortable with the 'gigantic abstraction' of the monumental Bruckner and also with the 'mystic' Bruckner, chose the relatively little-known earliest version, presumably because traditional and modern performance styles did not mark it so heavily.[18]

Nonetheless, the 1873 version has begun to accumulate some recordings since Teldec first released Inbal's account in 1983. Table 15.5 gives details of three accounts including Norrington, with the timings for the first movement. A strange picture they present, reminiscent in some details of the case of the slow movement of the Eighth Symphony. That Norrington would be the fastest of the three is predictable; that there would be a twelve-minute discrepancy with Tintner seems faintly incredible. On the relatively virgin territory of the 1873 score, battle would seem to be truly joined between mystics and the new modernizers.

A notable feature of all three performances is the care taken in the opening paragraph to give full value to the silent beats and bars; the kind of clipping characteristic of the various readings of the Fifth's opening movement is largely absent, in recognition that there is a qualitative difference between pauses that scroll off different types of material and those that constitute natural breaks within melodic paragraphs. Conspicuously all three conductors practise restraint in handling the many expressive hairpins that characterize the two-bar units of the second subject; the kind of rubato characteristic of Furtwängler is notably absent; indeed when Bruckner asks for rubato at bar 705, both Norrington and Tintner assume that it is a substitute for rallentando.

Nonetheless there is a drastically different approach to pulse between Norrington and Tintner. This becomes particularly apparent in the development, where Norrington's tendency to leap forward at M and N (more a matter of urgency of articulation than tempo) builds an impressive climax at O. None of this is present in Tintner, who throughout exhibits that trait also noted above in the later Wand. The natural tendency of his rubato is to relax, leading to a sense of lethargy in handling an already slow tempo as well as a tendency to anticipate Bruckner's marked slowing downs (as before bar 76). This is different from planned slowing down, in which all three indulge from time to time, most notably at the hushed end of the development, and at the visionary 'Wagnerian' episodes. Inbal is particularly striking at such moments, because they run counter to his policy of playing the music straight at a uniform tempo. When he points the change from the *Tristan* reference to the Second Symphony at bar 469, the effect is particularly striking and prepares the further slight pulling back at the 'Magic Sleep' reference at bar 479.

There are occasional interpretative moments in Norrington which confirm the discomfort with the sublime implied in his sleeve note. The chorale phrase at 235 leaps forward eagerly as though reluctant to sink into solemnity at a moment that can probably bear it. This is of a piece with his urgent treatment of the trumpet fanfares in the previous section, which are more lightly tongued than in Tintner. The brass playing is in general a distinctive aspect of Norrington, and quite consistent with his comments on the qualities of less 'supercharged' instruments. There are many moments in both Inbal and Tintner where detail in the brass section is slightly cloudy. One passage that shows the virtues of Norrington's instruments is the elaborate trombone passage in bars 410–19. These decorations of otherwise simple brass block sonorities were probably never a convincing idea, and Bruckner dropped them in 1877. In Inbal's account, they are rather absorbed in the whole brass sonority, and it may be that the recording is partially responsible for this, since it has an intermittent cloudiness, preventing the opening viola figure from fully registering. The trombone figures are clearer in Tintner, partly because his slower speed gives them more time to register, but they are even clearer in Norrington, where the non-melodic trumpets blare less than their modern equivalents, a feature that is also noticeable at the trombone rodomontade at bar 641 (also cut in 1877). Occasionally Norrington's brass lacks the weight of the others when Bruckner demands *fff* as at Q, but on the whole the narrow-bore instruments emerge quite well from comparison.

The encounter of Bruckner with period instruments does not tell us very much that could not have been deduced from other conductors operating with traditional orchestras. There is a leaner-sounding Bruckner performance tradition that includes conductors such as Knappertsbusch who remained faithful to the disciples' scores, modernists such as Rosbaud and Boulez, and figures schooled in early music performance. Neither period instruments nor the pre-Haas editions seem to be intrinsically part of the tradition, however, which represents a gathering of features and a reconfirmation of the directness seen intermittently in the thirties recordings of figures such as Karl Böhm. The truly lost tradition would seem to be Furtwängler's unique style of rubato that almost convinces that there really is a technical dimension to conducting beyond time-beating, that the conductor is ultimately a performer rather than a vehicle of the mystic vision. Neither there nor in the generalized plainness characteristic of a great deal of contemporary Bruckner do I find much evidence of a glossy 'Wagnerized' style that embraces even the 'original versions'. It may even be truer to say that the distinction is not merely to be made between a monumental present and a former tradition of dramatic, 'mercurial' Bruckner. Within the style that has evolved since the fifties, there is both a mystic-monumental approach and a swifter alternative, but both have been increasingly caught up in the search for unified tempi that may never have been Bruckner's intention.

16 The musical image of Bruckner

CHRISTA BRÜSTLE

Bruckner reception has long exhausted itself in footnotes to hermeneutics and criticism and in the circumstances of, and commentaries on, performances. The need for a classification of Bruckner literature according to sociological criteria and authors' intentions has only been answered hesitantly.[1] Not until the 1980s did works appear with important consequences for the analysis of authors' strategies. Mathias Hansen stated then that 'The complicated history of the effect of Anton Bruckner's work is an unparalleled result of the accumulation and intertwining of irrational meanings, which revealed their concrete intentions with ever less pretence since the twenties and were completely exposed under German Fascism.'[2] By 1991, when the first study of Bruckner anecdotes appeared, reappraisal of Bruckner reception history and its ideology still hardly registered.[3] It still dealt mainly in documenting the dates of reception, which was undeniably necessary and useful. Far-reaching discussions then began with international conferences in the USA and Britain in 1994 and 1996.

Why question the views, intentions, actions, and effects of authors? Is it mostly just a matter of eliciting politico-ideological implications of Bruckner reception and letting them run towards National Socialism? This would certainly be too simple and one-sided. If it is assumed that biographies or general accounts of artists not only represent but also construct and (re)constitute reality, then it is a major purpose of music history to investigate how and why this happened.

It seems to me of extraordinary importance to trace as precisely as possible the strategies of past interpreters because we cannot just describe the origins and development of specific themes but must attempt to clarify them and adopt a distanced and critical attitude that can prevent us becoming entangled in the interpretations and strategies of Bruckner authors. Allied to this is the basic problem that the real historical personality of Bruckner is (comparatively) hard to grasp. We have relied for long on relatively unreliable sources and on accounts from the first half of the twentieth century. To doubt these is not to repudiate or dismantle Bruckner himself but to be aware that his image is largely formed from individual, partly personal interests and by the political, religious, or cultural views of the authors.

Idealization of Bruckner

A fundamental trait of Bruckner biography is the separation of the 'composer of genius' from the everyday man particularly in the sphere of Bruckner's 'faith': because he was a pious Catholic, 'religion' turns up in his works, because he was a believer, he dedicated his Ninth Symphony to his 'dear God', etc.[4] Such undiscriminating extrapolation from sources that reveal him as a practising Catholic is not false or unusual considering the clichés about other Christian composers (e.g. Bach). But the linking of artistic genius to earthly existence on the level of private 'belief' yields far-reaching consequences for reception even in the obituaries: 'If in the more harmless cases the talk is of "divinely gifted" or the "manifestation of God or the divine in Bruckner", in a few articles a messianic dimension is conferred on the composer by citing events and people from the life and social milieu of Jesus Christ and transferring them to Bruckner'; this dimension was already crossed with the image of the martyr.[5] As the Bruckner literature unanimously asserted from the beginning, the 'martyrdom that he had to suffer in the world' began with his move from Linz to Vienna in 1868. His ambition 'to count as a composer [of symphonies]' and his faith in Wagner turned the world against him and brought indescribable grief.[6] But he carried on *firm in belief* in God and on his own path. A fundamental feature of this *tale* is that although he pursued his goals without wavering, he never achieved a breakthrough, that to the end he remained an *unknown genius*.[7]

Bruckner's *via dolorosa* is no longer believable. From the middle of the 1880s at the latest, the composer numbered among the famous personalities of Austro-German musical life – but the picture of the eternally defeated composer is still fixed in the popular imagination. In this context he is an archetype: people who themselves labour under psychological strain and seek ethical or moral standpoints seem to have been fixated on Bruckner from time immemorial.

The artist's 'suffering' is admittedly a specific attribute of 'genius' in the nineteenth century and Beethoven too was revered as saint and martyr (as in Wagner's essay of 1870). Schopenhauer provided an appropriate model. In the tension between will and intellect in which genius exists, there occurs in 'individuals of genius' a certain melancholy mood 'more or less useless' for normal everyday life. The genius lives 'essentially alone', exists 'in contradiction and conflict with his times', experiences 'emotions of the most varied kind' about 'trifles', and has a 'childlike character'.[8] Schopenhauer saw a similar fundamental disposition in the lives of Christian saints and mystics. 'A saint may be full of the most absurd superstition, or, on the other hand, may be a philosopher; it is all the same. His conduct alone [asceticism, monkhood, suffering, martyrdom] is evidence that he is a saint.' The ideal condition aspired to by the artistic genius as by the saint or philsosopher is the 'redemption' from the blind drive of the 'will to live'.[9]

In the development of the idealized image of Bruckner – which reached its first climax between 1921 (the twenty-fifth anniversary of his death) and 1924 (the centenary of his birth) – it almost seemed as if Schopenhauer had portrayed Bruckner. Thus Max Auer wrote in 1923: 'Up to his maturity he scarcely came into contact with the great world . . . He remained an original in everything human . . . he enjoyed the humble earthly joys that life brought him with the naivety of a child whom the world views from a quite different viewpoint than modern man. Had Schopenhauer known him, he must have thought Bruckner the epitome of his treatment of genius.'[10]

Thus one can understand nowadays how idealization of Bruckner largely developed in tandem with the belief that he really had incorporated Schopenhauer's ideal. Because the Bruckner disciples were intimate with Wagner's adaptation of Schopenhauer, the 'pure genius' was increasingly mixed with the 'pure redeemer': everything suggested that in Bruckner an ideal figure from Wagner had come to life. 'So here saint and artist appears before us in the person of Bruckner in the moment of creation: "Durch Reinheit wissend!"'[11] We will return later to Bruckner as 'Parsifal of music history'.

In this context a further aspect of the stylization of the artist should be dealt with. At an early stage Bruckner the mystic had joined with the genius and saint. In 1896, Max Graf spoke of Bruckner's 'mystic language of profundity' in *Die klingende Welt* and invoked his 'elemental force . . . the enigmatic relationships of the notes, the transformation of form, the cabbalistic design of the notes, whose secret doors open wide'.[12] Already 'Bruckner the mystic' was separated like an archetype from the present and presented as antidote to modernity, civilization, and the 'artistic ecstasies of over-civilized or weary spirits'.[13] This was aimed against the modernism of the nineteenth century, i.e. against Liszt and Wagner (and above all Richard Strauss), so that the image of Bruckner and his works was played off against those for whom he had the greatest respect. This tendency was gradually incorporated – mainly after 1918 – into the war against twentieth-century 'modernism'.[14] The 'Bruckner phenomenon' soon resembled an 'erratic block' that was to repel superficiality, 'sensationalism . . . anxiety, despair, inner turmoil . . . lawlessness, [and] arbitrariness'.[15] To the question, 'What is Bruckner's standing today?' Alfred Heuss, editor of the *Zeitschrift für Musik*, which he dedicated in 1921 to 'fighting for German music and musical culture', responded: 'A Bruckner too strides with steady feeling through the god-forsaken atonal sea and from the opposite shore greets a purified, devout, child-like, and strong art.'[16]

For Ernst Kurth (1886–1946), who grew up in Vienna and studied with Guido Adler, the mystic was the starting-point of his comprehensive and singular survey of the composer's life and work. He ranked Bruckner as a 'true mystic': this 'mediaeval' or 'gothic man' stood diametrically opposed to the modern 'man of reason'. Bruckner's 'existence was more closely woven into the riddles of life'; his nature traced 'directly the fundamental stirrings of creative power itself'. On the one hand a certain 'primeval calm' and 'stillness beyond time' (the property of the mystic and fed by a secret power) had led to complete independence from the circumstances of life and time. On the other, the extraordinary psychic constitution of the mystic required the absorption and conquest of his historical surroundings (Bruckner would be 'both fulfilment and conqueror of Romanticism'). Bruckner and his works might be not only a mirror of their age but beyond this a prophetic medium of visions transcending time.[17]

Kurth's metaphysical viewpoint and transformation of Bruckner's compositional personality belonged to cultural currents that had already appeared in the nineteenth century as alternatives to modernism and continued in the first half of the twentieth. These included the invocation of the Middle Ages as 'mythical golden age' and the belief that a new, integrated experience of the transcendental world could be revealed by mixing art with religion.[18] Space does not permit investigation of the enormous relevance of 'mysticism' in theology, philosophy, psychology, and especially in the Expressionistic literature and art of the twenties, or of that period's fascination with new interpretations of 'Gothic'. But it may be noted that 'Bruckner the mystic' represented a thoroughly contemporary construct that was also responsible for the equally virulent idea of 'The Decline of the West'.[19] 'Bruckner the mystic' was a 'product of the last days', whose effects still remained open, as Ernst Kurth claimed: 'if *Tristan* and *Parsifal* are truly the twilight of the culture, then Bruckner would belong to the most terrible part of its end: a last mighty appearance of all the former starting power amidst the final tragedy, interwoven with it, and sacrificed to the great event of passing away ... Granted that our position in cultural history is not to be read into Bruckner, he still teaches us that there are many possibilities.'[20]

I called 'Bruckner the mystic' a construct, and the transformation of a 'pronounced Catholic' into a mystic is actually a biographical interpretation, and not only in Ernst Kurth.[21] This raises the question of what consequences such an idealized image (however nuanced) should and did have, as well as the opposite problem that other unpleasant, contradictory qualities were ignored in such a presentation of an artist. The repercussions of the apologetics that explained Bruckner as a saint and medium and his music as spiritual message included manifold demands for a correct attitude towards him. Criticism was excluded as hostility. Humble reverence, devotion to the music, a certain hagiographical tone in the literature, the formation of communities of admirers, have to a considerable extent shaped the history of Bruckner reception until today.[22] If Kurth in 1925 maintained that 'Bruckner's fundamental emotion is celebration' and contained 'a complete contrast to the neurotic man of the twentieth century', it is hardly astonishing that Bruckner events should be like church services: 'A Bruckner festival means worship of Bruckner, experience of the deity.'[23] The tendentious ideal should underpin the authenticity of the 'experience'.

When we turn to aspects omitted from this picture, we are confronted with reinterpretations and with omissions of specific biographical traits. In the apologetic, idealizing literature Bruckner's secular behaviour – his human, sensuous, pleasure-loving side, his ordinary conduct, his pragmatic thinking – is either avoided and left to popular biographies and the like, and/or transformed into 'childlike behaviour' so that it can be integrated with, or confirmed by, the picture of genius taken from Schopenhauer: the 'earthly joys that life offered him' were enjoyed 'with the naïveté of a child'.[24] Both strategies afforded an escape from a logically consistent moral and ethical judgement of Bruckner's behaviour, for the mainly Christian conservative biographers ought sometimes to have had problems with discrepancies between secular, religious, and artistic levels in Bruckner and also with contradictions in the biographical information. In their memoirs Bruckner's pupils obviously could not suppress ambiguous feelings about his relationships with women, specific traits of his personality, and his immoderate consumption of alcohol. Admittedly a fundamentally reverent attitude always prevailed in the end, but Bruckner's 'strangeness and coarseness' were deliberately glossed over or turned into an anecdote.[25]

This aspect was always presented on a different literary-biographical level. In the Bruckner literature, above all in Göllerich and Auer, Bruckner the man is depicted by a mixture of almost belletrist biography, light reading, 'funny stories about Bruckner', and homily, which aimed to suggest that the matter can be bypassed in a 'relaxed' manner.[26] The basic tendency of Bruckner literature after his death was already expressed by August Stradal in 1902: 'within these narrow bounds Anton Bruckner's image should appear only in his gigantic greatness, and everything mortal, petty, and ephemeral that clings to him should disappear'.[27]

Bruckner as 'Wagner's longed-for second Beethoven'

A year after Wagner's death, the Viennese monthly *Deutsche Worte* published an article about Bruckner (on the seventy-first birthday of Wagner) written by August Göllerich, still a member of Liszt's closest circle.[28] What Bruckner's later 'official biographer' wrote in 1884 is certainly a partisan 'call to arms', but here too a tendency that turned into a 'certainty' for many after Bruckner's death made an early appearance. Göllerich had canvassed for Bruckner as 'Wagner's longed-for second Beethoven' and claimed that the 'Brucknerian symphony' stood for 'something completely new... which Wagner desired and whose absence in *pure* instrumental music after Beethoven he regretted'. Two paths diverged: Bruckner took that of instrumental music and his 'creations, and in the strict sense only they', are 'to be added to Beethoven's legacy'; 'but the path that led from Beethoven's Ninth Symphony to Liszt's symphonic poems and finally climaxed in music drama belonged to a second sphere that stood for itself, which conquered the music of our century through Berlioz, Liszt, and Wagner'.[29]

Göllerich seems to have known how to impress Bruckner.[30] Other friends or followers of the composer were less unanimous or certain at the time about the historical place of his works.[31] It is well known that programmatic explanations to the works which Bruckner himself partly suggested were then extended to prove him a 'New German'. Wagner himself, however, had rejected this compromise, of which Bruckner's supporters were well aware.[32] The irritations released by Bruckner's music in this way settled only with increased distance from Wagner, even if his ideals remained in the foreground.[33]

Such a change can be discerned in the journalist and critic Rudolf Louis (1870–1914), a convinced Wagnerian who at first took a sceptical view of Bruckner. In his dissertation of 1893, he located Bruckner among the 'humorous' in music. He was a 'half-genius' (a 'humorous composer') because in a mood of 'resignation' he forced an indescribable content striving for eternity on to the Beethovenian symphony. He was 'formless' because he 'submitted slavishly to the conventional form', i.e. in Louis' opinion he failed to create a form appropriate to his content, as Liszt or Wagner had done. In symphonic poem and music drama a 'form-giving principle' was created by or in alliance with the poem, and so according to Louis only the 'modern progressive genres' after Beethoven properly constituted 'dramatic music'.[34] In his obituary of Bruckner Louis still maintained that the composer had an 'original talent' but only ranked 'among the "satellites" to Wagner's sun'.[35] And in 1904 – still doubtful – he asked about the meaning of Bruckner: 'Does he not perhaps already proclaim a reaction against the newer kind of programme music, to which in a certain sense we can even ascribe the scenic-dramatic works of Wagner, in favour of a new mastery of absolute instrumental music?' Or is he 'a completely isolated special case, an anomaly as it were [who] will have no influence on the further development of our art?'[36] Then in his biography of Bruckner that appeared a year later Louis formally withdrew the charge of being a Wagner epigone, having attained the insight that 'Wagner's assumption about the death of the symphony with Beethoven was actually incorrect; absolute instrumental music was certainly possible on the basis of the new music.' Bruckner's symphonies were 'pure music' but with concrete content; 'only this can never be adequately described in words, let alone expressed completely. This music is the direct outflow and revelation of an uncommonly rich and complex intellectual life, which was . . . so unconscious as to have been communicable in no other way than in tones.'[37] This content for Louis was now Bruckner's merit and rather more than 'a play of tonal forms', as he adds in repelling the 'formal aesthetic' of Hanslick.[38] That Bruckner remained 'a composer of absolute instrumental music' in spite of Liszt and Wagner was no longer interpreted by him as resignation or backwardness but as steadfastness. According to Louis this was not based on a deliberate decision; rather Bruckner was conscious neither of the temptations to which he might have succumbed nor of his incontestability. What mattered for Louis was 'to recapture for music the innocence of unconsciousness' and that could only be done by 'one who had not yet lost this innocence'.[39] Bruckner had dared to venture into Klingsor's magic garden, so to speak, and had remained unaffected – with which his role as 'Parsifal of music history' gradually became evident.

If Louis' view of Bruckner's historical position had gradually become clearer, it was hardly based on analysis of the works. His descriptions of the symphonies were restricted to bare commentaries on their origins; the First he called a 'monstrosity', 'colossal', and 'gigantic, displaying a 'bizarre lack of restraint . . . without order, moderation, and economy', and was 'really an impossible work'. Bruckner had indeed worked his way up in its successors but never mastered the writing of finales: 'formally they certainly lagged behind what we expect of well-constructed symphonic movements'.[40] It may have been such remarks that in the last resort caused Louis' Bruckner book to be rated an 'accident' of early Bruckner reception.

At the beginning of the twentieth century, however, there also appeared a Bruckner admirer who left Louis' explanations far behind in his analytical conclusions, the journalist and pedagogue August Halm (1869–1929).[41] He had encountered Bruckner's works while studying Protestant theology at Tübingen (1887–91/92) and reckoned that although the Austrian symphonist showed a 'spiritual affinity with Beethoven', it was the 'pupil who probably achieved something greater still, towering above the master in stature and energy because he tried to be more daring'.[42] This was the basis, according to Halm, of Bruckner's formal mastery and exemplary qualities, which had hitherto escaped recognition for lack of an adequate intellectual and musical approach. It was Halm's highest role to create the basis for it. He pursued this on the practical level at the Freie Schulgemeinde in

Wickersdorf, a reformed-syllabus institution in Thuringia which he founded in 1906 with Gustav Wyneken, an almost messianic, not uncontroversial 'leading figure' of the youth movement.[43] In his writings, in which Bach, Beethoven, and Bruckner took the central place, Halm's approach set out a new musico-aesthetic point of view.[44] This consisted of rehabilitating and newly ennobling the standing of 'absolute music' or 'pure instrumental music' after Wagner without recourse to Brahms or Hanslick, who were excluded as strict opposites to Bruckner. At the same time Halm rejected hermeneutic interpretations such as he found in Paul Bekker. In the area of tension between 'form with (or as) content' and 'content without programme' Halm achieved an explanation of music as 'drama of forces' and a psychological interpretation whose starting-point was the fundamental elements of composition (harmony, melody, rhythm, etc.). Form – Halm's 'ideal forms' were fugue and sonata form – was objectively an idea predetermined historically in conformity with natural law, to which the material subordinated itself or, more precisely, in which the material 'grasped' itself as basis for realization. 'Musical form [for Halm] is the sonic embodiment of rationality... In art we are witnesses to a "fragment of world order", which is governed by universal laws. For music, the laws are those of tonality, the source of logic in music... The belief in laws as the source of musical rationality and basis for analysis also becomes a basis for aesthetic pronouncements. Music that transgresses the laws is irrational, illogical, and hence aesthetically inferior.'[45]

The real masters of fugue and sonata form for Halm were Bach and Beethoven, and he saw in Bruckner the synthesis of these composers, which followed both from the fact that Bruckner expanded Beethoven's sonata form, and from his granting the shaping of themes and melodies more room in sonata form. Through this he drew nearer to Bach.[46] Halm proceeded from a definite idea of 'sonata form': two themes or 'principles' first were opposed or, more precisely, followed one another, and needed a 'syntactic tension'; in the development they were brought into a relationship; the reprise signified a 'purified return' to the opening.[47] In Beethoven's symphonies Halm saw only the crucial first step towards this formula. Bruckner was the first to 'comprehend' it completely. He presented the individual 'groups' of sonata form in all 'honesty' and before the development added the third main group, which resolved the dialectic of the first two themes and set the music in motion again after the second lyrical theme, which was 'of a static character'.[48]

On the one hand stood the various themes (a theme being 'something complete in construction, something settled... a law') that he 'personified' as dramatic characters that moved on the stage of sonata form, on the other their motivation, the harmonic field of tension, the cadence.[49]

Harmony characterized the groups of sonata form and structured them. In this respect Bruckner had fulfilled 'Beethoven's premonition of form-creating harmony'.[50] Because of his extraordinary mastery of harmony it had been possible for Bruckner to compose his themes as 'finished shapes'. They arose from the harmonic structure but represented more than just the surface of the harmonies. In his melodic style Bruckner came 'nearer than any other' to Bach 'from the other side'.[51]

Apart from the fact that Halm treated Bruckner's themes like Wagnerian leitmotifs and 'dramatized' sonata form, he described the composer as someone who thought and acted analytically and who expanded symphonic form group by group. This led Halm to assume that an analyst could take the reverse path. In the best cases he might experience the music compositionally.[52]

The theses and arguments on which Halm's Bruckner interpretation was based were at the time as impressive as effective. Above all they should have refuted criticism of Bruckner's 'formlessness', but also opposed the opinion that his music was only a translation of Wagner into the realm of the symphony and 'theatre music without action and scene'.[53] Halm's views about Bruckner's music originated topoi of Bruckner reception that seemed to reveal the 'content' of the music as constants. Thus he interpreted Bruckner's symphonic openings as follows: 'In Bruckner for the first time we completely feel the sanctity of the original; we believe that we inhale something like the breath of creation when we are engulfed by the first sounds of his Seventh, Ninth, or Fourth Symphony. We feel that it is not the start of a piece of music but of music itself . . . *Bruckner begins with what must have happened for history to exist*.'[54] The impression arises of a Bruckner beyond history and time, whose works were unconditional 'natural creations' with roots in paradise, in which the surmounting of Wagner and Beethoven was revealed. Moreover it was in his finales that 'absolute plainness became a factor in art, in its temporal appearance; a musical ecstasy . . . raised the plain to the highest heights, to the level of the mythical'. The world of Bruckner's music for Halm is transformed from the human into a 'realm of objective intellect', a 'higher kingdom of divinely achieved reality'.[55] Bruckner's works were set in the context of cult and rite in complete correspondence with Halm's characterization of him as a 'priestly artist' whom Halm served as 'preacher' and 'educator'.[56]

Halm's 'energetic' theory of music was expanded by Kurth, who taught for a time in Wickersdorf. For him too form took central place in Bruckner. Like the origin of a melody, the birth of form was firstly a 'fundamental event of a force' incomprehensible in itself 'beyond the spatial and temporal form of representation, towards which we are initially forced when it rises into the phenomenal world'. Form is thus 'a concept to be grasped not statically but dynamically', and Bruckner had 'renewed not form but forming'. The composer had thus 'reawakened' the idea of form 'to the fundamental idea of life'.[57]

Beyond their general analytical approach, Halm and Kurth were united by a reconstruction of the 'idea of absolute music', to which was linked a continuation of the 'myth of German music'.[58] Bruckner came to hold a key function in this. In his works 'Tonkunst' appears to have attained (and guaranteed) a new cosmological totality that Wagner had admittedly pursued with the 'heteronomous' means of the *Gesamtkunstwerk*, but had attempted to grasp in vain. No doubt Bruckner showed a 'kinship' with Wagner, but even for Kurth Bruckner's 'surmounting of Romanticism' was also 'redemption' of Wagner. In Ernst Bloch's précis of Halm, Bruckner had 'finally detached the gains of Wagner's style, "descriptive" music, from the tax of the programme or music drama'; he was 'the purification of Wagner'.[59]

Bruckner – 'German' and 'Austrian'

There would have been nothing wrong in viewing Bruckner as a genuine 'Austrian composer', as indeed partly happened, but this was long seen in relation to an all-embracing 'German' cultural history; the 'Austrian' in Bruckner's music was viewed by many as only one aspect or as local colour (similar to 'South German').[60] Almost as stereotyped were references to nature, sounds of the homeland, or folk music.

Bruckner and Wagner supporters who stood up for their 'masters' in the last years of the nineteenth century, and thus during Bruckner's lifetime, were naturally more pompous about the 'German-ness' of the composer. For example, Josef Schalk thought in 1885 that it 'might have been a drawback to Bruckner's recognition that his music is more German than anything we have hitherto possessed in pure instrumental music'.[61]

After 1918 and the foundation of the first Austrian Republic, a little more was made of Bruckner the 'Austrian'.[62] Franz Gräflinger brought out Bruckner's attachment to his homeland: 'Just as Bruckner the man is only to be understood properly if we can assess and typify him as a true Austrian, so we must also view his works as products that grew on the most intimate terms with the soil on which they were created. Bruckner's music is rooted through and through, it sounds and breathes the breath of home.'[63] According to the author this home is German-Austrian, however, and even for the Austrian Gräflinger Bruckner was the revered 'German master'.[64]

Something similar was also to be found among authors who traced an 'Austrian line' of the symphony. For Paul Bekker, who combined it with the development of a generic history of the symphony as idealistic 'symbolization of the nation', the *German* symphonists were divided into three groups: middle-German (Mendelssohn, Schumann, Brahms), new German (Liszt, Berlioz, Wagner, and followers), and Austrian (Schubert, Bruckner, Mahler).[65] Alfred Orel referred to this in 1925 in a style-critical investigation that to some extent can be read as pendant and in part also as opposite pole to Kurth's *Bruckner*. Orel maintained for instance that there was no justification for 'drawing the connecting line from Bach to Bruckner too strongly'; Viennese Classicism should be seen as the foundation for Bruckner's style: 'The style of the Viennese Classicists, the ground on which Romantic compositional technique grew, stands in this respect in opposition to the old Classicism of the age of Handel and Bach, so that it is in its essence thoroughly homophonic, while counterpoint stamped its characteristic mark on the earlier period. The polyphony of Viennese Classicism is completely different from the older Classicism.'[66] Moreover Wagner's influence should be rejected from the line joining 'late (Romantic) Beethoven' to Bruckner and the connection between Schubert and Bruckner brought out. Orel, however, scarcely provided concrete analytical grounds for this; the closeness of Schubert and Bruckner was attributed primarily to their common working-out and artistic integration of folksong and folk art.[67]

For the 1920s there thus existed a double-sided picture: on the one hand Bruckner belonged in the 'history of German composition and music' (variously interpreted or constructed).[68] On the other stood the attempt to integrate Bruckner into an Austrian cultural history, by which the young Austrian Republic addressed the problem of newly defining its own cultural tradition.[69] Separating the Austrian from the German (and Austria from Germany) was problematic, especially since this in no way met with unanimous approval among the population. In Austria there was a counterforce not to be underrated that took the view that Versailles had 'brutally and senselessly torn apart' a unity that 'organically' belonged together and aspired to become one from 'natural necessity': 'the German Empire and the non-viable German Austria that had been thrown back on its own resources and surrendered to systematic stripping of its German characteristics!'[70]

The 'Bruckner movement' of the twenties and thirties developed in this field of tension. The communities of admirers in Austria and Germany – mainly joined since 1929 in the Internationale Bruckner-Gesellschaft (IBG) under the leadership of the Austrian biographer of Bruckner Max Auer – mutually saw in the composer a symbol of German-Austrian attachment. 'We love in Anton Bruckner the German kind of Austrian, we honour him as one who is the mediator for us between Germans and Austrians... We are united forever by the great musical line that leads on the common path from Austria to Germany'; so ran the message of 1924 in the Berlin Reichstag to honour the centenary of Bruckner's birth.[71]

Conversely, during the Austrian celebrations for the Bruckner Jubilee a call went out to support the restoration of the Bruckner organ in St. Florian, an appeal to all who 'treasured German culture'.[72] In 1930 when the IBG celebrated its first 'international' Bruckner festival in Munich, Max Auer explained: 'We now recognize as a national duty the distribution of the riches that the master left us to all tribes of his people but also to proclaim the gospel of his gladdening art to all artistic peoples so that it makes its reconciling and unifying effect on them. What politics and diplomacy have torn asunder culture must reunite.'[73]

The propagation of Bruckner in the Third Reich

In the succeeding years Munich developed into the 'capital of the Bruckner movement'. It was also the scene on 2 April 1932 for the inaugural presentation of the new *Bruckner-Gesamtausgabe* in Germany by comparing the first published version and the so-called 'original version' of the Ninth Symphony in a demonstration concert (under the baton of Siegmund von Hausegger, who soon ranked as 'official' Bruckner conductor).[74]

In October 1933 the second International Bruckner Festival also assembled in Munich in full knowledge that Hitler's 'seizure of power' had created a new situation. Now the festivities took place under the 'honorary protection' of Munich's prominent Nazis. In his festival address the art historian Oskar Lang (1884–1950), a member of the board of the IBG, made it unmistakably clear that Bruckner was an absolutely perfect artistic figure for the National Socialist state: 'In him live, both strong and uncorroded by foreign influences, the typical natural strengths of the German man: the wild monster of heroic blood and the humble fervour of faith of the pure godseeker ... In Bruckner's music the German nature, inwardly understood, has found a new symbolic character of universal validity ... I see in Bruckner the last wholly great representative of our German Teutonic art, entirely unbroken in his instincts, weakened by no cultural over-refinement, the prototype of a coming world view, the representative of a new world feeling. Bruckner was a music *against* his age, he must become one *for* the age!'[75]

The topics that Lang elaborated in his address were all known: Bruckner as visionary mystic, pious believer, German man and artist in union with people and homeland, intuitive creator. Adapted to the National Socialist world view, Bruckner met the ideal of the 'religious, patient, national-socialist man' that Alfred Rosenberg had invoked in 1933.[76] That his descent had been traced back a year earlier to 'Lower Austrian peasants' was almost a confirmation of the cultural-political goals according to which 'a recreation and rebirth of German culture' must be allied to the 'return to the peasantry, to blood and soil'.[77]

Thus if we speak of the 'monopolizing' of Bruckner in the Third Reich, it doesn't entirely accord with the actual events. Certainly the composer was monopolized, but by whom? Was it not the many Bruckner followers who had first propagated an image of the composer that ultimately assumed their political convictions? And did not a kind of 'transfer' then ensue, a presentation of Bruckner that directly provoked the Nazi cultural and political seizure and so in a certain sense could have seemed like a historically justified fulfilment of all hopes – even Bruckner's – of 'final recognition'? Already in 1935 Karl Grunsky, leader of the Swabian Bruckner admirers and convinced National Socialist, maintained 'that the Führer of the German Reich recognizes and favours the Bruckner movement'.[78] If the editor of the new *Bruckner-Gesamtausgabe* himself, Robert Haas (1886–1960), had expressed the view in 1934 that Bruckner's 'world view' was 'entirely founded on the German character, [that] its musical setting allowed the German soul to pour forth untroubled, [that] every cosmopolitan refinement and foreign admixture of blood was missing from objective necessity, and [that] even the formative experience of Catholicism had left no trace', then it not only is a falsified picture but corresponds completely and entirely to a 'Germanized' picture long before the self-proclaimed specialists in 'racial research' occupied themselves with Bruckner.[79]

As climax to Bruckner's 'recognition' in Nazi Germany the Bruckner community planned for the fortieth anniversary of his death in 1936 to combine a festival of the IBG with a ceremonial dedication of a bust in the Walhalla, in the collection of marble busts of 'great Germans' set up in the middle of the nineteenth century in a classical building above the Danube near Regensburg. Actually the setting-up of the bust was proposed by the IBG in 1933 (and even earlier by the Linz Liedertafel *Frohsinn* in 1930); in 1935 and early 1936 the positive signals from the Bavarian authorities, who still had responsibility for the Walhalla at that time, grew more frequent. Why the plan could not be realized in 1936 but only a year later resided *inter alia* in the realization by Hitler and Goebbels of the political symbolic force of such an event. They now moved everything to stage a great act of state.[80]

If the close links of Austria with Mussolini had delayed an aggressive 'politics of union', towards the end of the year there were signs of a marked improvement in German–Italian relationships. Mussolini himself spoke in Milan on 1 November 1936 of the 'Rome–Berlin axis'. This development finally meant the possibility of *Anschluss* for Austria and accordingly also the realization of Hitler's plans for expansion. A long-drawn-out demonstration of German and Austrian desire for unity in the summer of 1937 – two months before the state visit of the Duce – would strengthen the political 'strategy of fraternization'.

The dedication of the Bruckner bust thus developed into a highly political act, the first symbolic 'fetching home' of an Austrian into the German Reich. Goebbels stressed in his festival address on 6 June 1937 that 'Anton Bruckner, as a son of the Austrian land, is particularly destined to symbolize in our time too the inextinguishable intellectual and spiritual community of fate that embraces our entire German folk.' The propaganda minister drew on the current clichés; the new perceptions about Bruckner's 'peasant ancestral heritage' – the 'blood-and-race tinged elemental powers of his humanity' – were as familiar to him as talk about Bruckner's 'pure joy in the world' or his 'firm belief in God' (*Gottglaube*), which Goebbels – like many other Bruckner apologists before him – regarded as linked not to Catholicism, but to the 'absolutely religious'.[81] Moreover Goebbels referred to the current very real questions about the first *Bruckner-Gesamtausgabe* and gave it a measure of state protection. He made it known that 'the Führer and his government' had decided 'to put a considerable sum at the disposal of the Internationale Bruckner-Gesellschaft for as many years as it takes to edit the original versions of all of his symphonies, until the complete works of the master were available in the form intended by him'. Not only was the *Gesamtausgabe* awarded a subvention from the German Reich but an end was declared at the highest official level to the campaign waged in the Austro-German press over the so-called 'original versions'. Goebbels even connected this to his ban of 1936 on music or art criticism, for 'if in the *new* Germany the public consideration of art is to be steered by law into an orderly course, we also believe that by this we have conveyed a debt of gratitude to the lonely struggling master who suffered from his tormentors until his death'.

It is hardly astonishing that the IBG and its Musikwissenschaftlicher Verlag – the editorial bases of the *Gesamtausgabe* in Vienna and Leipzig – had managed to obtain the support of the propaganda minister. For the arguments *for* the *Gesamtausgabe* were more than conspicuously entangled with ideas and ideals that claimed the highest priority in Nazi cultural politics.[82] It was not only enough that the 'original versions' vouched for authenticity in contrast to the first published versions of Bruckner's works as well as testifying in their 'organ-like monumentality' to Bruckner's independence from Wagner, but the 'original versions' were supposedly also free from 'alien influences' and from 'falsifying interventions', and only the 'purified scores' corresponded to Bruckner's 'final intentions'.[83] That a conflict about the *Gesamtausgabe* had nevertheless climaxed among Brucknerians in 1935–6 lay much less in philological positions than in the problematizing of Bruckner's reception of Wagner. Since the champions of the 'original versions' rejected as arrangements the scores that appeared during his life or shortly after his death because they stood *inter alia* in too close proximity to Wagner, the older generation of Wagnerians (e.g. Karl Grunsky or Max von Millenkovich-Morold) as well as the circle around the former Bruckner pupils Schalk and Löwe had spoken out against the new tendencies of the *Gesamtausgabe*.[84]

The struggle over the 'original versions' threatened to escalate, dividing the Bruckner Society, and Alfred Orel, the joint editor of the *Gesamtausgabe*, had made critical remarks about Haas and his actions.[85] A search began for ways to bring these arguments to a close 'from higher standpoints'.[86] These efforts were successful, as Goebbels' Walhalla address showed, and the original version of the Fifth Symphony obviously left a great impression on Hitler himself when it was performed in his presence on the evening of the dedication.[87] Three months later the 'original' finale of the same symphony – with the distinctive wind contrasts ('organ-like blocks') and the 'monumental' chorale ending – rang out at Hitler's 'cultural address' during the Nuremberg party congress.[88] This reveals why Bruckner's music was so highly prized: because of its 'absolute religious content', it was functionally integrated within the pseudo-religious Nazi cult, and underpinned the Nazis' aesthetic predisposition to gigantomania.

The propagation of Bruckner in the Third Reich was therefore already carried out with great success before 1938. After the *Anschluss* hardly anyone took exception to the transformation of the IBG into the Deutsche Bruckner-Gesellschaft and to Goebbels' naming of Wilhelm Furtwängler as its new president.[89] There were just as few questions about the 'final victory of the original versions' when Goebbels explained at the Düsseldorf Reichsmusiktage in 1939: 'Now the great masters of the stature of a Gluck, Haydn, Mozart, Schubert, Hugo Wolf, and Bruckner also belong purely outwardly to us . . . Besides we can detect a regularly increasing organic process of recovery in this sector of our musical creation and performance after the eradication of the Jews from what was then called Austrian music.'[90]

In Hitler's plans for cultural 'life after the war' Bruckner played a central role. Then the personal link of the Führer with his Upper Austrian compatriot would be fully demonstrated for the first time and Bruckner would be presented as a uniquely Nazi cult figure. In the monastery at St. Florian a centre of the Greater German Radio was set up and a Bruckner Orchestra and Choir newly founded in 1942. It was planned to have a 'Bruckner Bayreuth' there with an adjoining training school.[91] For a time the Deutsche Bruckner-Gesellschaft (DBG) envisaged resettlement to Linz or St. Florian, and the Bruckner-Verlag was to be moved to Braunau am Inn, Hitler's birthplace. In Linz – now the centre of 'Gau Oberdonau' – which Hitler wanted to rebuild to his own design as the central National-Socialist city of culture, a Bruckner concert hall was also planned as well as a great commemorative column with a monumental statue of Bruckner.[92]

A few closing remarks

In the literary Bruckner reception of the first half of the twentieth century, 'Bruckner' was developed increasingly into a symbol of conservatism, of the anti-modern, and finally into a crude celebration of the pre-civilized. Even today we can agree with Mathias Hansen: 'The *de facto* unbroken continuation, deviating only in incidentals, of a regressive understanding of Bruckner reaches far into the sixties; indeed, individual offshoots have survived into the present and, it is to be feared, also into the indefinite future.'[93]

That Bruckner's works themselves had once caused difficulties even for experienced conductors, or had been out of line with the symphonic expectations of the nineteenth century, has evidently been quickly forgotten. And to what extent Bruckner then was 'progressive', and remained 'progressive' – as opposed to Brahms – in the eyes of his followers (although he was honoured for his steadfastness in the face of the 'progressive' influence of Wagner) is in principle still part of the paradoxical constellations of Bruckner reception history.[94]

Apart from the question of Bruckner's 'modernity' in the nineteenth century there arises today the hitherto little-touched-on problem of the effect of his works on the history of the symphony in the twentieth and twenty-first centuries. And in this connection too, peculiar fault-lines may arise between 'modern' and 'conservative' or 'traditional'. Even a brief glance should provide a few clues to this.

When Dika Newlin's book *Bruckner – Mahler – Schoenberg* appeared, for the first time a connection was hinted at between Bruckner and the new music of the twentieth century, the 'neo-Viennese school' as she formulated it.[95] In this Bruckner admittedly was less of an initiator than a 'conserver' and transmitter of older traditions. In Newlin's eyes Bruckner was important in passing on the fundamental bass theory of his teacher Simon Sechter to Schoenberg who then passed it on to his pupils.[96] Beyond that Bruckner was (with Brahms) 'the chief link between the Viennese Classicists and their modern counterpart'; Schoenberg, to be sure, emphasized (as we know) 'Brahms the Progressive' (1933).[97]

The Mahler revival of the sixties and seventies and above all Adorno's book on Mahler then caused a polarization in the view of Bruckner and

Mahler; Bruckner's 'affirmation' and 'pre-critical attitude' was contrasted with Mahler's 'contemporary consciousness' of the invalidity of this 'unbrokenness', though this was also partly a reaction to the devalued picture of Mahler that had dominated the Bruckner literature for a long time.[98] It seems as if this dichotomy has only gradually been resolved in the investigations of the compositional connections between Mahler and Bruckner.[99] At any rate it remained doubtful for a long time how far Bruckner also had a positive effect in this connection.[100]

To compose symphonies and at the same time to invoke Bruckner stood even more thoroughly condemned as 'reactionary' when 'objectivity' in music was preferred and 'Romantic powers of expression' were more or less obsolete. That applied in part to the twenties and also to the fifties of the past century. Whether the Bruckner follower Richard Wetz (1875–1935) was forgotten only because 'modern' composers were preferred to him is questionable.[101] He belonged in the twenties to the Bruckner apologists and also wrote a surviving Bruckner book in this tone.[102] In his three symphonies (originating between 1915 and 1922) Wetz seems to have aimed to be an immediate continuation of Bruckner, as a result of which he actually ended up on the margin of music history in the early twentieth century.[103]

In looking at Scandinavia or Great Britain from a continental perspective it becomes clear that not only the dependence on the nineteenth-century symphony and in particular Bruckner's kind of symphony but also its revival was increasingly pushed into the cold.[104] A composer like Robert Simpson (1921–97), who campaigned throughout his life not only for Sibelius and Nielsen but also for Bruckner and quoted from him, ranks in British musical life as a disputatious champion of traditional compositional and symphonic categories. This appears to have changed since the late 1980s.[105] The composer Wolfgang Rihm incensed his audiences *inter alia* because he placed himself 'consciously in the tradition of Beethoven, Bruckner, Mahler, and Hartmann'; but in Rihm it was also clear that his own personal powers of expression necessitated this recourse, which eventually gained acceptance.[106] Perhaps in Bruckner it is precisely the 'contemporary, peculiar tone' mediated by tradition, the personal voice that is of interest until today – beyond everything that his apologists have told us.

(*Trans. John Williamson*)

Notes

1   Introduction: a Catholic composer in the age of Bismarck

1   E.g. William M. Johnston, *The Austrian Mind: An Intellectual and Social History 1848–1938* (Berkeley and Los Angeles, 1972), pp. 134–5.

2   'Bruckners gründerzeitliche Monumentale Symphonie: Reflexionen zur Heteronomie kompositorischer Praxis', in *Musik-Konzepte 23/24: Anton Bruckner*, ed. Heinz-Klaus Metzger and Rainer Riehn (Munich, 1982), p. 88.

3   Constantin Floros, 'On Unity between Bruckner's Personality and Production', in *PAB*, p. 286.

4   Ibid., pp. 286–8, citing Erwin Ringel, 'Psychogram für Anton Bruckner', in *Bruckner-Symposion, 'Bruckner, Liszt, Mahler und die Moderne' (Linz 1977): Bericht*, ed. Franz Grasberger (Linz, 1978), pp. 19–26.

5   Martin Geck, *Von Beethoven bis Mahler: die Musik des deutschen Idealismus* (Stuttgart, 1993), pp. 386–7; see the reservations of Manfred Wagner, *Anton Bruckner: Werk und Leben* (Vienna, 1995), pp. 70–3.

6   Peter Gülke, *Brahms, Bruckner: zwei Studien* (Kassel, 1989), p. 88. For a consideration of Bruckner's 'necrophilia' from a more mundane Austrian perspective, see Elisabeth Maier, 'A Hidden Personality: Access to an "Inner Biography" of Anton Bruckner', in *BS*, p. 51.

7   See Frederic Morton, *A Nervous Splendour: Vienna 1888/1889* (London, 1979), pp. 18–20, 44–5, 97–8, 276–8, and 295.

8   Nagler, 'Bruckners gründerzeitliche Monumentale Symphonie', pp. 96–101.

9   Gülke, *Brahms, Bruckner*, pp. 91–4.

10   Pieter M. Judson, 'Rethinking the Liberal Legacy', in *Rethinking Vienna 1900*, ed. Stephen Beller (New York and Oxford, 2001), p. 61.

11   Geck, *Von Beethoven bis Mahler*, pp. 381–5.

12   Ibid., pp. 383–4; Nagler, 'Bruckners gründerzeitliche Monumentale Symphonie', pp. 104–10. 'Gründerzeit' denotes the period of industrialized expansion that began in the mid 1860s in Germany and Austria.

13   Gülke, *Brahms, Bruckner*, pp. 102–3.

14   Nagler, 'Bruckners gründerzeitliche Monumentale Symphonie', pp. 101 and 112–13; Gülke, *Brahms, Bruckner*, p. 94.

15   James Shedel, '*Fin de Siècle* or *Jahrhundertwende*? The Question of an Austrian *Sonderweg*', in *Rethinking Vienna 1900*, p. 83.

16   Nagler, 'Bruckners gründerzeitliche Monumentale Symphonie', p. 97; Morton maintains that Bruckner was 'no anti-Semite' in spite of his connections to Schönerer: *A Nervous Splendour*, p. 162. For a biographer who concludes that the exclusively 'religious' nature of Bruckner's anti-Semitism was 'harmless', see Karl Grebe, *Anton Bruckner* (Reinbek bei Hamburg, 1995), p. 66. For the degree to which Bruckner remains concealed behind his friends and biographers over the Vincent affair, see Maier, 'A Hidden Personality', pp. 46–7.

17   Judson, 'Rethinking the Liberal Legacy', p. 68.

18   Shedel, '*Fin de Siècle* or *Jahrhundertwende*?', pp. 97–9.

19   Péter Hanák, *The Garden and the Workshop: Essays on the Cultural History of Vienna and Budapest* (Princeton, NJ, 1998), p. 174.

20   John W. Boyer, *Political Radicalism in Late Imperial Vienna: Origins of the Christian Social Movement, 1848–1897* (Chicago and London, 1981), pp. 77 and 122.

21   Ibid., p. 78.

22   Ulrike Tanzer, 'Anti-clericalism in Literary Journalism of the Liberal Era: Ferdinand Kürnberger, Friedrich Schlögl, Daniel Spitzer and Ludwig Anzengruber', in *Catholicism and Austrian Culture*, ed. Ritchie Robertson and Judith Beniston (Edinburgh, 1999), pp. 65–78; Lucian Hölscher, 'The Religious Divide: Piety in Nineteenth-century Germany', in *Protestants, Catholics and Jews in Germany, 1800–1914*, ed. Helmut Walser Smith (Oxford and New York, 2001), p. 46.

23   Boyer, *Political Radicalism*, pp. 31 and 137.

24   Monika Glettler, 'Die *Monarchia Austriaca* und die deutsche Musik', in *Anton Bruckner: Tradition und Fortschritt in der Kirchenmusik des 19. Jahrhunderts*, ed. Friedrich W. Riedel (Sinzig, 2001), pp. 29–46.

25   See Wolfgang Altgeld, 'Religion, Denomination and Nationalism in Nineteenth-Century Germany', in *Protestants, Catholics and Jews*, pp. 49–65.

26 'Students and Friends as "Prophets" and "Promoters": the Reception of Bruckner's Works in the *Wiener Akademischer Wagner-Verein*', in *PAB*, pp. 317–27.

27 'The Annexation of Anton Bruckner: Nazi Revisionism and the Politics of Appropriation', *MQ* 78 (1994), 584–604; reprinted in *BS*, pp. 72–90.

28 Erwin Doernberg, *The Life and Symphonies of Anton Bruckner* (London, 1960), p. 122; Benjamin M. Korstvedt, '"Return to the Pure Sources": the Ideology and Text-Critical Legacy of the First Bruckner *Gesamtausgabe*', in *BS*, pp. 91–109; Günter Brosche, 'Ideologische Einflüsse auf das Nachleben Anton Bruckners', in *Österreichische Musik – Musik in Österreich. Theophil Antonicek zum 60. Geburtstag*, ed. Elisabeth Theresia Hilscher (Tutzing, 1998), pp. 451–61; Christa Brüstle, 'Politisch-ideologische Implikationen der ersten Bruckner-Gesamtausgabe', in *B-P*, pp. 192–201.

29 Manfred Wagner, 'Response to Bryan Gilliam regarding Bruckner and National Socialism', *MQ* 80 (1996), 118–23.

30 Leon Botstein, 'Music and Ideology: Thoughts on Bruckner', *MQ* 80 (1996), 1–11.

31 Glettler, 'Die *Monarchia Austriaca* und die deutsche Musik', pp. 45–6; Bryan Gilliam, 'Bruckner's Annexation Revisited: a Response to Manfred Wagner', *MQ* 80 (1996), 126–8.

32 Gilliam, 'Bruckner's Annexation Revisited', 129.

33 Botstein, 'Music and Ideology', p. 9.

34 Ibid.

35 Thomas Leibnitz, *Die Brüder Schalk und Anton Bruckner: dargestellt an den Nachlassbeständen der Musiksammlung der Österreichischen Nationalbibliothek* (Tutzing, 1988).

36 Thomas Leibnitz, 'Anton Bruckner and "German Music": Josef Schalk and the Establishment of Bruckner as a National Composer', in *PAB*, pp. 328–40.

37 Gilliam, 'Bruckner's Annexation Revisited', 130.

38 Botstein, 'Music and Ideology', 10; Benjamin M. Korstvedt, 'Anton Bruckner in the Third Reich and After: An Essay on Ideology and Bruckner Reception', *MQ* 80 (1996), 149 and 159.

39 See Richard Taruskin, *Text and Act: Essays on Music and Performance* (New York and Oxford, 1995), pp. 164–72.

40 Wagner, 'Response to Bryan Gilliam', 120.

41 Geck, *Von Beethoven bis Mahler*, pp. 384–5; Albrecht von Massow, 'Anachronismus als Moderne: zur Eigenart eines kompositorischen Prinzips in der Musik Anton Bruckners', in *B-P*, pp. 156–57.

42 Michael Bringmann, 'Kirchliche Monumentalarchitektur im späten 19. Jahrhundert', in *Anton Bruckner: Tradition und Fortschritt*, pp. 49–51.

43 Winfried Kirsch, 'Anmerkungen zu einem Spätwerk: Anton Bruckners 150. Psalm', in *Anton Bruckner: Studien zu Werk und Wirkung (Walter Wiora zum 30. Dezember 1986)*, ed. Christoph-Helmut Mahling (Tutzing, 1988), p. 98.

44 Ilona Sármány-Parsons, 'Religious Art and Modernity in the Austro-Hungarian Empire around 1900', in *Catholicism and Austrian Culture*, p. 95.

45 '*Volksconcerte* in Vienna and Late Nineteenth-Century Ideology of the Symphony', *Journal of the American Musicological Society* 50 (1997), 426–39.

2 Musical life in Upper Austria in the mid-nineteenth century

1 For the church music repertoire in St. Florian see Walter Pass, 'Studie über Bruckners ersten St. Florianer Aufenthalt', in *Bruckner-Studien*, ed. Othmar Wessely (Vienna, 1975), pp. 13–42.

2 *Göll-A*, I, p. 141.

3 See Franz Zamazal, 'Johann Baptist Schiedermayr: ein Vorgänger Bruckners als Linzer Dom- und Stadtpfarrorganist', in *Bruckner-Symposion, 'Musikstadt Linz – Musikland Oberösterreich' (Linz 1990): Bericht*, ed. Othmar Wessely *et al.* (Linz, 1993), pp. 119–60.

4 Othmar Wessely, 'Das Linzer Musikleben in der ersten Hälfte des 19. Jahrhunderts', *Jahrbuch der Stadt Linz* (1953), 205.

5 *Göll-A*, I, p. 164.

6 See Walter Deutsch, 'Eine Ländlersammlung aus Windhaag', in *Bruckner-Symposion, 'Bruckner und die Musik der Romantik' (Linz 1987): Bericht*, ed. Renate Grasberger *et al.* (Linz, 1989), pp. 120–52; Othmar Wessely, 'Zu Bruckners Windhaager Jahren', in *Bruckner-Symposion, 'Anton Bruckner – Persönlichkeit und Werk' (Linz 1992): Bericht*, ed. Renate Grasberger *et al.* (Linz, 1995), pp. 49–56.

7 Friedrich Eckstein, *Alte unnennbare Tage: Erinnerungen an siebzig Lehr- und Wanderjahre* (Vienna, 1935; repr. Vienna, 1988), p. 156.

8 See Elisabeth Maier and Franz Zamazal, *Anton Bruckner und Leopold von Zenetti* (Graz, 1980).

9 Letter of 30 July 1852, in *H-S1*, p. 2.

10 Letter from Ferdinand Ruckensteiner, 17 December 1855, in *H-S1*, p. 5.

11 *Linzer Zeitung*, 19 September 1867.

12 *Linzer Zeitung*, 27 July 1858, p. 669 quoted from the *Wiener Zeitung*.

13 *Linzer Zeitung*, 3 December 1861, p. 1165, quoted from the *Wiener Zeitung*.

14 Letter to the Linzer Musikverein, 6 November 1863, in *H-S1*, p. 39.

15 Letter to Rudolf Weinwurm, 7 June 1860, in *H-S1*, p. 18.

16 Letter to Rudolf Weinwurm, 10 February 1861, in *H-S1*, p. 21.

17 *Linzer Zeitung*, 30 November 1864.

18 *Linzer Zeitung*, 20 December 1864.

19 See Andrea Harrandt, '"Vivat! Und nochmals Vivat!": Rudolf Weinwurm und sein Preischor Germania', in *Österreichische Musik – Musik in Österreich: Beiträge zur Musikgeschichte Mitteleuropas (Theophil Antonicek zum 60. Geburtstag)*, ed. Elisabeth Theresia Hilscher (Tutzing, 1998), pp. 385–94.

20 *Linzer Zeitung*, 8 June 1865.

21 Letter to Rudolf Weinwurm, 18 October 1864, in *H-S1*, p. 47.

22 Letter to the Dom-Musikverein, Salzburg, 22 June 1861, in *H-S1*, p. 24.

23 Letter to Rudolf Weinwurm, 29 January 1865, in *H-S1*, p. 51.

24 Letter to Anton M. Storch, 11 December 1866, in *H-S1*, p. 64.

25 Letter to Johann Herbeck, 30 April 1866, in *H-S1*, p. 55.

26 Letter from Johann Herbeck to Bruckner, 10 June 1868, in *H-S1*, p. 89.

27 Letter to Hans von Bülow, 20 June 1868, in *H-S1*, p. 91.

28 Letter from Johann Herbeck to Bruckner, 20 June 1868, in *H-S1*, p. 92.

29 Letter to the Episcopal Ordinariate, Linz, 24 July 1868, in *H-S1*, pp. 93–4.

30 *Alpenbote*, 24 September 1868.

31 *Linzer Zeitung*, 7 April 1868.

32 *Linzer Zeitung*, 13 May 1868.

33 Letter from Alois Weinwurm to Bruckner, 8 November 1868, in *H-S1*, p. 98.

3 Bruckner in Vienna

1 *Linzer Zeitung*, 14 February 1867, quoted from the *Fremdenblatt*.

2 Letter to Moritz von Mayfeld, 13 July 1869, in *H-S1*, p. 110.

3 Management of the Gesellschaft der Musikfreunde to Bruckner, 15 January 1891.

4 Letter to the Ministry for Culture and Education, 11 May 1870, in *H-S1*, p. 117.

5 Letter to Moritz von Mayfeld, 13 February 1875, in *H-S1*, p. 154.

6 Letter of Johann E. Habert to Bernhard Deubler, 22 October 1890, in *H2*, no. 901022.

7 *Neue Freie Presse*, 11 January 1870.

8 *Vaterland*, 20 June 1872.

9 See Andrea Harrandt, 'Students and Friends as "Prophets" and "Promoters": The Reception of Bruckner's Works in the *Wiener Akademischer Wagner-Verein*', in *PAB*, pp. 317–27.

10 It was during this stay in Bayreuth that Bruckner dedicated the Third Symphony to Richard Wagner.

11 See Franz Grasberger, 'Anton Bruckners II. Symphonie', in *Bruckner-Studien*, ed. Othmar Wessely (Vienna, 1975), 303–21.

12 *Neue Freie Presse*, 28 October 1873.

13 *Fremdenblatt*, 28 October 1873; F. G. [= Franz Gehring], in *Deutsche Zeitung*, 28 October 1873.

14 *Neue Freie Presse*, 18 December 1877.

15 *Wiener Zeitung* (*Abendpost*), 17 December 1877.

16 C. B., in *Deutsche Zeitung*, 4 February 1880.

17 Franz Gehring, in *Deutsche Zeitung*, 22 February 1881.

18 *Vaterland*, 3 March 1881.

19 *Neue Freie Presse*, 13 February 1883.

20 On the occasion of the piano performance of the second movement of the Seventh Symphony and the third movement of the Fourth Symphony on 4 November 1884 by Josef Schalk at the Wiener Akademischer Wagner-Verein (*Neue Zeitschrift für Musik*, 5 December 1884).

21 *Wiener Salonblatt*, 28 December 1884.

22 *Deutsche Kunst- und Musikzeitung*, 1 January 1885.

23 *Deutsche Zeitung*, 23 March 1886.

24 *Neue Freie Presse*, 30 March 1886.

25 *Die Presse*, 3 April 1886.

26 *Deutsche Zeitung*, 25 March 1886.

27 *Deutsche Zeitung*, 27 January 1888.

28 Letter to Hermann Levi, August 1888, in *H2*, no. 880800.

29 Letter to Hans von Wolzogen, 1 January 1889, in *H2*, no. 890101/2.

30 h-m., in *Deutsche Zeitung*, 17 October 1889 (the reference is to the First Symphonies of Brahms and Schumann respectively).

31 *Neue Freie Presse*, 24 December 1890.

32 *Deutsche Zeitung*, 23 December 1890.

33 *Ostdeutsche Rundschau*, 21 December 1890.

34 h-m., in *Deutsche Zeitung*, 14 December 1891.

35 Letter of Helm to Bruckner, 5 January 1893, in *H2*, no. 930105.

36 *Neue Freie Presse*, 23 December 1892.
37 E. v. H. and h-m., 'Programm-Wünsche', in *Deutsche Zeitung*, 29 September 1893.
38 *Deutsche Zeitung*, 30 November 1894.
39 *Deutsche Zeitung*, 11 January 1896.
40 Unsigned obituary, *Neue Freie Presse*, 12 October 1896.
41 *Deutsche Zeitung*, 13 October 1896.

4 Bruckner's large sacred compositions

1 *Göll-A*, IV/2, pp. 141–2. The German 'kirchlich' ('und kirchli' is' do' nöt!') has been translated as 'ecclesiastical' with a view to taking full advantage of the musical, religious, and sociological overtones the English word provides. Although questions of venue and function may well have occupied the composer, there is no way to know the extent to which Bruckner intended to differentiate, for example, between 'kirchlich' and 'geistlich'. The latter, with reference to music might be translated as 'sacred' or 'religious', terms that are used interchangeably in this article without regard to issues of liturgical function.

Göll-A is the source of much of the biographical information in the remainder of this essay. The concert in question took place on 14 December 1884; August Böhm, *Geschichte des Singvereines der Gesellschaft der Musikfreunde in Wien* (Vienna, 1908), *Beilage*, p. 55.
2 Comment by [Ludwig Speidel] in an otherwise favourable review of the first performance of the Mass, *Fremdenblatt*, 20 June 1872. For a selection of reviews of the F minor Mass see Paul Hawkshaw (ed.), *ABSW*, XVIII, *Kritischer Bericht* (Vienna, forthcoming).
3 The specific relationship between the Te Deum and the Ninth Symphony has recently been discussed by John A. Phillips, 'The Facts behind a "Legend": the Ninth Symphony and the Te Deum', in *PAB*, pp. 270–81. Phillips points out that, regardless of the state of completion of the instrumental Finale, in Bruckner's mind there was a symbiotic programmatic and musical relationship between the Te Deum and the symphony. On a broader scale, assessments of Bruckner's sacred music as 'symphonies for the church' or of his symphonies as 'Masses for the concert hall' are commonplace in the literature. See, for example, Leopold Nowak, 'Symphonischer und kirchlicher Stil bei Anton Bruckner', in *Über Anton Bruckner: gesammelte Aufsätze 1936–1984* (Vienna, 1985), pp. 47–54.

4 See, for example, Leopold M. Kantner, 'Die Frömmigkeit Anton Bruckners', in *Anton Bruckner in Wien: eine kritische Studie zu seiner Persönlichkeit* (Graz, 1980), pp. 229–78.
5 See Karl Gustav Fellerer, 'Bruckner und die Kirchenmusik seiner Zeit', in *Anton Bruckner: Studien zu Werk und Wirkung*, ed. Christoph-Hellmut Mahling (Tutzing, 1988), pp. 41–62. Bruckner had no qualms about allowing the same piece to serve both church and concert hall. The second performance of the D minor Mass, for example, took place under his direction in the Redoutensaal in Linz in 1868. A performance of the Mass in F minor in the Grosser Musikvereinsaal, Vienna, 23 March 1893, was one of the most successful public appearances of his career. Three 'religious' but 'non-liturgical' works mentioned in this chapter (*Entsagen* WAB 14, *Festgesang* WAB 15, and *Festkantate* WAB 16) are also considered in the context of Bruckner's secular vocal music by Crawford Howie in Chapter 6.
6 'Large' is something of a misnomer in that the pieces vary considerably in dimension, both in terms of performance forces and duration. There are also two Kyrie fragments, WAB 139 (1845–8?) and 140 (*Missa pro Quadragesima,* 1845–6?), and a Requiem fragment, WAB 141 (September, 1875).
7 It is known to have been performed at Vespers in St. Florian on selected feasts between 1852 and 1855: Paul Hawkshaw, 'Bruckners Psalmen', in *B-P*, p. 73.
8 Except Psalm 146, the early history of which is a mystery: see Paul Hawkshaw, 'The Enigma of Anton Bruckner's Psalm 146', in *Musica Conservata: Günter Brosche zum 60. Geburtstag*, ed. Josef Gmeiner, Zsigmond Kokits, Thomas Leibnitz, and Inge Pechotsch-Feichtinger (Tutzing, 1999), pp. 105–19; Hawkshaw, 'A Composer Learns his Craft: Anton Bruckner's Lessons in Form and Orchestration with Otto Kitzler, 1861–3', in *PAB*, 17; and 'Die Psalmkompositionen Anton Bruckners', in *Bruckner Vorträge: Tagung Wien 1999*, ed. Elisabeth Maier, Andrea Harrandt, and Erich Wolfgang Partsch (Vienna, 2000), pp. 8–10. The third article has reproductions of handwritten programmes for music evenings at the monastery.

Festgesang was composed in 1855 for the name day of Jodok Stülz, *Stiftsdechant* in St. Florian, and the *Festkantate* was commissioned for the corner-stone-laying ceremony of the new cathedral in Linz in 1862: Franz Zamazal, 'Festgesang (WAB 15)' and 'Festkantate (WAB 16)', in *Anton Bruckner:*

ein Handbuch, ed. Uwe Harten (Salzburg and Vienna, 1996), pp. 151–3. *Entsagen* was composed for the name-day ceremony of Prelate Michael Arneth in St. Florian, possibly in 1851; Hofkapellmeister Joseph Hellmesberger planned to use the Te Deum for the biretta ceremony of the new Viennese Cardinal Ganglbauer in 1884, though he eventually decided against it owing to its length; and Psalm 150 was intended for the opening ceremony of the International Music and Theatre Exhibition, Vienna, 1892, but the piece was not finished in time: Elisabeth Maier, 'Entsagen (WAB 14)', 'Psalm 150 (WAB 38)', and 'Te Deum (WAB 45)', *Anton Bruckner: ein Handbuch*, pp. 145, 345, and 439–41.

9 An autograph note on the title page over the inscription *A[d]. M[ajorem]. D[ei]. G[loriam].* indicates that the Kyrie and Gloria were added in 1845, though they cannot be located today. There is also a lost Requiem from 1845 (*Göll-A.* I, p. 280). Given the two fragments that exist (see Table 4.1), it is clear that Bruckner was more active as a church composer during his Kronstorf and early St. Florian years than his surviving repertoire indicates. One wonders what he destroyed in the process of moving to Belvedere in 1895.

10 St. Florian Bibliothek 20/66.

11 See above, Chapter 2, p. 17.

12 The parts are kept in the Wels Stadtarchiv 2692.

13 *Liber usualis* (Tournai, 1947), p. 64. Elisabeth Maier has observed that there is also an audible relationship between the opening phrase and the plainchant *Kyrie Deus Sempiterne*: Elisabeth Maier, 'Der Choral in den Kirchenwerken Bruckners', in *Bruckner-Symposion, 'Anton Bruckner und die Kirchenmusik' (Linz 1985): Bericht*, ed. Othmar Wessely (Linz, 1988), p. 119. See also Keith William Kinder, *The Wind and Wind-Chorus Music of Anton Bruckner* (Westport, Conn., 2000), pp. 2–3.

14 Zenetti, who was an important influence on the aspiring musician, lived in Enns, so lessons required a considerable expenditure of time and effort on Bruckner's part. See Elisabeth Maier and Franz Zamazal, *Anton Bruckner und Leopold von Zenetti* (Graz, 1980); Walter Schulten, 'Anton Bruckners künstlerische Entwicklung der St. Florianer Zeit (1845–1855)', Ph.D. thesis (University of Mainz, 1956), contains an exhaustive investigation of Bruckner's Marpurg studies.

15 An extensive performance archive of scores and parts as well as weekly lists of music performed at the liturgies survive today at the monastery. For a discussion of the musical activities at St. Florian see Walter Pass, 'Studie über Bruckners ersten St. Florianer Aufenthalt', in *Bruckner-Studien*, ed. Othmar Wessely (Vienna, 1975); and Schulten, 'Anton Bruckners künstlerische Entwicklung'. Contrary to views expressed in much of the Bruckner literature, Renaissance music was performed only rarely at the monastery while Bruckner was resident there.

16 Preserved under signature 20 in the St. Florian library.

17 Elisabeth Maier, 'Requiem in d-Moll (WAB 39)', in *Bruckner-Handbuch*, p. 350. Bruckner continued to use the Mozart Requiem as a model well into the 1870s; Timothy L. Jackson, 'Bruckner's *Oktaven*: The Problem of Consecutives, Doubling, and Orchestral Voice-leading', in *PAB*, pp. 37–45.

18 As a general rule, text setting did not come easily to Bruckner in his early works. His surviving composition scores from the period demonstrate that he often laboured over issues of declamation, not always with meritorious results; see Paul Hawkshaw, 'The Enigma of Psalm 146', pp. 112–14.

19 *Göll-A*, II/1, p. 70.

20 Ibid., p. 156.

21 Ibid., pp. 186–8.

22 The author is grateful to Dr Friedrich Buchmayr, monastery librarian, for the information that St. Florian is in possession of more than one hundred first editions and early copies of both sacred and secular music of Schubert.

23 Othmar Wessely, 'Bruckners Mendelssohn Kenntnis', in *Bruckner-Studien*, p. 88. While he lived in St. Florian Bruckner also travelled to Linz to study and hear performances. On one of these occasions in 1847 or 1848 he may have heard *St Paul*; he certainly studied the work in St. Florian. See Leopold Nowak, 'Mendelssohns *Paulus* und Anton Bruckner', in *Über Anton Bruckner*, pp. 191–4.

24 There was little call for Bach's liturgical music in St. Florian. Bruckner encountered some of his fugues in his investigations of Marpurg and presumably studied some of the organ music with Kattinger.

25 See Othmar Wessely, 'Zur Geschichte der Equals', in *Beethoven-Studien* (Vienna, 1970), pp. 341–60. Trombone Aequale, of which Bruckner composed two (WAB 114 and 149), were performed at funerals in St. Florian – one of the many rhetorical connections between trombones and death in Bruckner's experience.

26 The secular cantata *Heil, Vater! Dir zum hohen Feste* (WAB 61) has a melodic fragment that first appears in the second movement and recurs thereafter; Kinder, *Wind and Wind-Chorus Music*, p. 19.

27 He sent the piece to Assmayr on 30 July 1852; see *H-S1*, p.2.

28 The clash is emphasized by a glaring cross relation between g♯ of the chorale's cadential chord in bar 9 and g♯ of the opening chord of the first chorus in the next bar. It is difficult to imagine that Assmayr was impressed by Bruckner's voice-leading, at least in this instance.

29 Layers of handwriting in the two manuscript sources demonstrate that Bruckner worked on them over an extended period of time, perhaps after he had moved to Linz. For a discussion of the various theories about the genesis of the work, see Hawkshaw, 'The Enigma of Psalm 146', pp. 105–12. The Psalm survives in a fragmentary autograph composition score and a copy in the Music Collection of the Austrian National Library, Mus. Hs. 40.500 and 6011 respectively, neither of which is dated.

30 *Göll-A*, II/1, p. 184.

31 Bruckner completed his studies with Sechter in March 1861 and started with Kitzler before the end of the same year. In between there was a brief flurry of compositional activity that included two important motets, *Afferentur Regi* (WAB 1) and *Ave Maria [à.7]* (WAB 6), and possibly work on the *Festkantate* (WAB 16). For more on Sechter and Kitzler see Ernst Schwanzara, *Anton Bruckner: Vorlesungen über Harmonielehre und Kontrapunkt an der Universität Wien* (Vienna, 1950), pp. 17–34; and Paul Hawkshaw, 'A Composer Learns his Craft: Lessons in Form and Orchestration, 1861–3', pp. 3–29.

32 Bruckner only began to use the standard nineteenth-century score order with woodwinds at the top and strings at the bottom, for example, after working with Kitzler.

33 Kitzler conducted *Tannhäuser* in Linz on 13 February 1863. Bruckner prepared the Liedertafel *Frohsinn* to sing the 'Pilgrims' Chorus'; see Otto Kitzler, *Musikalische Erinnerungen mit Briefen von Wagner, Brahms, Bruckner und Richard Pohl* (Brünn [Brno], 1904), pp. 29–31.

34 *Um Mitternacht* (WAB 89), *Herbstlied* (WAB 73), and *Germanenzug* (WAB 70). Although it is a chronological inaccuracy, the Mass is usually referred to as No. 1 in concert programmes; the Masses in E and F minor are Nos. 2 and 3 respectively. The numbering dates from Bruckner's time and stems from the fact that, for the remainder of his life, he regarded the end of the Kitzler studies as the beginning of his career as a professional composer.

35 Letter to Rudolf Weinwurm, 26 December 1864, *H-S1*, p. 47.

36 In the autograph score (Austrian National Library, Mus. Hs. 19.483) the woodwind of bars 100–9 are scored for organ, which was no doubt used for the first performance in the Linz Cathedral. He rescored the part for woodwind for performances where the organ was not available or where its pitch didn't match that of the orchestra. The woodwind interpolation proved practical: in Bruckner's experience orchestral pitch had already climbed above that of most organs by 1865. See the letter to Weinwurm of 21 January 1865, *H-S1*, p. 59.

37 See Othmar Wessely, 'Vergangenheit und Zukunft in Bruckners Messe in D Moll', *Österreichische Musikzeitschrift* 29 (1974), 412–18 for an extensive discussion of Bruckner's rhetorical gestures in a historical context. In particular Wessely connects the falling semitones to the Baroque gesture of the *passus duriusculus*.

38 *Linzer Abendboten*, cited in *Göll-A*, III/1, pp. 297–9.

39 *Göll-A*, III/1, p. 299.

40 Ibid., pp. 300–1.

41 Auer, *Bruckner als Kirchenmusiker*, p. 38. It is not uncommon to find, especially in the German literature, analyses of the Mass movements in the terminology of sonata form; i.e. the opening of the Gloria is referred to as the *Hauptsatz* and the 'Gratias' as the *Nebensatz*; see Horst-Günther Scholz, *Die Form der reifen Messen Anton Bruckners* (Berlin, 1961).

42 See Ludwig Speidel's remark about the Wolf's Glen scene in a review of the Credo of the F minor Mass, note 2.

43 The earthquake metaphor was already present in the *Missa solemnis*, and trombone chorales had found their way into the Requiem and the *Missa solemnis* setting of 'mortuorum' ('of the dead') in the Credo; see note 24.

44 The reference is to the 1882 version (bar 49 in 1866). Kinder (*Wind and Wind-Chorus Music*, p. 55) connects the opening phrase of the Gloria to the plainchant Gloria VIII in the *Liber usualis*, p. 37.

45 Witt was founder of the German Cecilian
Society that saw Gregorian chant and the
music of Palestrina as models for a church
music renaissance. For more on Bruckner's
relationship with the Cecilianists see Karl
Gustav Fellerer, 'Bruckners Kirchenmusik
und der Cäcilianismus', *Österreichische
Musikzeitschrift* 29 (1974), 404–12.
46 *ABSW*, XVIII (Vienna, 1960), Preface.
47 *Neue Freie Presse*, 29 June 1872; the call for
a concert performance of the Mass became a
recurring theme in Viennese criticism. See
the chapter on reviews in *ABSW*, XVIII,
Kritischer Bericht.
48 Bruckner had not used obbligato solo
instruments to accompany singers in such an
extended passage since his St. Florian days.
One wonders whether an encounter with the
Missa solemnis during his Linz years opened
his eyes to new possibilities in this regard. A
similar passage occurs with a violin solo at
'Christe eleison' (Kyrie, bars 36–54);
Bruckner would return to this kind of writing
with passages in the Te Deum (bars 191–204
and 273–86) and Psalm 150 (bars 109–42).
49 Hans Ferdinand Redlich (ed.), *Mass in F
Minor* (London, 1967), Foreword, p. 31.
50 *Liber usualis*, p. 26.
51 See the list of performances in Theophil
Antonicek, *Anton Bruckner und die Wiener
Hofmusikkapelle* (Graz, 1979), pp. 142–4.
52 *Göll-A*, IV/2, p. 143.
53 For more on the revisions see Leopold
Nowak, 'Bruckners Formveränderungen an
seiner e-Moll-Messe', in *Über Anton Bruckner*,
pp. 200–3 and Paul Hawkshaw, 'An Anatomy
of Change: Anton Bruckner's Revisions to the
Mass in F Minor', in *BS*, pp. 1–31. Robert
Haas, unaware of the 1883 changes to the
autograph score of the F minor Mass,
incorrectly dated the first version 1881 in his
edition in the first Bruckner Collected
Edition.
54 *Göll-A*, III/1, pp. 88 criticizes Bruckner's
early fugues for their extended passages of
parallel thirds and sixths, and Maz Graf,
'Anton Bruckner: der Entwicklungsgang', *Die
Musik* 1 (1901–2), 581, laments the lack of
technical freedom in the voice leading, short
phrases, and standard contrapuntal
progressions in the fugue of Psalm 146.
55 See for example Fritz Grüninger, *Anton
Bruckner: der metaphysische Kern seiner
Persönlichkeit und seiner Werke*, 2nd edn
(Augsburg, 1949).
56 *EKB*, vol. II, p. 1201. Kurth went on to
suggest that a major accomplishment of
Bruckner's mature sacred music was a

successful blend of romantic melodic style
with plainchant.

5 Bruckner and the motet

1 It may have been written slightly later,
during his period as a choirboy at St. Florian
(1837–40), but certainly pre-dates his teacher
training year (1840–1). For a facsimile of the
autograph of the revised 1891 version see
Göll-A, II/1, p. 230; also A. C. Howie, 'The
Sacred Music of Anton Bruckner', Ph.D. thesis
(University of Manchester, 1969), pp. 213–44;
Leopold Nowak, 'Die kleinen
Kirchenmusikwerke Anton Bruckners', in
Über Anton Bruckner: gesammelte Aufsätze
(Vienna, 1985), pp. 245–6; Nowak, 'Anton
Bruckners Kirchenmusik', in
*Bruckner-Symposion, 'Anton Bruckner und die
Kirchenmusik' (Linz 1985): Bericht*, ed. Othmar
Wessely (Linz, 1988), pp. 85–93; Helmut
Loos, 'Zu Bruckners Kirchenmusik', in *B-P*,
pp. 64–70; Hartmut Krones, '"Und 1000 Jahre
sind ihm wie ein Tag": Kirchenmusik in
Österreich 996–1996', *Österreichische
Musikzeitschrift* 51 (1996), 705–6.
2 WAB 3 was printed in *Göll-A*, III/2,
pp. 140–1. Auer considered it a later
composition, dating from the Linz years,
but this must be ruled out on stylistic
grounds. *Asperges me* is sung during the
distribution of holy water at the Sunday
services during Lent.
3 All five settings were published by Gross of
Innsbruck in 1893.
4 It may have been performed together with
Bruckner's 1852 *Magnificat* at St. Florian on
1 August 1854. The work was printed in
Göll-A, II/2, pp. 255–8.
5 *Göll-A*, II/2, pp. 141–4.
6 The first piece was printed in *Göll-A*, II/2,
pp. 83; in *ABSW*, XXI/1 (Vienna, 1984), 52–3,
Hans Bauernfeind supplied the missing bass
part of the second.
7 See Harry Slapnicka, *Bischof Rudigier: eine
Bildbiographie* (Linz, 1962) and 'Bischof
Rudigier und die Kunst', in *Bruckner-
Symposion Linz 1985*, pp. 23–31; also Elisabeth
Maier, '"Kirchenmusik auf schiefen Bahnen":
zur Situation in Linz von 1850 bis 1900', in
*Bruckner-Symposion, 'Musikstadt Linz –
Musikland Oberösterreich' (Linz 1990): Bericht*,
ed. Othmar Wessely *et al.* (Linz, 1993),
pp. 109–17.
8 One smaller sacred piece from the Linz
period which has been lost is *Litanei* (WAB
132). For a successful performance of it in
Linz in 1858 see Sechter's letter of 26
September to Bruckner (*H-S1*, pp. 13–14).

9   For a facsimile of the autograph of
Afferentur regi see Max Auer, *Anton Bruckner
als Kirchenmusiker* (Regensburg, 1927), p. 64.
See also Wolfgang Hoffmann,
'"Sextaccord"-Folgen im geistlichen
Vokalschaffen Anton Bruckners', *B-J
1994/95/96* (1997), 157–73.

10   *Frohsinn*, with Bruckner at the organ,
gave it its first performance in Linz Parish
Church on 6 February 1865. There is a
facsimile of the autograph in *Göll-A*, III/2,
pp. 219–24.

11   Bruckner referred to the 1868 setting of
Pange lingua as 'my favourite *Tantum ergo*' in a
letter of 18 October 1892; it was to be
performed 'very slowly and solemnly'; see
Max Auer (ed.), *Anton Bruckner: gesammelte
Briefe (Neue Folge)* (Regensburg, 1924),
pp. 264–5.

12   This 'correction' was amended in the
Gross edition of 1895 and subsequent
editions of the piece. Prior to its publication
in Franz X. Witt, *Eucharistische Gesänge* 5
(1888), it appeared in the supplement of Witt
(ed.), *Musica Sacra* 18 (1885), p. 44. Witt
made some rhythmical changes in bars 9–11.
For an account of Bruckner's reaction, see
Friedrich Eckstein, *Erinnerungen an Anton
Bruckner* (Vienna, 1923), pp. 13–17.

13   For a facsimile of the autograph of
the 1868 *Pange lingua* see *Göll-A*, III/1,
p. 500.

14   As editor of the *Fliegende Blätter für
katholische Kirchenmusik* and the *Cäcilienverein*
catalogue (a kind of repertoire codex
including only those church music works
which adhered to strict Cecilian principles),
Witt's reform ideas became even more
radical. Habert effectively prevented Witt
from gaining a foothold in Austria. For an
overview of Cecilianism in Austria, see Otto
Biba, 'Der Cäcilianismus', in
Bruckner-Symposion (Linz 1985), pp. 123–8;
Josef Moser, 'Zum Thema Kirchenmusik:
cäcilianische Bestrebungen in der Diözese
Linz', in *Oberösterreichische Heimatblätter* 39
(1985), 62–85; Maier, '"Kirchenmusik auf
schiefen Bahnen"', 115–17; Hartmut Krones,
'Bruckners Kirchenmusik im Spiegel der
Cäcilianismus', in *Anton Bruckner: Tradition
und Fortschritt in der Kirchenmusik des 19.
Jahrhunderts*, ed. Friedrich W. Riedel (Sinzig,
2001), pp. 91–104; Hubert Unverricht (ed.),
*Der Caecilianismus: Anfänge – Grundlagen –
Wirkungen* (Tutzing, 1988).

15   For a facsimile of the autograph see Auer,
Anton Bruckner als Kirchenmusiker, p. 64, and
Göll-A, III/2, pp. 239–44.

16   The dedicatee of *Iam lucis* was the abbot
of Wilhering Abbey, and Robert Riepl, a priest
in the abbey, supplied the text; see G. K.
Mitterschiffthaler, 'Die Beziehungen Anton
Bruckners zum Stift Wilhering', in *Bruckner
Studien*, ed. Othmar Wessely (Vienna, 1975),
p. 128. It was first published in Linz in 1868
and was printed again later, in a transposed
version and with four of the original eight
verses omitted, in the Viennese magazine *An
der schönen blauen Donau* in May 1886.

17   There is an entry in the Hofkapelle
schedule for 8 December 1873 which clearly
refers to a performance of this setting of
Christus factus est. See Theophil Antonicek,
Anton Bruckner und die Wiener Hofmusikkapelle
(Graz, 1979), for detailed information about
Bruckner's appointment at the
Hofmusikkapelle. See also Walburga
Litschauer, 'Bruckner und die Wiener
Kirchenmusiker', in *Bruckner-Symposion (Linz
1985)*, pp. 95–101; Leopold M. Kantner
discusses the typical *Hofkapelle* repertoire in
'Kirchenmusikalische Strömungen bis
Bruckner', in *Bruckner-Symposion (Linz 1985)*,
pp. 53–7.

18   See Imogen Fellinger, 'Die drei Fassungen
des "Christus factus est"', in
Bruckner-Symposion (Linz 1985), pp. 145–53.

19   Elisabeth Maier identifies the similarity of
the opening phrase to the second, third, or
eighth psalm-tone or the 'Alleluia' of the
*Officium in festo immaculatae Conceptionis
Beatae Mariae Virginis* ('Der Choral in den
Kirchenwerken Bruckners', in
Bruckner-Symposion (Linz 1985), p. 118).
Hartmut Krones also discusses the three-note
head-motive of this opening phrase in the
context of Bruckner's use here and elsewhere
of what Constantin Floros has called the
'tonal symbol of the cross' in
'Musiksprachliche Elemente aus Renaissance
und Barock bei Anton Bruckner',
*Bruckner-Symposion, 'Bruckner – Vorbilder und
Traditionen' (Linz 1997): Bericht*, ed. Uwe
Harten (Linz, 1999), p. 57.

20   Bruckner sent a signed copy of the work
to Rudigier, its dedicatee, on 30 May 1878
(see *H-S1*, p. 178).

21   See *H-S1*, pp. 181ff. for the text of this
letter, dated Vienna, 25 July 1879. Traumihler
asked Bruckner to make some changes,
particularly in the middle section. Bruckner
complied and on 28 July added the
organ-accompanied versicle 'Inveni David'.
See *Göll-A*, II/1, p. 269, and Nowak, 'Die
Motette "Os justi" und ihre Handschriften', in
Über Anton Bruckner, pp. 246–9.

22 The text of *Os justi* is from the *Missa de Doctoribus*. Although there appears to be no pre-existent model for the 'Inveni David' versicle, the melody for the 'Alleluia' is taken from the 'Alleluia' of the Introit *In medio ecclesiae* in the *Commune Doctorum*; see Maier, 'Der Choral in den Kirchenwerken Bruckners', p. 117. There is a facsimile of the autograph of the first version of the motet in *Göll-A*, IV/1, between pages 568 and 569.

23 Erwin Horn suggests that just as Bruckner sublimated his feelings for Aloisia Bogner when he wrote *Entsagen*, so in this *Ave Maria*, he put his obvious affection for Luise Hochleitner on one side: 'separated from the private connection . . . it is "religious" in the best sense of the word and can be conducive to religious edification at any time. Its religious "worth" is in no way diminished by the presence of other resonating factors'; see Horn, 'Eros und Marienlob: Gedanken zu Anton Bruckners Marienmotetten', in *B-J 1989/90* (1992), 225.

24 Timothy L. Jackson – in 'The Enharmonics of Faith: Enharmonic Symbolism in Bruckner's *Christus factus est* (1884)', *B-J 1987/88* (1990), 19 – argues that it is the 'overwhelming significance of this "rising" D♭ become C♯ that "raises" Jesus' name above all others' ('super omne nomen').

25 The work was first published in a facsimile of the autograph in *Göll-A*, IV/2, pp. 496 and 497.

26 Maier suggests that Bruckner's harmonization of *Veni creator* is closer to a Lutheran chorale harmonization, with pauses coming at the end of each line. In addition Bruckner has 'compromised' the modality of the piece by harmonizing the first syllable of 'Creator' with an A major chord. See Maier, 'Der Choral in den Kirchenwerken Bruckners', 114–15. For the use of plainsong in Austrian abbeys and large churches, St. Florian in particular, during the nineteenth century, see Franz K. Prassl, 'Die österreichische Choralpflege im 19. Jahrhundert', in *Bruckner-Symposion (Linz 1997)*, pp. 35–51.

27 A revised version of the E minor Mass was performed on the final day of the celebrations, 4 October 1885 (see *H-S1*, p. 264).

28 This doxology is taken from the fourth psalm tone in the *Tonus solemnis* (see Maier, 'Der Choral in den Kirchenwerken Bruckners', 118). The text of *Ecce sacerdos magnus* is taken from the *Responsory for the Reception of a Bishop*.

29 *Virga Jesse floruit*, the setting of a text from the Feast of the Blessed Virgin, was dedicated to the memory of Traumihler. Its first performance was probably as a gradual during the F minor Mass, which Bruckner conducted in the Hofkapelle on 8 December 1885.

30 The text of *Ave regina coelorum* is taken from a Lenten antiphon, but the plainsong comes from a gradual verse with 'Alleluia' in the *Missa de Sancta Maria ab Adventu usque ad Navitatem Domini*. See Elisabeth Maier, 'Der Choral in den Kirchenwerken Bruckners', 115.

31 For this 'inner compulsion' see Auer (ed.), *Bruckner: gesammelte Briefe*, pp. 257 and 259.

32 This is particularly relevant in the first verse where the B dominant seventh chord at 'morte' is followed by the first inversion E♭ major chord at 'vitam' (bars 25–9). Timothy Jackson refers to the sketches in noting that the corrections Bruckner made to the music and metrical numbers 'testify eloquently to Bruckner's considerable effort in setting the last line of text', the enharmonic passage in particular. See Timothy L. Jackson, 'Bruckner's Metrical Numbers', *NCM* 14 (1990–1), 114 and 118.

6   Bruckner and secular vocal music

1 Gernot Gruber, 'Nachmärz und Ringstrassenzeit', in *Musikgeschichte Österreichs 3: von der Revolution zur Gegenwart*, ed. Rudolf Flotzinger and Gernot Gruber (Vienna – Cologne – Weimar, 1995), pp. 24–6.

2 Hans Commenda, *Die Geschichte des Oberösterreichischen Sängerbundes* (Linz, 1953), p. 29.

3 *Frohsinn* was founded in 1845, *Sängerbund* in 1857. Because of their similar repertories, they frequently joined forces. See Karl Kerschbaum, *Chronik der Liedertafel 'Frohsinn' in Linz über den 50jährigen Bestand vom 17. März 1845 bis anfangs März 1895* (Linz, 1895); Andrea Harrandt, 'Aus dem Archiv der Liedertafel "Frohsinn"; zum Chorwesen im 19. Jahrhundert', in *Bruckner-Symposion, 'Musikstadt Linz – Musikland Oberösterreich' (Linz 1990): Bericht*, ed. Othmar Wessely *et al.* (Linz, 1993), pp. 57–70.

4 See Andrea Harrandt, 'Bruckner und das bürgerliche Musiziergut seiner Jugendzeit', in *Bruckner-Symposion, 'Bruckner und die Musik der Romantik' (Linz 1987): Bericht*, ed. Renate Grasberger *et al.* (Linz, 1989), pp. 93–103; 'Bruckner and the *Liedertafel* Tradition: His Secular Music for Male Voices, *Choral Journal* 37 (1996), 15–21; 'Bruckner und die

Chormusik seiner Zeit', *Oberösterreichische Heimatblätter* 51 (1997), 184–95; Erich Wolfgang Partsch, 'Bruckner-Pflege in Steyr bis zur Jahrhundertwende', *Internationale Bruckner-Gesellschaft Mitteilungsblatt* 35 (1990), 5–10.

5 See Angela Pachovsky, 'Anton Bruckners weltliche Chorwerke: zum Inhalt von Band XXIII/2 der Bruckner-Gesamtausgabe', in *Bruckner-Tagung Wien 1999: Bericht*, ed. Elisabeth Maier, Andrea Harrandt, and Erich Wolfgang Partsch (Vienna, 2000), pp. 35–46.

6 *Göll-A*, I, pp. 229–35.

7 See *H-S1*, p. 1.

8 *Der Lehrerstand* was possibly performed by the St. Florian *Liedertafel* in the late 1840s. See Christoph Meran and Elisabeth Maier, 'Anton Bruckner und Charles O'Hegerty: zur Geschichte eines lange verschollenen Bruckner-Autographs', *B-J 1994/95/96* (1997), 195–210, for further information about *Des Dankes Wort* written during the St. Florian period for Count Charles O'Hegerty of Tillysburg.

9 The text for *Sternschnuppen* was provided by Ernst Marinelli (1824–87), for whom see *Anton Bruckner: ein Handbuch*, ed. Uwe Harten (Salzburg and Vienna, 1996), p. 271. *Ständchen* is discussed in *Göll-A*, II/1, pp. 47–51.

10 The original manuscript (Oberösterreichisches Landesarchiv, Linz) lacks date and title-page. A facsimile of a page (in Pachovsky, 'Bruckners weltliche Chorwerke', p. 38) reveals the insertion of metrical numbers which Bruckner began to use during his period of study with Kitzler. The first performance probably took place in 1898 with new words by Anton August Naaf – 'Dir holde Heimat soll erklingen' – and sung by the *Schubertbund* in Vienna.

11 See Paul Hawkshaw, 'The Manuscript Sources for Anton Bruckner's Linz Works: a Study of his Working Methods from 1856 to 1868', Ph.D. thesis, University of Columbia (1984), pp. 255 and 262.

12 Letter to Rudolf Weinwurm dated Linz, 3 October 1861, *H-S1*, pp. 25–6.

13 Hawkshaw, 'Manuscript Sources', p. 223.

14 *Göll-A*, III/1, p. 254.

15 *H-S1*, p. 63.

16 Ibid., 64.

17 See Fritz Racek, 'Ein neuer Text zu Bruckners "Vaterländisches Weinlied"?', in *Bruckner-Studien*, ed. Franz Grasberger (Vienna, 1964), pp. 83–6.

18 See *H-S1*, p. 114, for the second letter, which is dated 24 November 1869. Bruckner

was mistaken in believing that Joseph Mendelssohn, the author of the poem, was Felix Mendelssohn's grandfather.

19 The text of *Das hohe Lied* was provided by Heinrich von der Mattig, the pseudonym of Dr Heinrich Wallmann (1827–98), an army doctor, writer and journalist. In 1902 it was edited for publication by Hans Wagner, who dispensed with the humming parts and retained only one solo tenor part, redistributing material among the chorus.

20 The text of the original version, *Nachruf*, was provided by Wallmann. See also *H-S1*, p.176.

21 Wallmann was responsible for the text of *Abendzauber*. In the first edition of the work (Vienna, Universal Edition, 1911), Viktor Keldorfer provided a text underlay derived from the words of the solo part. As Bruckner did not provide any specific syllabic underlay for the yodelling voices, Keldorfer also added 'yodelling syllables corresponding to the typical way of singing in the Austrian alpine districts'.

22 See *Göll-A*, IV/1, pp. 520–1, where the date of composition is given wrongly as 11 November 1878.

23 See *H-S1*, p.197 for Bruckner's letter to August Göllerich sen., the dedicatee, dated 17 February 1882, to which he attached the finished chorus. According to Franz Bayer, the original words were provided by Wallmann, but the chorus was later furnished with another text by Kerschbaum, edited by Keldorfer, and published by Universal Edition in 1911.

24 Quoted by Andrea Harrandt in 'Bruckner und das bürgerliche Musiziergut', 97.

25 The advert appeared in the *Deutsche Zeitung*, which also reported the decision on 16 April 1882. Auer, who erroneously assigned an earlier date to the piece, commended its 'powerful folk-like' quality; *Göll-A*, III/1, p. 105; also III/2, p. 191 for a facsimile of the autograph.

26 The second setting of *Um Mitternacht* was dedicated to the Strasbourg Male Voice Society, which published a facsimile edition of the piece in 1886. Angela Pachovsky compares the two settings in 'Bruckners weltliche Chorwerke', pp. 42–3.

27 According to the autograph, *Das deutsche Lied* was composed on 29 April. For extracts from contemporary reviews of the work, see Harrandt, 'Bruckner und das bürgerliche Musiziergut', 97–8, and Elisabeth Hilscher, 'Bruckner als Gelehrter – Bruckner als Geehrter', in *Bruckner-Symposion, 'Anton*

Bruckner als Schüler und Lehrer' (Linz 1988): Bericht, ed. Othmar Wessely *et al.* (Linz, 1992), pp. 120–1.

28 The first version is described on the manuscript title-page as an 'attempted musical setting of a short poem in the chamber style'. The second version, written about a month later, added a dedication to Knauer. The work received its definitive title in its third version, dedicated to Friedrich Mayr, who was later to succeed Arneth as prelate of St. Florian. See *Göll-A*, I, pp. 283–300 for a facsimile; also Leopold Nowak, '*Vergissmeinnicht* von Anton Bruckner', in *Über Anton Bruckner*, pp. 249–53.

29 The text of the cantata, which Bruckner dedicated to Arneth on his name-day, is taken from Redwitz's poem, *Amaranth*. See *Göll-A*, II/2, pp. 47–58 for a facsimile.

30 *Heil, Vater! Dir zum hohen Feste* was performed in revised versions on at least two other occasions with altered texts (by Marinelli and by Beda Piringer). The published autograph facsimile (*Göll-A*, II/1, pp. 112–30) is of the second version; see Hawkshaw, 'Manuscript Sources', pp. 214–21; Franz Zamazal, 'Bruckners Namenstag-Kantate für Propst Michael Arneth (1852)', *B-J 1989/90* (1992), 205–12. *Göll-A*, II/2, pp. 241–54 has a facsimile of the manuscript of *Sankt Jodok spross* in which the piano part is incomplete.

31 See *Göll-A*, III/2, pp. 197–216 for a facsimile of the autograph score of *Preiset den Herrn*; also Hawkshaw, 'Manuscript Sources', pp. 189–91 and 269–70.

32 For Silberstein, the Wiener Männergesangverein, and the various socio-political issues which provide a backcloth to Bruckner's two settings, see Johannes-Leopold Mayer, 'Die Zwielichtigkeit des Erfolges: Anton Bruckners *Helgoland* im historischen Umfeld des Wiener Männerchorwesens', *B-J 1980* (1980), 21–6; Alexander L. Ringer, '*Germanenzug* bis *Helgoland*: zu Anton Bruckners Deutschtum', in *B-P*, pp. 25–34.

33 See *H-S1*, p. 35–7; also *Göll-A*, III/1, pp. 208–9 for a facsimile of *Germanenzug* in Silberstein's handwriting.

34 See *H-S1*, pp. 40 and 42–3; Paul Hawkshaw, 'From Zigeunerwald to Valhalla in Common Time: The Genesis of Anton Bruckner's *Germanenzug*', *B-J 1987/88* (1990), 21–3.

35 Bruckner was convinced that *Germanenzug* marked the true beginning of his career as a recognized composer. His first

published work, it was certainly the most popular and probably the most frequently performed of his works during his lifetime; after his death and at least up until the outbreak of the 1914–18 war, hardly a year passed without a public performance. The Akademischer Gesangverein under Eduard Kremser performed the vocal quartet from the chorus at Bruckner's funeral.

36 See Franz Gräflinger, *Anton Bruckner: gesammelte Briefe* (Regensburg, 1924), pp. 64–6; Max Auer, *Anton Bruckner: gesammelte Briefe – neue Folge* (Regensburg, 1924), p. 274; *Göll-A*, IV/3, pp. 331 and 341–2 for letters to Viktor Christ, Cyrill Hynais and Eduard Kremser.

37 Ringer, '*Germanenzug* bis *Helgoland*', p. 31.

38 See Wolfgang Grandjean, 'Anton Bruckners "Helgoland" und das Symphonische', *Die Musikforschung* 48 (1995), 349–68; Mayer, 'Die Zwielichtigkeit des Erfolges', 22.

39 Bruckner probably intended to dedicate both 'Mild wie Bäche' and 'Wie des Bächleins Silberquelle' to Arneth, who was no doubt the 'father' mentioned in the text of the former. The text of the latter is the same as that of *Ständchen* (WAB 84). The author of the poems is unknown but was probably Marinelli. There are facsimiles of the sketches of both pieces in *Göll-A*, II/2, 59–60, and 65–6. There is a facsimile of the original manuscript of 'Frühlingslied' in *Göll-A*, II/1, pp. 41–3.

40 *H-S1*, p. 14.

41 See *Göll-A*, III/1, p. 56 and *ABSW* XXIII/1, vii.

42 *Göll-A*, III/1, p. 514.

43 Walther Dürr, 'Das romantische Lied', in *Bruckner-Symposion (Linz 1987)*, p. 165.

44 See above and note 25 for discussion of the choral version. There are facsimiles of both versions in *Göll-A*, III/2, pp. 191–2.

7 The Brucknerian symphony: an overview

1 Deryck Cooke, 'Anton Bruckner (1824–96)', in *The Symphony*, ed. Robert Simpson, 2 vols. (Harmondsworth, 1966), I, pp. 283–306.

2 See Warren Darcy, 'Bruckner's Sonata Deformations', in *BS*, p. 260.

3 Manfred Wagner, 'Zum Tremolo in der Musik Anton Bruckners', in *Bruckner-Studien*, ed. Othmar Wessely (Vienna, 1975), pp. 328–40 and 342–6.

4 Adolf Nowak, 'Die Wiederkehr in Bruckners Adagio', in *Anton Bruckner: Studien zu Werk und Wirkung (Walter Wiora zum 30.*

Dezember 1986), ed. Christoph-Helmut Mahling (Tutzing, 1988), p. 168.
5 Dika Newlin, *Bruckner – Mahler – Schoenberg*, 1st edn (New York, 1971), pp. 52–3.
6 See Thomas Röder, *Auf dem Weg zur Bruckner-Symphonie* (Stuttgart, 1987), p. 132.
7 Wendelin Müller-Blattau, 'Chor- und Orchestersatz im *Te Deum* von Anton Bruckner', in *Anton Bruckner: Studien zu Werk und Wirkung*, pp. 149–58.
8 Ibid., pp. 157–8.
9 Carl Dahlhaus, *Nineteenth-Century Music*, trans. J. Bradford Robinson (Berkeley, 1989), p. 333.
10 Manfred Wagner, *Anton Bruckner: Werk und Leben* (Vienna, 1995), pp. 4–5; cf. the same author in *Bruckner: eine Monographie* (Mainz, 1983), p. 359.
11 *Schematismus und Evolution in der Sinfonik Anton Bruckners* (Munich and Salzburg, 1983), p. 88.
12 'Thesen über Bruckner', in *Musik-Konzepte 23/24: Anton Bruckner*, ed. Heinz-Klaus Metzger and Rainer Riehn (Munich, 1982), pp. 7–11; translated as 'Bruckner Propositions (I)', *Bruckner Journal* 1/1 (1997), 4–5 and 'Bruckner Propositions (II)', *Bruckner Journal* 1/2 (1997), 8–9.
13 Rainer Boss, *Gestalt und Funktion von Fuge und Fugato bei Anton Bruckner* (Tutzing, 1997), pp. 171–2.
14 Othmar Wessely, 'Bruckners Mendelssohn Kenntnis', in *Bruckner-Studien*, ed. Othmar Wessely (Vienna, 1975), pp. 98–9; Leopold Nowak, 'Mendelssohns *Paulus* und Anton Bruckner', in *Über Anton Bruckner: gesammelte Aufsätze 1936–1984* (Vienna, 1985), pp. 191–4.
15 E.g. the idea of 'rotational form' in Warren Darcy, 'Bruckner's Sonata Deformations', in *BS*, pp. 264–6.
16 'Zur Stellung der "Nullten" Symphonie in Bruckners Werk', in *Anton Bruckner: Studien zu Werk und Wirkung*, pp. 70–3.
17 See Peter Gülke, *Brahms, Bruckner: zwei Studien* (Kassel, 1989), pp. 103–4; for how the Wagnerians dealt with the problem, see Stephen M. McClatchie, 'Bruckner and the Bayreuthians; or, *Das Geheimnis der Form bei Anton Bruckner*', in *BS*, pp. 110–21.
18 Graham H. Phipps, 'Bruckner's Free Application of Strict Sechterian Theory with Stimulation from Wagnerian Sources: an Assessment of the First Movement of the Seventh Symphony', in *PAB*, pp. 228–58.
19 See also Timothy L. Jackson, 'Schubert as "John the Baptist to Wagner-Jesus": large-scale Enharmonicism in Bruckner and his Models', *B-J 1991/92/93* (1995), 61–107.

20 Mathias Hansen, 'Bruckners "Ton": das Streichquintett im Umfeld der Sinfonien', in *B-P*, p. 102.
21 Joseph C. Kraus, 'Phrase Rhythm in Bruckner's Early Orchestral Scherzi', in *BS*, pp. 278–97.
22 Floros, 'Thesen über Bruckner', p. 9.

8 Bruckner's symphonies – a reinterpretation: the dialectic of darkness and light

1 John 8: 12.
2 Job 10: 21: 'The land of darkness and the shadow of death'; Isaiah 9: 2: 'The people that walked in darkness have seen a great light: they that dwell in the land of the shadow of death, upon them hath the light shined'; Luke 1: 79: 'To give light to them that sit in darkness and in the shadow of death, to guide our feet into the way of peace'.
3 Quoted in Hans Hubert Schönzeler, *Bruckner* (London, 1970), 80.
4 Genesis 1: 2–4.
5 August Halm, *Die Symphonie Anton Bruckners* (Munich, 1914), p. 43, quoted in Dika Newlin, *Bruckner – Mahler – Schoenberg*, rev. edn (London, 1979), p. 83. The second quotation is from Derek Watson, *Bruckner*, 2nd edn (Oxford, 1996), p. 74.
6 *Anton Bruckner: Sein Leben und Werk*, 2nd edn (Vienna, 1934), p. 424, quoted in Newlin, *Bruckner–Mahler–Schoenberg*, p. 83.
7 Robert Simpson, *The Essence of Bruckner*, 3rd edn (London, 1992), p. 210.
8 That the pairing of themes originated in Bruckner's reaction to a body lying in state amid the sounds of a grand ball from an adjacent mansion is well known. The anecdote is from *Göll-A*, IV/2, p. 663.
9 'Media vita morte sumus' is from an antiphon *c.* 911 AD attributed to Notker Balbulus of the monastery of St Gall, Switzerland, and appears in the *Book of Common Prayer* ('Burial of the Dead') as 'In the midst of life we are in death.'
10 In the same way as writing is understood as an absence of the voice, but the voice is not an absence of writing; see Jacques Derrida, *Of Grammatology*, trans. Gayatri Chakravorty Spivak (Baltimore, 1976), pp. 144 and 295.
11 Ibid., and *Writing and Difference*, trans. Alan Bass (London, 1978).
12 Simpson, *Essence*, p. 204. The metaphor of the cathedral was common in the critical reception of Bruckner in the 1920s.
13 Oxford University Press (originally published in 1843).
14 Simpson, *Essence*, p. 232; a reference to the Eighth Symphony follows.

15 Ernst Bloch, *Essays on the Philosophy of Music*, trans. Peter Palmer (Cambridge, 1985), p. 41.

16 Rose Rosengard Subotnik, *Developing Variations: Style and Ideology in Western Music* (Minneapolis, 1991), p. 21. She is explaining ideas from Adorno based on her own translation of passages from his *Einleitung in der Musiksoziologie* (Reinbek bei Hamburg, 1968), pp. 223–5 and 232, *Moments Musicaux* (Frankfurt am Main, 1964), pp. 182–3, and from *Philosophy of Modern Music*, trans. Anne G. Mitchell and Wesley V. Blomster (New York, 1973), pp. 55–6.

17 Quotations from Bloch, *Essays*, pp. 41–2.

18 Subotnik, *Developing Variations*, p. 23, referring to Adorno's *Einleitung*.

19 Ibid., p. 217, referring to Adorno's *Philosophie*.

20 Simpson, *Essence*, p. 172.

21 Susan McClary, *Feminine Endings: Music, Gender, and Sexuality* (Minneapolis, 1991), p. 15.

22 Ibid., p. 114.

23 See Max von Oberleithner, *Meine Erinnerungen an Anton Bruckner* (Regensburg, 1933), excerpted in Stephen Johnson, *Bruckner Remembered* (London, 1998), pp. 99–100.

24 'Bruckner Propositions (II)', *Bruckner Journal* 1/2 (1997), 8–9. Floros' 'Propositions' were originally published as 'Thesen über Bruckner', in *Musik-Konzepte 23/24: Anton Bruckner*, ed. Heinz-Klaus Metzger and Rainer Riehn (Munich, 1982), pp. 5–14.

25 See Derrick Puffett, 'Bruckner's Way: the Adagio of the Ninth Symphony', *Music Analysis* 18 (1999), 13–14.

26 A. Crawford Howie, 'Traditional and Novel Elements in Bruckner's Sacred Music', *MQ* 67 (1981), 554.

27 Erwin Doernberg, *The Life and Symphonies of Anton Bruckner* (London, 1960), p. 109.

28 In Karl Grunsky (ed.), *Bruckners Sinfonien* (Berlin, 1907), p. 165; cited by Benjamin M. Korstvedt, *Bruckner: Symphony No. 8* (Cambridge, 2000), p. 54.

29 This is not the only way in which Bruckner changes his motives, but it is the way that is relevant to my argument. Another type of change to motives has been interpreted as mutation by Werner Korte in *Bruckner und Brahms: die spätromantische Lösung der autonomen Konzeption* (Tutzing, 1963).

30 See also Constantin Floros, *Brahms und Bruckner: Studien zur musikalischen Exegetik* (Wiesbaden, 1980), pp. 186–8.

31 Carl Dahlhaus, *Nineteenth-Century Music*, trans. J. Bradford Robinson (Berkeley, 1989), p. 272.

32 Ibid.

33 Simpson, *Essence*, pp. 151 and 156.

34 Watson, *Bruckner*, p. 109.

35 Matthew 17: 2.

36 Linda Murray, *The High Renaissance and Mannerism: Italy, the North and Spain 1500–1600* (London, 1977), pp. 68–70; monochrome illustration, 69. For a colour illustration, see Marco Albertario, *Raphael* (Milan, 1996), p. 55.

37 Doernberg, *Bruckner*, p. 194.

38 I am indebted to Stan and Carmen Hawkins for providing me with this information.

39 *Briefe Hugo Wolfs an Emil Kauffmann*, ed. Edmund Hellmer (Berlin, 1903), p. 82.

40 Alan E. Brooke, 'John', in Arthur S. Peake, ed., *A Commentary on the Bible* (London, 1919), p. 746.

41 Watson, *Bruckner*, p. 111.

42 Ibid., p. 118.

43 Simpson, *Essence*, p. 131.

44 Eero Tarasti, *Myth and Music: a Semiotic Approach to the Aesthetics of Myth in Music* (The Hague, 1979), p. 92.

45 Simpson, *Essence*, 103.

46 Deryck Cooke, 'Bruckner', *The New Grove Late Romantic Masters* (London, 1985), p. 53.

47 Ibid., p. 50.

48 Gregory Bateson, *Steps to an Ecology of Mind*, rev. edn (Chicago and London, 2000), p. 113.

49 Gilles Deleuze and Félix Guattari, *A Thousand Plateaus: Capitalism and Schizophrenia*, trans. Brian Massumi (Minneapolis, 1987), p. 22.

50 Ibid.

51 Evidence for this claim is provided by the work of German critical scholarship in the nineteenth century; see Rowland Williams, 'Bunsen's Biblical Researches', in Frederick Temple, Rowland Williams, Benjamin Jowett, *et al.*, *Essays and Reviews* (London, 1860; repr. Farnborough, 1970), pp. 50–93.

52 Quoted by Korstvedt, *Bruckner: Symphony No. 8*, p. 7. This statement originally appeared in 'Anton Bruckner', *Die Zeit* 7 (1896) and is reprinted in *Heinrich Schenker als Essayist und Kritiker: gesammelte Aufsätze, Rezensionen und kleinere Berichte aus den Jahren 1891–1901*, ed. Hellmut Federhofer (Hildesheim, 1990), pp. 200–1.

53 Puffett, 'Bruckner's Way', 9 and 33.

54 Deleuze and Guattari, *A Thousand Plateaus*, p. 22; a rhizome is an underground stem with a mixture of roots and shoots.

55 Simpson, *Essence*, p. 232.

56 Ibid., p. 128.

57 Watson, *Bruckner*, pp. 66–7.

58 Newlin, *Bruckner–Mahler–Schoenberg*, p. 96.

59 Simpson, *Essence*, p. 164.

60 Ibid., pp. 167–8.

61 Ernst Kurth, *Selected Writings*, ed. and trans. Lee A. Rothfarb (Cambridge, 1991), p. 203.

62 Doernberg, *Bruckner*, p. 136.

63 Bryan Gilliam, 'The Two Versions of Bruckner's Eighth Symphony', *NCM* 15 (1991–2), 59–69, in particular 66.

64 Ibid.

65 Ibid., n. 22.

66 The original coda of this work was revised; see Arthur D. Walker, 'Foreword', *Overture in G minor by Anton Bruckner* (London, 1971), pp. iii–iv.

67 Deleuze and Guattari, *A Thousand Plateaus*, p. 12.

68 Doernberg, *Bruckner*, p. 220.

69 Deleuze and Guattari, *A Thousand Plateaus*, p. 9.

70 Robert S. Hatten, 'The Expressive Role of Disjunction: a Semiotic Approach to Form and Meaning in the Fourth and Fifth Symphony', in *PAB*, 145–84.

71 'Bruckner Propositions (II)', 9.

72 Newlin, *Bruckner–Mahler–Schoenberg*, p. 92.

73 'Zur Stellung der "Nullten" Symphonie in Bruckners Werk', in *Anton Bruckner: Studien zu Werk und Wirkung (Walter Wiora zum 30. Dezember 1986)*, ed. Christoph-Helmut Mahling (Tutzing, 1988), pp. 63–79, in particular 69–79. I am grateful to John Williamson for bringing this to my attention.

74 Cited by Peter Palmer, 'Ludwig Wittgenstein's Remarks on Bruckner', in *PAB*, pp. 353–62; the remarks are in Ludwig Wittgenstein, *Vermischte Bemerkungen*, ed. Georg Henryk von Wright (Frankfurt am Main and Oxford, 1977).

75 Martin Pulbrook, '"Death, Release and Resolve": an Analysis of Anton Bruckner's Seventh Symphony', *Maynooth Review* 9 (1983), 93, n. 4.

76 *Meine Erinnerungen an Anton Bruckner* (Vienna, 1901), cited in Johnson, *Bruckner Remembered*, p. 33.

77 See Elisabeth Maier, 'A Hidden Personality: Access to an "Inner Biography" of Anton Bruckner', in *BS*, pp. 32–53, in particular 51.

78 Newlin, *Bruckner–Mahler–Schoenberg*, p. 81.

79 Cooke, 'Bruckner', 20.

9 Programme symphony and absolute music

1 Rebecca Grotjahn, *Die Sinfonie im deutschen Kulturgebiet 1850 bis 1875: ein Beitrag zur Gattungs- und Institutionengeschichte* (Sinzig, 1998).

2 Matthias Wiegandt, *Vergessene Symphonik? Studien zu Joachim Raff, Carl Reinicke und zum Problem der Epigonalität in der Musik* (Sinzig, 1997).

3 See F. E. Kirby, 'Beethoven's Pastoral Symphony as a *Sinfonia Caracteristica*', *MQ* 56 (1970), 605–23.

4 Grotjahn, *Die Sinfonie*, p. 271.

5 *EKB*, vol. I, pp. 256–65; see Carl Dahlhaus, *The Idea of Absolute Music*, trans. Roger Lustig (Chicago, 1989), pp. 40–1, and 'Bruckner und die Programmusik: zum Finale der Achten Symphonie', in *Anton Bruckner: Studien zu Werk und Wirkung (Walter Wiora zum 30. Dezember 1986)*, ed. Christoph-Helmut Mahling (Tutzing, 1988), pp. 7–32.

6 *Brahms und Bruckner: Studien zur musikalischen Exegetik* (Wiesbaden, 1980), pp. 155–6 and 158–9. That Bruckner sometimes thought of Berlioz, Liszt, and Wagner as a group does not make them indispensable for understanding his music; see Martin Geck, *Zwischen Romantik und Restauration: Musik im Realismus-Diskurs 1848–1871* (Kassel and Stuttgart, 2001), p. 130.

7 Leopold Nowak, 'Anton Bruckner, der Romantiker', in *Über Anton Bruckner: gesammelte Aufsätze* (Vienna, 1985), pp. 157–9.

8 Walter Wiora, 'Über den religiösen Gehalt in Bruckners Symphonien', in *Anton Bruckner: Studien zu Werk und Wirkung*, pp. 274–5 and 269.

9 Floros, *Brahms und Bruckner*, p. 174; letter of 19 September 1876, in *H-S1*, p. 2.

10 Ernst Decsey, *Bruckner: Versuch eines Lebens* (Stuttgart and Berlin, 1919), pp. 131–2; Max Auer, *Bruckner: sein Leben und Werk*, 2nd edn (Vienna, 1934), p. 192.

11 *H-S1*, p. 228.

12 Floros, *Brahms und Bruckner*, p. 173.

13 Joseph von Eichendorff, *Werke*, ed. Ansgar Hillach, 3 vols. to date (Munich, 1970), vol. III: *Geschichte der poetischen Literatur Deutschlands*, p. 779; Jean Paul, *Werke*, ed. Norbert Miller and Gustav Lohmann, 6 vols. (Munich, 1959–63), vol. V: *Vorschule der Ästhetik*, p. 91.

14 *Göll-A*, IV/1, p. 519; Decsey, *Bruckner*, p. 197; Auer, *Bruckner*, pp. 197–8.

15 For the 'Promethean' interpretation of Josef Schalk, see Benjamin M. Korstvedt,

Bruckner: Symphony No. 8 (Cambridge, 2000), pp. 49–51.

16 Floros, *Brahms und Bruckner*, p. 183, citing an often-quoted letter.

17 Korstvedt, *Bruckner: Symphony No. 8*, p. 52.

18 *Göll-A*, IV/3, p. 15; Dccsey, *Bruckner*, pp. 216–17; Friedrich Eckstein, *Alte unnennbare Tage* (Vienna, 1936; repr. 1988), p. 145.

19 *Göll-A*, IV/3, p. 18.

20 Thomas Röder, 'Anton Bruckners Glaube', in *B-P*, pp. 61–2.

21 Eckstein, *Alte unnennbare Tage*, p. 145.

22 'Der deutsche Michael erwacht: zur Bruckner-Rezeption im NS-Staat', in *B-P*, pp. 206–7.

23 Heinrich Heine, *Werke und Briefe*, ed. Hans Kaufmann, 2nd edn, 10 vols. (Berlin and Weimar, 1972), vol. V, p. 34.

24 Dümling, 'Der deutsche Michael erwacht', p. 207.

25 See Hermann Kretzschmar, 'Anton Bruckner, Symphony No. 4', in *Music Analysis in the Nineteenth Century*, ed. Ian Bent, 2 vols. (Cambridge, 1994), vol. II: *Hermeneutic Approaches*, pp. 109–17.

26 See Gerold Wolfgang Gruber, 'Brahms und Bruckner in der zeitgenössischen Wiener Musikkritik', in *Bruckner-Symposion, 'Johannes Brahms und Anton Bruckner' (Linz 1983): Bericht*, ed. Othmar Wessely (Linz, 1985), p. 207.

27 Floros, *Brahms und Bruckner*, pp. 174–9, in particular 178. Auer explains this tale as an example of the Austrian fondness for concealing serious matters with a jest (*Bruckner*, p. 195).

28 See Floros, *Brahms und Bruckner*, p. 178; Robert S. Hatten, 'The Expressive Role of Disjunction: a Semiotic Approach to Form and Meaning in the Fourth and Fifth Symphonies', in *PAB*, pp. 166–7.

29 François René de Chateaubriand, *Génie du Christianisme*, ed. Pierre Reboul, 2 vols. (Paris, 1966), vol. I, p. 401.

30 Constantin Floros, 'Zur Deutung der Symphonik Bruckners: das Adagio der Neunten Symphonie', *B-J 1981* (1982), 89–96.

31 *EKB*, vol. II, pp. 733–7.

32 Paul Thissen, *Zitattechniken in der Symphonik des 19. Jahrhunderts* (Sinzig, 1998).

33 Hans-Joachim Hinrichsen takes an even more sceptical view of the Wagnerian origins of this 'quotation', pointing out that it also has associations with the Kyrie of the D minor Mass; see 'Bruckners Wagner-Zitate', in *B-P*, pp. 124–5.

34 These criticisms draw on Hinrichsen, 'Bruckners Wagner-Zitate', pp. 115–33; Thissen, *Zitattechniken*, pp. 109–32, and Wolfram Steinbeck, '"Dona nobis pacem": religiöse Symbolik in Bruckners Symphonien', in *B-P*, pp. 87–96. They do not deny the existence of an 'intertextual pool' (Hatten, 'The Expressive Role of Disjunction', p. 179), but see it in conjunction with a 'common stylistic heritage' and strategies of coherence rather than as a programmatic narrative.

35 Floros, *Brahms und Bruckner*, pp. 168–70 and 207; Dahlhaus, 'Bruckner und die Programmusik', pp. 15–16.

36 Hinrichsen, 'Bruckners Wagner-Zitate', pp. 116 and 121; Peter Gülke, *Brahms – Bruckner: zwei Studien* (Kassel, 1989), p. 136.

37 Robert Schollum, 'Umkreisungen: Anmerkungen zum Beginn des Adagio der Neunten Symphonie Bruckners', in *B-J 1981* (1992), p. 101; Röder, 'Anton Bruckners Glaube', pp. 61–3.

38 Dahlhaus, 'Bruckner und die Programmusik', p. 32.

39 Floros, *Brahms und Bruckner*, pp. 16–17 and 156; Dahlhaus, 'Bruckner und die Programmusik', pp. 28–32.

40 Carol S. Bevier, 'The Program Symphonies of Joseph Joachim Raff', Ph.D. dissertation, North Texas State University (1982), pp. 29–30.

41 Wiegandt, *Vergessene Symphonik?*, p. 308.

42 Floros, *Brahms und Bruckner*, p. 181.

43 Hatten, 'The Expressive Role of Disjunction', pp. 146–7; Timothy L. Jackson, 'The Finale of Bruckner's Seventh Symphony and the Tragic Reversed Sonata Form', in *BS*, p. 143. Jackson does not use 'programmatic' here in quite the same sense as Floros, and 'affective-rhetorical' may be closer to the kind of analysis that he proposes.

44 See Warren Darcy, 'Bruckner's Sonata Deformations', in *BS*, pp. 276–7.

10 Bruckner editions: the revolution revisited

I would like to thank my colleagues Paul Hawkshaw, Thomas Röder, and William Carragan for their helpful comments and suggestions about various aspects of this article, and Crawford Howie for his bibliographic assistance.

1 The term 'Bruckner Problem' was made famous by Deryck Cooke's 'The Bruckner Problem Simplified', in *Vindication: Essays about Romantic Music* (Cambridge, 1982), pp. 43–71; originally published in *The Musical Times* 110 (1969), 20–2, 142–4, 362, 479–82, and 828.

2 See Leopold Nowak, 'Die Anton Bruckner Gesamtausgabe: ihre Geschichte und Schicksale', in *B-J 1982/83* (1984), 33–67, and William Carragan, 'The Early Version of the Second Symphony', in *PAB*, pp. 85–8.

3 Letter to Wilhelm Tappert, 12 October 1877, in *H-S1*, pp. 175–6 and in Max Auer (ed.), *Anton Bruckner: gesammelte Briefe – neue Folge* (Regensburg, 1924), pp. 144–5.

4 See, in particular, Manfred Wagner, *Der Wandel des Konzepts: zu den verschiedenen Fassungen von Bruckners Dritter, Vierter und Achter Sinfonie* (Vienna, 1980), and Timothy Jackson, 'Bruckner's Metrical Numbers', *NCM* 14 (1990–1), 101–31, and 'Bruckner's *Oktaven*: The Problem of Consecutives, Doubling, and Orchestral Voice-leading', in *PAB*, pp. 30–66.

5 *IX. Symphonie D-moll, Finale (unvollendet): Rekonstruction der Autograph-Partitur nach den erhaltenen Quellen*, ABSW, Supplement to IX, ed. John A. Phillips (Vienna, 1994) and *II. Symphonie C-moll: Fassung von 1872*, ABSW, II/1, ed. William Carragan (Vienna, forthcoming).

6 A seminal early collection is *Bruckner-Symposion, 'Die Fassungen' (Linz 1980): Bericht*, ed. Franz Grasberger (Linz, 1981).

7 Tabulations of details of instrumentation in the first published versions of the Sixth, Eighth, and Ninth Symphonies may be found in Wolfgang Doebel, *Bruckners Sinfonien in Bearbeitungen: die Konzepte der Bruckner-Schüler und ihre Rezeption bis zu Robert Haas* (Tutzing, 2001), pp. 451–70.

8 The 1888 version of the Fourth Symphony will be published as *Anton Bruckner: IV Symphonie Es-Dur, Fassung von 1888*, ABSW, IV/3, ed. Benjamin M. Korstvedt (Vienna, in preparation); also see Korstvedt, 'The First Printed Edition of Anton Bruckner's Fourth Symphony: Collaboration and Authenticity', *NCM* 20 (1996–7), 3–26.

9 Influential English-language statements of this position may be found in Cooke's 'The Bruckner Problem Simplified' and in his article on Bruckner in *The New Grove Dictionary of Music and Musicians*, ed. Stanley Sadie, 20 vols. (London, 1980), vol. III, pp. 352–71, as well as in Robert Simpson, *The Essence of Bruckner*, 3rd edn (London, 1992). Erwin Doernberg, *The Life and Symphonies of Anton Bruckner* (London, 1960) contains an early, partisan exposition; see pp. 113–24.

10 Cooke, 'The Bruckner Problem Simplified', p. 53

11 *'zum erstenmal den von Bruckner festgelegten Text'* – Pamphlet advertising Haas' edition of

the Sixth Symphony (1935), reproduced in Nowak, 'Die Anton Bruckner Gesamtausgabe', p. 57, emphasis in the original.

12 'Wichtige Aufgaben der Musikwissenschaft gegenüber Anton Bruckner', *Zeitschrift für Musikwissenschaft* 1 (1919), 293–5.

13 'Bruckner-Ausgaben (eine Erwiderung)', *Zeitschrift für Musikwissenschaft* 1 (1919), 422–4. Göhler also published two brief replies to Orel: a 'Nachschrift' appended to Orel's article (*Zeitschrift für Musikwissenschaft* 1 (1919), 424–5) and a brief comment published in the 'Mitteilungen' section of *Zeitschrift für Musikwissenschaft* 1 (1919), 735.

14 'Original und Bearbeitung bei Anton Bruckner', *Deutsche Musikkultur* 1 (1936–7), 193–222. On the circumstances of Orel's removal see Christa Brüstle, *Bruckner und die Nachwelt: zur Rezeptionsgeschichte des Komponisten in der ersten Hälfte des 20. Jahrhunderts* (Stuttgart, 1998), pp. 166–9.

15 From Goebbels' address at the installation of the Bruckner bust in Walhalla on 6 June 1937; quoted in Paul Ehlers, 'Das Regensburger Bruckner-Erlebnis', *Zeitschrift für Musik* 104 (1937), 747; also see the translation of this speech by John Michael Cooper in *MQ* 78 (1994), 605–9 and Bryan Gilliam's discussion of the event in 'The Annexation of Anton Bruckner: Nazi Revisionism and the Politics of Appropriation', *MQ* 78 (1994), 584–604.

16 Nowak, 'Die Anton Bruckner Gesamtausgabe', p. 39.

17 See Doebel's discussion of Haas' interpretation of the percussion in *Bruckners Sinfonien in Bearbeitungen*, pp. 395–8.

18 See Carragan, 'The Early Version of the Second Symphony', pp. 85–8; Benjamin M. Korstvedt, *Bruckner: Symphony No. 8* (Cambridge, 2000), pp. 104–6; and Doebel, *Bruckners Sinfonien in Bearbeitungen*, pp. 302–401.

19 This position has recently received a lengthy and detailed restatement in Doebel's *Bruckners Sinfonien in Bearbeitungen*.

20 Noteworthy examples include Egon Wellesz, 'Anton Bruckner and the Process of Musical Creation', *MQ* 24 (1938), 265–90; Gertrud Staub-Schläpfer, 'Einige Glossen zur "Originalfassung" von Bruckners 8. Sinfonie', *Schweizerische Musikzeitung* 79 (1939), 542–7; Werner Wolff, *Anton Bruckner: Rustic Genius* (New York, 1942), pp. 261–70; Emil Armbruster, *Erstdruckfassung oder "Originalfassung"?: ein Beitrag zur Brucknerfrage am fünfzigsten Todestag des Meisters* (Leipzig, 1946); and Joseph Braunstein, Notes to Anton

Bruckner, Symphony No. 8 in C minor (1890 version), Vienna Pro Musica Orchestra, cond. Jascha Horenstein (Vox CDX2 5504).

21 Important contributions include Brüstle, *Bruckner und die Nachwelt*; Brüstle, 'Politisch-ideologische Implikationen der ersten Bruckner-Gcsamtausgabe', in *B-P*, pp. 192–201; and Morten Solvik, 'The International Bruckner Society and the N.S.D.A.P.: A Case Study of Robert Haas and the Critical Edition', *MQ* 82 (1998), 362–82. Also see Benjamin M. Korstvedt's '"Return to the Pure Sources": the Ideology and Text-critical Legacy of the First Bruckner *Gesamtausgabe*', in *BS*, pp. 91–109; 'Anton Bruckner in the Third Reich and after: an Essay on Ideology and Bruckner Reception', *MQ* 80 (1996), 132–60; and 'The First Edition of Anton Bruckner's Fourth Symphony: Authorship, Production, and Reception', Ph.D. thesis, University of Pennsylvania (1995), esp. pp. 7–241. Also important and somewhat different in approach is Nowak's 'Die Anton Bruckner Gesamtausgabe'.

22 See Korstvedt, 'The First Edition of Anton Bruckner's Fourth Symphony' as well as the overview offered in Thomas Röder, 'Neues zur Fassungsfrage bei Anton Bruckner', *Neues musikwissenschaftliches Jahrbuch* 8 (1999), 115–35. Paul Hawkshaw offers a measured view of the editorial issues raised by the re-evaluation of the first published versions in 'The Bruckner Problem Revisited', *NCM* 21 (1997–8), 96–107.

23 This score was owned by Ferdinand Löwe's son and surfaced under unusual circumstances in 1940; see Brüstle, *Bruckner und die Nachwelt*, pp. 159–67. It has since returned to an unknown private collection, but a complete set of photos is preserved in the Wiener Stadt- und Landesbibliothek; see Korstvedt, 'The First Printed Edition of Anton Bruckner's Fourth Symphony', pp. 7–16.

24 *III. Symphonie D-moll, Revisionsbericht*, *ABSW*, Supplement to III, ed. Thomas Röder (Vienna, 1997) and *IX. Symphonie D-moll, kritischer Bericht*, *ABSW*, Supplement to IX, ed. Benjamin Gunnar Cohrs (Vienna, 2001).

25 Haas reportedly made this assertion in a lecture before the first Viennese performance of his edition of the Fifth Symphony; see Paul Stefan, 'Um Bruckner', *Die Stunde*, 15 March 1936.

26 See 'The Bruckner Problem Simplified', p. 61 and Redlich, Preface to *Anton Bruckner: Symphony No. 4 in E flat major, 'Romantic'* (London, [1955]), pp. v–vi.

27 Paul Hawkshaw, 'Bruckner', in *The New Grove Dictionary of Music and Musicians*, ed.

Stanley Sadie and John Tyrrell, 2nd edn, 29 vols. (London and New York, 2001), vol. IV, p. 467; also see his 'The Bruckner Problem Revisited', 101–3.

28 The text of this document has been widely reproduced. Two recent sources are Mantred Wagner, *Bruckner: eine Monographie* (Mainz, 1983), pp. 300–1 and Rolf Keller, 'Die letztwilligen Verfügungen Anton Bruckners', in *B-J 1982/83* (1984), 98–9. The instructions regarding his manuscripts are found in the fourth section of the will. A recent and careful appraisal of the will and its implications is found in Hawkshaw, 'The Bruckner Problem Revisited', 96–107.

29 *Bruckner und die Nachwelt*, p. 183.

30 The phrase was Haas'; see Alfred Orel, 'Original und Bearbeitung bei Anton Bruckner', p. 201, and Doebel, *Bruckners Sinfonien in Bearbeitungen*, p. 263.

31 'Bericht zur Gesamtausgabe der Werke Anton Bruckners', 25 April 1938; quoted in Brüstle, 'Politisch-ideologische Implikationen', p. 198 and in Solvik, 'The International Bruckner Society and the N.S.D.A.P.', 369.

32 In February 1940 the Reich Ministry of *Volksaufklärung* and Propaganda actually urged a ban on public debate of the 'original versions' until a 'conclusive scholarly resolution' was reached; see Günter Brosche, 'Ideologische Einflüsse auf das Nachleben Anton Bruckners', in *Österreichische Musik – Musik in Österreich: Theophil Antonicek zum 60. Geburtstag*, ed. Elisabeth Theresia Hilscher (Tutzing, 1998), pp. 458–9, and Brüstle, *Bruckner und die Nachwelt*, p. 160, n. 94.

33 For a full discussion of this see Brüstle, *Bruckner und die Nachwelt*, pp. 123–236, and Korstvedt, 'The First Edition of Anton Bruckner's Fourth Symphony', pp. 83–185.

34 Doebel, for example, describes these developments as 'opposition' to Haas and Nowak and 'vehement' support for the Schalk and Löwe 'party', oddly reviving the positions taken in the 1930s; see *Bruckners Sinfonien in Bearbeitungen*, pp. 409–15.

35 'Ideologische Einflüsse auf das Nachleben Anton Bruckners', p. 451.

36 *John Wayne's America: the Politics of Celebrity* (New York, 1997), p. 26.

37 'Myth and Historiography', in *Myth and Modern Philosophy* (Philadelphia, 1990), pp. 9–10; quoted in Arved Ashby, 'Schoenberg, Boulez, and Twelve-tone Composition as "Ideal Type"', *Journal of the American Musicological Society* 54 (2001), 619.

38 Robert Pascall, 'The Editor's Brahms', in *The Cambridge Companion to Brahms*, ed.

Michael Musgrave (Cambridge, 1999), p. 252; also see his 'Brahms and the Definitive Text', in *Brahms: Biographical, Documentary and Analytic Studies*, ed. Robert Pascall (Cambridge, 1982), pp. 59–75.

39 'Overriding the Autograph Score: The Problem of Textual Authority in Verdi's *Falstaff*', *Studi Verdiani* 8 (1992), 13–51.

40 Ibid., 19–29.

41 Ibid., 21–2.

42 Jerome McGann, *A Critique of Modern Textual Criticism* (Chicago and London, 1983; reprint. Charlottesville, 1992), p. 42.

43 On this point see Peter Shillingsburg, 'An Inquiry into the Social Status of Texts and Modes of Textual Criticism', *Studies in Bibliography* 42 (1989), 55–79.

44 'Public and Private in the Study of Manuscripts', *Text* 6 (1994), 51.

45 'The Editor's Brahms', p. 251.

46 *A Critique of Modern Textual Criticism*, p. 75.

47 *The Critical Editing of Music: History, Method, and Practice* (Cambridge, 1996), p. 19.

48 *H-S1*, p. 217 and Auer (ed.), *Bruckner: gesammelte Briefe*, p. 164.

49 *H-S1*, p. 224 and Auer (ed.), *Bruckner: gesammelte Briefe*, pp. 169–70.

50 This is clear, for example, in the 1888 version (i.e. the first published version) of the Fourth Symphony.

51 Peter Gülke, 'The Orchestra as Medium of Realization: Thoughts on the Finale of Brahms's First Symphony, on the Different Versions of Bruckner's Sixth Symphony, and on "Part One" of Mahler's Fifth Symphony', *MQ* 80 (1996), 272.

52 For the first suggestion, see Rudolf Stephan, 'In und Jenseits der Tradition: zur sechsten Symphonie Anton Bruckner', *Österreichische Musikzeitschrift* 51 (1996), 31; for the second, see Simpson, *Essence*, pp. 168–9. William Carragan examined how various conductors handled tempi in the first movement in 'Tempo studies on Bruckner's Sixth and Eighth Symphonies', a paper read at 'The Wagnerian Symphony', a conference held in Troy, New York, 22 November 1996.

53 See Gülke, 'The Orchestra as Medium of Realization' as well as Constantin Floros, 'Historische Phasen der Bruckner-Interpretation', in *Bruckner-Symposion, 'Bruckner-Interpretation' (Linz 1982): Bericht*, ed. Franz Grasberger (Linz, 1982), pp. 93–102, and William Carragan's 'Reconstructing Bruckner's Tempos', *American Record Guide* (Nov./Dec. 1996), 73–5 and 177 and 'Tempo Studies on Bruckner's Fourth Symphony', unpublished paper read at 'Perspectives on Anton Bruckner', a conference at the University of Manchester, April 1996, all of which incorporate studies of historical recordings.

54 On this point, see Korstvedt, 'Anton Bruckner in the Third Reich and after', 149–50, and on the evolution of performing styles see Robert Philip, *Early Recordings and Musical Style: Changing Tastes in Instrumental Performance, 1900–1950* (Cambridge, 1992).

55 Richard Taruskin has argued for the positive role of unfamiliarity in historically informed performance and for the aesthetic ends of this pursuit; see 'The Limits of Authenticity: a Contribution', in *Text and Act: Essays on Music and Performance* (New York and Oxford, 1995), pp. 77–81.

11 Bruckner and the symphony orchestra

1 See Max Auer, 'Anton Bruckner, die Orgel und Richard Wagner', *Zeitschrift für Musik* 5 (1937), 477–81; Alfred Lorenz, 'Zur Instrumentation von Anton Bruckners Symphonien', *Zeitschrift für Musik* 4 (1936), 1318–25.

2 See Auer, 'Anton Bruckner, die Orgel und Richard Wagner', 477.

3 Ibid., 478.

4 The passage is bars 175–200 in *ABSW*, V (Vienna, 1951).

5 See Auer, 'Anton Bruckner, die Orgel und Richard Wagner', 478.

6 See Lorenz, 'Zur Instrumentation von Anton Bruckners Symphonien', 1381.

7 See ibid., 1325. Compare this for example with Goebbels' views at the 1937 Regensburg Bruckner Festival; see *Goebbels Reden*, ed. Helmut Heiber, 2 vols. (Düsseldorf, 1971), vol. I, pp. 281–6.

8 See for example Ingrid Fuchs, 'Klingt Bruckner "wagnerisch"?' and Gerda Lechleitner, 'Bruckner – Wagner: ein messbarer Unterschied', in *Bruckner-Symposion, 'Bruckner, Wagner und die Neudeutschen in Österreich' (Linz 1984)*, ed. Othmar Wessely (Linz, 1986), pp. 111–22 and 123–47.

9 Gerald Abraham, *A Hundred Years of Music*, 1st edn (London, 1938), p. 193.

10 Alfred Einstein, 'Bruckner, Anton', in *The Grove Dictionary of Music and Musicians*, 3rd edn, ed. H. C. Colles, 5 vols. (London, 1927), vol. I, p. 482; Hans Redlich, 'Bruckner, Anton', in *The Grove Dictionary of Music and Musicians*, 5th edn, ed. Eric Blom, 9 vols. (London, 1954), vol. II, p. 971.

11 See Deryck Cooke, 'Anton Bruckner', in *The New Grove Late Romantic Masters* (London, 1980); Denis Arnold, 'Bruckner, Anton' in *The Oxford Companion to Music* (Oxford, 1983), p. 278; Donald Jay Grout and Claude Palisca, *A History of Western Music*, 5th edn (New York, 1996), p. 592; Derek Watson, *Bruckner*, 2nd edn (Oxford, 1996), p. 64; Hans-Hubert Schönzeler, *Bruckner* (London, 1970), p. 164.

12 See for example Bryan Gilliam, 'The Annexation of Anton Bruckner: Nazi Revisionism and the Politics of Appropriation', in *BS*, pp. 72–90.

13 See Alexander Rehding, 'Trial Scenes at Nuremberg', *Music Analysis* 20 (2001), 239–67; Stephen McClatchie, *Analyzing Wagner's Operas: Alfred Lorenz and German Nationalist Ideology* (Rochester, 1998); McClatchie, 'Bruckner and the Bayreuthians; or, *Das Geheimnis der Form bei Anton Bruckner*', in *BS*, pp. 110–21. Auer's engagement with contemporary politics took a different form, emphasizing suggestive parallels between the growth of the Bruckner movement in the 1930s and the spiritual rebirth of the German nation under National Socialism. See for example *Göll-A*, IV/4, pp. 61–2, translated in Benjamin M. Korstvedt, 'Anton Bruckner in the Third Reich and After: An Essay on Ideology and Bruckner Reception', *MQ* 80 (1996), 136.

14 See Paul Hawkshaw, 'A Composer Learns his Craft: Anton Bruckner's Lessons in Form and Orchestration with Otto Kitzler, 1861–63', in *PAB*, pp. 3–29.

15 See for example bars 318–50 of the first movement.

16 Kurth advances a similar notion in his distinction between lengthwise and crosswise profiles (*Längsschnitt, Querschnitt*). He regarded Bruckner's forms as compounds of symphonic waves (*Wellen*), which in their lengthwise profile are constructed from the build-up and dissipation of tiers (*Schichtungen*); *EKB*, vol. I, pp. 279–355. This passage from the Sixth Symphony is considered in pp. 291–308.

17 Persistently in the second statement, the theme is accompanied by free rhythmic imitations in the horns, a common Brucknerian habit. Generally in this analysis I will consider such instances to be amplifications of an existent stratum, rather than as a separate stratum, unless the imitations proliferate to form a substantial part of the texture, as is the case in bars 159–82.

18 See for example *EKB*, vol. I, pp. 279–89.

19 As for example in Simpson's idea that the symphonies embody a 'patient search for pacification', rather than the dynamic 'struggle–victory' archetype of the Beethovenian symphony, or more recently Benjamin Korstvedt's contention that 'the final tonic major [in the Eighth Symphony] is not wrested from the darkness with Beethovenian might, but granted to us with awesome ease'; see Robert Simpson, *The Essence of Bruckner*, 1st edn (London, 1967), pp. 198–9 and Benjamin M. Korstvedt, *Bruckner: Symphony No. 8* (Cambridge, 2000), p. 49.

20 On Bruckner's relation to the Baroque, see for example Carl Dahlhaus, 'Bruckner und der Barock', *Neue Zeitschrift für Musik* 124 (1963), 335–6.

21 See Paul Hawkshaw, 'The Bruckner Problem Revisited', *NCM* 21 (1997–8), 96–107 and especially p. 106.

12 Between formlessness and formality: aspects of Bruckner's approach to symphonic form

I would like to thank William Carragan for his careful reading of and thoughtful responses to a draft of this essay.

1 *Wiener Abendpost*, 28 October 1873; reprint in *Göll-A*, IV/1, p. 252.

2 *Wiener Allgemeine Zeitung*, 30 March 1886; reprint in *Göll-A*, IV/2, p. 438.

3 *Wiener Salonblatt*, 28 December 1884; reprint and trans. in *The Music Criticism of Hugo Wolf*, ed. and trans. Henry Pleasants (New York, 1979), p. 99.

4 Max Kiel, 'Ist Bruckner Formlos?', *Neue Musik-Zeitung* 23 (1902), 176.

5 'Der erste Satz von Bruckners Neunter: ein Bild höchster Formvollendung', *Die Musik* 18 (1925–6), 210–34 and 104–12. On the ideological context of Grunsky's project, see Stephen McClatchie, 'Bruckner and the Bayreuthians; or, *Das Geheimnis der Form bei Anton Bruckner*', in *BS*, pp. 110–21.

6 On the Seventh, see Leopold Nowak, 'Das Finale von Bruckners VII. Symphonie' (1956), in *Über Anton Bruckner* (Vienna, 1985), pp. 30–4, esp. p. 30. For a critical study of the formal evolution of Bruckner's Finales see William Carragan, 'Structural Aspects of the Revisions of Bruckner's Symphonic Finales', in *Bruckner-Symposion, 'Fassungen, Bearbeitungen, Vollendungen' (Linz 1996)*, ed. Uwe Harten *et al.* (Linz, 1998), pp. 177–88.

7 'Zur Klärung der Wagnerkontroverse' (1896); reprint in Christian von Ehrenfels, *Philosophische Schriften*, vol. II, *Ästhetik*, ed. Reinhard Fabian (Munich, 1986), p. 107.

8 Rudolf Louis, *Der Widerspruch in der Musik: Bausteine zu einer Ästhetik der Tonkunst auf realdialektischer Grundlage* (Leipzig, 1893), p. 103; quoted in Christa Brüstle, *Bruckner und die Nachwelt* (Stuttgart, 1998), p. 20.

9 Quoted in Margaret Notley, 'Bruckner and Viennese Wagnerism', in *BS*, p. 61.

10 Franz Schalk, 'A. Bruckner: Betrachtungen und Erinnerungen (1921)', *Die Musik* 24 (1931–2), 882; reprint in Lili Schalk (ed.), *Franz Schalk: Briefe und Betrachtungen* (Vienna and Leipzig, 1935), p. 89.

11 Halm, *Von zwei Kulturen der Musik* (Munich, 1913; 3rd edn, Stuttgart, 1947), p. 253; quoted from Carl Dahlhaus, *The Idea of Absolute Music*, trans. Roger Lustig (Chicago and London, 1989), pp. 123–4.

12 *EKB*, vol. I, pp. 241–2.

13 'Bruckner, Josef Anton', *Die Musik in Geschichte und Gegenwart*, 17 vols. (Kassel, 1949–86), vol. II, cols. 369–71.

14 See Donald J. Grout and Claude V. Palisca, *A History of Western Music*, 6th edn (New York, 2001), pp. 561–2; Leon Plantinga, *Romantic Music* (New York, 1984), p. 437.

15 See '"Urfassung" und "Endfassung" bei Anton Bruckner', in *Über Anton Bruckner*, pp. 34–7.

16 Blume's position on Bruckner's schematicism found considerable acceptance in its day; see Werner Korte, *Bruckner und Brahms: die spätromantische Lösung der autonomen Konzeption* (Tutzing, 1963), pp. 44–6, 54, 61–4. More recent scholars have contested and refined Blume's position: e.g. Wolfram Steinbeck, 'Form als Schema bei Anton Bruckner: zum Adagio der VII. Symphonie', in *Analysen: Beiträge zu einer Problemgeschichte des Komponierens (Festschrift für Hans Heinrich Eggebrecht zum 65. Geburtstag)*, ed. Werner Breig, Reinhold Brinkmann, and Elmar Budde (Stuttgart, 1984), pp. 304–23; Steinbeck, *Anton Bruckner: Neunte Symphonie D-Moll*, Meisterwerke der Musik 60 (Munich, 1993), pp. 25–49; Bo Marschner, 'Schema und Individualität in der Formbildung Bruckners anhand seiner Reprisenkonzeption ab der Vierten Symphonie', in *Bruckner-Symposion, Fassungen, Bearbeitungen, Vollendungen' (Linz 1996)*, ed. Uwe Harten *et al.* (Linz, 1998) pp. 17–24.

17 Wolfram Steinbeck, 'Bruckner, (Joseph) Anton', in *Die Musik in Geschichte und Gegenwart*, rev. edn, Personenteil, 6 vols. to date (Kassel, 2000), vol. III, col. 1090.

18 'Bruckner: Romantic Symphony in E flat Major, no. 4', in *Essays in Musical Analysis*, 6 vols. (Oxford, 1935–9), vol. II, p. 73.

19 'Issues in Composition', in *Between Romanticism and Modernism: Four Studies in the Music of the Later Nineteenth Century*, trans. Mary Whitall (Berkeley and Los Angeles, 1980), p. 44.

20 August Halm, *Die Symphonie Anton Bruckners* (Munich, 1913), pp. 62–4.

21 'Mahler and Episodic Structure: the First Movement of the Seventh Symphony', in *The Seventh Symphony of Gustav Mahler: a Symposium*, ed. James L. Zychowicz (Madison, Wisc., 1990), p. 31. Also see Dika Newlin's suggestion that Bruckner's third themes derive from Beethoven's codetta themes in *Bruckner – Mahler – Schoenberg* (New York, 1971), p. 90; and Friedrich Blume's comments in *Classic and Romantic Music: A Comprehensive Survey*, trans. M. D. Herter Norton, 1st edn (New York, 1970), p. 153.

22 See Rey M. Longyear and Kate R. Covington, 'Sources of the Three-Key Exposition', *Journal of Musicology* 6 (1988), 448–70.

23 James Webster, 'Schubert's Sonata Form and Brahms's First Maturity (II)', *NCM* 3 (1979–80), 61.

24 'Beethoven's Ninth Symphony: Its Place in Musical Art', in *Essays in Musical Analysis*, vol. II, p. 5.

25 For further discussion of the technique of *Steigerung*, see below, Chapter 13, pp. 198–9.

26 *Mahler: A Musical Physiognomy*, trans. Edmund Jephcott (Chicago and London, 1992), p. 27.

27 See Constantin Floros, 'Die Zitate in Bruckner's Symphonik', in *B-J 1982/83* (1984), 7–18; Egon Voss, 'Wagner Zitate in Bruckners Dritter Sinfonie?', *Die Musikforschung* 49 (1993), 403–6; and Hans-Joachim Hinrichsen's nicely critical 'Bruckners Wagner-Zitate', in *B-P*, pp. 115–33.

28 James Buhler, '"Breakthrough" as Critique of Form: the Finale of Mahler's First Symphony', *NCM* 20 (1996–7), 135–7.

29 James Webster, 'Sonata Form', in *The New Grove Dictionary of Music and Musicians*, ed. Stanley Sadie and John Tyrrell, 2nd edn, 29 vols. (London and New York, 2001), vol. XXIII, p. 688.

30 The term 'sonata principle' seems to have been coined independently by Wilfrid Mellers, in Alec Harman and Wilfrid Mellers, *Man and His Music: The Story of Music Experience in the West*, vol. III, *The Sonata Principle, from c. 1750*, 1st edn (London, 1957), and Edward Cone, in *Musical Form and Musical Performance* (New York, 1968) – see pp. 76–8. My quotation is from Charles

Rosen, *Sonata Forms* (New York, 1980; rev. edn, 1988), pp. 284–5. James Hepokoski's critical history 'Beyond the Sonata Principle', *Journal of the American Musicological Society* 55 (2002), 91–154 appeared only after I had finished work on the present article.

31 See Benjamin M. Korstvedt, '"Harmonic Daring" and Symphonic Design in the Sixth Symphony: an Essay in Historical Musical Analysis', in *PAB*, pp. 185–205.

32 For a more extensive analysis of the passage, see Korstvedt, *Bruckner: Symphony No. 8* (Cambridge, 2000), pp. 34–6.

33 Louis, *Der Widerspruch in der Musik*, p. 103; quoted in Brüstle, *Bruckner und die Nachwelt*, p. 20.

34 Korte, *Bruckner und Brahms*, p. 61.

35 'Sonata Forms', in *The Forms of Music* (New York, 1956), p. 232.

36 Robert Simpson, *The Essence of Bruckner*, 3rd edn (London, 1992), p. 175; for more examples, see pp. 26–7, 170, and 209.

37 *Musical Form and Musical Performance* (New York, 1968), p. 82.

38 'The New Musical Horizon' (1937), in *Roger Sessions on Music* (Princeton, 1979), p. 47.

39 *The Classical Style*, rev. edn (London, 1976), p. 120. See also Mark Evan Bonds, *Wordless Rhetoric: Musical Form and the Metaphor of the Oration* (Cambridge, Mass., 1991), pp. 23–6.

40 'Issues in Composition', p. 42.

41 Review of Bruckner's Eighth Symphony, *Neue Freie Presse*, 23 December 1892; translation as in Eduard Hanslick, *Music Criticisms 1846–1899*, trans. Henry Pleasants (Baltimore, 1950), pp. 288–9 (modified).

42 'Anton Bruckners Stellung in der Musikgeschichte', in *In Memoriam Anton Bruckner*, ed. Karl Kobald (Vienna, 1924), p. 12.

43 *Classic and Romantic Music*, pp. 143–4.

44 Adler, 'Bruckners Stellung', p. 12.

45 Ibid., pp. 12 and 13.

46 'Liszts Faust-Symphonie und die Krise der symphonischen Form', in *Über Symphonien: Festschrift Walter Wiora zum 70. Geburtstag*, ed. Christoph-Hellmut Mahling (Tutzing, 1979), p. 132.

47 Theodor Helm, 'Anton Bruckner als Tondichter', *Oesterreichische Musik und Theaterzeitung*, 1–15 November 1896; cited in Rudolf Louis, *Anton Bruckner*, rev. edn (Munich, 1918), p. 342.

48 *The Romantic Generation* (Cambridge, Mass., 1995), p. 50.

49 Ibid., p. 51.

50 *Musical Elaborations* (New York, 1991), p. 102.

13 Formal process as spiritual progress: the symphonic slow movements

I would like to thank Kevin Salfen for reading a draft of this chapter.

1 Bernhard Paumgartner, 'Das Instrumental Ensemble', in *Musica aeterna*, ed. Gottfried Schmid, 2 vols. (Zurich, 1950), vol. II, pp. 13–14.

2 August Halm, *Die Symphonie Anton Bruckners* (Munich, 1923), pp. 117–18.

3 I have chosen not to discuss the slow movements of the two unnumbered symphonies. Bar numbers are for the collected edition begun under the supervision of Leopold Nowak; I refer to the Linz version (1866) of the First Symphony and the second versions of both the Fourth (1878–80) and Eighth Symphonies.

4 See Margaret Notley, 'Late-Nineteenth-Century Chamber Music and the Cult of the Classical Adagio', *NCM* 23 (1999–2000), 33–61.

5 On *unendliche Melodie*, see Ernst Kurth, *Romantische Harmonik und ihre Krise in Wagners 'Tristan'*, 2nd edn (Berlin, 1923), pp. 444–571. Kurth uses figures from the Vienna version of this Adagio as one of his examples; see ibid., pp. 558–9. See also *EKB*, vol. II, p. 759.

6 *EKB*, vol. I, pp. 564–5.

7 Review in *Deutsche Zeitung*, 17 December 1891, 1–2.

8 Walter Wiora, 'Über den religiösen Gehalt in Bruckners Symphonien', in *Religiöse Musik in nicht-liturgischen Werken von Beethoven bis Reger*, ed. Günther Massenkeil, Klaus Wolfgang Niemöller, and Walter Wiora (Regensburg, 1978), p. 160; reprinted in *Anton Bruckner: Studien zu Werk und Wirkung (Walter Wiora zum 30. Dezember 1986)*, ed. Christoph-Hellmut Mahling (Tutzing, 1988), pp. 235–75.

9 Interestingly, Helm included the Benedictus in a group of 'Adagios' by Beethoven. See Notley, 'Late-Nineteenth-Century Chamber Music', 41.

10 Wiora, 'Über den religiösen Gehalt in Bruckners Symphonien', pp. 170–9.

11 *EKB*, vol. I, pp. 587–8.

12 Wiora, 'Über den religiösen Gehalt in Bruckners Symphonien', p. 176.

13 See Notley, 'Late-Nineteenth-Century Chamber Music'.

14 Reinhold Brinkmann, *Late Idyll: the Second Symphony of Johannes Brahms*, trans. Peter

Palmer (Cambridge, Mass. and London, 1995), p. 144.

15 Walther Vetter, 'Das Adagio bei Anton Bruckner', *Deutsche Musikkultur* 5 (1940–1), 121–32.

16 Quoted in *Göll-A*, IV/3, p. 293.

17 See the discussion in Margaret Notley, '*Volksconcerte* in Vienna and Late Nineteenth-Century Ideology of the Symphony', *Journal of the American Musicological Society* 50 (1997), 432–9.

18 See the review of Brahms' Third Symphony quoted in Notley, '*Volksconcerte*', 437.

19 Heinrich Christoph Koch, *Musikalisches Lexikon* (1802; reprint Hildesheim, Zurich, and New York, 1964), p. 1386.

20 For a discussion of the Adagio of Bruckner's Eighth and the aesthetics of the sublime, see Benjamin M. Korstvedt, *Bruckner: Symphony No. 8* (Cambridge, 2000), pp. 54–67.

21 Arnold Schering, 'Über den Begriff des Monumentalen in der Musik', reprinted in his *Von grossen Meistern der Musik* (Leipzig, 1940), pp. 10, 12, and 14.

22 Ibid., p. 15.

23 Ibid., p. 17.

24 Kurth has written the most eloquent commentary on Bruckner's construction of intensifications and smaller-scale 'waves'. For a recent treatment of Kurth, see Wolfgang Krebs, 'Zum Verhältnis von musikalischer Syntax und Höhepunktsgestaltung in der zweiten Hälfte des 19. Jahrhunderts', *Musiktheorie* 13 (1998), 31–41.

25 Wiora, 'Über den religiösen Gehalt in Bruckners Symphonien', p. 177.

26 Vetter, 'Das Adagio bei Anton Bruckner', p. 125.

27 *EKB*, vol. II, p. 1002.

28 Wolfram Steinbeck, '"Dona nobis pacem": religiöse Symbolik in Bruckners Symphonien', in *B-P*, pp. 87–96.

29 *EKB*, vol. II, p. 737.

30 Wolfram Steinbeck, *Anton Bruckner: Neunte Symphonie d-Moll* (Munich, 1993), p. 25.

31 *EKB*, vol. II, p. 719.

14 Bruckner and harmony

1 See Edward Laufer, 'Some Aspects of Prolongational Procedures in the Ninth Symphony', in *BS*, pp. 209–55.

2 Smith's system was first presented in Charles J. Smith, 'Prolongations and Progressions as Musical Syntax', in *Music Theory: Special Topics*, ed. Richmond Browne (New York, 1981), pp. 139–74, and later revised in Charles J. Smith, 'The Functional Extravagance of Chromatic Chords', *Music Theory Spectrum* 8 (1986), 94–139.

3 Throughout this essay, roman numerals are case sensitive to the modality of the chord, and all assume an integrated major-minor context. Therefore, in the key of C major-minor, VII refers to a B major triad, ♭VI to an A♭ major triad, ♭iii to an E♭ minor triad, etc.

4 Smith, 'Functional Extravagance', 126–7.

5 Daniel Harrison, *Harmonic Function in Chromatic Music* (Chicago and London, 1994), pp. 116–17.

6 The idea that harmonic function is not a property of chords themselves, but is instead a phenomenon that exists in the motion of one chord to the next is appropriated from Harrison, *Harmonic Function*, passim.

7 Once again, this explanation and language is clearly indebted to Harrison, *Harmonic Function*.

8 I use the terms 'basic idea' and 'contrasting idea', as well as other formal terminology, in the sense defined in William Caplin, *Classical Form: A Theory of Formal Functions for the Instrumental Music of Haydn, Mozart, and Beethoven* (New York and Oxford, 1998).

9 I have discussed the ubiquity of this progression in Bruckner's oeuvre elsewhere; see Kevin J. Swinden, 'Harmonic Tropes and Plagal Dominant Structures in the Music of Anton Bruckner', Ph.D. dissertation, State University of New York at Buffalo (1997).

10 The omnibus was first introduced in Victor Fell Yellin, 'The Omnibus Idea', paper presented at the annual meeting of the American Musicological Society, Dallas, 1972. Yellin eventually expanded this paper in *The Omnibus Idea* (Warren, Mich., 1998), reviewed by Paula J. Telesco in *Music Theory Spectrum* 23 (2001), 129–36. See also Paula J. Telesco, 'Enharmonicism and the Omnibus Progression in Classic-Era Music', *Music Theory Spectrum* 20 (1998), 242–79, and Robert W. Wason, *Viennese Harmonic Theory from Albrechtsberger to Schenker and Schoenberg* (Ann Arbor, 1985), pp. 15–19.

11 Telesco, 'Enharmonicism', 259.

12 Yellin, *Omnibus Idea*, p. 73 refers to omnibus progressions in the first movement of Bruckner's Seventh Symphony, but he does not discuss any in particular, nor does he refer to their precise location.

13 Ibid., pp. 73–5.

14 Richard Cohn, 'Maximally Smooth Cycles, Hexatonic Systems, and the Analysis of Late Romantic Triadic Progressions', *Music Analysis* 15 (1996), 9–40; also Cohn, 'As

Wonderful as Star Clusters', *NCM* 22 (1998–9), 213–32.

15 Substantial work on neo-Riemannian transformations of seventh-chord cycles has been done by Adrian P. Childs, 'Moving beyond Neo-Riemannian Triads: Exploring a Transformational Model for Seventh Chords', *Journal of Music Theory* 42 (1998), 181–91.

16 Jack Douthett, personal correspondence to Richard Cohn, cited in Richard Cohn, 'Weitzmann's Regions, My Cycles, and Douthett's Dancing Cubes', *Music Theory Spectrum* 22 (2000), 95–6.

17 The choice of <1> was fairly arbitrary in this instance; selecting to interpret the E as <0> has no bearing on the present discussion. However, defining the <0,0,0,0> and <1,1,1,1> cases as fully-diminished seventh chords permits a complete cycle through 16 (2^4) recognizable harmonic chords, including two diminished sevenths, four half-diminished sevenths, four dominant sevenths, four minor sevenths, and two French sixth chords. There would be four distinct regions possible with this construction, but only two regions that would be mutually exclusive; each region would share half of its members with another of the four possible regions.

18 Hugo Riemann, *Katechismus der Musik* (Berlin, 1890), pp. 123–7.

19 David Kopp, 'A Comprehensive Theory of Chromatic Mediant Relations in Mid-Nineteenth-Century Music' Ph.D. dissertation, Brandeis University (1995), pp. 148–50.

15 Conductors and Bruckner

1 Daniel Barenboim, 'Mystische Erfahrung', in *Bruckner-Symposion, 'Bruckner Interpretation' (Linz 1982): Bericht*, ed. Othmar Wessely (Linz, 1983), pp. 29–30.

2 Tess James, 'Celibidache and Bruckner', *Music Theory Online* 4/5 (1998), http://smt.ucsb.edu/mto/issues/mto.98.4.5/mto.98.4.5.james.html# AUTHORNOTE.

3 Bruckner, Symphony No. 4, cond. Sergiu Celibidache, EMI, 7243 5 56690 2 5.

4 Bruckner, Symphony No. 4, cond. Karl Böhm, Iron Needle, IN 1414. See Benjamin M. Korstvedt, 'Anton Bruckner in the Third Reich and After: An Essay on Ideology and Bruckner Reception', *MQ* 80 (1996), 160; although Korstvedt notes the influence of the Schalk score on this performance, Böhm was a self-proclaimed exponent of the 'original versions'; see Karl Böhm, *'Ich erinnere mich ganz genau': Autobiographie*, ed. Hans Weig (Zurich, 1968), pp. 78–81.

5 Bruckner, Symphony No. 4, cond. Karl Böhm, Decca, 425 036–2.

6 Korstvedt, 'Anton Bruckner in the Third Reich and After', 149; Leon Botstein, 'Music and Ideology: Thoughts on Bruckner', *MQ* 80 (1996), 10.

7 Botstein, 'Music and Ideology', 8–10; Taruskin, *Text and Act: Essays on Music and Performance* (New York and Oxford, 1995), pp. 164–72.

8 Korstvedt, 'Anton Bruckner in the Third Reich and After', 150–1 and 159.

9 Constantin Floros, 'Historische Phasen der Bruckner-Interpretation', in *Bruckner-Symposion (Linz 1982)*, p. 96.

10 Harry Halbreich, 'Verlangt Bruckner ein einheitliches Tempo?', *B-J 1981* (1982), 191–204; *H-S1*, 217 and 225.

11 Bruckner, Symphony No. 7, cond. Karl Böhm, Archipel Records, ARPCD 0040.

12 Bruckner, Symphony No. 7 (and Mahler, *Das Lied von der Erde*), cond. Hans Rosbaud, Vox, CDX2 518; cond. Nikolaus Harnoncourt, Teldec, 3984-24488-2; cond. Sir Simon Rattle, EMI, 7243 5 56425 2 3.

13 Adolf Nowak, 'Die Wiederkehr in Bruckners Adagio', in *Anton Bruckner: Studien zu Werk und Wirkung (Walter Wiora zum 30. Dezember 1986)*, ed. Christoph-Helmut Mahling (Tutzing, 1988), p. 159.

14 Floros, 'Historische Phasen', pp. 97–9.

15 The 1938 Jochum recording – Music & Arts, CD-1086(1) – presents considerable evidence for consistency.

16 That this was entirely conscious is suggested by Mark W. Kluge ('Eugen Jochum Conducts Bruckner's Fifth Symphony: The Historic 1938 Telefunken Recording', notes to Music & Arts, CD-1086(1), p. 8), where he quotes Jochum, 'About the Phenomenology of Conducting', in *The Conductor's Art*, ed. Carl Bamberger (New York, 1965).

17 Benjamin M. Korstvedt, *Bruckner: Symphony No. 8* (Cambridge, 2000), pp. 98–103.

18 Roger Norrington, 'En route to the Wagner Symphony', note accompanying Bruckner, Symphony No. 3, EMI, 7243 5 56167 2 2, pp. 8–10; 'Performing Brahms', in Michael Musgrave (ed.), *The Cambridge Companion to Brahms* (Cambridge, 1999), pp. 234–9.

16 The musical image of Bruckner

1 See Winfried Kirsch, 'Die Bruckner-Forschung seit 1945 (I–IV): eine kommentierte Bibliographie', *Acta Musicologica* 53 (1981), 157–70; 54 (1982), 208–61; 55 (1983), 210–44, 56 (1984), 1–29;

Renate Grasberger, *Bruckner-Bibliographie (bis 1974)* (Graz, 1985).

2 Mathias Hansen, *Anton Bruckner* (Leipzig, 1987), p. 19.

3 Renate Grasberger and Erich Wolfgang Partsch, *Bruckner – skizziert: ein Porträt in ausgewählten Erinnerungen und Anekdoten* (Vienna, 1991).

4 See Thomas Röder, 'Anton Bruckners Glaube', in *B-P*, pp. 50–63.

5 Manfred Wagner, 'Die Nekrologe von 1896: rezeptionsstiftend? – oder Wie Klischees von Anton Bruckner entstanden', in *Musik-Konzepte 23/24: Anton Bruckner*, ed. H.-K. Metzger and R. Riehn (Munich, 1982), p. 138.

6 E.g. Franz Brunner, *Dr. Anton Bruckner: ein Lebensbild* (Linz, 1895), p. 14; *Göll-A*, I, p. 39.

7 Emphases mine; see for example Max Auer, 'Anton Bruckner: zum 100. Geburtstag am 4. September'; Siegfried Kallenberg, 'Das Unrecht an Bruckner', *Zeitschrift für Musik* 91 (1924), 481–6 and 487–8.

8 Arthur Schopenhauer, *The World as Will and Representation*, trans. E. J. F. Payne, 2 vols. (New York, 1966), vol. II, pp. 383–4, 389–90, 393.

9 Ibid., vol. I, p. 383.

10 Max Auer, *Anton Bruckner: sein Leben und Werk* (Zurich, Leipzig, and Vienna, 1923), pp. 5–6.

11 *Göll-A*, II/1, p. 237.

12 *Die Gesellschaft: Monatsschrift für Literatur, Kunst und Sozialpolitik* (1896), 1402 and 1404.

13 Max Graf, 'Anton Bruckner', *Die Musik* 1 (1901–2), 28.

14 See Martin Eybl, 'Das bedrohliche Neue: konservative Konzepte von Musikgeschichte in Wien', in Anselm Gerhard (ed.), *Musikwissenschaft – eine verspätete Disziplin? Die akademische Musikforschung zwischen Fortschrittsglauben und Modernitätsverweigerung* (Stuttgart and Weimar, 2000), pp. 119–27.

15 See Franz Müller, 'Warum lieben wir Bruckner?', in *In Memoriam Anton Bruckner*, ed. Karl Kobald (Zurich, Vienna, and Leipzig, 1924), p. 198.

16 Alfred Heuss, 'Wie steht es heute um Bruckner: allerlei Brucknerfragen', *Zeitschrift für Musik* 91 (1924), 493.

17 *EKB*, vol. I, pp. 1–17.

18 See Peter Wapnewski, 'Der Merker und der Mittler, Richard Wagner und sein Mittelalter', in *Mittelalter-Rezeption (I): gesammelte Vorträge des Salzburger Symposions 'Die Rezeption mittelalterlicher Dichter und ihre Werke in Literatur, bildender Kunst und Musik des 19. und 20. Jahrhunderts'*, ed. Jürgen Kühmel *et al.* (Göppingen, 1979), pp. 7–38.

19 In his *Bruckner* Kurth refers in many formulations to Oswald Spengler's *Der Untergang des Abendlandes* (1918); but Spengler according to Kurth had 'completely overlooked Bruckner's importance' (*EKB*, vol. I, p. 594).

20 *EKB*, vol. I, pp. 594–5.

21 Ernst Kurth in a letter to Max Auer of 30 October 1927 (Österreichische Nationalbibliothek, Musiksammlung, F 31 Auer 381); see Oskar Lang, *Anton Bruckner: Wesen und Bedeutung* (Munich, 1924); Fritz Grüninger, *Anton Bruckner: der metaphysische Kern seiner Persönlichkeit* (Augsburg, 1930).

22 Christa Brüstle, *Anton Bruckner und die Nachwelt: zur Rezeptionsgeschichte des Komponisten in der ersten Hälfte des 20. Jahrhunderts* (Stuttgart, 1998), pp. 73–4.

23 *EKB*, vol. I, p. 290; Fritz Grüninger (ed.), *1. Badisches Brucknerfest 6. bis 10. November 1929* (Karlsruhe, 1929), p. 14.

24 Auer, *Anton Bruckner*, p. 5.

25 See Klose, *Meine Lehrjahre bei Bruckner*, p. 153; also Grasberger and Partsch, *Bruckner – skizziert*, p. 214.

26 See also Manfred Wagner, 'Gefahr der Anekdote', in *Bruckner-Symposion 1977: Bericht*, ed. Franz Grasberger (Linz, 1978), pp. 27–33.

27 August Stradal, 'Anton Bruckner: eine Studie', *Neue Zeitschrift für Musik* 69 (1902), 315.

28 See Franz Zamazal, 'Göllerich – Auer – Gräflinger', *Bruckner-Symposion, 'Bruckner-Freunde – Bruckner-Kenner' (Linz 1994): Bericht*, ed. Othmar Wessely *et al.* (Linz, 1997), pp. 113–31.

29 August Göllerich, 'Anton Bruckner', *Deutsche Worte* 4 (1884), 147–8.

30 See Bruckner's astonished reaction to the talk of the 'second Beethoven' in *Göll-A*, I, p. 29, and the letter from Bruckner to Göllerich of 7 July 1885, in *H-S1*, p. 270.

31 See Theodor Helm, 'Anton Bruckner', in *Musikalisches Wochenblatt* 17 (1886), 4–6, 34–5, 46–8, 60–1; and 27 (1896), 679–81, 694–9.

32 See Wagner's essay 'Über die Anwendung der Musik auf das Drama', *Bayreuther Blätter* 2 (1879), 313–25; also Josef Schalk, 'Beiträge zur Charakteristik der Zeit, XXV: Lichtblicke aus der Zeitgenossenschaft – Anton Bruckner', *Bayreuther Blätter* 7 (1884), 334: 'Attempts to explain the content of purely symphonic pieces of music I frankly confess to finding futile.'

33 See Rudolf Flotzinger, 'Bruckner – Hausegger – Wagner', *Bruckner-Symposion,*

'Bruckner, Wagner und die Neudeutschen in Österreich' (Linz 1984): Bericht, ed. Othmar Wessely (Linz, 1986), pp. 201–10, in particular p. 208.

34 Rudolf Louis, *Der Widerspruch in der Musik: Bausteine zu einer Ästhetik der Tonkunst auf realdialektischer Grundlage* (Leipzig, 1893), p. 103.

35 Rudolf Louis, 'Anton Bruckner', *Allgemeine Musik-Zeitung* 23 (1896), 617.

36 Rudolf Louis, *Anton Bruckner* (Berlin, 1904), p. 36: see also Louis, 'Anton Bruckner: der Mann und sein Werk', *Neue Musik-Zeitung* 23 (1902), 180–1, 200–1, 215–17.

37 Rudolf Louis, *Anton Bruckner* (Munich, 1905), pp. 224–5 and 210.

38 See Eduard Hanslick, *Vom Musikalisch-Schönen*, ed. Dietmar Strauss, 2 vols. (Mainz, 1990), vol. I, p. 75.

39 Louis, *Anton Bruckner* (1905), p. 226.

40 Ibid., pp. 192 and 196.

41 See August Halm, 'Melodie, Harmonie und Themenbildung bei Anton Bruckner', *Neue Musik-Zeitung* 23 (1902), 170–4, 196–8, 211–14, 227–8; *Von zwei Kulturen der Musik* (Munich, 1913); *Die Symphonie Anton Bruckners* (Munich, 1914).

42 *Die Symphonie Anton Bruckners*, p. 81.

43 See Lee A. Rothfarb, 'Musik und Theologie: August Halm am Kreuzungspunkt seines beruflichen und schöpferischen Weges', *Musik in Baden-Württemberg* 3 (1996), 115–34 (I am grateful to Lee Rothfarb for sending me the English manuscript of his essay entitled 'Music and Theology: August Halm's Crossroads of Career and Creativity' which I quote later); Rothfarb, 'The "New Education" and Music Theory, 1900–1925', in *Music Theory and the Exploration of the Past*, ed. Christopher Hatch and David W. Bernstein (Chicago and London, 1993), pp. 449–72.

44 See August Halm, *Von Form und Sinn der Musik: gesammelte Aufsätze*, ed. S. Schmalzriedt (Wiesbaden, 1978); also Rudolf Stephan, 'Über August Halm', in *August-Halm-Preis 1989 für Ernest Bour: Festschrift*, ed. Volker Scherliess (Trossingen, 1989), pp. 6–13.

45 Rothfarb, 'Music and Theology'.

46 Halm, *Die Symphonie Anton Bruckners*, pp. 199–200.

47 The remark about two principles attributed to Beethoven, about whose meaning there was then no unanimity, Halm interpreted as a 'psychological' contrast of themes: see Arnold Schmitz, *Beethovens 'Zwei Prinzipe': ihre Bedeutung für Themen- und Satzbau* (Berlin and Bonn, 1923).

48 Halm, *Die Symphonie Anton Bruckners*, pp. 47–56.

49 Ibid., p. 27; see also August Halm, *Harmonielehre* (Leipzig, 1900).

50 Halm, *Die Symphonie Anton Bruckners*, p. 182. In his essay 'Melodie, Harmonie und Themenbildung bei Anton Bruckner' (see above, n. 41) Halm deals with harmonic function. For him it has tonal importance in homophonic and polyphonic composition, dynamic significance in underlining *crescendo* and *diminuendo*, and an articulating function in relation to symphonic form. Harmony 'serves' the form according to one of his principal theses.

51 Halm, *Die Symphonie Anton Bruckners*, pp. 200–1.

52 See Lee A. Rothfarb, 'Zwischen Originalität und Ideologie: die Musik von August Halm (1869–1929)', *Musik in Baden-Württemberg* 5 (1998), 175–99.

53 Hugo Riemann, *Handbuch der Musikgeschichte*, 2 vols. in 5 parts (Leipzig, 1904–13), vol. II /3, p. 240.

54 Halm, *Die Symphonie Anton Bruckners*, p. 42.

55 Ibid., p. 128 and p. 223. The 'plain' (*das Kunstlose*) is the symphonic apotheosis that Bruckner knew how to organize in the Finale without the aid of rhetoric (words or texts), unlike Beethoven.

56 See Halm, *Von Form und Sinn der Musik*, pp. 176–81.

57 *EKB*, vol. I, pp. 239–42; see also Stephen Parkany, 'Kurth's *Bruckner* and the Adagio of the Seventh Symphony', *NCM* 11 (1987–8), 262–81.

58 See Carl Dahlhaus, *The Idea of Absolute Music*, trans. Roger Lustig (Chicago and London, 1978), pp. 39–41 and 122–7.

59 Ernst Bloch, *Geist der Utopie*, 2nd edn (Frankfurt am Main, 1985), p. 97.

60 Somewhat in the sense of Victor Zuckerkandl, when he said that 'community of musical language' is also 'community of civilization' and accordingly that 'the music of Austria is a special type of German music'; see *Vom musikalischen Denken: Begegnung von Ton und Wort* (Zurich, 1964), p. 227.

61 Josef Schalk, 'Anton Bruckner und die moderne Musikwelt: Vortrag gehalten im Wiener Akademischen Wagner-Verein', *Deutsche Worte* 5 (1885), 474. See also Thomas Leibnitz, 'Anton Bruckner "Deutscher" oder "Österreicher": Deutungen, Vereinnahmungen, Hintergründe', in *Österreichische Musik – Musik in Österreich: Beiträge zur Musikgeschichte Mitteleuropas (Theophil Antonicek zum 60. Geburtstag)*, ed. Elisabeth Theresia Hilscher (Tutzing, 1998),

pp. 463–76; also Brüstle, *Anton Bruckner und die Nachwelt*, pp. 60–2.

62 See also Rudolf Flotzinger, 'Bruckners Rolle in der Kulturgeschichte Österreichs', in *B-P*, pp. 9–24; Gottfried Scholz, 'Wer gilt als österreichischer Komponist? Der Österreich-Begriff im Wandel der Geschichte als Problem nationaler Musikgeschichtsschreibung', *Bericht über den Internationalen musikwissenschaftlichen Kongress Bayreuth 1981*, ed. Christoph-Hellmut Mahling and Sigrid Wiesmann (Kassel, 1984), pp. 445–9.

63 Franz Gräflinger, *Anton Bruckner: Leben und Schaffen* (Berlin, 1927), p. 313.

64 Ibid., p. iv.

65 Paul Bekker, *Die Sinfonie von Beethoven bis Mahler* (Berlin, 1918), pp. 37–9; W. Steinbeck, 'Symphonie der Nationen: zur Frage einer "österreichischen Symphonik"', in *Bruckner-Symposion, 'Entwicklungen, Parallelen, Kontraste – Zur Frage einer "österreichischen Symphonik"' (Linz 1993): Bericht*, ed. Otto Wessely *et al.* (Linz, 1996), pp. 69–74.

66 Alfred Orel, *Anton Bruckner: das Werk, der Künstler, die Zeit* (Vienna and Leipzig, 1925), pp. 165 and 52.

67 Orel strengthened a cliché that was to have long-lasting effect. Only recently have basic studies been undertaken into this connection, e.g. Franz Grasberger, 'Schubert und Bruckner', *Schubert-Kongress Wien 1978: Bericht*, ed. Otto Brusatti (Graz, 1979), pp. 215–28; Timothy L. Jackson, 'Schubert as "John the Baptist to Wagner-Jesus": large-scale Enharmonicism in Bruckner and his Models', *B-J 1991/92/93* (1995), 61–107.

68 Even foreign voices subscribed to this: see Peter Jost, 'Die französische Symphonie im 20. Jahrhundert', *Die Musikforschung* 47 (1994), 132.

69 See Carl Dahlhaus, 'Musikgeschichte Österreichs und die Idee der deutschen Musik', in *Deutschland und Österreich: ein bilaterales Geschichtsbuch*, ed. R. A. Kann and F. E. Prinz (Vienna and Munich, 1980), pp. 322–49; Rudolf Flotzinger and Gernot Gruber, *Musikgeschichte Österreichs*, vol. III: *Von der Revolution 1848 zur Gegenwart*, 2nd edn (Vienna, 1995), pp. 173–5.

70 Anton Reichel, 'Deutsch-Österreichs künstlerische Sendung', *Neue Musik-Zeitung* 42 (1921), 214.

71 Speech by the Reich Chancellor Wilhelm Marx, who led a contemporary Berlin Bruckner society: cited according to an undated document in Historisches Archiv der Stadt Köln, Nachlass Marx, No. 260, provided by Stehkämper with the information

11 October 1924; see *Der Nachlass des Reichskanzlers Wilhelm Marx*, 5 vols., ed. Hugo Stehkämper (Cologne, 1968–97), vol. IV, p. 33. In *Göll-A*, IV/4, p. 76 the date of the event is June 1924, but see also the report in *Die Musik* 16 (1923–4), 533–4.

72 *Göll-A*, II/1, p. 358. See *Die Musik* 17 (1924–5), 238: in Germany President Ebert made a contribution of 500 gold marks.

73 *Bruckner-Blätter* 3 (1931), 3. When Kurth attempted to found a Swiss Bruckner society, 'there was a fair amount of fuss then in the press and elsewhere, that it [the IBG] was a German National and Austrian affair, that it was an attempt to drag the Swiss in, that it was a biased organization only "international" in name' (letter from Kurth to Auer of 31 December 1928, Österreichische Nationalbibliothek, Musiksammlung, F 31 Auer 381).

74 See Christa Brüstle, 'Siegmund von Hausegger: a Bruckner Authority from the 1930s', in *PAB*, pp. 341–52.

75 Oskar Lang, 'Bruckners Bedeutung im deutschen Geistesleben', *Deutsche Zeitschrift* 48 (1934–5), 10–16.

76 See Rosenberg, 'Um die nationalsozialistische Weltanschauung', *Völkischer Beobachter*, 18 November 1933.

77 See Alfred Rosenberg, 'Bauerntum und Kultur', *Deutsche Kultur-Wacht* 2 (1933), 2. For many years there had been controversy about Bruckner's peasant origins. For a new genealogy of the composer, see Ernst Schwanzara, 'Neue Bruckner-Forschungen: die Vorfahren stammen aus Niederösterreich', *Neues Wiener Tagblatt*, 9 January 1932, 'Anton Bruckners Urahnen – niederösterreichische Bauern: Richtigstellung eines Irrtums', *Bruckner-Blätter* 5 (1933), 11–13, 22, also *Göll-A*, IV/4, pp. 135–222.

78 Report on the Freiburg Bruckner Festival, *Zeitschrift für Musik* 102 (1935), 750–1.

79 Robert Haas, *Anton Bruckner* (Potsdam, 1934), p. 6; R. Zimmermann, *Um Anton Bruckners Vermächtnis: ein Beitrag zur rassischen Erkenntnis germanischer Tonkunst* (Stuttgart, 1939); Morten Solvik, 'The International Bruckner Society and the N.S.D.A.P: A Case Study of Robert Haas and the Critical Edition', *MQ* 83 (1998), 362–82.

80 Hitler's 'takeover' of the Walhalla followed on 21 May 1936 and was directly linked to his decision to set up the Bruckner bust: Friedrich Heer, *Der Glaube des Adolf Hitler: Anatomie einer politischen Religiosität* (Munich and Esslingen, 1968), p. 309 (also pp. 27, 34, and 309–10). For Hitler and Bruckner see also Henry Picker, *Hitlers*

Tischgespräche im Führerhauptquartier
(Frankfurt am Main and Berlin, 1993),
p. 336.
81 See for example Max Auer, *Anton Bruckner: sein Leben und Werk* (Vienna, 1934),
p. 397.
82 See also Brüstle, 'Politisch-ideologische Implikationen der ersten Bruckner-Gesamtausgabe', in *B-P*, pp. 192–201.
83 An anti-Semitic subtext of the quarrel about the *Bruckner-Gesamtausgabe* referred to Bruckner's pupil Ferdinand Löwe, but also was directed against Universal Edition as inheritor of the first published editions; see Benjamin M. Korstvedt, '"Return to the Pure Sources": the Ideology and Text-Critical Legacy of the First Bruckner *Gesamtausgabe*', in *BS*, pp. 91–109, and Brüstle, 'Politisch-ideologische Implikationen der ersten Bruckner-Gesamtausgabe', in *B-P*,
pp. 192–201.
84 See *Zeitschrift für Musik* 103 (1936), Bruckner Number. The opponents of the *Gesamtausgabe* also obtained support from the well-known Wagner expert Alfred Lorenz, in 'Zur Instrumentation von Anton Bruckners Symphonien', *Zeitschrift für Musik* 103 (1936), 1318, and 'Klangmischung in Anton Bruckners Orchester', *Allgemeine Musikzeitung* 63 (1936), 717–20. See also the recent account in Wolfgang Doebel, *Bruckners Symphonien in Bearbeitungen: die Konzepte der Bruckner-Schüler und ihre Rezeption bis zu Robert Haas* (Tutzing, 2001); also above, Chapter 11, pp. 138–41.
85 Alfred Orel, 'Original und Bearbeitung bei Anton Bruckner', *Deutsche Musikkultur* 1 (1936–7), 193–222.
86 In the Leipzig branch of the Musikwissenschaftlicher Verlag the following was considered at the end of 1936: 'At the moment we are mulling over the problem of how to make the whole complex of the original versions comprehensible to the highest levels of the Party and win them to our side . . . For example, we must under all circumstances be punctual in convincing Goebbels of the importance and necessity of the original versions' (letter of Hilde Wendler to Max Auer of 1 December 1936, Österreichische Nationalbibliothek, Musiksammlung, F 31 Auer 560). One result was the brochure *Anton Bruckner: Wissenschaftliche und künstlerische Betrachtungen zu den Originalfassungen* (Vienna, 1937).
87 See Paul Ehlers, 'Das Regensburger Bruckner-Erlebnis', *Zeitschrift für Musik* 104 (1937), 745–8.

88 Goebbels regarded Bruckner's music as 'magnificent music for Party occasions', as he noted in 1938: *Die Tagebücher von Joseph Goebbels: sämtliche Fragmente*, Part I/*Aufzeichnungen 1924–1941*, ed. Elke Fröhlich *et al.*, 4 vols. (Munich, 1987), vol. III, pp. 465, 491 and vol. IV, p. 55.
89 Auer gave up his position to the celebrated conductor; see Auer's announcement 'Furtwängler setzt den Schlusspunkt zum Streit um die Fassungen bei Bruckner', *Zeitschrift für Musik* 106 (1939), 81–2.
90 Speech by Goebbels at the Düsseldorf Reichsmusiktage in May 1939; sound recording of the *Original-Tondokumente zur Ausstellung 'Entartete Musik'*, ed. Albrecht Dümling (Düsseldorf, 1988). In April 1938 Robert Haas, the editor of the *Gesamtausgabe*, had 'dedicated this "monumental work" to the German people and our leader Adolf Hitler'; see Brüstle, *Bruckner und die Nachwelt*, pp. 306–11. Haas was a party member from 1933 and thus belonged to the 'illegal National Socialists' in Austria before 1938; see Pamela M. Potter, *Most German of the Arts: Musicology and Society from the Weimar Republic to the End of Hitler's Reich* (New Haven and London, 1998), p. 115.
91 Hanns Kreczi, *Das Bruckner-Stift St. Florian und das Linzer Reichs-Bruckner-Orchester (1942–1945)* (Graz, 1986).
92 Ingo Sarlay, *Hitlers Linz: die Stadtplanung von Linz an der Donau 1938–1945*, dissertation, University of Graz (1985), and *Baukunst im Dritten Reich – Hitlers Linz* (Graz, 1987). See also Albrecht Dümling, 'Der deutsche Michel erwacht: zur Bruckner-Rezeption im NS-Staat', in *B-P*, pp. 202–14.
93 Hansen, *Bruckner*, p. 312.
94 See also Floros, *Brahms und Bruckner*, pp. 12–13 and 34–5.
95 Dika Newlin, *Bruckner – Mahler – Schoenberg*, 1st edn (New York, 1947), p. 1.
96 Robert W. Wason, *Viennese Harmonic Theory from Albrechtsberger to Schenker and Schoenberg* (Ann Arbor, 1985), p. 84; Ulrich Krämer, *Alban Berg als Schüler Arnold Schönbergs: Quellenstudien und Analysen zum Frühwerk* (Vienna, 1996).
97 Newlin, *Bruckner – Mahler – Schoenberg*, p. 102; Arnold Schoenberg, 'Brahms the Progressive', in *Style and Idea*, ed. Leonard Stein, trans. Leo Black, 2nd edn (London and Boston, 1975), pp. 398–441.
98 Bekker, *Die Sinfonie von Beethoven bis Mahler*, pp. 54–6. In the Bruckner literature of the twenties and early thirties the negative evaluation of Mahler predominated (against

the background of anti-Semitic resentment), in so far as he was mentioned; Orel dealt with Mahler in comparative detail in *Anton Bruckner: das Werk, der Künstler, die Zeit*, pp. 195–7.

99 Hansen, *Bruckner*, p. 316.

100 E.g. Hans F. Redlich, *Bruckner and Mahler*, rev. edn (London, 1963); Rudolf Stephan, 'Zum Thema "Bruckner und Mahler"', in *Vom musikalischen Denken: gesammelte Vorträge*, ed. Rainer Damm and Andreas Traub (Mainz, 1985), pp. 91–7; Constantin Floros, 'Von Mahlers Affinität zu Bruckner', *Bruckner-Symposion, 'Bruckner, Liszt, Mahler und die Moderne' (Linz 1986): Bericht*, (Linz, 1989), pp. 109–17; Timothy L. Jackson, 'Die Wagnersche Umarmungs-Metapher bei Bruckner und Mahler', in *B-P*, pp. 134–52.

101 The author of the liner notes of the CD of Wetz's First Symphony in C minor op. 40 is of the opinion that this composer was forgotten in the face of so many 'uninteresting' modern composers; CD of 1995, Cracow Philharmonic Orchestra conducted by Roland Bader, cpo, 999 272–2.

102 Richard Wetz, *Anton Bruckner: sein Leben und Schaffen* (Leipzig, 1922), a small reader in which the author provides no analytical or technical information.

103 Fred K. Prieberg, *Musik im NS-Staat* (Frankfurt am Main, 1982), p. 187; Erik Levi, 'Richard Wetz (1875–1935): a Brucknerian Composer', in *PAB*, pp. 363–94.

104 Jürgen Schaarwächter, *Die britische Sinfonie 1914–1945* (Cologne, 1995).

105 See S. Phillippo, 'Assessing Robert Simpson: the Perpetual Striver', *The Musical Times* 139 (1998), 30. On Simpson and Bruckner, see Stephen Johnson, 'Robert Simpson's Ninth', *The Musical Times* 128 (1987), 196–9.

106 Wolfgang Rihm, *ausgesprochen: Schriften und Gespräche*, ed. Ulrich Mosch, Veröffentlichungen der Paul Sacher-Stiftung 6, 2 vols. (Winterthur, 1997), vol. II, p. 289.

Select bibliography

Antonicek, Theophil, *Anton Bruckner und die Wiener Hofmusikkapelle* (Graz, 1979).

Auer, Max, *Anton Bruckner: sein Leben und Werk* (1st edn, Zurich, Leipzig, and Vienna, 1923; rev. edn Vienna, 1934).

Anton Bruckner als Kirchenmusiker (Regensburg, 1927).

Auer, Max (ed.), *Anton Bruckner: gesammelte Briefe (Neue Folge)* (Regensburg, 1924).

Benjamin, William E., 'Tonal Dualism in Bruckner's Eighth Symphony', in W. Kinderman and H. Krebs (eds.), *The Second Practice of Nineteenth-Century Tonality* (Lincoln, Nebr. and London, 1996), pp. 237–58.

Boss, Rainer, *Gestalt und Funktion von Fuge und Fugato bei Anton Bruckner* (Tutzing, 1997).

Botstein, Leon, 'Music and Ideology: Thoughts on Bruckner', *The Musical Quarterly* 80 (1996), 1–11.

Brosche, Günter, 'Ideologische Einflüsse auf das Nachleben Anton Bruckners', in E. T. Hilscher (ed.), *Österreichische Musik – Musik in Österreich. Theophil Antonicek zum 60. Geburtstag* (Tutzing, 1998), pp. 451–61.

Brüstle, Christa, *Anton Bruckner und die Nachwelt: zur Rezeptionsgeschichte des Komponisten in der ersten Hälfte des 20. Jahrhunderts* (Stuttgart, 1998).

'Politisch-ideologische Implikationen der ersten Bruckner-Gesamtausgabe', in A. Riethmüller (ed.), *Bruckner-Probleme: internationales Kolloquium 7.–9. October 1996 in Berlin* (Stuttgart, 1999), pp. 192–202.

'Siegmund von Hausegger: A Bruckner Authority from the 1930s', in C. Howie, P. Hawkshaw, and T. [L.] Jackson (eds.), *Perspectives on Anton Bruckner* (Aldershot, 2001), pp. 341–52.

Carragan, William, 'The Early Version of the Second Symphony', in C. Howie, P. Hawkshaw, and T. [L.] Jackson (eds.), *Perspectives on Anton Bruckner* (Aldershot, 2001), pp. 85–8.

Cooke, Deryck, 'The Bruckner Problem Simplified', *The Musical Times* 110 (1969), 20–2, 142–4, 362, 479–82, and 828; repr. in *Vindication: Essays about Romantic Music* (Cambridge, 1982), pp. 43–71.

Dahlhaus, Carl, 'Bruckner und die Programmusik: zum Finale der Achten Symphonie', in C.-H. Mahling (ed.), *Anton Bruckner: Studien zu Werk und Wirkung (Walter Wiora zum 30. Dezember 1986)* (Tutzing, 1988), pp. 7–32.

Darcy, Warren, 'Bruckner's Sonata Deformations', in T. L. Jackson and P. Hawkshaw (eds.), *Bruckner Studies* (Cambridge, 1997), pp. 265–77.

Decsey, Ernst, *Bruckner: Versuch eines Lebens* (Berlin, 1919).

Doebel, Wolfgang, *Bruckners Sinfonien in Bearbeitungen: die Konzepte der Bruckner-Schüler und ihre Rezeption bis zu Robert Haas* (Tutzing, 2001).

Doernberg, Erwin, *The Life and Symphonies of Anton Bruckner* (London, 1960).

Dümling, Albrecht, 'Der deutsche Michel erwacht: zur Bruckner-Rezeption im NS- Staat', in A. Riethmüller (ed.), *Bruckner-Probleme: internationales Kolloquium 7.–9. October 1996 in Berlin* (Stuttgart, 1999), pp. 202–14.

Finscher, Ludwig, 'Zur Stellung der "Nullten" Symphonie in Bruckners Werk', in C.-H. Mahling (ed.), *Anton Bruckner: Studien zu Werk und Wirkung (Walter Wiora zum 30. Dezember 1986)* (Tutzing, 1988), pp. 63–79.

Floros, Constantin, *Brahms und Bruckner: Studien zur musikalischen Exegetik* (Wiesbaden, 1980).

'Historische Phasen der Bruckner-Interpretation', in F. Grasberger (ed.), *Bruckner-Symposion, 'Bruckner-Interpretation' (Linz 1982): Bericht* (Linz, 1982), pp. 93–102.

'Thesen über Bruckner', in H.-K. Metzger and R. Riehn (eds.), *Musik-Konzepte 23/24: Anton Bruckner* (Munich, 1982), pp. 5–14.

'On Unity between Bruckner's Personality and Production', in C. Howie, P. Hawkshaw, and T. [L.] Jackson (eds.), *Perspectives on Anton Bruckner* (Aldershot, 2001), 285–98.

Flotzinger, Rudolf, 'Bruckners Rolle in der Kulturgeschichte Österreichs', in A. Riethmüller (ed.), *Bruckner-Probleme: internationales Kolloquium 7.–9. October 1996 in Berlin* (Stuttgart, 1999), pp. 9–24.

Gilliam, Bryan, 'The Two Versions of Bruckner's Eighth Symphony', *19th Century Music* 15 (1991/92).

'The Annexation of Anton Bruckner: Nazi Revisionism and the Politics of Appropriation', *The Musical Quarterly* 78 (1994), 584–604; repr. in T. L. Jackson and P. Hawkshaw (eds.), *Bruckner Studies* (Cambridge, 1997), pp. 72–90.

Glettler, Monika, 'Die *Monarchia Austriaca* und die deutsche Musik', in F. W. Riedel (ed.), *Anton Bruckner: Tradition und Fortschritt in der Kirchenmusik des 19. Jahrhunderts* (Sinzig, 2001), pp. 29–46.

Göllerich, August, *Anton Bruckner: ein Lebens- und Schaffens-Bild*, ed. and completed by Max Auer, 4 vols. (Regensburg, 1922–37).

Gräflinger, Franz (ed.), *Anton Bruckner: gesammelte Briefe* (Regensburg, 1924).

Grandjean, Wolfgang, 'Anton Bruckners "Helgoland" und das Symphonische', *Die Musikforschung* 48 (1995), 349–68.

Grasberger, Franz, 'Anton Bruckners II. Symphonie', in Othmar Wessely (ed.), *Bruckner-Studien* (Vienna, 1975), pp. 303–21.

Grasberger, Franz (ed.), *Bruckner-Symposion, 'Bruckner, Liszt, Mahler und die Moderne' (Linz 1977): Bericht* (Linz, 1978).

Bruckner-Symposion, 'Die Fassungen' (Linz 1980): Bericht (Linz, 1981).

Bruckner-Symposion, 'Bruckner-Interpretation' (Linz 1982): Bericht (Linz, 1982).

Grasberger, Renate, *Bruckner-Bibliographie* (Graz, 1985).

Bruckner-Ikonographie 1: um 1854 bis 1924 (Vienna, 1990).

Grasberger, Renate and Partsch, Erich Wolfgang, *Bruckner – skizziert: ein Porträt in ausgewählten Erinnerungen und Anekdoten* (Vienna, 1991).

Grasberger, Renate (ed.), *Werkverzeichnis Anton Bruckner* (Tutzing, 1977).

Bruckner-Symposion, 'Zum Schaffensprozess in den Künsten' (Linz 1995): Bericht (Linz, 1997).

Grasberger, Renate *et al.* (eds.), *Bruckner-Symposion, 'Bruckner und die Musik der Romantik' (Linz 1987): Bericht* (Linz, 1989).

Bruckner-Symposion, 'Anton Bruckner – Persönlichkeit und Werk' (Linz 1992): Bericht (Linz, 1995).

Gülke, Peter, *Brahms, Bruckner: zwei Studien* (Kassel, 1989).

Haas, Robert, *Anton Bruckner* (Potsdam, 1934).

Halm, August, *Die Symphonie Anton Bruckners*, 2nd edn (Munich, 1923).

Von zwei Kulturen der Musik (Munich, 1913; 3rd edn, Stuttgart, 1947).

Hansen, Mathias, 'Die faschistische Bruckner-Rezeption und ihre Quellen', *Beiträge zur Musikwissenschaft* 28 (1986), 53–61.

Anton Bruckner (Leipzig, 1987).

Harrandt, Andrea, and Schneider, Otto (eds.), *Briefe 1852–1886*, Anton Bruckner Sämtliche Werke, vol. XXIV/1 (Vienna, 1998).

'Students and Friends as "Prophets" and "Promoters": the Reception of Bruckner's Works in the *Wiener Akademischer Wagner-Verein*', in C. Howie, P. Hawkshaw, and T. [L.] Jackson (eds.), *Perspectives on Anton Bruckner* (Aldershot, 2001), pp. 317–27.

Briefe 1887–1896, Anton Bruckner Sämtliche Werke, vol. XXIV/2 (Vienna, forthcoming).

Harten, Uwe (ed.), *Anton Bruckner: ein Handbuch* (Salzburg, 1996).

Harten, Uwe *et al.* (eds.), *Bruckner-Symposion, 'Fassungen, Bearbeitungen, Vollendungen' (Linz 1996): Bericht* (Linz, 1998).

Bruckner-Symposion 'Bruckner – Vorbilder und Traditionen' (Linz 1997): Bericht (Linz, 1999).

Bruckner-Symposion, 'Künstler-Bilder' (Linz 1998): Bericht (Linz, 2000).

Hatten, Robert S., 'The Expressive Role of Disjunction: a Semiotic Approach to Form and Meaning in the Fourth and Fifth Symphony', in C. Howie, P. Hawkshaw, and T. [L.] Jackson (eds.), *Perspectives on Anton Bruckner* (Aldershot, 2001), pp. 145–84.

Hawkshaw, Paul, 'The Date of Bruckner's "Nullified" Symphony in D Minor', *19th Century Music* 6 (1982–83), 252–63.

'The Manuscript Sources for Anton Bruckner's Linz Works: a Study of His Working Methods from 1856 to 1868', Ph.D. thesis, University of Columbia (1984).

'From Zigeunerwald to Valhalla in Common Time: the Genesis of Anton Bruckner's *Germanenzug*', *Bruckner-Jahrbuch 1987/88* (1990), 21–30.

'The Bruckner Problem Revisited', *19th Century Music* 21 (1997–8), 96–107.

'Bruckners Psalmen', in A. Riethmüller (ed.), *Bruckner-Probleme: internationales Kolloquium 7.–9. October 1996 in Berlin* (Stuttgart, 1999), pp. 71–84.

'The Enigma of Anton Bruckner's Psalm 146', in J. Gmeiner *et al.* (eds.), *Musica Conservata: Günter Brosche zum 60. Geburtstag* (Tutzing, 1999), pp. 105–19.

'Die Psalmkompositionen Anton Bruckners', in E. Maier, A. Harrandt, and E. W. Partsch (eds.), *Bruckner Vorträge: Tagung Wien 1999* (Vienna, 2000), pp. 7–20.

'A Composer Learns his Craft: Anton Bruckner's Lessons in Form and Orchestration with Otto Kitzler, 1861–63', in C. Howie, P. Hawkshaw, and

T. [L.] Jackson (eds.), *Perspectives on Anton Bruckner* (Aldershot, 2001),
pp. 3–29.

Hinrichsen, Hans-Joachim, 'Bruckners Wagner-Zitate', in A. Riethmüller (ed.),
Bruckner-Probleme: internationales Kolloquium 7.–9. October 1996 in Berlin
(Stuttgart, 1999), pp. 115–71.

Hoffmann, Wolfgang, '"Sextaccord"-Folgen im geistlichen Vokalschaffen Anton
Bruckners', *Bruckner-Jahrbuch 1994/95/96* (1997), 157–73.

Howie, A. Crawford, 'The Sacred Music of Anton Bruckner', Ph.D. thesis,
University of Manchester (1969).

'Traditional and Novel Elements in Bruckner's Sacred Music', *The Musical
Quarterly* 67 (1981), 544–67.

Anton Bruckner: a Documentary Biography, 2 vols. (Lewiston and Lampeter,
2002).

Howie, A. Crawford, Hawkshaw, Paul, and Jackson, Timothy [L.] (eds.),
Perspectives on Anton Bruckner (Aldershot, 2001).

Jackson, Timothy L., 'Bruckner's Metrical Numbers', *19th Century Music* 14
(1990–1), 101–31.

'Schubert as "John the Baptist to Wagner-Jesus": large-scale Enharmonicism
in Bruckner and his Models', *Bruckner-Jahrbuch 1991/92/93* (1995),
61–107.

'The Finale of Bruckner's Seventh Symphony and Tragic Reversed Sonata Form',
in T. L. Jackson and P. Hawkshaw (eds.), *Bruckner Studies* (Cambridge, 1997),
pp. 140–208.

'Bruckner's *Oktaven*: the Problem of Consecutives, Doubling, and Orchestral
Voice-leading', in C. Howie, P. Hawkshaw, and T. [L.] Jackson (eds.),
Perspectives on Anton Bruckner (Aldershot, 2001), pp. 30–66.

'Die Wagnersche Umarmungs-Metapher bei Bruckner und Mahler', in
A. Riethmüller (ed.), *Bruckner-Probleme: internationales Kolloquium 7.–9.
October 1996 in Berlin* (Stuttgart, 1999), pp. 134–52.

Jackson, Timothy L. and Hawkshaw, Paul (eds.), *Bruckner Studies* (Cambridge,
1997).

Johnson, Stephen (ed.), *Bruckner Remembered* (London and Boston, 1998).

Kantner, Leopold M., 'Die Frömmigkeit Anton Bruckners', in *Anton Bruckner in
Wien: eine kritische Studie zu seiner Persönlichkeit* (Graz, 1980), pp. 229–78.

Kinder, Keith William, *The Wind and Wind-Chorus Music of Anton Bruckner*
(Westport, Conn., 2000).

Kirsch, Winfried, 'Die Bruckner-Forschung seit 1945 (I–IV): eine kommentierte
Bibliographie', *Acta Musicologica* 53 (1981), 157–70; 54 (1982), 208–61; 55
(1983), 210–44; 56 (1984), 1–29.

'Anmerkungen zu einem Spätwerk: Anton Bruckners 150. Psalm', in C.-H.
Mahling (ed.), *Anton Bruckner: Studien zu Werk und Wirkung (Walter Wiora
zum 30. Dezember 1986)* (Tutzing, 1988), pp. 81–99.

Kopfermann, Michael, 'Über den Anfang des ersten Satzes von Bruckners
VIII. Symphonie: analytische Ausführungen', in H.-K. Metzger and
R. Riehn (eds.), *Musik-Konzepte 23/24: Anton Bruckner* (Munich, 1982),
pp. 23–70.

Korstvedt, Benjamin M., 'The First Edition of Anton Bruckner's Fourth
    Symphony: Authorship, Production, and Reception', Ph.D. dissertation
    (University of Pennsylvania, 1995).
  'Anton Bruckner in the Third Reich and after: an Essay on Ideology and
    Bruckner Reception', *The Musical Quarterly* 80 (1996), 132–60.
  'The First Printed Edition of Anton Bruckner's Fourth Symphony:
    Collaboration and Authenticity', *19th Century Music* 20 (1996–97), 3–26.
  '"Return to the Pure Sources": the Ideology and Text-critical Legacy of the First
    Bruckner *Gesamtausgabe*', in T. L. Jackson and P. Hawkshaw (eds.), *Bruckner
    Studies* (Cambridge, 1997), pp. 91–109.
  Bruckner: Symphony No. 8 (Cambridge, 2000).
  '"Harmonic Daring"and Symphonic Design in the Sixth Symphony: an Essay in
    Historical Musical Analysis', in C. Howie, P. Hawkshaw, and T. [L.] Jackson
    (eds.), *Perspectives on Anton Bruckner* (Aldershot, 2001), pp. 185–205.
Korte, Werner, *Bruckner und Brahms: die spätromantische Lösung der autonomen
    Konzeption* (Tutzing, 1963).
Kreczi, Hanns, *Das Bruckner-Stift St. Florian und das Linzer Reichs-Bruckner-
    Orchester (1942–1945)* (Graz, 1986).
Krones, Hartmut, 'Bruckners Kirchenmusik im Spiegel des Cäcilianismus', in
    F. W. Riedel (ed.), *Anton Bruckner: Tradition und Fortschritt in der Kirchenmusik
    des 19. Jahrhunderts* (Sinzig, 2001), pp. 91–104.
Kurth, Ernst, *Bruckner*, 2 vols. (Berlin, 1925; repr. Hildesheim and New York,
    1971).
Laufer, Edward, 'Some Aspects of Prolongational Procedures in the Ninth
    Symphony', in T. L. Jackson and P. Hawkshaw (eds.), *Bruckner Studies*
    (Cambridge, 1997), pp. 209–55.
  'Continuity in the Fourth Symphony (First Movement)', in C. Howie,
    P. Hawkshaw, and T. [L.] Jackson (eds.), *Perspectives on Anton Bruckner*
    (Aldershot, 2001), pp. 114–44.
Leibnitz, Thomas, *Die Brüder Schalk und Anton Bruckner: dargestellt an den
    Nachlassbeständen der Musiksammlung der Österreichischen Nationalbibliothek*
    (Tutzing, 1988).
  'Anton Bruckner and "German Music": Josef Schalk and the Establishment of
    Bruckner as a National Composer', in C. Howie, P. Hawkshaw, and T. [L.]
    Jackson (eds.), *Perspectives on Anton Bruckner* (Aldershot, 2001), pp.
    328–40.
Lieberwirth, Steffen (ed.), *Anton Bruckner – Leben, Werk, Interpretation, Rezeption:
    Kongressbericht zum V. Internationalen Gewandhaus-Symposium anlässlich der
    Gewandhaus-Festtage 1987* (Leipzig, 1988).
Loos, Helmut, 'Zu Bruckners Kirchenmusik', in A. Riethmüller (ed.),
    Bruckner-Probleme: internationales Kolloquium 7.–9. October 1996 in Berlin
    (Stuttgart, 1999), pp. 64–70.
Lorenz, Alfred, 'Klangmischung in Anton Bruckners Orchester', *Allgemeine
    Musikzeitung* 63 (1936), 717–20.
  'Zur Instrumentation von Anton Bruckners Symphonien', *Zeitschrift für Musik*
    103 (1936), 1318–25.

McClatchie, Stephen M., 'Bruckner and the Bayreuthians; or, *Das Geheimnis der Form bei Anton Bruckner*', in T. L. Jackson and P. Hawkshaw (eds.), *Bruckner Studies* (Cambridge, 1997), pp. 110–21.

Mahling, Christoph-Hellmut (ed.), *Anton Bruckner: Studien zu Werk und Wirkung: Walter Wiora zum 30. Dezember 1986* (Tutzing, 1988).

Maier, Elisabeth, and Zamazal, Franz, *Anton Bruckner und Leopold von Zenetti* (Graz, 1980).

   Anton Bruckner: Stationen eines Lebens (Linz, 1996).

   'A Hidden Personality: Access to an "Inner Biography" of Anton Bruckner', in T. L. Jackson and P. Hawkshaw (eds.), *Bruckner Studies* (Cambridge, 1997), pp. 32–53.

Massow, Albrecht von, 'Anachronismus als Moderne: zur Eigenart eines kompositorischen Prinzips in der Musik Anton Bruckners', in A. Riethmüller (ed.), *Bruckner-Probleme: internationales Kolloquium 7.–9. October 1996 in Berlin* (Stuttgart, 1999), pp. 153–71.

Metzger, Heinz-Klaus and Riehn, Rainer (eds.), *Musik-Konzepte 23/24: Anton Bruckner* (Munich, 1982).

Nagler, Norbert, 'Bruckners gründerzeitliche Monumentalsymphonie: Reflexionen zur Heteronomie kompositorischer Praxis', in H.-K. Metzger and R. Riehn (eds.), *Musik-Konzepte 23/24: Anton Bruckner* (Munich, 1982), pp. 86–118.

Newlin, Dika, *Bruckner–Mahler–Schoenberg* (New York, 1971; rev. edn, London, 1979).

Notley, Margaret, 'Bruckner and Viennese Wagnerism', in T. L. Jackson and P. Hawkshaw (eds.), *Bruckner Studies* (Cambridge, 1997), pp. 54–71.

Notter, Werner, *Schematismus und Evolution in der Sinfonik Anton Bruckners* (Munich and Salzburg, 1983).

Nowak, Leopold, *Anton Bruckner: Musik und Leben* (Linz, 1973).

   Über Anton Bruckner: gesammelte Aufsätze 1936–1984 (Vienna, 1985).

Orel, Alfred, *Anton Bruckner: das Werk, der Künstler, die Zeit* (Vienna and Leipzig, 1925).

Parkany, Stephen, 'Kurth's *Bruckner* and the Adagio of the Seventh Symphony', *19th Century Music* 11 (1987–8), 262–81.

Partsch, Erich Wolfgang, 'Schubert, Bruckner, Mahler und die Frage nach einer "österreichischen" Linie in der Symphonik', *Nachrichten zur Mahler-Forschung* 31 (1994), 3–16.

Pass, Walter, 'Studie über Bruckners ersten St. Florianer Aufenthalt', in Othmar Wessely (ed.), *Bruckner-Studien* (Vienna, 1975), pp. 13–42.

Phillips, John A., 'The Facts behind a "Legend": the Ninth Symphony and the *Te Deum*', in C. Howie, P. Hawkshaw, and T. [L.] Jackson (eds.), *Perspectives on Anton Bruckner* (Aldershot, 2001), pp. 270–81.

Redlich, Hans Ferdinand, *Bruckner and Mahler*, rev. edn (London, 1963).

Riedel, Friedrich W. (ed.), *Anton Bruckner: Tradition und Fortschritt in der Kirchenmusik des 19. Jahrhunderts* (Sinzig, 2001).

Riethmüller, Albrecht (ed.), *Bruckner-Probleme: internationales Kolloquium 7.–9. October 1996 in Berlin* (Stuttgart, 1999).

Ringer, Alexander, '*Germanenzug* bis *Helgoland*: zu Bruckners Deutschtum', in A. Riethmüller (ed.), *Bruckner-Probleme: internationales Kolloquium 7.–9. October 1996 in Berlin* (Stuttgart, 1999), pp. 25–34.

Röder, Thomas, *Auf dem Weg zur Bruckner-Symphonie: Untersuchungen zu den ersten beiden Fassungen von Anton Bruckners Dritter Symphonie* (Wiesbaden, 1987).

'Neues zur Fassungsfrage bei Anton Bruckner', *Neues musikwissenschaftliches Jahrbuch* 8 (1999), 115–35.

'Anton Bruckners Glaube', in A. Riethmüller (ed.), *Bruckner-Probleme: internationales Kolloquium 7.–9. October 1996 in Berlin* (Stuttgart, 1999), pp. 50–63.

Röthig, Claudia Catharina, *Studien zur Systematik des Schaffens von Anton Bruckner auf der Grundlage zeitgenössischer Berichte und autographer Entwürfe* (Kassel, 1978).

Scheder, Franz, *Anton Bruckner Chronologie* (Tutzing, 1996).

Schipperges, Thomas, 'Zur Wiener Fassung von Anton Bruckners Erste Sinfonie', *Archiv für Musikwissenschaft* 97 (1990), 272–85.

Scholz, Horst-Günther, *Die Form der reifen Messen Anton Bruckners* (Berlin, 1961).

Schönzeler, Hans Hubert, *Bruckner*, 2nd edn (London, 1978).

Zu Bruckners IX. Symphonie: die Krakauer Skizzen (Vienna, 1987).

Simeone, Nigel, 'Bruckner's Publishers, 1865–1938', *Brio* 36 (1999), 19–38.

Simpson, Robert, *The Essence of Bruckner* (London, 1967; 3rd edn, London, 1992).

Solvik, Morten, 'The International Bruckner Society and the N.S.D.A.P.: a Case Study of Robert Haas and the Critical Edition', *The Musical Quarterly* 82 (1998), 362–82.

Steinbeck, Wolfram, 'Form als Schema bei Anton Bruckner: zum Adagio der VII. Symphonie', in *Analysen: Beiträge zu einer Problemsgeschichte des Komponierens (Festschrift Hans Heinrich Eggebrecht)* (Stuttgart, 1984), pp. 304–23.

'Zu Bruckners Symphoniekonzept oder Warum ist die Nullte "ungiltig"?', in *Probleme der symphonischen Tradition im 19. Jahrhundert, Kongress-Bericht Bonn 1989* (Tutzing, 1990), pp. 545–69.

Bruckner: Neunte Symphonie d-Moll (Munich, 1993).

'Symphonie der Nationen: zur Frage einer "österreichischen Symphonik"', in O. Wessely (ed.), *Bruckner Symposion, 'Entwicklungen, Parallelen, Kontraste. Zur Frage einer "österreichischen Symphonik', (Linz 1993): Bericht* (Linz, 1996), pp. 69–74.

'"Dona nobis pacem": religiöse Symbolik in Bruckners Symphonien', in A. Riethmüller (ed.), *Bruckner-Probleme: internationales Kolloquium 7.–9. Oktober 1996 in Berlin* (Stuttgart, 1999), pp. 87–96.

Tröller, Josef, *Bruckner: III. Symphonie d-Moll* (Munich, 1976).

Wagner, Manfred, 'Vorwort zu einer Bibliographie: dargestellt an jener über Anton Bruckner', *Die Musikforschung* 26 (1973), 225–35.

Der Wandel des Konzepts: zu den verschiedenen Fassungen von Bruckners Dritter, Vierter und Achter Sinfonie (Vienna, 1980).

'Musik von gestern – Provokation für heute: zum Einfluss Bruckners auf die musikalische Gegenwart', in H.-K. Metzger and R. Riehn (eds.), *Musik-Konzepte 23/24: Anton Bruckner* (Munich, 1982), pp. 71–85.

'Die Nekrologe von 1896: rezeptionsstiftend? – oder Wie Klischees von Anton Bruckner entstanden', in H.-K. Metzger and R. Riehn (eds.), *Musik-Konzepte 23/24: Anton Bruckner* (Munich, 1982), pp. 119–47.

Bruckner: eine Monographie (Mainz, 1983).

Anton Bruckner: Werk und Leben (Vienna, 1995).

Wagner, Manfred, Maier, Elisabeth, Mayer, Johannes-Leopold, and Kantner, Leopold M., *Anton Bruckner in Wien: eine kritische Studie zu seiner Persönlichkeit* (Graz, 1980).

Watson, Derek, *Bruckner*, 2nd edn (Oxford, 1996).

Weinman, Alexander, 'Anton Bruckner und seine Verleger', in F. Grasberger (ed.), *Bruckner-Studien: Leopold Nowak zum 60. Geburtstag* (Vienna, 1965), pp. 121–38.

Werner, Eric, 'The Nature and Function of the Sequence in Bruckner's Symphonies', in G. Reese and R. J. Snow (eds.), *Essays in Musicology in Honor of Dragan Plamenac* (Pittsburgh, 1969), pp. 365–84.

Wessely, Othmar (ed.), *Bruckner-Studien: Festgabe der Österreichischen Akademie der Wissenschaften zum 150. Geburtstag von Anton Bruckner* (Vienna, 1975).

Bruckner-Symposion, 'Die österreichische Symphonie nach Anton Bruckner' (Linz 1981): Bericht (Linz, 1983).

Bruckner-Symposion, 'Johannes Brahms und Anton Bruckner' (Linz 1983): Bericht (Linz, 1985).

Bruckner-Symposion, 'Bruckner, Wagner und die Neudeutschen in Osterreich' (Linz 1984): Bericht (Linz, 1986).

Bruckner-Symposion, 'Anton Bruckner und die Kirchenmusik' (Linz 1985): Bericht (Linz, 1988).

Bruckner-Symposion, 'Orchestermusik im 19. Jahrhundert' (Linz 1989): Bericht (Linz, 1992).

Staat – Kirche – Schule in Oberösterreich (Vienna, 1994).

Bruckner-Symposion, 'Entwicklungen, Parallelen, Kontraste: zur Frage einer "österreichischen Symphonik"' (Linz 1993): Bericht (Linz, 1996).

Bruckner Symposion, 'Bruckner-Freunde, Bruckner-Kenner' (Linz 1994): Bericht (Linz, 1997).

Wessely, Othmar, *et al.* (eds.), *Bruckner-Symposion, 'Anton Bruckner als Schüler und Lehrer' (Linz 1988): Bericht* (Linz, 1992).

Bruckner-Symposion, 'Musikstadt Linz – Musikland Oberösterreich' (Linz 1990): Bericht (Linz, 1993).

Bruckner-Symposion, 'Bruckner-Rezeption' (Linz 1991): Bericht (Linz, 1994).

Wiora, Walter, 'Über den religiösen Gehalt in Bruckners Symphonien', in G. Massenkeil, K. W. Niemöller, and W. Wiora, *Religiöse Musik in nicht-liturgischen Werken von Beethoven bis Reger* (Regensburg, 1978), pp. 157–84; repr. in C.-H. Mahling (ed.), *Anton Bruckner: Studien zu Werk und Wirkung (Walter Wiora zum 30. Dezember 1986)* (Tutzing, 1988), pp. 235–75.

Wolff, Werner, *Anton Bruckner: rustic Genius* (New York, 1942).

Zamazal, Franz, 'Bruckner im systematischen Gefüge der Gesellschaft seiner Zeit', *Bruckner-Jahrbuch 1980* (1980), 145–52.

'Bruckners Namenstag-Kantate für Propst Michael Arneth (1852)', in *Bruckner-Jahrbuch 1989/90* (1992), 205–12.

Index

[298]

31816369R00182

Printed in Great Britain
by Amazon